Sheffield Hallam University
Learning and IT
Collegiate Learni
Collegiate Crescent Campus
Sheffield   S10 2BP

KT-511-875

102 079 585 9

Sheffield Hallam University
Learning and Information Services
Withdrawn From Stock

FIRST AMENDMENT INSTITUTIONS

First Amendment Institutions

Paul Horwitz

HARVARD UNIVERSITY PRESS
Cambridge, Massachusetts, and London, England 2013

Copyright © 2013 by the President and Fellows of Harvard College

ALL RIGHTS RESERVED

Printed in the United States of America

Library of Congress Cataloging-in-Publication Data
Horwitz, Paul.
First Amendment institutions / Paul Horwitz.
p. cm.
Includes bibliographical references and index.
ISBN 978-0-674-05541-4 (alk. paper)
1. United States. Constitution. 1st Amendment.   2. Freedom of speech—United
States.   3. Freedom of the press—United States.   4. Freedom of religion—
United States.   5. Assembly, Right of—United States.   I. Title.
KF4770.H67 2012
323.440973—dc23   2012012114

SHEFFIELD HALLAM UNIVERSITY
LSL
342.73
Ho
COLLEGIATE LEARNING CENTRE

To Kelly

Contents

PART THREE: PROBLEMS AND PROSPECTS

Then came the churches
Then came the schools
Then came the lawyers
Then came the rules

Dire Straits, *Telegraph Road*

Acknowledgments

It's fitting, given the subject of this book, that it is the product of a great many institutions. Although all the material in this book is new, it represents the culmination of work I have been doing on the subject of First Amendment institutions practically since I entered teaching, as a visitor at the University of San Diego College of Law and a tenure-track professor at Southwestern Law School, with a brief visit at Notre Dame Law School. The majority of the work was completed at the University of Alabama School of Law, where I now teach. I thank all of those institutions. I am especially grateful to Alabama, its dean Kenneth Randall, my faculty colleagues, the wonderful library staff, my students, and my assistants Donna Warnack and Donna Tucker for their help and support. I am grateful to Elizabeth Knoll, my editor at Harvard, for her patience during the protracted gestation of the book. Two anonymous reviewers for the Press provided extraordinarily, and dauntingly, detailed comments on the manuscript. Their suggestions have much improved it. Alas, any faults that remain are mine.

I would like to thank the following journals for allowing me to explore some of the ideas presented in this book in previous articles: the *Boston College Law Review*, NEXUS, the *UCLA Law Review*, the *Notre Dame Law Review*, the *Harvard Civil Rights-Civil Liberties Law Review*, and the *Northwestern University Law Review*. I am grateful to those journals for supporting this work, and especially to the "Harvard Civil Rights-Civil Liberties Law Review" for publishing my article "Churches as First Amendment Institutions: Of Sovereignty and Spheres," from which I drew heavily in writing Chapter 7. Research assistance on the articles was contributed by Adam Cohen, Andy Hayden, Jennifer Michaelis, and Martha Rogers. Research assistance on the book was provided by Martha Rogers and Noah Jones, with help in its final stages by Michelle Marron, and Aisha Mahmood. I also owe thanks to a student of mine at Notre Dame, Angelen Brookshire, for introducing me to the work of Abraham Kuyper.

For comments on earlier articles and on some or all of the manuscript itself, I thank—among others—Larry Alexander, Carl Auerbach, Amy Barrett, Charles Barzun, Thomas Berg, Joseph Blocher, Bill Brewbaker, Peg Brinig, Al Brophy, Chris Cameron, Dale Carpenter, Doug Cassel, Marc DeGirolami, Michael C. Dorf, Michael B. Dorff, Fernand Dutile, Dave Fagundes, David Fontana, Amy Gajda, Rick Garnett, Cheryl Harris, John Harrison, Deborah Hellman, Rick Hills, John Jeffries, Bill Kaplin, Cathleen Kaveny, Leslie Kendrick, Sung Hui Kim, Michael Kirsch, Ron Krotoszynski, Chris Lund, Dan Markel, Diane Mazur, Michael McConnell, Scott Moss, John Copeland Nagle, Patricia O'Hara, Michael Olivas, Mike Pardo, Robert Post, Gowri Ramachandran, Angela Riley, John Robinson, Bob Rodes, Connie Rosati, Frederick Schauer, Richard Schragger, Micah Schwartzman, Maimon Schwarzchild, Paul Secunda, Steve Smith, Jason Solomon, Daniel Solove, Kelly Strader, Rob Vischer, Johan Van der Vyver, Leland Ware, James Weinstein, Adam Winkler, Nicholas Wolterstorff, and the late Fred Zacharias. The earlier articles, as well as portions of the manuscript of this book, were presented at the Arizona State University's Sandra Day O'Connor College of Law (under the auspices of the legal blog *Prawfsblawg*), Brigham Young University Law School, Chapman Law School, the University of Houston Law Center, the New England School of Law, Notre Dame Law School, UCLA Law School, the University of San Diego College of Law, Southwestern Law School, the University of St. Thomas Law School in Minnesota, the University of Virginia Law School, and Yale Law School; I appreciate the hospitality shown me on those occasions.

My dear friends Rick Garnett of Notre Dame and Nelson Tebbe of Brooklyn Law School generously organized a roundtable conference in the fall of 2011 to discuss the full book manuscript at Notre Dame Law School, under the generous sponsorship of Notre Dame's Program in Church, State, and Society, and with the participation of Joseph Blocher, Anuj Desai, Frederick Mark Gedicks, John Inazu, Randy Kozel, and Mark Tushnet. I could not think of a sweeter reminder that ideas emerge not from individuals alone, but from a network of friends and institutions.

Camille Smith, formerly an editor at Harvard University Press, provided freelance editing services on this book. She wrestled the manuscript down from an unruly behemoth to—well, to a smaller unruly behemoth. Despite its remaining flaws, she refined and improved the book immeasurably.

I owe a special debt of gratitude to two scholars, Robert Post and Frederick Schauer, whose work in this area has inspired so much of my own thinking. I hope I have built on and extended their work, but this book would not exist if they had not been there first.

As I write in Chapter 10, although this book focuses mostly on larger institutions like the press and universities, the family is the original institution, the little sovereign from which everything else flows. So it is here. My children, Samantha and Isaac, put up with my frequent physical or mental absences while I was writing this book. And my wife, Kelly Riordan Horwitz, whose own work as an elected member of the Tuscaloosa City Board of Education has taught me much about what institutions look like in practice, has been my best friend and touchstone in life. I lovingly and gratefully dedicate this book to her.

Introduction

A Day in the Life . . .

Your day begins like any other: in the company of others.

You and your spouse wake to the sound of the radio. As you prepare breakfast and get the children ready for school, NPR plays in the background. The headlines this morning start with yesterday's ruling by the Supreme Court, holding that civil rights laws cannot generally interfere with a church's decision on whom to hire or fire to perform key "ministerial" duties such as providing religious instruction to children in a church school.[1] Curious for more information, you turn surreptitiously to your iPhone (which is not allowed at the breakfast table—a family rule) and read in a *New York Times* story that one law professor has said of the decision, "Obviously, churches are not 'above the law.' . . . However, governments are not permitted to resolve essentially religious disputes and questions."[2] You find yourself agreeing with both parts of the quote—and wondering how both can be true.

Your mind wanders, as it will. As NPR drones on in the background— first with a story about the role of Super PACs in the Republican primaries,[3] then with a short item about a fringe candidate's complaint that he has been excluded from a debate on the local NPR station[4]—you wonder whether congressional Republicans have gotten anywhere with their plans to defund NPR following Juan Williams's dismissal from the network.[5] No matter; it's time for work.

You drop your two children off at school. You are a little worried about your 16-year-old. He was recently disciplined by the principal for taking part in a skit at a school assembly that the principal believed was loaded with subtle but offensive innuendo; the principal did not take kindly his defense that the skit was a political satire.[6] He was also caught recently trying to download materials at his local library that, when you were his age, would have been utterly beyond your comprehension.[7] You mutter a prayer for strength under your breath—and realize that you have forgotten it is Wednesday: your church study group will be meeting tonight.

You teach constitutional law at a local university. Your 19-year-old daughter attends the university as well and lives at home with you. By the time you drop her off on campus, edging your car around a small clump of Occupy Wall Street protesters, your mind is off somewhere else again, and you barely hear her shutting the car door. Your colleagues have been arguing with the dean of the law school over whether a candidate for a faculty position is really qualified for the job. As if that weren't bad enough, the dean has complained that you are the lowest grader in the law school and are hurting students' chances of getting jobs. You loathe grade inflation and wonder whether you can stand on your rights; tenure must be good for something, right?[8]

That night your spouse, a local newspaper reporter, shares her own problems. The mayor and some local business owners have complained about a story she wrote pointing to longstanding ties between the business owners and the mayor, who recently convinced the City Council to ease zoning restrictions in the downtown core. One of the business owners has threatened to sue. Once upon a time, her editor would have laughed off such threats.[9] But the newspaper was recently sold, and the new publisher is concerned about the cost of liability insurance.[10] In the meantime, the mayor has threatened to restrict her access to the press briefings he holds occasionally.[11] She asks you whether he can get away with it.

As the two of you drift off to sleep, your spouse's mind is filled with thoughts of the press, of editors and publishers, of the role of journalism, of her pride in contributing to the public's knowledge of current affairs and local government. Your thoughts, in these waning moments, are quite different. Phrases drift past your closed eyes in some Latinate script: "public forum," "content-neutral," "state actor," "neutral and generally applicable" . . . All is quiet.

. . . of Public Discourse—and the First Amendment

This book is about what happens when we take this story seriously. The day I have described is somewhat eventful, but not unusual. It is a day in the life of the real world of public discourse as a lived experience. It has touched on three of our central First Amendment freedoms: freedom of speech, of the press, and of religion. But it has not been a solitary day, filled with isolated individuals fighting against a monolithic and repressive state. It has been filled with the *institutions* that help make our First Amendment freedoms, and public discourse itself, possible and meaningful.

A central argument of this book thus focuses on a feature shared by much important First Amendment speech: it is *institutional*. Institutions form a central part of the infrastructure of public discourse, or what Jack Balkin has called the "infrastructure of free expression." They are places in which some of the most vital First Amendment activities occur. In Richard Garnett's words, they are "the scaffolding around which civil society is constructed, in which personal freedoms are exercised, in which loyalties are formed and transformed, and in which individuals flourish."[12] The object of this book is to help us see these institutions for what they are, understand how they function and how they help form the infrastructure of public discourse—and ask how the law of the First Amendment ought to respond to them.

That the day described above was full of what I will call "First Amendment institutions"—universities, schools, newspapers, churches, libraries, and so on—should be evident to every reader: given their infrastructural role, these institutions are pervasive in our lives and our actual experience of the world of speech and worship. What may be more surprising to nonlawyers, however, is just how little language the law has to express the same concepts and institutions—to reflect in its own language just what the lived experience of public discourse looks and feels like.

Imagine, for example, the following characters:

- Carla reports for the *Daily Star,* a local newspaper. A disgruntled employee at City Hall feeds her documents revealing that the mayor is distributing no-show municipal jobs in exchange for political contributions. The district attorney presses Carla to reveal her source before the grand jury. She refuses.

- Josh is a blogger. Most of his blog posts consist of his views on drinking, sports, and pop culture.
- Oxbridge is an old and prestigious private university. In keeping with its Quaker roots, it refuses to allow military recruiters on campus.
- Agricultural Tech is a state university. In keeping with the political views of its faculty, it refuses to allow military recruiters on campus.
- Floor-Mart is a major retail chain. It has fired Penelope, a cashier, because customers have objected to her unmarried pregnancy.
- God-Mart, a local megachurch, has fired Priscilla, a receptionist, because congregants have complained about the scandal of her unmarried pregnancy.

As "Sesame Street" used to ask, which of these things is not like the other? Which are the same, and which are different? And why?

How you answer these questions depends on how you carve up the world. Some—perhaps your spouse, in the story that opened this book—might focus on the subject involved: matters of public versus private concern, politics versus art, and so on. Others might focus on the institution in question: churches, newspapers, libraries, museums, retailers. Or it could be something less relevant. (Josh the blogger and Priscilla have red hair; the other individuals are blondes.) All of these distinctions make more or less sense in different circumstances. But we all use them.

Now imagine posing the same questions to lawyers or judges looking at these scenarios for purposes of the First Amendment. Their answers would be quite different from those of the average citizen. They would focus less on the real-world nature of these speakers and institutions, and more on the complex set of doctrines courts use to interpret the First Amendment. In formulating their answers, they would ask, Are some of the characters participating in a "public forum"? If so, what kind? A "limited public forum"? A "traditional public forum"? If government intervention is involved, what form does it take? Is the government regulating the "time, place, or manner" of the speech? Is it engaging in "content" or "viewpoint" discrimination? Is the speech "high-value" or "low-value"? Above all, the lawyer or judge would ask who is doing the speaking and who is doing the censoring. Is the speaker a "state actor" or a "private actor"? Is the censor the state or a private entity?

These distinctions are strikingly different from the ones average citizens would draw. Lawyers and judges see differences where laypeople see similarities, and vice versa. For legal professionals, somewhere between Grover and the bar exam, something changed in the way they view the world. Once we recognize this, we are on to something important—something that affects not only First Amendment law but the law more generally.

The Lure of Acontextuality

What changed, in brief, is this: in many ways, at many times, law is indifferent to context. Put more mildly, it is indifferent to what we might call real-world context and highly attentive to legal context. Lawyers do not see car accidents, for instance, in the visceral, physical way that laypeople do. They see concepts: "torts," "negligence," "damages," and so on. These concepts may in turn influence the layperson's thinking. In our litigious society, the first thing victims of car accidents often ask, after checking that their limbs are intact, is whom to sue. Still, real people start with real events, more or less. Lawyers, in contrast, get to "real things only indirectly, through categories, abstractions and doctrines."[13]

This way of carving up the world is widespread among First Amendment experts. They habitually ignore real-world context and focus instead on one central distinction: that between the speaker and the state. On one side is the speaker, often thought of as an individual soapbox orator, a "lone pamphleteer[ ] or street corner orator[ ] in the Tom Paine mold."[14] Even when the speaker is not one but many people, we describe it with individualistic language, as a single "parade," or "march," or "demonstration": a single entity with many legs but one voice. On the other side is the state—powerful, coercive, censorious, an imposing and undifferentiated mass. Most First Amendment doctrine begins with a speaker and a state censor.

In this book I focus on a particular aspect of law's indifference to context: its "institutional agnosticism." In Frederick Schauer's words, First Amendment doctrine "presupposes the undesirability of having a rule, principle, or doctrine for one institution that is not applicable to another."[15]

A worldview that divides the free speech universe between "speakers" and "the state" leaves little room for the special role institutions play in public discourse. From this perspective, the differences between Oxbridge and Agricultural Tech are more important than the similarities: one is a private speaker and the other is "the state." The similarities between Oxbridge and God-Mart are more important than the differences: both are private "speakers." And there is no difference between any of those institutions and Josh the blogger, or between a parade and a soapbox orator: they are all simply "speakers."

Identifying this pattern does not tell us whether it is a good or bad thing. There are strong arguments for this tradition of acontextuality and institutional agnosticism. Two concerns, in particular, are central to the courts' approach to the First Amendment. The first is fear of government censorship. If we allow legislatures or courts to draw lines on an institutional or contextual basis, we lose sight of a central lesson of the First Amendment: that government *any*where is a potential threat to free speech *every*where. We create "an opening for the dangers of government partisanship, entrenchment, and incompetence."[16] The second is fear that the state is incapable of drawing sound distinctions between speakers based on context or their institutional nature.

This second fear has driven judicial doctrine for decades. Consider the differences, if any, between Carla the reporter and Josh the blogger. Intuitively, most of us see *some* difference between a professional newsgathering organization like the *Star* and a pajama-clad blogger who takes to the Internet to share his views on various trivialities. But what if we are considering whether some speaker, individual or institutional, ought to enjoy a constitutional privilege as a "journalist" to refuse to disclose the identity of a confidential source to a grand jury? Then our commonsense intuitions may prove inadequate to the task. As the Supreme Court said in 1972, that question "would present practical and conceptual difficulties of a high order." This inquiry has only grown more complicated over the years. Both lone bloggers and mighty newspapers, for instance, publish over the Internet, using the same conduit to convey information. Perhaps the Court was prescient when it refused to "embark the judiciary on a long and difficult journey to such an uncertain destination" by creating such a privilege for anyone.[17]

The courts' tendency toward acontextuality is hardly unique to the First Amendment. Its traces are evident whenever lawyers and judges carve up the world according to legal categories rather than real-world contexts. Before we can reach any conclusions about whether this habit is good or bad, we must first recognize it *as* a habit. Once we do, we will see it everywhere. Indeed, its hold on the law is so strong that we might call it an obsession.

Just as we see this obsession everywhere, so we see its limits wherever we look. It is evident that the law—especially First Amendment law—does not and cannot always ignore the context of speech or the institutional nature of the speaker, and that it does not and cannot always treat the "state" as a monolithic entity. Again and again, courts abandon, or carve out exceptions to, the context-insensitive rules that they so often assert are the very foundation of the rule of law, and certainly of the First Amendment.

A few years ago, for example, the Supreme Court faced the question of whether public libraries could be required, as a condition of receiving public funding, to install Internet filters to ensure that patrons could not access obscene or child pornographic websites and that minors could not view harmful materials. The usual route to a decision would have led through the Court's public forum doctrine, which focuses on which *legal* category a state-owned speech "forum" falls into. But the Court was forced to concede that public forum doctrine was "out of place in the context of this case." Instead, it had to "examine the role of libraries in our society."[18]

These exceptions to the rule of acontextuality are as revealing as the rule itself. The law is often said to require generality and consistency of application. When courts cannot fulfill those requirements, we know something important is going on. When they flout those requirements but continue to insist that they *are* requirements, we know something has gone awry.

So it is with First Amendment law. The tensions created by the courts' efforts to follow a rule of rigid acontextuality, and the gaps and fissures created in the law when they cannot—when they are forced to admit that some standard doctrine is "out of place"—have led to increasing incoherence in First Amendment doctrine.[19] This suggests that First Amendment doctrine is in serious need of revision, that something deeper is going on that needs to be brought to the surface—or both.

The Institutional Turn

Seeing the world the way most of us see it, and not just the way lawyers and judges do, is the subject of this book. It is the story of a path not taken by the law.

This story is not new. There has been a long-running contest between the idea of law as a pure conceptual system and the idea of law as a contextual enterprise. It erupted in the early twentieth century, when the Legal Realists challenged what they saw as an unduly conceptual approach to law and rhapsodized about reorganizing the law around messy facts rather than pristine legal principles.[20] It persists to this day, as a wave of "New Legal Realists" urge an approach that focuses on "how law and social and institutional structures interact," and "takes its lead from the [real] world, not ethereal, dogmatic, and academic theorizing."[21] It is evident on the Supreme Court today, in the warring visions of Justice Antonin Scalia, who sees the "rule of law" as a formalist "law of rules," and Justice Stephen Breyer, who argues against "purely conceptual" approaches to the First Amendment and insists that courts "*should* distinguish among different speech-related activities."[22] Even the institutional orientation at the heart of this book is prefigured in earlier legal and political theory emphasizing that "government must recognize that it is not the sole possessor of sovereignty, and that private groups within the community are entitled to lead their own free lives and exercise within the area of their competence an authority so effective as to justify labeling it a sovereign authority."[23]

For the most part, however, the kind of approach I advocate is a minority position. It would be wrong to say that the legal conceptualists won: all but the most rigid legal formalists make allowances for context. But in the First Amendment as elsewhere in law, lawyers and judges rarely give primacy to context.

I argue that we should take context seriously. In particular, we should take seriously the simple fact that a good deal of the speech and conduct that makes up some of the most important aspects of the lived world of First Amendment activity takes place through *institutions*. Taking that institutional context seriously does not necessarily mean that courts should become particularists, sifting through the facts of every First Amendment case and engaging in a balancing of interests that shifts with every new dispute. In its own way, as we will see, the institutional approach, like current First Amendment doctrine, can itself be quite categorical in its approach.[24] But the categories with which we carve up the world of the First Amendment must change. They should be based on the richly complex world of free speech rather than the simplified legal picture of "speaker" and "state." They should pay due regard to the "infrastructure of free expression."

What would happen if we took an institutional turn in First Amendment law—that is, if we redrew our doctrinal categories in a way that recognized the centrality of certain institutions to public discourse? What if we replaced the iconic view of the lone pamphleteer or soapbox speaker versus the monolithic and censorious state with a view in which institutions are the major players? How might this improve First Amendment law? How might it make things worse, or create new reasons for concern? And what implications might that institutional turn have for law and legal theory as a whole?

I am not the only one asking such questions. Much of this book is inspired by the work of Frederick Schauer, who has argued that we ought to pay attention to the role of institutions in First Amendment law.[25] Other legal scholars have raised similar questions. Within certain doctrinal areas, such as freedom of the press or religion, or academic freedom, scholars have long been concerned with the features of different speech institutions, although few of them have connected this concern to broader currents in First Amendment theory. More generally, Robert Post has argued that if First Amendment doctrine is to escape incoherence, it must be reshaped to reflect the "material and normative dimensions of [different] forms of social order and of the relationship of speech to these values and dimensions."[26] This book is, in short, part of an emerging movement in First Amendment law and theory.

This movement also reflects the rise of an interest in institutions across a range of disciplines. From economics and history to sociology and anthropology, scholars are studying the role and nature of institutions in our society. Legal academics have come late to the party, as usual, but they too have felt a pull toward the institutional turn.

This is most evident in constitutional theory. There is a growing awareness that general rules of constitutional interpretation focused on broad legal categories cannot do all the work demanded of them. Some theorists have focused on the gap between the Constitution's text and its implementation by the courts.[27] Others have argued that law should become more "experimental": more focused on the evolution of law and legal norms through interactions between public and private institutions designed to encourage these institutions' "best practices."[28] In this book I aim to bring these streams of scholarship together and to show that they are tributaries of a wider institutional turn in legal theory.

If we take the institutional turn, the implications will be significant and wide-ranging. The list of potential changes in First Amendment doctrine is long:

- Granting the press new constitutional privileges to conceal sources and to engage in newsgathering practices without legal interference.
- Expanding universities' rights of academic freedom, including the right to engage in behavior such as enforcing speech codes and excluding student groups that they believe improperly restrict membership on religious or other grounds.
- Allowing libraries to follow their own policies on the use of Internet filters, even when the government demands the use of filters as a condition of funding.
- Treating religious entities as largely sovereign institutions, immunizing them from the application of civil rights laws and other statutes.
- Strengthening the rights of voluntary associations to operate without legal interference.
- Breaking down the legal divide between "public" and "private" entities and allowing some "state" institutions to operate at a remove from state control, even though the state funds those institutions.
- Rethinking some of our most sacred rulings in the area of race and civil rights in a way that may allow some institutions to openly discriminate on that basis.

The institutional turn does not *require* all these results, although I will argue for most of them. Even where it does not demand wholesale revision of results, however, it requires a dramatic refashioning of our *approach* to First Amendment institutions. The new approach will involve broad judicial deference to those institutions, recognition that they are, in effect, sovereign spheres in their own right, and a willingness to treat them not as *dependents,* subject to the doctrine laid down by the courts, but as *partners* in shaping First Amendment doctrine.

Preliminary Definitions

Before we can go further, we need to define First Amendment institutions. And before we can do that, we need to define institutions more generally.

The Nobel laureate Douglass C. North defines institutions as "the humanly devised constraints that structure human interaction. They are made up of formal constraints (e.g., rules, laws, constitutions), informal constraints (e.g., norms of behavior, conventions, self-imposed codes of conduct), and their enforcement characteristics."[29] This description includes a variety of abstract social practices and understandings, not just more specific entities like corporations or newspapers. It includes everything from the bookstore in which you may be standing right now, pondering whether to buy this book (you should, of course), to the organizational assumptions that allowed you to track down the book in the store ("fiction" vs. "nonfiction," "law" vs. "self-help"), to the very act of reading it, which is bounded by numerous conventions that allow you to do so in a coherent fashion.

These kinds of conventions and norms play a role in this book. But our definition is narrower. It focuses on what some institutional scholars call "organizations." Organizations are more concrete and specific than the kinds of abstract practices that institutional scholars sometimes talk about. They are "groups of individuals bound together by some common purpose to achieve certain objectives." These include "political bodies" like the Senate, "economic bodies" like corporations, "social bodies" like churches, and educational institutions like schools.[30] Of course, these entities are deeply influenced by the broader norms, practices, and traditions that infuse them. But I am mostly concerned here with the particular entities that embody these practices. When I refer to institutions, I generally mean these kinds of concrete entities, although I will sometimes use the term more broadly to discuss not only individual organizations—the *Washington Post,* the New York Public Library, Georgetown University—but the broader spheres of which they are a part: newspapers, libraries, universities, and so on.[31]

If these are "institutions," what is a "First Amendment institution"? We can begin with a working definition I have used elsewhere: a First Amendment institution is one "whose contributions to public discourse play a fundamental role in our system of free speech."[32] This in turn requires us to think about what "public discourse" means. That is a controversial question, for First Amendment theorists and others, and I address it in greater detail in Chapter 4. For now, let me offer a sketch of a definition.

A useful definition of public discourse has recently been supplied by Robert Post. Public discourse, he writes, means "those speech acts and media of communication that are socially regarded as necessary and proper means of participating in the formation of public opinion."[33] For Post, what is important about this definition is its link to the collective decision-making that he places at the heart of democratic government. Democratic government depends for its legitimacy on the people's belief that they are "potential authors of [the] law." In order for them to maintain this belief, they must be able to "participat[e] in the formation of public opinion." That process takes place through "communication in the public sphere." So public discourse is ultimately that set of communications in the public sphere, or media of communication within the public sphere, that contribute to the formation of public opinion, specifically about politics and democratic governance.[34]

I adopt Post's definition of public discourse, for the most part. But it is important to emphasize some key differences. First, while Post's understanding of public discourse places a heavy emphasis on the political process, stressing that its ultimate end is to make "government responsive to [the public's] views,"[35] I do not understand public discourse as being this limited. Its concern is not simply the political process, writ narrowly, but "the shaping of our shared culture."[36] Indeed, much of the argument of this book is that the state is just *one* part of a broader social infrastructure in which First Amendment institutions play a prominent role of their own. Second, the idea of public discourse plays a different and, in some respects, more modest role here than it does in Post's work. While speech that falls outside of "public discourse" may be presumptively entitled to much less protection under his approach, in my case the role of public discourse is simply to help us understand which institutions are "First Amendment institutions" and which are not. As I note below, the fact that a speaker is not a First Amendment institution does not mean it will not receive substantial constitutional protection.

Third, while Post derives much of his understanding of public discourse from theory, my understanding of public discourse is more sociological than theoretical in orientation: it is more about public discourse as we generally observe it around us than about public discourse in some ideal state.

Broad as my definition of public discourse may be, not every speech act fits within it. A blog post about why *Avatar* is an awful movie may be public discourse; an argument about the environmental politics of *Avatar* is surely public discourse; even *Avatar* itself, God help us, is public discourse. But my text message asking a friend, "Since we're not doing anything Friday, would you like to go see that awful movie *Avatar* again?" is not. Nor would I be engaged in public discourse if I showed up with a gun in my hand and ordered the ticket-taker at the movie theater to give me the day's receipts from *Avatar.* But public discourse is a broad realm nonetheless.

Individuals contribute to public discourse too, of course. The conventional picture of a First Amendment speaker is that of a single person urging political or social change. If I stand on a soapbox at a busy street corner demanding reform of the health care system, I am engaging in public discourse. The passers-by may ignore me; they may scoff; they may argue back. A few may join me. Together, we may form a successful new movement. Or we may fail. But surely our individual efforts will constitute public discourse.

But neither social change nor public discourse takes place at the individual level alone. If we were to imagine a modern-day version of Tom Paine, the pamphleteer whose words helped launch the American Revolution, we would quickly realize that many institutions contributed to his speech. Unless he emerged full-grown into the political landscape, like Athena from Zeus's skull, his ideas would come from somewhere. And that somewhere would be a series of institutions. He might have learned how to form his words and communicate them to others at school. He might have refined his ideas, and his ability to express them, at a college or university. The books he drew on to form those ideas might have been borrowed from a library. His views might have been nurtured in a faith community like a church. And an array of institutions might be involved in carrying his words to others: newspapers, book publishers, television stations, the Internet. Nor would those institutions simply convey his views unaltered: they would be analyzed, distorted, refined, and answered in a public conversation taking place in and through the same institutions.

So one lesson of the institutional approach to the First Amendment is that there *are* no "lone pamphleteers," no Tom Paines, without institutions to mold and guide them and to transmit their views. Human beings are social creatures; before they have something worth saying, their identities and views must first be formed, and much of the process of identity formation takes place in and through institutions. For their speech to be public discourse, and not just a lonely monologue, we need institutions.

And not just any institutions. Some institutions are connected to the First Amendment in a special way. They play a fundamental role, not just an incidental or occasional one, in our system of public discourse and the law of free speech that helps it to flourish. These are what I call "First Amendment institutions."

It doesn't take an expert on free speech to identify them. Indeed, that's the point. We all know these institutions well, because they are woven into the fabric of our everyday existence: The press. Universities. Libraries. Churches. Perhaps public schools. Possibly that vague amalgamation called the Internet. (There are also borderline cases, such as families and corporations; we will get to them later.)

It is also easy to describe what gives those institutions their special connection to the First Amendment. The exercise of fundamental First Amendment freedoms—of speech, association, and religion—is central to their existence. Conversely, a gym is certainly a place where speech occurs. It can even be a site of public discourse; what could be more natural than gabbing about politics over a *schvitz*? But we can imagine the same institution carrying on without public discourse—there are times we wish our benchmate in the sauna would shut up about politics, already. By contrast, we cannot imagine a newspaper without public discourse. Even in the electronic age, if anything the reverse is true: it is hard to imagine public discourse without newspapers.

First Amendment institutions are thus not merely sites in which public discourse takes place. They are also places in which public discourse is *formed* and *disseminated,* in social ways and for social purposes. Their social nature is just as important as the experience of individuals within them.

We may think of libraries, for example, as catering to individuals, and the library experience as a fundamentally solitary and private one. The essayist Alfred Kazin, who learned about the world in the reading room of the New

York Public Library, wrote: "How lucky I was to grow up in the Depression, when my country was poor and there was money for libraries."[37] But libraries are also social enclaves and institutional enterprises. They are both repositories and conversations. They allow the dead to congregate with the dead, the dead to speak to the living, and the living to know one another. Civilizations are constructed, and reconstructed, in libraries.

Similar points can be made about other First Amendment institutions. They are not places in which speech takes place in an atomistic fashion, with individual speakers addressing individual listeners; if anything, they help us to see that very little public discourse fits that atomistic model. A good deal of speech involves individuals. But many of our most important communications occur in and through institutions. These institutions are central to public discourse and its infrastructure. They make public discourse possible just as surely as roads and railway lines make commerce possible.[38]

For our purposes, two central qualities of First Amendment institutions are worth singling out. First, they are relatively *stable and established*. Note the word "relatively." Although the framers of the Constitution saw fit to single out freedom of the "press" in the Bill of Rights, newspapers today are quite different from those of two hundred years ago. Given the trouble newspapers are in today, their remaining employees may chuckle sourly at the notion that they work in a "stable" profession. But stability is not synonymous with stasis. As an institution, newspapers—and journalism more broadly—are far from static. But they *are* relatively stable. They are a long-recognized, albeit evolving, institution with a venerable history and well-established traditions.

Second, First Amendment institutions are *self-regulating*. Their actions and policies are influenced by norms and practices that have been deeply woven into each institution during its long history. Libraries and newspapers are vital First Amendment institutions, but for the most part librarians and journalists don't do what they do *because of* the First Amendment. They do it because they are following a set of professional norms that have been drilled into them by training, experience, and institutional culture.

The self-regulating quality of First Amendment institutions is a central concern of this book. It allows us to see public discourse as something whose rules are defined as much by the institutions that contribute to it as by the First Amendment itself. If the First Amendment is the first line of public discourse's operating system, the institutions provide most of the code that follows. They fill in the gaps and lay out the rules and mechanisms by which public discourse is actually conducted.

This working definition of First Amendment institutions—what they are, why they are important, and how they function—leaves many questions to be answered. Even at this early stage, however, we can make two observations.

First, nothing should be too startling about the notion of First Amendment institutions. Intuitively, most of us already carve up the world in something like this fashion. Our perceptual landscape is dotted with libraries, schools, universities, newspapers, and other central speech institutions. But judges and lawyers see the world differently, according to uniquely *legal* concepts and categories. Given the doctrinal confusion and contradictions into which these concepts and categories have led us, it is worth reconsidering the way we carve up the world. Thus, a major task of this book is to make the commonsense intuition that First Amendment institutions exist, and are important, more visible to the legal viewpoint.

Second, viewing the First Amendment through an institutional lens gives us a new perspective on the complex relationship between law and the real-world entities it purports to govern. In truth, the two govern each other. Law regulates our culture, but it is also determined by our culture. This insight helps us to understand that law cannot be simply a top-down regulatory strategy, but is always formed at least in part from the bottom up. It is not a single empire[39] with jurisdiction over every human activity, including those we think of as being "public" or "political"; it is just one of many realms, one of many separate but interconnected spheres in which law and the other norms that govern us are made.[40] This understanding allows us to think more clearly about how law might be built, or rebuilt, from the bottom up.

Implications and Directions

Treating First Amendment institutions as important elements of our social infrastructure that the law ought to acknowledge has a number of implications.

Public vs. Private

First Amendment institutionalism should lead us to think very differently about the perennial legal distinction between "public" and "private." This is the distinction that places "state actors" on one side and private, or nongovernmental, actors on the other. It is what leads courts—at least in theory—to conclude that Harvard University is more like Wal-Mart than it is like the University of Michigan, and that the University of Michigan is more like the Michigan Department of Motor Vehicles than it is like Princeton University.

This distinction has been under attack for years. Some critics advocate eliminating it in order to subject government speech to the full range of First Amendment doctrines.[41] Others argue that we should treat private actors more like state actors, so that some private acts of "censorship" can be regulated under the First Amendment.[42] Still others believe the distinction is worth preserving but requires reshaping.[43] But the critics are united in their belief that the distinction is problematic.

First Amendment institutionalism argues that this distinction is often less important than the basic idea of thinking about institutions, public *or* private, in terms of their functions and roles in society. In many circumstances, it is more useful to think about what *kind* of institution we are dealing with than about whether it is a "state actor" or a "private actor." Sometimes a university is a university, no matter who signs the checks.

In truth, the law sometimes recognizes that not all state actors are the same, and that some of them resemble private actors more closely than they do "the government." But its insistence on carving up the world according to purely *legal* categories prevents it from acknowledging this fact unabashedly. That is one reason the public-private distinction in constitutional law is so tangled and confused. The institutional turn may help untangle it.

Institutional Autonomy and Judicial Deference

Focusing on institutions may also help us rethink the way First Amendment law is generated. The conventional view is that it is generated by the courts themselves, which lay down the law from some Olympian summit where they breathe the air of pure reason (or pure politics). That's an understandable perspective, but it is mistaken. Judges are social creatures, like the rest of us. However rigorously they strive for acontextuality, their decisions are inevitably influenced by the function and purpose of the institutions that come before them. When Chief Justice William Rehnquist observed, in *United States v. American Library Association,* that the Court was obliged to consider "the role of libraries in our society," he was not recommending that the justices look deep within their souls to find the answer, or even that they consult a legal textbook.[44] He meant that the Court had to ask how and why libraries function in the real world. However awkwardly the Court may have answered the question in that case, it was asking the right question.

The answers to that sort of question may come from the judges' own experience with public discourse, or they may come from the institutions themselves, through the arguments they make to the courts. Regardless, when courts recognize that First Amendment doctrine must draw on the actual role and function of First Amendment institutions, they are treating those institutions as partners in shaping the law. We might say, adapting a phrase popular in contemporary constitutional theory, that there is a First Amendment "outside the courts" which influences the development of the First Amendment *inside* the courts.[45]

When we combine that idea with the two defining traits of First Amendment institutions—stability and self-regulation—we have a new way of thinking about what the "First Amendment outside the courts" requires. In a nutshell, it requires institutional autonomy and judicial deference. If First Amendment institutions are partners with the courts in the development of First Amendment law, then they deserve considerable autonomy to shape their own destiny and regulate their own practices. The *New York Times* did not need the First Amendment to tell it that its reporter Jayson Blair had transgressed the norms of the profession by plagiarizing and fabricating stories, nor did it need the courts to order it to cast out the transgressor and attempt to correct any mistakes. In taking those steps the *Times* was simply following its own institutional traditions.

Thus, rather than think of First Amendment institutions as legal subjects that depend on the courts to tell them what the law is, we might think of them as legally autonomous entities that collaborate with courts in defining the law—as institutions that "create[ ] law as fully as does the judge."[46] From this perspective, the proper posture of the courts toward these institutions is one of strong deference. In shaping their institutional rights, the courts must give them room to develop their *own* visions of what the First Amendment means, even if that vision is different from the one courts would choose themselves.[47]

INSTITUTIONAL PLURALISM

So far, we have focused on diversity *between* First Amendment institutions—the idea that a newspaper is different from a library, that each has its own culture and self-regulatory practices and its own function in contributing to public discourse. For these purposes, the University of California is closer to Harvard University than it is to other state government bodies. But we must also consider diversity *within* institutions. Within overarching institutions like "the press" or "the university," individual entities are not all the same. Some journalistic entities may strive to be fair and balanced, while others favor the partisan approach typical of the press in earlier periods. (And some may call themselves "fair and balanced" but still practice partisanship.) Some universities may adopt an unfettered model of learning and teaching, while others favor a more restrictive model that includes, say, speech codes. Some libraries may understand their function as providing a neutral repository for knowledge, while others may see themselves as politically engaged actors.

The institutional turn celebrates diversity within as well as between institutions. It recognizes that although particular First Amendment institutions may share common roles and purposes, they may see those roles and purposes in different ways. Call this "institutional pluralism."[48] Within broad limits, the individual institutions that make up overarching institutional categories such as journalism or the academy may arrive at different rules, practices, and visions of their mission. Courts should leave plenty of room for institutional pluralism.

THE LIMITS OF INSTITUTIONAL AUTONOMY

Given the diversity of First Amendment institutions, it is fair to ask whether an approach that grants them considerable judicial deference and institutional autonomy is so capacious as to be unworkable. Critics might argue that the institutional turn, in its eagerness to escape the snares of acontextuality, fails to see the dangers of *over*contextualizing. In focusing so closely on institutions, it neglects the central problem that the First Amendment was meant to address: the threat of the state as censor.[49] Or critics might argue that giving First Amendment institutions such broad autonomy will end in lawlessness. Could a newspaper, for instance, ban women from the newsroom? Could a university impose speech regulations on students, or forbid interracial dating? These criticisms raise an important question: What are the *limits* of an institutional approach to the First Amendment?

The institutional turn allows for more than one possible answer to this question, ranging from almost complete institutional autonomy to a much milder form of judicial deference. I will argue that the courts ought to defer substantially, but not totally, to the self-regulatory norms and practices of First Amendment institutions.

I can say a little more by way of preview. First, the suggestion that First Amendment institutions ought to enjoy substantial legal autonomy is not as radical as it may seem. When courts require the government to give a compelling justification for restrictions on the First Amendment freedoms of individuals or institutions—what lawyers call "strict scrutiny"—they are effectively granting these "speakers" autonomy. When courts decline to second-guess whether a particular religious claimant, individual or corporate, is adhering to that religion's doctrine,[50] they are acknowledging institutional pluralism. When they allow First Amendment doctrine to be shaped by institutional concerns such as the role of libraries in society, they weave institutional autonomy and judicial deference into the fabric of First Amendment law.

Second, there *are* limits to institutional autonomy. Most legal scholars who favor the institutional turn agree that in order to be entitled to judicial deference, an institution must be acting in something like its proper institutional role. What that means in particular cases will be closely tied to the function of that institution within the infrastructure of public discourse. A library that removes books according to standard professional criteria deserves presumptive deference; not so a library that claims legal immunity in holding a book-burning party in the town square.

Third, rather than think of the legal limits on First Amendment institutions' autonomy as being set once and for all, we might think in terms of regulation from the bottom up, based on the "best practices" each institution develops over time. Even if we believe there must be limits to institutional autonomy—so that, for example, a newspaper cannot invoke its institutional status to shield itself from antidiscrimination laws—we can still view those limits as subject to ongoing negotiation between courts and institutions. The principle of institutional pluralism suggests that not all individual First Amendment institutions—not all individual newspapers or churches—will share the same precise norms; courts should leave room for disagreement rather than cut off the conversation prematurely. But courts might give less deference to institutions' "worst practices" while leaving room for the evolution of *best* practices. This approach raises many practical questions. But it gives us a start toward a genuinely responsive, contextual, and institutionally sensitive approach to the relationship between First Amendment institutions and the courts.

Finally, to say that First Amendment institutions ought to enjoy substantial legal autonomy is not to say that they are perfect or that they should be immune from criticism. Of course these institutions will not always behave as they should. Their expertise, their self-regulatory practices, and their distinctive contributions to public discourse suggest that they, and not the courts, should have the primary responsibility to make decisions within their own proper spheres. But we should encourage those institutions to engage in internal debate over their practices, and reform them when necessary. And those institutions should welcome *public* criticism of their actions. As citizens responsible for the shape and future of our system of public discourse, we ought to be deeply engaged in monitoring and criticizing the actions of First Amendment institutions, even—*especially*—if courts themselves are constrained from doing so.[51]

INDIVIDUALS AND FREE SPEECH LAW

Because the focus of this book is on the central infrastructural role played by First Amendment institutions in our system of public discourse, readers may naturally wonder what is left of the individual speaker. As central as institutions may be to public discourse, not every speech act on matters of public concern involves institutions. Individuals may wonder what is to become of *their* First Amendment protections.

Let me be clear on this point. Nothing in what I write is intended to eliminate vigorous protections for individual speakers or worshippers. Indeed, it may be that many of the acontextual, institutionally indifferent legal rules that currently populate First Amendment law—the rule of content-neutrality, the protection of individual speakers in public forums, and so on—make better sense in this context than they do where First Amendment institutions are concerned. Furthermore, as I argue much later in the book, maintaining strong protection for individual speech acts under current doctrine, or for institutional speech—say, commercial speech—by institutions that do not fall within the definition of "First Amendment institutions," may be a necessary backdrop to First Amendment institutionalism itself. Some institutions are clearly not First Amendment institutions; others, like blogs and other aspects of discourse on the Internet, may not yet meet the definition, but might be thought of as "emerging" First Amendment institutions whose evolving culture and self-regulatory practices might one day merit a substantial amount of legal autonomy. In the meantime, even if they do not deserve to be thought of as entitled to legal "autonomy," they may well still merit strong legal *protection*. Nothing I say here is meant to suggest otherwise.

To be sure, there are good reasons to criticize current First Amendment rules even as they apply to the speech acts of individuals, or of institutions that do not belong within the select group of "First Amendment institutions."[52] That is not my focus here. My goal in this book is twofold: to bring attention to the central infrastructural role played by First Amendment institutions in public discourse and think about how the law might reflect that role, and more generally to encourage us to think about how First Amendment law might be more responsive to the real world of public discourse and less fixated on acontextual legal rules. It is intended in part as an institutionally oriented *supplement* to current First Amendment law, and in part as a provocation, a goad to further thinking about First Amendment law and theory. That should be more than enough for one book.

Summary of the Book

In keeping with the theme of lawmaking from the bottom up, Part One of the book offers a mixed theoretical and practical introduction to First Amendment institutionalism. In Chapter 1, I provide a basic guide to First Amendment theory and doctrine. It should be of special value to those who are relatively unfamiliar with First Amendment law; even for those who are, however, it provides a backdrop for the ensuing discussion. In Chapter 2, I discuss the "lure of acontextuality" and its role in First Amendment law, as well as the problems and tensions that result when acontextuality confronts specific facts and cases—especially those involving First Amendment institutions—that do not fit well within general doctrinal rules. In Chapters 3 and 4, I introduce First Amendment institutionalism itself, and the institutional turn in law and other fields of which it is a part.

Part Two examines First Amendment institutions on the ground. Starting with some of the most important and intuitively obvious First Amendment institutions, I examine their roles and their capacity for self-regulation, discuss the ways in which current doctrine succeeds or fails in acknowledging them, and offer suggestions for reform. Along the way, I use some of these institutions to shed light on broader questions about First Amendment institutionalism, and note some areas in which established First Amendment institutions, like the press, may raise questions about "emerging" institutions, like the blogosphere. The final chapter in Part Two, Chapter 10, discusses what I call the borderlands of First Amendment institutionalism: institutions that are unquestionably important to public discourse but whose social or legal status as "First Amendment institutions" is unclear.

Part Three is intended less as a summation than as a jumping-off point for further discussion. In Chapter 11, I examine some of the strongest potential criticisms of First Amendment institutionalism. Some of those criticisms are powerful indeed, and even those who are completely convinced by my arguments in this book will need to reckon with them. But they should not end the conversation. There are still good reasons to ask whether the current approach to First Amendment law does all it should, and to see where the institutional turn might take us. In Chapter 12, I seek to spark still other conversations by linking the institutional turn in the First Amendment to a host of emerging movements elsewhere in constitutional law and theory. These movements suggest that the institutional turn I argue for in First Amendment law supports—and can draw support from—a number of similar developments in contemporary legal thought. For this reason, too, there may be good reason to at least begin the job of *imagining* an institutional First Amendment.

One last note by way of preface is necessary. It concerns the sources and methods I use in this book and the approach to constitutional interpretation they suggest. It is, in a word, eclectic. In this, it is not unorthodox. The sources and methods of constitutional interpretation I employ are all conventional ones: text, history, structure, tradition, judicial precedents, political theory, public policy, and so on. To be clear, however, mine is not an originalist approach. I treat history here as relevant to the enterprise of understanding the First Amendment, but not dispositive. Certainly I do not focus narrowly on the original public understanding of the First Amendment. As most students of the Constitution are aware, however, history can function at a variety of levels of generality or specificity in helping us to understand what the Constitution means—or could mean. Readers will find within these pages ample historical support for the institutional turn, ample evidence of a longstanding recognition of the importance and independence of the institutions we will discuss here. But history is only one element of my argument.

This is not a perfectionist account. I do not presume that First Amendment institutionalism will dissolve all the problems of current First Amendment theory and practice. Rather, I hope to start a productive conversation—not only about the First Amendment, but about constitutional law and theory more broadly. First Amendment institutionalism is just one of a number of emerging legal theories that embrace a shared role for legal and social institutions in our constitutional and political culture. If most of us are not solitary Tom Paines, but instead live in and among an intricate web of institutions, then the institutional turn may have important lessons for all of us.

I

From Acontextuality to Institutionalism

I

The Conventional First Amendment

Before we can take the institutional turn, we must understand where the First Amendment is today: its leading values, theories, and judicial doctrines. Not all of those issues and debates will directly impact our discussion of First Amendment institutions. But they provide a useful background for those who are unfamiliar with the First Amendment's immense literature and jurisprudence, and help us to see what current approaches get right and what they miss. In looking at them, we will see a common thread: they routinely emphasize the individual and deemphasize the institutional.

Values and Theories

Discussions of the First Amendment often begin with the justifications behind First Amendment rights themselves.[1] I focus in this chapter on free speech.[2] Five of the most prominent justifications for freedom of expression are the arguments from truth, democracy, self-realization or autonomy, civic courage, and distrust of government.

The most influential is the *argument from truth*. One of its leading advocates was John Milton, who asserted, "Let [Truth] and Falsehood grapple; who ever knew Truth put to the worse, in a free and open encounter?"[3] In *On Liberty*, John Stuart Mill went a step further, arguing that even some false speech must be protected to "promote[ ] a reexamination that vitalizes truth."[4] This was one of the first arguments to appear in First Amendment jurisprudence, which emerged in the wake of the First World War.[5] Its most celebrated expression is Justice Oliver Wendell Holmes's dissent in *Abrams v. United States*. Arguing against the conviction of several individuals who had demonstrated in favor of the Russian Revolution and against American participation in the Great War, Holmes wrote that "only the present danger of immediate evil or an intent to bring it about" could justify Congress's imposition of restrictions on freedom of speech. He added: "When men have realized that time has upset many fighting faiths, they may come to believe . . . that the ultimate good desired is better reached by free trade in ideas—that the best test of truth is the power of the thought to get itself accepted in the competition of the market, and that truth is the only ground upon which their wishes safely can be carried out. That at any rate is the theory of our Constitution. It is an experiment, as all life is an experiment."[6]

Holmes's metaphor of a marketplace of ideas has become a central concept in First Amendment jurisprudence. Despite widespread criticism,[7] it remains a mainstay of the Supreme Court[8] and, to a lesser extent, the legal academy.[9] The basic concept is easy enough to grasp. If enough voices can speak freely enough, the ultimate result will be our collective arrival at the truth. That hope justifies freedom of speech, including "freedom for the thought that we hate."[10]

The *argument from democracy* turns not on the truth as such, but on the processes by which we collectively deliberate and decide on matters of public concern. Its leading champion is Alexander Meiklejohn. Drawing on the tradition of the New England town meeting, Meiklejohn saw free speech as involving "a group of free and equal men, cooperating in a common enterprise, and using for that enterprise responsible and regulated discussion." The goal of this kind of discussion is not speech itself, but "wise decisions" attained through responsible public deliberation. As Meiklejohn put it, "What is essential is not that everyone shall speak, but that everything *worth saying* shall be said."[11]

This argument gives a powerful but limited scope to free speech. Speech that is relevant to public deliberation on matters of public concern should be strongly protected; "all relevant information" must be made "available to the sovereign electorate so that they, in the exercise of their sovereign powers, can decide which proposals to accept and which proposals to reject."[12]

Because our political leaders are the people's servants, the state cannot censor information that the people need to decide whether to retain or replace those leaders. We must be able to criticize our leaders freely and without fear of government sanction. On the other hand, speech that is not relevant to collective political deliberation, or that violates the rules of civil debate, may be restricted. "Private" speech, including commercial speech, artistic expression, and much else besides, receives less protection than that accorded to public and political speech.[13]

The argument from democracy has critics,[14] but also followers. They include some of the leading modern theorists of free speech, like Cass Sunstein and Owen Fiss.[15] Some of Meiklejohn's followers have attempted to keep the baby with the bathwater, arguing, for example, that art often serves a political purpose and must be protected too.[16] Others have taken a stricter view, arguing that *only* clear political speech deserves First Amendment protection.[17] Even those who would soften Meiklejohn's narrowly politically oriented argument agree, however, that not all speech deserves protection.[18]

The argument from democracy has often been championed by the Supreme Court. The most famous example is *New York Times v. Sullivan*,[19] in which the Supreme Court reversed a libel judgment against the *New York Times* and a group of clergy who had placed an advertisement in the newspaper criticizing the conduct of public officials in Montgomery, Alabama, during the civil rights movement. In doing so, the Court effectively constitutionalized defamation law, which previously had been the province of the common law.

In one of the most influential opinions in First Amendment history, Justice William Brennan wrote that the "central meaning" of the First Amendment is that for democracy to function properly, "criticism of official conduct" must enjoy a strong "constitutional shield." The First Amendment represents "a profound national commitment to the principle that debate on public issues should be uninhibited, robust, and wide-open."[20] The argument from democracy remains popular and perhaps predominant on the Supreme Court, as its recent willingness to strike down campaign finance laws partly on this basis suggests.[21]

The *argument from self-realization or autonomy* holds that the true value of free speech lies in what it means for each of us individually. For champions of this idea, who include Thomas Emerson, C. Edwin Baker, and Martin

Redish,[22] the good to be realized from freedom of speech is self-realization, self-expression, or individual autonomy.[23] Protected speech includes not only matters of public concern, but any speech that fully develops and expresses a person's innermost self.

A high-water mark for this argument is *Cohen v. California*.[24] Cohen walked through a courthouse corridor wearing a jacket bearing the words "Fuck the Draft" and was convicted of disturbing the peace. Justice John Marshall Harlan acknowledged that the case might "seem at first blush too inconsequential to find its way into our books," but insisted that "the issue it presents is of no small constitutional significance." Underscoring the element of self-expression that drove the decision, he noted that while Cohen's speech might seem puerile, "'wholly neutral futilities come under the protection of free speech as fully as do Keats' poems or Donne's sermons.'" Harlan rhapsodized: "[W]hile the particular four-letter word being litigated here is perhaps more distasteful than most others of its genre, it is nevertheless often true that one man's vulgarity is another's lyric." Under the self-expression theory of free speech, the Constitution must leave "matters of taste and style . . . largely to the individual."[25]

Under this theory of freedom of speech, we protect speech "not as a means to achieve a collective good but because of its value to the individual."[26] It matters less that Cohen had something *political* to say than that he had something to say at all, and felt compelled to say it "lyrically," as it were. Free speech is essential to the "development of the individual's powers and abilities" and "control of his . . . own destiny through making [and expressing] life-affecting decisions."[27]

The *argument from civic courage* takes a somewhat different tack, holding that we should value free speech, including hateful speech, because it makes us more tolerant as individuals and as a society and thus makes us stronger and more capable citizens. This justification has been most fully developed by Lee Bollinger and Vincent Blasi, who argue that "if we are forced to acknowledge the right of detested groups to speak, we are taught the lesson that we should be tolerant of the opinions and behavior of those who are not like us."[28] This form of justification for free speech does not celebrate a speaker like Cohen for his talent at sewing four-letter words on his jacket, but instead focuses on the way our own reactions to Cohen's colorful language, and our willingness to protect it, "develop and demonstrate a social capacity to control feelings evoked by a host of social encounters."[29] Free speech is thus a rehearsal for the rough-and-tumble of social life.

The most famous judicial argument from civic courage can be found in the concurring opinion of Justice Louis Brandeis in *Whitney v. California*.[30] *Whitney*, like *Abrams*, involved radical political speech. Like Justice Holmes in *Abrams*, Brandeis urged that only an imminent and serious danger can justify repressing speech.[31] But he took a different route to this conclusion. Rather than emphasize free speech as a search for truth, Brandeis treated it as a proving ground for individuals and for democracy itself. The founders of the nation "valued liberty both as an end and as a means. They believed liberty to be the secret of happiness and courage to be the secret of liberty." "[T]he final end of the state" was "to make men free to develop their faculties." But these faculties can flourish only if people actually exercise them, even in the face of noxious speech. For Brandeis, "the greatest menace to freedom is an inert people," and "public discussion is a political duty." Freedom of speech functions to "free men from the bondage of irrational fears"[32] by demanding the courage to raise our voices in opposition. The Supreme Court has long since elevated Brandeis's concurrence to a central principle of the First Amendment.[33]

The *argument from distrust of government* focuses on the dangers of government regulation of speech, not the speech itself. The emphasis here is on the "checking value" of the First Amendment. The amendment's central concern is to provide a counterweight to "the inevitable temptation presented to those with power to act in corrupt and arbitrary ways."[34]

Distrust of government can be found everywhere in First Amendment doctrine.[35] It is expressed most clearly in a key aspect of modern First Amendment doctrine: government cannot regulate speech on the basis of its content. It cannot "adopt[ ] a regulation of speech because of disagreement with the message it conveys."[36]

Doctrine

The remainder of this chapter surveys some of the building blocks of First Amendment doctrine. The goal is to convey a *basic* sense of its fundamental doctrinal architecture and the standard distinctions the courts draw when confronting First Amendment claims—to show, in short, how the courts carve up the world of the First Amendment.

CONTENT NEUTRALITY

The central command of First Amendment doctrine is the rule of content neutrality.[37] Government can regulate speech in a content-*neutral* manner, but it can almost never regulate speech in a content-*based* manner.[38] "[A]bove all else, the First Amendment means that government has no power to restrict expression because of its message, its ideas, its subject matter, or its content."[39] This is "the most pervasively employed doctrine in the [modern] jurisprudence of free expression."[40]

The rule seems simple enough. Either a regulation of speech is content-based, in which case it is likely forbidden, or it is content-neutral, in which case it is likely permitted. The government is free to prohibit your neighbors from blaring music at high decibels at two in the morning, even though that music may have expressive value. But it is forbidden to ban *only* the playing of old Loggins and Messina records, simply because the government hates the music of Loggins and Messina.

As with any basic rule, the rule of content-neutrality has given rise to complications.[41] Unless interpreted with a mechanical literalism, it does not tell us whether content-based restrictions are ever permissible or content-neutral restrictions are ever forbidden. Nor does it tell us how to determine whether a particular restriction is content-based or content-neutral. This will often be an easy determination, but it need not be.[42]

Consider *Hill v. Colorado,* which dealt with a Colorado law aimed at protests in and around clinics, hospitals, and other facilities that provide abortions. The statute regulated "speech-related conduct within 100 feet of the entrance to any health care facility." Specifically, it restricted the ability to approach anyone near health care facilities "for the purpose of passing a leaflet or handbill to, displaying a sign to, or engaging in oral protest, education, or counseling with such other person" without that person's prior consent.[43]

A majority of the Supreme Court concluded that the statute was a content-neutral regulation of speech: it was directed at the "time, place, and manner" of the speech, not the content of the speech itself.[44] An individual would be equally in violation of the law for approaching a patient to say, "God hates abortion," "God loves abortion," or "Would you like to save money on your long-distance plan?" In a concurring opinion, Justice David Souter argued that "the key to determining whether" a law "makes a content-based distinction between varieties of speech lies in understanding that content-based discriminations are subject to strict scrutiny because they place the weight of government behind the disparagement or suppression of some messages, whether or not with the effect of approving or promoting others."[45]

To the three dissenters in the case, however, the statute's suppression of speech was obviously content-based. The statute was aimed only at protest, education, or counseling. It thus required anyone enforcing the law to examine the content of the speech to determine whether the law applied. For the dissenters, it "blink[ed] reality to regard this statute . . . as anything other than a content-based restriction upon speech in the public forum."[46]

In short, the very simplicity of the content-neutrality rule quickly leads to difficult questions about what constitutes a content-neutral or a content-based regulation of speech. (Or, to put it in terms more relevant to this book's argument, its simplicity can constrain the Court in cases in which the justices think the context demands a different result, leading them to complicate the doctrine in the course of distinguishing it.)

Beyond this, the justices have fractured on a host of subsidiary questions. The Court has suggested, for example, that speech regulations based on the speaker's *viewpoint* are even worse than content-based regulations. If a law banning discussion of abortion is bad, a law banning only speech that opposes (or supports) abortion rights is even worse. But the justices often disagree about when a law is a content regulation and when it is a viewpoint regulation.[47]

None of this goes to the *merits* of the content distinction in First Amendment doctrine. For example, does the division of speech regulations into impermissible content-based laws and permissible content-neutral laws encourage legislatures to craft sweeping content-neutral laws that end up restricting far *more* speech? Does it send the message that a restriction on speech will be permitted if only it is broad enough?[48] For now, however, our job is explanatory, not critical.

HIGH-VALUE VS. LOW- OR NO-VALUE SPEECH

An important qualification to the distinction between content-based and content-neutral restrictions focuses on the "value" of the restricted speech.

Even where content-based regulations are concerned, the courts will permit much more substantial regulation of so-called "low-value" speech. On this view, "not all speech is of equal First Amendment importance."[49] Some speech will be taken to be of low value, and thus subject to lesser First Amendment protection.[50] Other speech will, in effect, be treated as having *no* constitutional value. The Supreme Court advanced this proposition most clearly in *Chaplinsky v. New Hampshire:*

> There are certain well-defined and narrowly limited classes of speech, the prevention and punishment of which has never been thought to raise any Constitutional problem. These include the lewd and obscene, the profane, the libelous, and the insulting or "fighting" words—those which by their very utterance inflict injury or tend to incite an immediate breach of the peace. . . . [S]uch utterances are no essential part of any exposition of ideas, and are of such slight social value as a step to truth that any benefit that may be derived from them is clearly outweighed by the social interest in order and morality.[51]

By treating some categories of expression as entitled to little or no First Amendment protection, the doctrine of high-value and low-value speech serves as a pressure valve.[52] It eases the burden on the courts created by the broad distinction between content-based and content-neutral regulations.[53] By permitting the legislature to regulate "low-value" speech, it allows courts to uphold certain content-based speech regulations, as long as that speech forms "no essential part of any exposition of ideas."

This raises some difficult questions. How do we determine whether speech is of high or low value? Can we do so without making precisely the kinds of substantive judgments about content that the rule of content neutrality seems to place at the heart of the First Amendment? Even if it is a necessary part of free speech doctrine, does it serve as a nagging reminder of the ad hoc nature of the entire First Amendment enterprise?

We can say two things for certain about this distinction. First, the category of low-value speech has narrowed considerably in the decades since *Chaplinsky*. First the specific categories mentioned in that case and then others, such as commercial speech, have gradually come under the shelter of the First Amendment. In *R.A.V. v. City of St. Paul,* for example, the Court made clear that even laws proscribing "fighting words" may be infirm, at least if that law is aimed at only some forms of fighting words—in that case, racially charged hate speech—and not others.[54]

Second, the basis for the distinction between high- and low-value speech seems to be shifting. In *United States v. Stevens,* a recent decision involving what most would consider low-value speech—"crush videos," which cater to certain fetishists by showing actual instances of cruelty to small animals—the Court adopted a largely historical approach, stating that only a few "historic and traditional categories long familiar to the bar" qualify as low-value speech.[55] This approach is in some tension with the Court's previous characterization of low-value speech as of "slight social value" compared with the "social interest in order and morality." *Stevens* seemed to suggest that the category of low-value speech consists of a fixed set of historical exclusions from the usual coverage of the First Amendment, rather than a series of case-by-case, policy-oriented decisions identifying certain kinds of speech whose negligible benefits are outweighed by their significant harms.

Whether the distinction between high-value and low-value speech depends on the courts making ongoing substantive decisions about the social value of particular categories of speech, or whether the few remaining categories of low-value speech should be treated as just a set of contingent, historically fixed exclusions from the First Amendment—permanent exhibits in a Museum of Worthless Expression—is an open question. It is clear, however, that whether speech is of high or low value is a background question in every First Amendment case.

Public vs. Private Action, Individual vs. Corporate Speech

Two other key categorical distinctions implicate not only First Amendment doctrine but constitutional law in general. The first, state action doctrine, is, in a nutshell, the idea that the Bill of Rights constrains *state* actors, not *private* actors. If the government banned the broadcasting of the Dixie Chicks after their lead singer criticized President George W. Bush, that would be a clear violation of the First Amendment. If private listeners boycotted them and private record companies refused to release their music, the First Amendment would have nothing to say about it.

In a few cases the Supreme Court extended First Amendment protection to contexts in which private regulation was so comprehensive that the Court was willing to treat it as state action. The classic example involved the private regulation of speech in the old "company towns," where a private corporation controlled every aspect of public and private life.[56] The Court has long since retreated from this position, leaving most private action unregulated by the First Amendment.[57]

In an age in which government entanglement with private speakers and groups is pervasive, there will sometimes be difficult boundary questions concerning whether a particular actor is a "private" or "state" actor.[58] And in a few areas, the Court has tortured state action doctrine to extend the First Amendment to conduct it would otherwise be unable to address. For example, the Court has constitutionalized the law of defamation, primarily where public officials and speech on matters of public concern are involved, despite the fact that these suits usually involve private defendants.[59] Still, as permeable as the line between private and public may be, the courts continue to insist that it is an essential part of First Amendment inquiry.

Although the public-private distinction generally leaves private suppression of speech unregulated and government suppression of speech highly regulated, it can cut the other way. When government acts in a managerial role, regulating its own affairs rather than those of private individuals or groups, the writ of the First Amendment largely runs out.[60] Regulation *of* speech by government is subject to the strictures of the First Amendment; speech *by* government itself generally is not.[61] Government speech doctrine is arguably essential to government's functioning; it is also a hole in First Amendment doctrine through which one could drive a good-sized truck.

Thus, the public-private doctrine creates a vital set of distinctions for First Amendment law. On the one hand, it makes clear that public or state regulation of speech is subject to the strictures of the First Amendment, while private responses to speech are not. On the other, it makes clear that speech by government itself generally falls outside the amendment's scope, leaving private individuals without legal recourse when they object to that speech.[62]

An equally important distinction, but one the courts have generally refused to make, is between individual and group or corporate speech. Most recently, the Supreme Court has said that the "political speech of corporations or other associations should [not] be treated differently under the First Amendment simply because such associations are not 'natural persons.'"[63] Broadly speaking, the identity of a speaker and whether the speaker is an individual or a collectivity are matters of complete indifference to First Amendment law.

PUBLIC FORUM DOCTRINE

Just as the distinction between high- and low-value speech acts as a safety valve that relieves some of the pressure of the rule of content neutrality, so public forum doctrine eases the force of the public-private distinction in certain circumstances. It does so by creating a further distinction within the category of speech involving the government: namely, between speech *by* the government and *private* speech on government *property*. Government speech is assumed to be wholly within its own control. When the paradigmatic soapbox speaker mounts a platform in a park or on a street corner to address his fellow citizens, however, he is on government property. If the government's right to control its own affairs is not to overrun the right to gather and speak in public places, there must be a safety valve. The public forum doctrine serves that purpose.[64]

This doctrine's roots lie in *Hague v. CIO,* where the Court said that some government-owned sites, like streets and parks, "have immemorially been held in trust for the use of the public, and, time out of mind, have been used for purposes of assembly, communicating thoughts between citizens, and discussing public questions."[65] In these "quintessential public forums," government speech regulation will be held to a strict standard of scrutiny; it can, however, subject speakers to "time, place, and manner" restrictions as long as they are not aimed at the content of the speech and meet certain other requirements.[66]

Not all government property is treated as a quintessential public forum. It is one thing to speak up in the middle of a park and another to mount a protest in the middle of a busy government office. So the courts have come up with a variety of further distinctions. Some government property may not always have been an expressive forum, but once the government "designates" that property for general expressive activity, it is obliged to follow the rules that apply to traditional public forums. Meeting rooms in public universities are one example. The government can close these forums altogether, but as long as they remain open it must follow the rules. It may also open a "limited public forum," one that is open to certain kinds of speech, while restricting its use for other subjects. It is required to allow a wide spectrum of school-related speech at school board meetings, but not to permit someone to harangue a school board on foreign policy.[67]

Some government property is treated essentially the same as private property, and thus is largely free of First Amendment scrutiny. Although government offices are publicly owned, no citizen has the right to roam the corridors of the Hawaii Department of Health demanding to see President Barack Obama's birth certificate while government employees are trying to get their work done. The government is entitled to "reserve the forum for its intended purposes, communicative or otherwise." The only thing it can't do is impose an unreasonable regulation of speech, particularly one aimed at the viewpoint of the particular speaker: it can't allow citizens to roam a government office speaking in *support* of civil rights but ban them from wandering the office arguing *against* civil rights.[68]

Medium of Communication

Speech does not just take place on street corners, in one-to-one communications between a single speaker and a single audience. It takes place in print, on network and cable television, on the Internet, in movies, on billboards, and through other media. To a decreasing extent, different media of communication may be governed by different rules.

The classic example involves print and broadcasting. While print media such as newspapers have long been treated as fully protected under the First Amendment, laws regulating broadcasting have been reviewed under a more forgiving standard, largely on the grounds that the broadcast spectrum is limited and government needs greater discretion in managing this scarce resource in the public interest. The difference in treatment was glaringly apparent in a pair of cases decided in the late 1960s and early 1970s. In *Red Lion Broadcasting Co. v. FCC,* the Court relied on the spectrum scarcity and public interest arguments to uphold the so-called Fairness Doctrine, which required broadcasters to give equal time to the targets of criticisms aired on their stations. The Court said, "There is no sanctuary in the First Amendment for unlimited private censorship operating in a medium not open to all."[69] A few years later, however, in *Miami Herald Publishing Co.*

v. Tornillo, the Court rejected the idea that the legislature could impose a "right of reply" on newspapers.[70]

The justifications for treating broadcasting differently have fallen out of favor. The Federal Communications Commission later concluded that the Fairness Doctrine violates the First Amendment,[71] and it has fallen into desuetude. In a variety of cases touching on television, especially cable television, the Court has shifted to a medium-insensitive model under which broadcasting is treated more like print and other communications media.[72]

This shift is still a work in progress. Part of the reason for the Court's reticence has been its sense that it lacks the expertise to fully understand swiftly changing developments in communications technology.[73] Nevertheless, with respect to new communications media the Court has moved away from the "public regulation" model and toward a "free and independent media" model.[74] This is most evident with respect to the Internet, which the Court has treated more like the press and less like broadcasting.[75] Nevertheless, traces of medium-specificity remain in First Amendment law. It is evident—if not self-parodying—in statements like that of Justice Robert Jackson, who in a 1949 opinion wrote that each medium "is a law unto itself, and all we are dealing with now is the sound truck,"[76] or Justice Byron White, who, after arguing in one case that the law "must reflect the differing natures, values, abuses, and dangers" of different media of communication, notoriously concluded, "We deal here with the law of billboards."[77]

Standards of Review

The last bit of First Amendment mechanics involves the standards of review the courts use when judging restrictions on speech under the First Amendment. Content- or viewpoint-based regulations of speech are subject to strict scrutiny, under which the state must show that a regulation "is necessary to serve a compelling state interest and is narrowly drawn to achieve that end."[78] The state bears the burden of showing a close fit between means and ends: the regulation of speech must serve a compelling government interest that could not have been achieved by any more narrowly drawn law that would suppress less speech. This is an exceedingly heavy burden. Indeed, some justices have argued that even strict scrutiny does not capture the stringency with which courts should review content-based restrictions on speech.[79]

Content-neutral restrictions, in contrast, are subjected to intermediate scrutiny, under which the government must show that any speech-restrictive regulations are "justified without reference to the content of the regulated speech, that they are narrowly tailored to serve a significant governmental interest, and that they leave open ample alternative channels for communication of the information."[80] This is still a weighty burden, but it requires only that the government interest be "significant," not "compelling," and that "ample alternative channels" for the speech in question be left open, not that the regulation be drawn in the least restrictive manner possible.

Two examples of intermediate scrutiny will serve. First, recall the noise ordinance preventing your neighbors from blaring music at two in the morning. If it is directed at a particular speaker or at the content of that speech—if the law says, "No Loggins and Messina, or any other speech calling one's love object 'lady,' after midnight"—it is subject to strict scrutiny and will be struck down. But if the law is simply a "time, place, and manner" regulation having nothing to do with the *content* of the speech—such as "No loud noise after midnight"—it is subject to intermediate scrutiny and will survive if it serves a significant government interest, such as avoiding public nuisances, and leaves open alternative opportunities for expression. That is putting it mildly, however. Although intermediate scrutiny might seem to have some potential bite, virtually all "time, place, and manner" restrictions are upheld under this standard.[81]

The second example involves so-called symbolic speech or expressive conduct. During the Vietnam War, some protesters burned their draft cards, violating a law forbidding the cards' destruction. Such an act carries profound expressive meaning, at least if undertaken in public—at a protest march, for example. But it is not *only* expressive; it's also a physical act. Because almost any action can convey a message—shooting at the president is certainly one way to signal disapproval of his policies—not all expressive conduct can be given full First Amendment protection. In *United States v. O'Brien*,[82] the Court used intermediate scrutiny to uphold a statute criminalizing the burning of draft cards. If government aims at the *message* the card burner is trying to send, it is subject to strict scrutiny. If it aims only at the *conduct,* regardless of the message—making the card burner equally guilty whether he was trying to express opposition to the war or just to stay warm on a cold night—the law is subject to intermediate scrutiny. Conversely, although flag burning is also symbolic action, when the Supreme Court struck down a law forbidding the burning of the American flag, it made clear that the law was aimed at the message the defendant sought to send, not the act of flag-burning as such, and thus was subject to strict scrutiny.[83]

Broadly speaking, two traits run through all the theories and doctrines surveyed here. First, they are relatively individualistic. Most of them focus primarily on the classic model of a lone speaker arrayed against the terrible power of the state: they treat speech as something engaged in by and between private individuals, and they treat the possibility of state censorship as the primary threat to free speech.

Second, they are relatively indifferent to the context of the speech and to the identity, function, and nature of the speaker, as well as to the number of speakers. Whether the "speaker" is an individual, a group of parade marchers, a newspaper, or a media conglomerate is relatively unimportant. What matters is that the *government* is acting in a way that aims at the *content* of any speech other than low-value speech. And despite the occasional reference to "the law of billboards," the courts are mostly, and increasingly, insensitive to the particular nature or medium of the speech.[84] To put it in the terms I used in the Introduction, the Court seeks to make its doctrines generally applicable to a host of contexts and media. Even if the Court is dealing with "the sound truck" or the "billboard," it will approach the matter under general doctrinal categories—public forum doctrine, commercial speech doctrine, and so on.

This broad statement sets to one side the many complexities that have arisen as the courts attempt to apply their broad and acontextual approach to the First Amendment in real-world contexts. Nevertheless, it captures something important about conventional approaches to the First Amendment. It suggests that these approaches are both simplified and simplifying: in order to unify the vast landscape of First Amendment law and theory, they operate at a high level of abstraction. That means they inevitably neglect many important considerations. What these conventional approaches miss or obscure, and why they do so, is the subject of the next chapter.

2

The Lures and Snares of Acontextuality

As we saw in Chapter 1, Justice Oliver Wendell Holmes, Jr., is a pivotal figure in the development of First Amendment doctrine, and more broadly of American legal thought. Holmes often expressed himself in aperçus, so it is unsurprising that he means different things to different people. That's a lucky stroke for us, because Holmes provides both the central text *against* First Amendment institutionalism and the central text *for* it. More than that, he opens a window onto two very different ways of thinking about the relationship between law and the world.

The first text appears in Holmes's celebrated 1897 essay *The Path of the Law*. "One mark of a great lawyer," Holmes writes, "is that he sees the application of the broadest rules." He illustrates his point with a counterexample: "There is a story of a Vermont justice of the peace before whom a suit was brought by one farmer against another for breaking a churn. The justice took time to consider, and then said that he had looked through the statutes, and could find nothing about churns, and gave judgment for the defendant."[1]

The justice of the peace, in this telling, is worse than a rube: he comes off as a *nonlawyer*. Holmes's point is that "one can fail to see what the law really is by failing to discern what the law is at a sufficiently high level of generality."[2] The justice of the peace fails to see that there is "no morally relevant difference" between "butter churns and other objects broken maliciously by somebody else."[3] This is the world of rule-of-law values: of legal rules and norms whose broad applicability offer "clarity, publicity, stability, consistency, and prospectivity" to the law and its subjects.[4]

Now, we hardly need Holmes to tell us that there is no morally relevant difference between churns and other breakable objects for purposes of a tort action. But it is not so easy to determine when morally relevant differences *do* exist between two kinds of seemingly similar conduct that someone seeks to bring under the same legal principle. The question for lawyers is where and how to go about finding those differences. Do they come from the law itself, or from somewhere else? And if they come from somewhere else, should that affect the way lawyers see the world?

This brings us to the second text from Holmes. He once observed that in law, "We must think things not words." At least, he added, "we must constantly translate our words into the facts for which they stand, if we are to keep to the real and the true."[5] The question for us is whether law maintains a close connection between the words it uses and the facts for which they stand, or whether its words tend to come untethered from the social world. We must ask whether First Amendment law, and constitutional law more generally, have "become increasingly a doctrine of words merely, not of things," and if so, why.[6]

Lures

Few human activities cannot be described in legal terms. "American law," one writer has suggested, "is sweeping, pervasive, and all-encompassing."[7] But law's broad reach presents difficulties. The more activities it reaches, the more questions it raises about how those charged with applying the law can do so without entering a world full of particularities, of facts and contexts about which they know little. Judges may not know much about professional golf, for instance; yet if a case requires them to consider how a federal law requiring accommodations for persons with disabilities applies to professional golf, they will rule on the case despite their relative ignorance.[8] Furthermore, because predictability and generality are major virtues of the rule of law, judges will face a tension between their responsiveness to facts in particular cases and their desire to craft legal principles that can address wide swaths of human activity in a unified fashion.[9]

[43]

Judges and lawyers usually resolve this tension . . . well, like judges and lawyers. They see the world through *legal* categories. Where these categories come from—whether from the values that surround us in social life and the commonsense intuitions we bring to the world, or from "pure" principles derived from the law itself[10]—is less important than what happens once lawyers get hold of these distinctions. What they do is to put them in distinctly legal terms: to organize them around legal, rather than prelegal, categories.

Return to the justice of the peace and the churn. One path the judge in such a case could follow is to learn enough about churns to arrive at "a complete theory of churns and their place in farming culture."[11] But lawyers and judges rarely take that path. Instead, they ask what the relevant *legal* principles are. They think in terms of torts, or property, or malicious destruction, and they attempt to come up with a rule that will allow them to decide not only the case of the churn but any other case that involves the same legal categories.[12] In this way, they arrive at a stable and predictable set of categories that purports to apply across a wide variety of disputes and factual situations.

Consider a contemporary example: the Internet. If any field of legal scholarship has boomed in the last twenty years, it is Internet law. And yet some scholars consider the whole idea of "Internet law" absurd—because there is *just law*. "[T]he best way to learn the law applicable to specialized endeavors," Judge Frank Easterbrook writes, "is to study general rules"; there can no more be a law of the Internet than there is a "law of the horse."[13] Not everyone agrees.[14] But Easterbrook's dismissal of the very idea of Internet law captures an important tendency in legal thought. We should be concerned not with technical specifics, but with *legal* categories: jurisdiction, contracts, torts, crimes, and so on.[15]

There are compelling justifications for such an approach. For one thing, judges and lawyers cannot possibly be experts on every social activity they deal with. Moreover, they value predictability and generality in and of themselves—and quite rightly. They lean heavily on legal categories because they believe doing so is the best route to a stable system of legal principles. They also see this approach as necessary to the achievement of fairness. They do not want to treat those who sue because of a lost butter churn any differently from those who sue because of a lost tractor or a lost factory. Even if they trust *themselves* to make the right distinctions, they don't want to hand less reliable judges the discretion to treat people differently because of morally irrelevant factors.

Finally, some lawyers and legal philosophers believe this approach is necessary if law is to *be* law in a meaningful sense rather than something else—namely, politics. As Frederick Schauer puts it, "law, and especially constitutional law, have long been understood to be matters of principle and not of policy." This view is closely associated with the legal philosopher Ronald Dworkin, who believes legal interpreters ought to function at a relatively abstract level, asking whether legal principles demonstrate fit and integrity, rather than taking a policy- and fact-driven approach.[16] For other legal professionals, those working in a "formalist" vein, law must consist of a system of clear rules. Tinkering with these rules—creating myriad ad hoc exceptions because of particular sets of facts—undermines the rule of law.[17] In both schools of thought the same impulse is at work: a belief that for the legal system to function fairly and effectively, there can and must be clear and pure law, arrived at through clear and pure legal analysis.

These are perfectly sensible justifications for the way lawyers and judges work. But a sensible idea—that there is value in lawyers' working primarily with legal concepts and categories—can become an *idée fixe*. A well-worn path can become a rut; a taste can become a craving.

So it is in the law. Lawyers, judges, and scholars do not have just a *reason* to carve up the world into legal categories. They have an "*important psychological need*"—a "*deeply felt desire . . . to achieve noninstrumental certainty in the law*."[18] That no such thing might exist is as nothing in the face of the craving for certainty, predictability, and stability, which lawyers believe can only be found in legal analysis.

Call this phenomenon the *lure of acontextuality:* the attraction that lawyers and judges feel toward carving up the world into legal concepts and categories that transcend particular factual contexts.[19] The lure of acontextuality tells lawyers and judges they ought to be "stripped down like a runner,"[20] focusing on legal generalities and abstractions and avoiding an undue attachment to factual context.

We should not sneer at the lure of acontextuality. In many respects, trying to see the forest and not just the trees—trying to identify values that can unify and explain large segments of human activity—is not just the theoretical project of lawyers and judges; it is what it means to have a theory at all.[21] And focusing on forests rather than trees, even if it sometimes means obscuring apparent factual differences, can be an important way of ensuring the generality and predictability that are the hallmarks of the rule of law. Moreover, as we have seen, not all those differences are morally relevant: whether a tree has red or green leaves may be important to the arborist, but no one else. In short, before we can criticize the lure of acontextuality, we must first acknowledge its genuine importance.

Snares

Even so, we might ask: What *risks* does the lure of acontextuality pose for the law? When does the lure become a snare? The short answer is the one Holmes gave us: acontextuality becomes dangerous when it leads us to think words, not things. It ceases to be a reasonable solution to a problem, and threatens to become a problem in its own right, when the words that make up our legal categories and concepts stray from the real, the true, and the morally or functionally relevant.

Again, consider the examples of the churn and the Internet. The goal of acontextuality is to achieve a level of generality that allows us to treat similar conduct similarly. For that reason, Holmes ridiculed the justice of the peace's fruitless search for a law of the churn when he should have been looking at basic categories of tort law; and Judge Easterbrook urged us to view the Internet as something that could be addressed by the same general rules that govern other areas of human conduct. We should pitch our understanding at the level of abstraction at which "morally relevant differences" become apparent.[22]

But those morally relevant differences may not *be* apparent unless we are sufficiently educated about the facts and context surrounding particular activities. Our intuition tells us that whether our neighbor has maliciously destroyed a churn or a tractor should make no difference under the law. But our intuition may not be capable of doing the work we demand of it unless it is adequately informed as to the circumstances.

Worse still, it may lead us astray. We may fail to see morally relevant differences where they exist, or we may see morally relevant differences where none exist. To take a First Amendment example, the courts for years treated defamation cases the same regardless of whether the target of the speech was an anonymous citizen or the president of the United States. But in 1964, in *New York Times v. Sullivan* the Supreme Court concluded that the different identities of these plaintiffs was practically relevant to our system of public discourse. Some plaintiffs—public officials—may need to be subjected to greater levels of criticism if our public conversation about political matters is to remain "uninhibited, robust, and wide-open."[23]

In short, acontextuality may not guide our intuition enough to provide us with a basis for making relevant distinctions between different kinds of conduct covered by the law. "Competence with and immersion in a network of practical concerns" may be necessary for the legal concepts we use "to be intelligible."[24] Even if there is no "law of the churn," we still need to know enough about churns to decide what legal concept ought to govern them. Similarly, Judge Easterbrook may be right that the "law of the Internet" is no more necessary than the "law of the horse," but we will not know whether *either* category is necessary unless we know enough about both horses and the Internet to make this determination. The general concepts and categories of the law itself, if they become self-referential and come untethered from actual facts and social practices, cannot answer these kinds of questions. We need information about the nature of the activity we are judging and the activities we are comparing it to. So one snare of acontextuality is that carving up the world into legal categories may not help us to see the world as it really is and to make relevant distinctions between different kinds of conduct.

A similar argument has been made by Robert Post. Legal doctrine, he writes, "always presupposes a picture of how the world may be categorized so as to be rendered amenable to legal judgment." But even if this picture ought to be fairly abstract, it cannot be utterly disconnected from the social world. Ultimately, "all legal values are rooted in the experiences associated with local and specific kinds of social practices." Law is "a form of governance" and thus "does not deal with values as merely abstract ideas or principles. Values in the law function instead to signify concrete forms of actual or potential social life in which what we consider desirable may find realization."[25]

Put simply, law does not operate in a vacuum. It must have something to do with what we value *in the world*. Our sense of morally relevant differences in the law will depend on what we see as morally relevant differences in the "real" world. That will depend on the way we live and experience those differences, which will rest on a foundation of actual social practices. To forget this is to take a long step down the road of thinking words, not things.

This snare leads to another. We might call it the Procrustean bed problem, after the myth of Procrustes, who invited unwary guests to sleep on his iron bed—and either stretched or amputated them to fit it. Acontextuality purports to give us rules and concepts that will serve as a one-size-fits-all solution to a variety of categories of human conduct. Time and again, however, lawyers and judges find that the problem doesn't fit the solution.

This leaves them with two options. The first is to mold the facts to fit the rule, just as Procrustes molded his victims to fit his iron bed. The result will be similarly torturous: rather than changing the law to be responsive to the context, they will mutilate the facts and the context to fit the law. Law will be pure but not useful—or its usefulness will come at a great cost. The second option is to abandon acontextuality and recognize that particular facts and contexts demand different rules. The law will grow increasingly complex to respond to those various facts and contexts. In so doing, it will lose the very features that made acontextuality attractive in the first place: stability, predictability, and generality.

This snare grips even tighter when, as they often do, lawyers and judges try to do both. They may try to shape the law to respond to particular social facts and contexts without admitting that they are doing so. Or they may draw narrow exceptions without openly abandoning the general legal rules, concepts, and categories that are at the heart of the acontextual approach. They may insist that the rule of law remains a "law of rules,"[26] while creating so many exceptions and distinctions that the rules themselves become unintelligible.

The result will be incoherence, inconsistency, and illusion. The incoherence and inconsistency will stem from the fact that what purports to be a system of general legal rules and concepts is in fact a Swiss cheese, a collection of partial rules and partial exceptions with plenty of holes in between. The illusion will be the continued insistence that the law is pure and acontextual despite the implicit admission that this is impossible. Even as it continues to insist on its own purity and acontextuality, the law will either achieve that purity by sacrificing responsiveness to the real world, or abandon it without saying so openly. To the extent that the law takes either of these paths, it will become a machine for the manufacture of cognitive dissonance.

Again, the problem is not that the lure of acontextuality is irrational. The rule of law, and the generality it bespeaks, can be a tremendous virtue.[27] The problem is that acontextuality can *lead* to irrationality. Lawyers and judges want a system of general legal concepts and categories that offers them the hope of a fair, just, and general set of rules for the ordering of human affairs. But they also need to respond to the actual facts on the ground—tons of niggling details, most of which are irrelevant but some of which are crucial. They need to distinguish the relevant details from the irrelevant ones. But legal principles and categories alone will not help them do so. They want simultaneously to live in the real world and to rise above it. Try as they may, they can't do both. The lure of acontextuality is also a snare.

Lures and Snares of Acontextuality in First Amendment Law

First Amendment law is a prime example of both the lures and the snares of acontextuality. In principle, it is indifferent to the identity of the speaker and the social function and context of the speech. At the same time, in numerous cases it has been forced to acknowledge that different facts and contexts call for different results.

First Amendment doctrine thus faces a dual dilemma. In some cases, the courts are insensitive to contextual and institutional differences that should matter. In others, the courts *are* sensitive to differences in context, but feel compelled to shoehorn their decisions into an acontextual framework. The result is inconsistency, incoherence, and a lack of either candor or sound justification.

LURES

In First Amendment law, as we saw in Chapter 1, the Supreme Court draws some distinctions between types of speech, particularly between "high-value" and "no-value" or "low-value" speech. Some categories of speech, the Court said in *Chaplinsky*, "are no essential part of any exposition of ideas" and are "of such slight social value as a step to truth that any benefit that may be derived from them is clearly outweighed by the social interest in order and morality." These include "the lewd and obscene, the profane, the libelous, and the insulting or 'fighting' words."[28] This category also once included commercial speech.[29] Conversely, political speech lies "at the heart of the First Amendment."[30]

The truth is much more complex. Both the number and the relevance of the kinds of "low-value" speech identified by the Court have dramatically decreased in recent decades. In part under the influence of the lure of acontextuality—or what Daniel Farber calls "a formalist impulse toward uniformity"—the Supreme Court has progressively narrowed the reach of the "low-value" speech category in favor of a broader, more content- and context-independent approach to the First Amendment.[31]

Defamation has been constitutionalized since the Court's ruling in *New York Times v. Sullivan*. Obscenity has become more strongly protected over the last half-century.[32] The only sexual speech that is still entirely relegated to low-value status is child pornography, and even there the Court has struck down provisions aimed at real or "virtual" (computer-generated) child pornography that run afoul of other general doctrinal rules such as the rule disfavoring overbroad statutes.[33] Profane and "indecent" speech can be regulated in narrow circumstances, such as broadcasting when children may be watching or listening.[34] But this rule has come under fire on the Court,[35] and its members broadly agree that indecent or profane speech is permissible in most contexts.[36] Fighting words may still be prohibited, but the Court has struck down regulations aimed at particular fighting words because of their viewpoint.[37] Commercial speech is more susceptible to regulation than other forms of speech, at least if it is considered false or misleading. But the idea that commercial speech in general falls outside the scope of First Amendment protection has essentially disappeared.[38] Some justices believe there should be no distinction between nonmisleading commercial speech and any other protected speech.[39] In short, "low-value speech" as an unprotected category of expressive conduct has greatly diminished in the seventy years since *Chaplinsky*.[40]

As for "high-value" speech, although the Court continues to affirm the importance of political speech, such statements have less doctrinal impact than they used to. For one thing, distinguishing between high- and low-value speech means something only if there is such a thing as low-value speech, and increasingly there isn't. For another, the courts increasingly apply either strict or intermediate scrutiny in all speech cases, so the bite of judicial review is at least *potentially* present whether a case involves high- or low-value speech. Moreover, the acontextual approach makes it difficult to identify "high-value" speech in the first place, let alone to distinguish it from any other forms of speech. Some writers thus argue that the courts ought to focus only on the "government's reasons for regulating" speech, not on "the value inhering in some tangible form of speech or the communicative intentions of authors."[41] Finally, the Court has expanded the definition of high-value speech far beyond political speech to include artistic, scientific, and other forms of speech.[42] And it uses high-value speech as a default category, treating most speech as high-value unless it falls into one of the increasingly narrow exceptions, such as child pornography.[43]

The distinction between high- and low-value speech thus does much less work than it used to. Of course, even that distinction, although derived from some sort of calculus about the social value of that speech compared with its social costs, was fairly categorical in approach. It depended not on a nuanced consideration of the value of each individual instance of speech, but on whether that speech could be slotted into the broad labels of "high-value" or "low-value" speech. Even that minor departure from acontextuality has its detractors, however. Although the Court has pared down the general category of low-value speech substantially over time, some of its members have made clear their abhorrence of *any* method of distinguishing between high- and low-value speech that turns on a weighing of social costs and benefits.[44]

If distinctions based on the *value* of speech are doing little work in helping the courts to sort cases,[45] what is? One possibility is that the courts could focus on the identity of the speaker. By and large, however, they have not taken this approach. "The identity of the speaker," the Court has declared, "is not decisive in determining whether speech is protected."[46]

One prominent example is commercial speech, in which the Court has made clear that any limits on First Amendment protections must be based only on the nature of the speech or of the regulation, not on the identity of the speaker or the fact that it is operating for profit.[47] Another is the intersection between political speech and campaign finance laws, where the Court has said that what matters is that the speech in question is political speech, not the corporate or individual identity of the speaker.[48]

A third example involves the courts' treatment of the press. Their refusal to distinguish between the press and other speakers is remarkable because there is a strong textual basis for the distinction: the Press Clause of the First Amendment. If we could ever expect the courts to single out a particular speaker for protection based on its identity, surely the press qualifies.[49]

For the most part, however, the Supreme Court has refused to do so. As Chief Justice Warren Burger stated, "The First Amendment does not 'belong' to any definable category of persons or entities: It belongs to all who exercise its freedoms." Burger made clear that his reluctance to single out the press was based not just on the history of the Press Clause but on the dangers of straying from an acontextual approach to First Amendment doctrine. Such a move, he argued, would raise a "fundamental difficulty . . . of definition," requiring judges to wade into such "variables as content of expression, frequency or fervor of expression, or ownership of the techno-logical means of dissemination" of speech.[50]

In a number of areas, the Court has refused to make this move. First, it has declined to grant the press special privileges or immunities. In *Branzburg v. Hayes,* a fractured Court said that granting the press a privilege to maintain the confidentiality of sources would "present practical and concep-tual difficulties of a high order," including the necessity of defining "those categories of newsmen who qualified for the privilege."[51] Second, the Court has declined to give the press any special right of access under the Press Clause: a distinct right to attend government proceedings such as trials and hearings or a presumptive entitlement to visit government property such as prisons.[52] Third, it has refused to grant the press any special privileges under private law. While it has constitutionalized the law of defamation to ensure free and open criticism of public officials and discussion of matters of public concern, it has treated the press no differently from individual speakers in this area.[53] Similarly, it has held that a general claim of breach of contract applies to the press when it is accused of breaking a promise to maintain the confidentiality of a source, even if the media defendant asserts that it had sound journalistic reasons for doing so.[54]

On the other side of the coin, the courts' indifference to the speaker's identity or institutional role in a given context is also evident in their treat-ment of the "state." What is important here is not so much any contradiction between what the courts have done and what the Constitution says,[55] but the sheer clumsiness of "the state" as a sorting mechanism in First Amendment doctrine. Government actors come in all shapes and sizes and differ greatly with respect to function. The state is, to be sure, often that familiar figure: Big Brother, the regulator or censor. When government takes that form, it may make sense to treat different kinds of state actors—the federal government, state governments, local governments—alike.[56] But the state takes many other forms. It can be a publicly owned broadcaster, a public school, an arts funding council, a library, an employer, a public university, and so on.

Although, as we will see, the courts have often been forced—at no little cost to doctrinal consistency and coherence—to distinguish between these government roles in practice, in principle they treat them all the same, lumping them together under the general, and fundamentally *legal*, category of "the state." The state is often treated the same whether it is acting as a regulator or as something different, like a public library or school.[57]

Although the courts *do* sometimes distinguish between different forms of state actors, the Supreme Court has not made a serious effort to justify these distinctions, leaving them as little more than ad hoc exceptions. For the most part, the Court has offered only one serious distinction in its treatment of state actors for First Amendment purposes: the distinction between government regulation of speech and speech by government itself. The latter is generally considered to be beyond the purview of the First Amendment.[58] But that distinction is as subtle as a blunderbuss.

At least on its face, then, First Amendment doctrine is not driven by contextual factors such as the nature of the speech or the identity of the speaker. Instead, what is doing the doctrinal work in this area is a set of broader categories that are fundamentally legal and acontextual. In deciding First Amendment cases, the courts seek to abstract away from particular facts and situations, and identify general legal rules and concepts that apply regardless of context.

The leading example is the central rule in modern First Amendment doctrine: the distinction between content-based and content-neutral speech regulations. Content-based restrictions on speech are subject to strict scrutiny, while content-neutral restrictions are much more likely to be upheld.

One puzzle about the content distinction is that it may have a perverse effect. Both content-based and content-neutral regulations restrict the total amount of expression available to us.[59] But content-neutral regulations, which generally cover *more* speech, are subjected to a *lower* level of scrutiny, while content-based regulations, which generally cover *less* speech, are subjected to a *higher* level of scrutiny. Justice Louis Brandeis famously opined that the remedy for bad speech is *"more* speech."[60] Yet these differing levels of protection for content-based and content-neutral restrictions seem to make it easier for the government to ensure that we have *less* speech.

Geoffrey Stone has offered several explanations for this "seeming anomaly." The First Amendment, he argues, "is concerned not only with the extent to which a law reduces the total quantity of information, but also—and perhaps even more fundamentally—with at least three additional factors: distortion of public debate, improper motivation, and communicative impact." Content-based laws are more likely than content-neutral laws to reflect a government bias against particular viewpoints, which distorts public discussion; they are more likely to stem from improper motivations on the part of the officials regulating the speech; and they are more likely to be based on an impermissibly "paternalis[tic] or intoleran[t]" view of how listeners will react to the regulated speech.[61] Another reason may be that sweeping content-neutral speech restrictions create broad political coalitions that can effectively oppose such laws; in contrast, strict judicial scrutiny may be necessary to guard against content-based restrictions that only affect small or politically unpopular groups, and thus are easier to enact.

These are persuasive explanations.[62] But we can add yet another. If the lure of acontextuality expresses an "important psychological need" for lawyers and judges, perhaps this impulse is also at work in the courts' fixation on the distinction between content-based and content-neutral speech regulations. This distinction, by operating at a broad and abstract level, "accords with the persistent yearning in American constitutional culture to separate law from politics." It creates the "appearance of generality and universality," allowing judges to take comfort in the impartiality of their judgment. It does so by employing "increasingly general categories," "reified and abstract conceptions."[63] This approach is part of a broader jurisprudential pattern: a deeply felt desire to have general legal categories, rather than particularistic examinations of fact and context, do all the work.

The content distinction serves this impulse well. First, it makes the judicial task one of taxonomy rather than fine-grained analysis, reducing the judge's job to a series of mechanical slotting exercises.[64] Second, it converts a reasonable intuition—that we should be more suspicious of restrictions aimed at the content of speech than of restrictions in which the content of the speech is irrelevant—into a shortcut or heuristic, treating the general categories of content-based and content-neutral as stand-ins for more particular conclusions about whether a speech regulation should be presumptively suspect or not.

This shortcut often serves us well. But sometimes these broad categories do not fully capture what is going on in the real world. They may be blind to cases in which the factual context requires a departure from standard doctrine. In those cases, either the courts will end up with overly broad or overly narrow approaches to particular First Amendment problems, or the content distinction's "inability to make real world distinctions [will] be compensated for by highly technical, ad hoc exceptions."[65] The content distinction is thus a prominent example of the lure of acontextuality: the desire to use *legal* categories to carve up the world.

Another example can be found in public forum doctrine. We might view the emergence of this doctrine as both a manifestation of the lure of acontextuality and a solution to the problems the lure of acontextuality leaves in its wake.

Begin with the latter point. One function of public forum doctrine is to allow courts to soften the impact of another acontextual doctrine: the rule that the government has the right to control the use of its own property.[66] That rule, like many general legal categories, does not cut finely enough. It fails to distinguish between cases in which the government is acting as the manager of its own affairs and those in which it is regulating the affairs of others, including the public.[67] In particular, it does not, by itself, distinguish between speech *by* the government on its own property and speech by the *public* on government property. Public forum doctrine is thus necessary to ensure that, for example, the public can continue speaking in parks and on the streets with full assurance of First Amendment protection.

Of course, this doctrine does not capture the many varieties of government property. So the Supreme Court has served up a smorgasbord of further categories: public forums, limited public forums, nonpublic forums, non-forums, and so on. The more categories the Court comes up with, the more it is criticized for "the blurriness, the occasional artificiality, and the frequent irrelevance, of the categories within the public forum classification."[68]

From another perspective, the artificiality of the distinctions drawn in public forum doctrine is not a bug, but a feature. Judges *want* "artificial" categories to do their work for them; they don't trust their own ability to use "natural" categories. Thus, public forum doctrine, with its focus on legal slotting mechanisms only loosely connected to the real-world complexities of speech by government and public speech on government property, is not only a response to problems created in First Amendment doctrine by other acontextual rules, but a specifically *acontextual* response. In responding to a genuine dilemma—how to have general rules permitting government to control its own property without sacrificing the public's use of parks and other government-owned sites of public discourse—the courts turn to "formalistic labels."[69]

A final example of the lure of acontextuality involves the mother of all distinctions in constitutional doctrine: the public-private distinction. Given our general understanding of the Constitution as protecting individual constitutional rights against government incursion rather than private action, there is sound justification for the courts' focus on "state action." My intention is not to bury the public-private distinction, but to consider how and why it operates.

In a word, it operates acontextually.[70] As Frederick Schauer observes, "Although governmental action comes in many different institutional forms, the doctrine treats them all as essentially equivalent. . . . [S]tate action doctrine employs the same factors to determine the existence of state action regardless of the institutional settings in which they occur."[71] It sees all state actors as censors or regulators, no matter how much they differ in nature or kind. In this, it is "lawlike to the core."[72]

Much of the criticism of the public-private distinction, and state action doctrine in general, centers around the argument that there *is* no such distinction.[73] Both because of the expansive reach of the modern regulatory state and because public law defines our private entitlements in the first place, the two are inextricably intertwined.[74] The present concern regarding state action doctrine and the public-private distinction, however, is not with their conceptual underpinnings, but with the crude way in which the courts employ them. Even if there are good reasons for the basic distinction between "state actors" and "private actors," we can still worry that it is not fine-grained enough to address the sheer variety of state actions and state actors.

Defenders of these doctrines sometimes concede this point, but argue that this coarse distinction is necessary if we are to maintain a distinction "between constitutional and ordinary law."[75] That argument makes clear what is at work in the state action and public-private concepts: the desire to rescue law from context, and principle from policy, by sorting various actors and activities into broad "legal" categories. The mother of all doctrinal categories in constitutional law is, it would appear, the child of acontextuality.

SNARES

That the lure of acontextuality can also be a snare is glaringly obvious in modern First Amendment doctrine. The problem, simply put, is that "context matters."[76] Any system that uses a broad and capacious set of categories and classifications will necessarily miss some of the details that distinguish different contexts and actors from one another. Sometimes those details will not be "morally relevant" ones: a traffic law shouldn't treat drivers of blue cars differently than drivers of green cars. But when our legal categories do miss morally relevant details, either making a false distinction between two actors or wrongly lumping them together, there is a problem. And if the failure to spot those morally relevant details stems from the fact that the courts routinely employ purely legal categories that omit such details, the problem may be systemic.

Nothing I have said so far should be especially controversial. Lawyers and judges know perfectly well that their categories cannot possibly capture all that goes on in the real world. Outside of judicial confirmation hearings, no one truly believes that "knowing" and "applying" the law, in a mechanical fashion that draws only on legal categories, fully describes the judicial task. Defenders of this approach might argue that the benefits of the acontextual approach outweigh the costs.[77] Before we can agree with this conclusion, however, we need to know more about the causes and consequences of acontextuality in First Amendment law. We have already discussed the reasons for this categorical approach; now we turn to its consequences.

Courts regularly stray from the acontextual path, admitting that their general legal categories are inadequate for deciding a host of First Amendment cases. Almost at will, they make exceptions and qualifications to the broad rules that ostensibly guide them. This not only tells us something about the messy nature of First Amendment doctrine. When considered from within the framework of acontextuality, it tells us a great deal about *why* the doctrine is so messy.

Consider three examples. *Arkansas Educational Television Commission v. Forbes* involved a dispute between a political candidate and the Arkansas Educational Television Commission (AETC), which operated five noncommercial stations that comprised the Arkansas Educational Television Network (AETN). The AETC's professional staff "exercise[d] broad editorial discretion in planning the network's programming" in order to "insulate its programming decisions from political pressure." In planning a series of televised debates between candidates for federal office in the period leading up to the 1992 elections, the staff decided to limit participation to the candidates who represented major parties or had "strong popular support."[78] This decision effectively excluded Ralph Forbes, an independent candidate. Forbes sued.

The lower courts' struggle to figure out which categorical box the case fit into illustrates both the lures and snares of acontextuality. On the case's first go-round, the United States Court of Appeals for the Eighth Circuit concluded in a rather categorical fashion that the commission should be classified as a "state actor"—and thus, following the traditional understanding of the state, as a potential censor. As a result, it held that Forbes had "a qualified right of access created by AETN's sponsorship of a debate."[79] The case returned to the district court, which focused on two other general doctrines: public forum law and the content distinction. It concluded that the debate should be treated as a nonpublic forum, leaving only the question whether Forbes's exclusion was solely viewpoint-related. Since it believed there were viewpoint-neutral reasons to exclude him, it ruled for the broadcaster.[80] The Eighth Circuit reversed again, and again the appeals court's reasoning focused on broad conceptual categories. The court conceded that the broadcaster's decision to exclude Forbes was "exactly the kind of journalistic judgment routinely made by newspeople." But it said this was the wrong category into which to slot the defendant: "[A] crucial fact here is that the people making this judgment were not ordinary journalists: they were employees of the government. The First Amendment exists to protect individuals, not government. The question of political viability [on which the decision to exclude Forbes turned] is, indeed, so subjective, so arguable, so susceptible of variation in individual opinion, as to provide no secure basis for the exercise of governmental power consistent with the First Amendment."[81]

Moreover, it concluded, the debate should be classified not as a nonpublic forum, but as a limited public forum. Given that conclusion, the fact that the public broadcaster had exercised journalistic judgment was irrelevant. The only question was whether the "government," understood as a general legal category, could on its own authority "define a class of speakers so as to exclude a person who would naturally be expected to be a member of the class on no basis other than party affiliation."[82]

The lure of acontextuality is clearly at work here. Both the district court and the appeals court acted as if simply slotting the case into particular legal concepts and categories—public forum, state actor, content-neutrality—would resolve it, no matter the particular facts. More than that, the Eighth Circuit feared the consequences of doing anything else. Despite its admission that the decision to exclude Forbes had been a routine exercise of "journalistic judgment," it felt obliged to classify public broadcasters not as "ordinary journalists," but as government employees. Slotting them into this category turned a routine exercise of professional judgment into a potential threat in future cases: any approach that privileged this kind of professional judgment would be dangerous if applied across the entire range of state actors or government employees. From that perspective, the court had no choice but to forbid Forbes's exclusion from the debate—not for the sake of the facts, but for the sake of the *doctrine*.

The Supreme Court reversed. Tellingly, it began by asking "whether public forum principles apply to the case at all." Public forum doctrine, it declared, "should not be extended in a mechanical way" from the traditional context of "streets and parks" to the "very different context of public television broadcasting." In that context, the "broad right of access for outside speakers" demanded by public forum doctrine "would be antithetical, as a general rule, to the discretion that stations and their editorial staff must exercise to fulfill their journalistic purpose." Similarly, the Court said that the restrictions against viewpoint-based speech restrictions that operate within public forum doctrine were a poor fit with the case, given "the nature of editorial discretion" being exercised by the broadcaster. The risks of untrammeled discretion that so concerned the Eighth Circuit were necessary in order to serve the broadcaster's journalistic purpose.[83]

Although it recognized the snares of acontextuality in the case, the Court could not fully escape its lures. "The special characteristics of candidate debates," it said, "support the conclusion that the AETC debate was *a forum of some type.*" But it concluded that the debate was best classified as a non-public forum, and thus one in which "AETC could exclude Forbes in the reasonable, viewpoint-neutral exercise of its journalistic discretion."[84] The Court rescued the case from one imperfect legal category by slotting it into another one.

Forbes illustrates both the lures and the snares of acontextuality: the psychological need for an ordered and fundamentally legal approach, and the admission that those categories may not aptly describe either the dispute or the disputants. Both the Supreme Court and the lower courts were driven to view the case through the lens of broad legal categories, like public forum doctrine or the state action doctrine, and struggled to fit the parties into those slots. But the facts defied such facile characterizations. Not all government employees are the same; not all government forums fit neatly into public forum doctrine. What made those legal categories inapt was the intrusion of nonlegal categories like "journalist." As Frederick Schauer has put it, "Although the doctrinal structure of the majority opinion is focused on public forum doctrine, and to some extent on the idea of viewpoint discrimination, in the end it is the institutional character of public broadcasting as broadcasting"—what Schauer calls "state journalism *as journalism,* as opposed to state journalism as an enterprise of the state"—"that appears to have determined the outcome of the case."[85] The Court reached the right result—but only by distorting its own doctrine.

The same contortions can be found in our second example. *National Endowment for the Arts v. Finley* involved government decisions concerning publicly funded art. Congress amended the statute governing the National Endowment for the Arts, the nation's primary distributor of public arts funding, to require it to ensure that "artistic excellence and artistic merit are the criteria by which [grant] applications are judged, taking into consideration general standards of decency and respect for the diverse beliefs and values of the American public."[86] Four controversial performance artists sued, charging that they had been denied grants on political grounds and that the statute was unconstitutionally vague and violated the general rule against viewpoint-based speech restrictions by government.[87]

Viewed through the lens of acontextual First Amendment doctrine, *Finley* presented a clear case against the statute. It involved government employees sifting among private speech acts and making funding determinations based on a relatively standardless set of criteria. It invoked "decency" as a possible basis for denying funding, although indecent speech is not generally among the remaining categories of low-value speech.[88] The case hit all the right buttons: state action, content discrimination, and possible viewpoint discrimination.

Nevertheless, the Court upheld the statute. "Any content-based considerations that may be taken into account in the grant-making process," it said, "are a consequence of the nature of arts funding." "The 'very assumption' of the NEA is that grants will be awarded according to the 'artistic worth of competing applicants,'" it added, "and absolute neutrality is simply 'inconceivable.'" The unusual context of arts funding decisions made the case distinguishable from other cases in which it had applied public forum doctrine and the content distinction more rigidly.[89]

The Court's decision provoked anguished responses. Justice Antonin Scalia, the foremost advocate on the Supreme Court of an acontextual approach to constitutional law, concurred in the judgment, but for very different reasons. What mattered to him was not the *unique* status of arts funding decisions, but the *general* principle that government can choose to subsidize or not subsidize whatever speech it likes. In his view, the categorical legal distinction between "'abridging' speech and funding it" was a "fundamental divide" that did all the necessary work in the case.[90]

Justice David Souter dissented. Where Justice Scalia would have upheld the statute, Souter would have struck it down, but for equally categorical reasons. To him, there was no difference between this and any other government statute that engaged in viewpoint discrimination or was unconstitutionally vague. The Solicitor General had suggested at oral argument that "there is something unique . . . about the Government funding of the arts for First Amendment purposes." Justice Souter recoiled from this suggestion, arguing that First Amendment doctrine "forecloses any claim that the NEA and the First Amendment issues that arise under it are somehow unique."[91]

Like *Forbes, Finley* illustrates both the lures and the snares of acontextuality in First Amendment law. The categorical doctrinal tools available to the Court seemed to compel the conclusion that the statute violated the First Amendment. Again, however, the Court recognized that those tools could not do all the work demanded of them. Instead, "the nature of art [did] the work in *Finley* that the nature of journalism did in *Forbes*."[92] Strikingly, the majority in *Finley* followed the same rhetorical pattern as the majority in *Forbes*, referring to the party in terms of its *function*—as a journalist, or an arts funder—rather than simply calling it the "government," as the concurring and dissenting justices did.[93] In both cases, against the great weight of acontextual First Amendment doctrine, context mattered.

A third case shows the same dynamic at work. In *United States v. American Library Association*,[94] the question was whether public libraries could be forced to install Internet filters as a condition of the receipt of government funds. Government funding cases always raise difficult questions. Although the government is generally free to attach strings to the funds it gives out, it is barred from attaching "unconstitutional conditions": conditions that force private individuals or groups to sacrifice their constitutional rights in order to receive public benefits.[95] This is a notoriously difficult area of constitutional law. A further wrinkle raised by the case was how to characterize public libraries for purposes of public forum law.

In effect, however, the Supreme Court treated a contextual or institutional question as taking precedence over either of those doctrinal questions. It drew expressly on both *Forbes* and *Finley,* saying that in such cases, "forum analysis and heightened judicial scrutiny were incompatible with the role" played by each institution—in this case, with "the discretion that public libraries must have to fulfill their traditional missions." Standard public forum doctrine was "out of place in the context of this case." Instead, the Court said, it was required to "first examine the role of libraries in our society."[96]

The outcome of *American Library Association,* which—wrongly, in my view—upheld the funding condition, is less important for our purposes than its striking, if at times grudging, departure from common modes of thinking about the First Amendment. As Lillian BeVier, whose work argues powerfully for an acontextual approach, has written, although the "doctrinal choices" available to the Court "were straightforward, familiar, and comparatively clear, . . . several members of the Court neither sought guidance from nor appeared willing to have their analyses constrained by either established law or customary methodologies of First Amendment decision making."[97] For BeVier, this is cause for lament. She argues defensively that the majority opinion written by Chief Justice William Rehnquist "reflects a different, and more restrained, view of the Court's role in the sort of First

Amendment case represented by *American Library* than any of the separate opinions."⁹⁸ This is true in roughly the same sense that one might prefer to be blown to bits by a grenade rather than a nuclear bomb. Rehnquist's opinion, like the opinions in *Forbes* and *Finley*, struggles to fit the case within the usual constraints of First Amendment doctrine, but ultimately leaves the doctrine in tatters.

These examples are infrequent but representative. Much of the time the Court finds its way to an answer in First Amendment cases without having to stray too far from the standard doctrinal concepts and categories it has laid down. When a case comes along that challenges those concepts and categories, however, the cracks and fissures in the doctrine become all too obvious, especially if the Court tries to slot its decision into the preexisting legal framework. Then the lures of acontextuality become snares.

Why the Snares *Are* Snares

Naturally, the Supreme Court cannot possibly capture all the complexities of the real world in its legal doctrines. To say that generality is essential to the rule of law is not the same thing as saying it is perfectly attainable. From a common-law lawyer's perspective, those cracks and fissures are just the law "work[ing] itself pure."⁹⁹ They may show the challenges posed by an acontextual approach to the law, but they are not conclusive evidence that it should be abandoned. This argument is certainly defensible. Many people who advocate an acontextual approach to the law understand that it can only be an aspiration.

But this isn't the only way of thinking about it. The cracks and fissures we see in First Amendment doctrine tell us something important about legal doctrine and its development. They suggest that the tension between the lures and snares of acontextuality is deep and probably inevitable.

The cracks and fissures tell us, first, that the snares of acontextuality really are snares, not just growing pains. They show not just that an acontextual approach to the law is bound to be imperfect, but that such an approach tends repeatedly and perhaps fatally to undermine itself. They also suggest that there is room for alternative approaches. They invite us to think more closely about other ways that lawyers and judges could carve up the world. Let us begin that task by considering just what it is about the snares of acontextuality that makes them snares.

If, as most lawyers and judges would concede, pure acontextuality is impossible—if particular factual circumstances demand acknowledgment—then there are two possible responses. Both of them are deeply unsatisfactory, at least to those who feel the urge to achieve a pure, noninstrumental approach to the law. Both of them, indeed, threaten to capsize the whole project of acontextuality.

The first response is simply to make exceptions to general doctrine in order to address facts, contexts, and institutions that don't conform to that doctrine. Call this the exception strategy. If we view these simply *as* exceptions—regrettable but necessary carve-outs from the general rules that do not seriously impair the law's generality and acontextuality—they may not seem too troubling. Just as one swallow does not a summer make, so one narrow exception to public forum doctrine (or two, or three . . .) does not make public forum doctrine useless. But that response is insufficient. The exception strategy tells us a great deal about the weakness of the underlying general rules to which it is an exception. The more exceptions are necessary to a general rule, the less likely it is that the rule is actually serving its purpose—that it is actually achieving anything like generality.

The exception strategy also tells us something about the gap between legal language and the real world. As Frederick Schauer points out, "exceptions show how the meaning of a legal rule is related to the meaning of the language that law employs." They reveal the "larger relationship between law and a background social landscape whose most important elements are the language a society uses and the categories it deploys to carve up the world."[100] They suggest the ways in which law is "situat[ed] . . . in a world it both reflects and on which it is imposed."[101]

In other words, exceptions, like gasping canaries in coalmines, can be a good indicator of problems with the rules they are meant to preserve. The more of them there are, the more we must question whether the rules are working. If a principal value of legal rules is their generality, then the fact that a host of exceptions is needed to keep the acontextual enterprise going undermines that value. The more ad hoc the exceptions seem, the more likely it is that the general rule has failed to capture important and recurring aspects of the real world. The profusion of exceptions to the general doctrinal rules of the First Amendment suggests that acontextuality in First Amendment law is in grave condition.

A second response, which we may label the preservationist strategy, consists of attempting to perform surgery on the rules themselves. The goal is not so much to carve out exceptions to the general rules as to redraw the boundaries of those rules to absorb the exceptions. This is the evolutionary process of the common law in a nutshell: rewriting the law's operating system on the fly, using each new case as a basis for figuring out how the rules need to be modified to properly account for different circumstances.

There is something to be said for this approach, just as there is something to be said for the adaptability of any evolutionary system. But it is ultimately unsuccessful. The problem comes when lawyers' and judges' desire for an acontextual approach becomes paramount. Then it isn't simply a matter of the law evolving in a way that takes account of contexts it hadn't yet recognized or embraced. It is a matter of the law straining to bring those contexts within an acontextual set of concepts and categories. The goal in such cases will be twofold: to recognize new contexts and circumstances, but, and perhaps above all, to do so in a way that preserves the underlying acontextual structure of the law.

We can see this kind of impulse at work in First Amendment doctrine, and we can see the kinds of problems it breeds. Take public forum doctrine. The Court thought it had found a useful category in public forum doctrine: simple, parsimonious, and clear. But that category proved insufficient. So various public forum subcategories began to proliferate. That meant they could no longer provide what the doctrine was supposed to furnish in the first place: a clear, general, consistent, and predictable way for courts to reach the same outcomes in similar cases.[102] Finally, the courts were forced to concede that public forum doctrine, despite its goal of general applicability, was "out of place" in certain circumstances, such as those involving public libraries.[103] Yet in the very case in which it made that admission, the Supreme Court persisted in struggling to find a way to shoehorn the new context into its existing doctrine. Public forum doctrine was preserved, in a sense, but only at the cost of its coherence and predictability. The Court burned the village in order to save it.

The problem with the preservationist strategy, in short, is that sometimes it succeeds only at the cost of its own failure. It puts the acontextualist in an awkward, if not self-defeating, position. The judge strains so hard to fit a previously unrecognized social or factual context into the preexisting legal framework that the old framework loses its cardinal virtues: generality, consistency, predictability, and purity.[104]

Not every new case results in so dramatic a moment. Sometimes the old categories work—well enough, anyway. Sometimes they succeed in capturing a new context without undermining the old legal concepts. But not always. Often the very effort to preserve law's purity—its acontextuality—undermines that purity. That the law will reach a breaking point seems inevitable. Neither the exception strategy nor the preservationist strategy can postpone this moment forever. The snares of acontextuality really *are* snares.

For a host of reasons—practical, jurisprudential, and psychological—lawyers and judges seek a path through the law that is as pure, and as purely legal, as possible. They are not interested in the "law of the churn." They want a set of legal rules, concepts and categories, and doctrines that give them the same road map no matter what factual or social terrain they are wandering through.

There are sound reasons to favor such an approach. Predictability, stability, simplicity, and generality are desirable qualities in the law. So are restraint and institutional competence. Those who favor an acontextual approach believe that only fundamentally *legal* concepts and categories will restrain judges, and that anything other than those concepts and categories will fall outside lawyers' and judges' competence and lead to error and abuse.

But there are serious problems with this approach. Sometimes it will lead to a state of crisis. The further down the acontextual path we go, the more likely we are to reach a point at which our existing legal concepts and categories fail to acknowledge the wealth of facts and contexts that make up our lived reality.

Even once that point is reached, law may soldier on for some time in a relatively acontextual form. The existing concepts and categories will no longer be able to do all that we want, but the degree of cognitive dissonance this presents may not be too great at first. Eventually, however, as the gap between what law promises and the problems that reality confronts us with widens, the dissonance will become impossible to ignore.

At such moments, law may reach a tipping point at which the benefits of departing from settled ways of thinking and acting begin to outweigh the costs of making that change. Then we can imagine taking a new road. It is no longer a matter of carving out exceptions here and there, or of attempting to salvage the old legal categories, but of finding new categories to work with altogether. Acontextuality, after all, is not the only aspiration of the law. Another is responsiveness: the need to account for and respond to the circumstances of life as it is actually lived.[105]

To see this more clearly, recall the evolutionary model of the common law that we discussed earlier. According to evolutionary theory, things do not evolve in a gradual and incremental fashion forever. There are moments at which old evolutionary paths end and strikingly different new ones begin: when "long periods of stasis are followed by rapid" and radical change.[106] In this pattern of "punctuated equilibrium," new evolutionary paths emerge and then achieve stability over time. Of course, the success of any particular new path is not guaranteed: some new species die out. But there comes a point at which dramatic evolutionary change seems necessary and unavoidable. That prospect can be unsettling. But uncertainty may be preferable to trying to hang onto the old order even as it becomes increasingly incoherent. At these moments, the agony of death is also a prelude to the promise of rebirth.

Many students of the First Amendment believe we have reached such a moment. Robert Post has written that the Supreme Court's First Amendment jurisprudence "dances now macabrely on the edge of complete doctrinal disintegration," largely because the Court "has labored within the dominant First Amendment paradigm and hence has fruitlessly struggled to craft a doctrine that would reflect a universal and generic constitutional value for speech."[107] In Frederick Schauer's view, we may have reached the point of "intractable tension between free speech theory and judicial methodology."[108]

So this may be an especially opportune moment. If First Amendment doctrine is in crisis, then we may be entering a period in which evolutionary punctuation is possible. The fact that the old model seems to be failing may make us more willing to think productively about what might replace it. It may be time to give the Vermont justice of the peace his due.

3

Taking the Institutional Turn

There is an alternative to the standard way of carving up the world that lawyers and judges use. It is a way we might reconceive the concepts and categories we use in viewing the world through the First Amendment lens—or, to put it differently, a way we might begin to see the world *as it is* and adjust the First Amendment to fit its framework. This is the institutional turn.

Lawyers and judges will always carve up the world according to various concepts and categories. How could they not? Law is meant to order human activity, and making sense of things will always involve categorization. The problem is *how* legal minds carve up the world. I have argued that they do so—or at least *yearn* to do so—acontextually. That is, rather than focus on concepts and categories drawn from social life and the everyday world, they focus on broad concepts and categories drawn from legal thought itself. They do not see churns and farmers, but torts, property, and malicious intent. They do not think things, but words, particularly *legal* words: terms of art that are prominent in the lawyer's vision of the world but less so in the layperson's.

Moreover, this acontextual legal vision of the world is, for the most part, imposed from the top down. That is, law uses its own concepts and categories to impose order on the world. It is prescriptive, not responsive. It proceeds without a "bottom-up appreciation of individuals, social contexts, and the dynamics of institutional processes."[1]

But these approaches are bound to be incomplete, at least. The real world of human activity has a way of defying such simple categories. In the end, attempts to dig the acontextual approach halfway out of this dilemma only sink it deeper in the mire. It is time, then, to reconsider how we think about the law and how we carve up the world of public discourse. The institutional turn offers one way of doing so.

I offer two basic premises. First, law should be responsive to context, specifically including institutional context. That does not mean it must absolutely forswear general rules or categories in favor of particularistic, case-by-case analysis. The problem is not the use of categories, even acontextual legal ones, as such; the problem arises when the lures of the acontextual approach become so strong that the urge toward generality verges on pathology.[2] As we will see in the next chapter, the institutional turn itself can make productive use of broad categories. But the categories it uses must be better able to take into account some of the contexts and particulars of life as it is lived. In particular, for purposes of this book, law's categories should be capable of recognizing some of the most prominent contexts and institutions in which public discourse occurs.

Second, the law should be built from the bottom up, or at least as much from the bottom up as from the top down. That is, law should not simply be a matter of legal institutions—particularly the Supreme Court—stating a broad rule drawn from general legal categories and applying it more or less mechanically to every new factual situation. It should be built from the perspective of important speech institutions, not imposed upon them.

Responsiveness

First Amendment law must be *responsive*. It must fully account for the variety of factual circumstances and contexts, including institutions, in which public discourse actually takes place. Its decision-makers must demonstrate a "commitment to a style of legal reasoning that reaches beyond mere rule-following and seeks to ground law and legal decisions in their individual and social consequences."[3]

One way to illuminate this idea is with a metaphor loosely adapted—very loosely adapted, to be clear—from the German theorist Jürgen Habermas. Habermas describes a conflict between the world of "systems" and what he calls the "lifeworld."[4] The lifeworld, as William Forbath explains, is "the realm in which communicative action unfolds: it is the background of tradition, culture, and language, the framework of shared understandings, values and norms, that makes communicative action possible." It includes "the 'informal' institutions of family, religion, and civic associations," in which "individuals construct their identities and group their solidarities."[5] It is, so to speak, the "real world" of public discourse.

Against this Habermas contrasts the "system," which "in modern western societies . . . is constituted by the market and the bureaucratic state," including the law. Unlike the lifeworld, which consists of a broad set of tacit social norms and understandings, the system is thoroughly rationalized and rationalizing in nature.[6] Systems supply the rationalizing impulse that allows us to function in a complex society, but they also undermine the qualities—"independence, mutual trust," and so on—that the lifeworld requires.[7]

As Robert Post puts it, the modern state "so pervasively deploys law as a method of channeling behavior that it has become very common to protest that contemporary law actually undermines culture." Law's tendency to see everything through the lens of legal concepts and categories—what I have called its urge toward acontextuality—"does not enforce the norms of an ambient culture, but instead deracinates and suppresses culture."[8]

Let us engage in a bit of creative plundering. Redrawing Habermas's labels a little, let us imagine two realms, two ways of thinking about the world. Call them the "lifeworld" and the "law-world."

The lifeworld is what we see around us in everyday life. When we draw connections between different phenomena, we do so through common sense, intuition, and the categories that make the most sense to us. When we witness a car accident, we will probably not care that one vehicle is red and the other blue. But we may care that it *is* a car accident, not a natural disaster; that it involves, say, a subcompact versus an SUV; or that one driver is mature and experienced and the other young and inexperienced.

Similarly, when we encounter a speech act, a variety of aspects of that act may be pertinent. We may or may not care that one speaker is the government or receives government funds. But we may care a great deal about how and where the speech occurs: in a newspaper, in a private conversation, in the quiet spaces of a library, and so on. These categorizations may be imperfect, but they will be highly salient to us—and they will draw on our nonlegal, social understanding of the world.

Against the lifeworld, imagine the law-world. This is the lawyer's vision of the world, which sees things in terms of concepts and categories drawn from the law itself, not directly from the lifeworld. Its picture of a car accident is a matrix of tortfeasors and blameless victims (or contributorily negligent co-tortfeasors). Its cars are not red and blue, but not subcompacts and SUVs either, just motor vehicles. Its bloody, vivid injuries are "damages."

Similarly, the law-world's vision of a speech act is regulated by standard legal distinctions. It asks what general doctrinal category—public forum, content distinction, and so on—best fits the speech act as a *legal* matter. It is largely indifferent to the institutional character of the speaker, beyond wanting to know whether a state actor is involved.

The law-world, with its devotion to acontextuality, corresponds to what Philippe Nonet and Philip Selznick have called the "autonomous" stage of law, in which law "insulates itself" and "accepts a blind formalism as the price of integrity."[9] Decisions under this regime are "made strictly according to *legal* rules."[10] "The task of the judiciary," in this view, "is to maintain fidelity to a system of certain and definite rules" rather than to make the law fit social realities.[11] As Robert Kagan notes, however, such a "commitment to uniform rule application often undermines its own commitment to treating like cases alike."[12]

The institutional turn's first premise is that we must move from law-world to lifeworld. The law's categories should be drawn from life's categories, not insulated from them. Law should be responsive, able to adapt to the realities and needs of the lifeworld. It should be "open to pragmatic and functional demands" and interested in practical problem-solving "even at the expense of established patterns of formal legalistic rules and procedures."[13]

Moving from law-world to lifeworld, or from an autonomous to a responsive model of law, has its costs.[14] What law gains by becoming more responsive it loses in regularity, formality, and clarity. Tradeoffs are required. But the benefits may outweigh the costs. First Amendment doctrine is currently in a poor state: too complex, too inconsistent, and too incoherent to be genuinely stable or predictable. Where the outcomes of First Amendment disputes *are* predictable, it is not the legal categories of the law-world that make them so, but the categories and intuitions of the lifeworld.[15] It may be time to focus on what we are *actually* doing in First Amendment law, not what we *say* we are doing.

Moreover, at a certain point the autonomous and acontextual categories of the law-world end up undermining themselves. As we create more exceptions to the general doctrinal categories or stretch the doctrine into grotesque shapes to account for those exceptions, the costs of acontextuality grow. Moving toward a more consciously responsive approach to the law in this area may seem radical, but it is no more radical than, and may be preferable to, sticking loyally to increasingly inadequate ways of carving up the world of the First Amendment.

Law from the Bottom Up

Responsiveness alone is not enough to give us the First Amendment law we need. Before the law can respond to different speech contexts and institutions, it needs to be able to *listen* to them. It needs an ongoing dialogue with those institutions. Above all, it needs to be able to respond productively to institutional pluralism and institutional change.

The possibility of doing law in a way that is more "open-textured, participatory, bottom-up, consensus-oriented, contextual, flexible, integrative, and pragmatic"[16] has been explored by a number of scholars. The vehicles for bottom-up lawmaking they have proposed vary, but I will focus on some common threads.

One label that has been offered for a bottom-up system of thinking about the law and legal doctrine is "reflexive law."[17] Reflexive law focuses on coordination rather than control. It is interested in harnessing the *self*-regulatory capacities of institutional actors, within and outside the government, rather than using the law to regulate those activities more directly.[18]

Another label, one on which reflexive law often draws, is "autopoiesis," the idea that society is not a single system but a variety of subsystems, including politics, education, the legal system, and so on. Each subsystem operates according to its own norms, and each interacts only imperfectly with the others. Thus, the best way to regulate is not directly, but by "specifying procedures and basic organizational norms geared toward fostering self-regulation within [these] distinct spheres of social activity."[19] The goal of an autopoietic approach is to encourage these actors to internalize basic norms of self-regulation within their own subsystems rather than imposing a single top-down set of rules that applies to all.

Finally, consider what some call "democratic experimentalism" and others "new governance." Democratic experimentalism is a "new model of institutionalized democratic deliberation that responds to the conditions of modern life."[20] Under this model, the primary job of courts and other central authorities is to coordinate local institutions as those institutions formulate and share their own ways of addressing legal and social problems. Out of this experimentation and information-sharing, an evolving set of "best practices" emerges, which can then be enforced by the courts.[21] Rather than issuing strong formal rules, the courts lay down general standards that can be met in a variety of ways, thus leaving it to the local actors to craft specific legal norms and instructional practices that meet those standards.

Similarly, new governance is "an umbrella term covering a kind of interaction between the state, regulated entities, and other stakeholders that has a number of desiderata—public participation, data provision, transparency, benchmarking, sharing of best practices, fora for deliberation on ends and means, and autonomy and flexibility for those subject to regulation."[22] Instead of imposing top-down solutions to problems, law "can actively involve firms in the legal process, including the processes of interpreting and complying with legal norms."[23] As with reflexive law, the role of central regulators in the new governance model is less to "run things" than to encourage and "monitor self-regulation."[24]

The goal of democratic experimentalism or new governance is to replace a regulatory model in which the government comes up with legal norms and imposes them on everyone with a more collaborative model, in which institutions with a stake in particular legal and social problems partner with regulators to come up with solutions. The regulators give them room to do so and use what they learn from those institutions to shape broad new legal standards that are capable of ongoing revision.

These approaches have been employed in a number of areas in recent years. Consider, for example, the law of sexual harassment in the workplace. The Supreme Court has largely refused to lay down categorical rules concerning how employers should address sexual harassment, recognizing that a "constellation of surrounding circumstances, expectations, and relationships" would make any single rule difficult for courts to formulate and enforce.[25] Instead, it has established a legal safe harbor for employers that take reasonable care to avoid and remedy harassment.[26] That doesn't mean anything goes. As courts learn from employers' experience, they will be able to reject some measures as insufficient to address the problem, while encouraging all employers to adopt the best practices that have emerged. These practices may in turn be superseded by later solutions. Employers can experiment with ways to address sexual harassment, and courts can learn from those local experiences.[27]

These approaches share several features. They focus on participation, not command-and-control regulation. They believe that "intermediary institutions" should be involved in forming regulatory standards, rather than simply having courts or some other regulatory authority "regulate social behavior directly."[28] And they believe in giving local institutions room "for experimental elaboration and revision [of their activities] to accommodate varied and changing circumstances."[29]

Christine Parker has argued that for law to fully respond to the conditions of a pluralistic society, "it must be both reflexive *and* responsive."[30] It must be aware of myriad social contexts and institutions, and eager to respond to them rather than forcing them onto the Procrustean bed of a single autonomous vision of law. At the same time, its responses must be bottom-up rather than top-down: it must be capable of learning from those institutions' expertise and attempts at self-regulation, and of incorporating those evolving practices into its own regulatory efforts.

That insight underlies the two premises I have offered here: law must be responsive to particular social contexts and institutions, and it should frame its responses in a bottom-up rather than a top-down fashion. These premises offer us one possible path out of the frail state to which the lure of acontextuality has arguably brought First Amendment theory and doctrine. That path is the institutional turn.

The Institutional Turn

The institutional turn is a move away from an approach to First Amendment law that is insufficiently attentive to the existence and nature of a variety of what we might call "First Amendment institutions." It recommends that the law actively take these institutions into account, treating them as "morally relevant" for purposes of the definitions and distinctions drawn in First Amendment doctrine.

The institutional approach rejects, or at least treats as seriously incomplete, the misleading dichotomy between the state and individual private speakers, as well as other distinctions that are largely indifferent to context and grounded in the typical thinking of the law-world, such as the somewhat mechanical distinction between content-based and content-neutral speech regulations. It urges us instead to base our legal distinctions and categories on the lifeworld of public discourse—a world that prominently includes particular speech institutions.

The institutional turn is consistent with the premises of responsiveness and bottom-up lawmaking. It is responsive because it focuses on the actual institutional contexts in which public discourse takes place rather than on some idealized vision of "speech" shorn of context. It is a bottom-up approach because it envisions legal standards emerging from the institutions themselves rather than being imposed on them by the courts in a one-size-fits-all manner.

Before we can fully evaluate this approach, we must understand a little more about current work on the nature of institutions. This work has occurred across a variety of scholarly fields and has been grouped together under the general rubrics of "New Institutionalism," "neoinstitutionalism," or the "New Institutional Economics."[31] Although much about these ideas is indeed new, the study of institutions dates back at least to the late nineteenth and early twentieth centuries. In 1909, for example, the economist Thorstein Veblen wrote, "Not only is the individual's conduct hedged about and directed by his habitual relations to his fellows in the group, but these relations, being of an institutional nature, vary as the institutional scene varies."[32]

What *is* new about New Institutionalism is its dynamic focus, its theoretical sophistication, and its practical utility. It contends that "actors are not isolated individuals," but "members of complex organizations whose motivations, behaviors, and knowledge are heavily affected by their institutional settings." It observes that because individuals lack perfect information or decision-making capacity, they must "rely on institutions to simplify and regularize a complex environment because their own ability to process information is inherently limited."[33]

Several implications follow from this insight. The New Institutionalists pay careful attention to the rules and norms that "constrain and structure behaviors within a given institution."[34] They also focus on the "habitual adherence to certain cultural values, routines, or patterns" of individuals within institutions and organizations—the way "institutions are culturally constituted and justified." They understand institutions in a dynamic fashion: not as monolithic or isolated, but rather as "engaged in a continual dialectic exchange with the surroundings they inhabit."[35] They treat law as taking place not in a vacuum but within "an institutional setting—legislatures, government agencies, business firms, or non-commercial private organizations."[36] They see not only institutions and organizations but also the individuals within them as having an "identity," one shaped both by the broader norms of the institution or organization and by the individuals' specific roles within it.[37] Like institutional change, role identity is dialectical: "the role shapes the role player to meet institutional needs," while at the same time "the player may shape the role according to her interests."[38]

First Amendment Law

What does the institutional turn mean for the theory and practice of First Amendment law? What new doctrinal paths does it recommend?

First, it requires us to make room in First Amendment doctrine for the prominent role of institutions in the formation and dissemination of public discourse. Paying more attention to the role of institutions not only will reduce the pathologies of acontextuality; it is a good in itself. It recognizes something that current doctrine sometimes obscures: speech does not take place in a vacuum, an environment artificially emptied of everything except archetypal state censors and individual soapbox speakers. Some of the most important speech occurs in and through institutions.

More to the point, it occurs in and through *particular* institutions. It may be an accident of history that certain institutions—universities or newspapers, for example—have emerged as sites for important public discourse. But it is not a *random* accident, and there is certainly nothing random about the recurring importance of particular institutions as sites for important speech. The same vital speech does not occur today through a newspaper, tomorrow through a bowling league, and the next day through a Mom-and-Pop business. Instead, the same kinds of important speech acts emerge, day after day, from the same specific institutions. Some institutions may evolve over time, some may drop out of the picture, and new ones may emerge. But many institutions have remained fairly stable, discernible, and central locations of public discourse for centuries. There is ample reason to take these institutions seriously as subjects of the First Amendment.

Second, the institutional turn requires us to think about both institutional stability and institutional change.[39] Today's universities differ from yesterday's universities in some important respects; they are continually, if slowly, rethinking their particular norms and practices. Similarly, today's newspapers look different from yesterday's newspapers, both in the platforms they use—moving, say, from typeset print to the Internet—and in the role they play in public discourse.[40] But change is not the whole story. These institutions have, for a long time, been both subject to change *and* relatively stable. Speech institutions naturally evolve, just as public discourse does. But they do so, for the most part, gradually and incrementally. We should give due regard to both their stability and their evolving nature.

Third, the institutional turn requires us to recognize that each of these institutions plays a particular role in public discourse. A single, acontextual set of legal doctrines cannot account for all of these institutions and their different roles. First Amendment doctrine must become more aware of and responsive to the lifeworld of public discourse, including the particular roles and purposes of different speech acts and speech institutions.

Fourth, the institutional turn requires First Amendment law to be not only responsive but reflexive. Important First Amendment institutions like libraries, newspapers, and churches are not only, or even primarily, regulated from the outside; they are also self-regulating, through their own norms, standards, practices, and cultures.

The law should not view these self-regulating practices as a threat to its authority. To the contrary, they are essential to each institution's self-definition and to its capacity to evolve to meet new social challenges as part of its institutional role within society as a whole. Newspapers evolved, for example, in a complex and ongoing system of interaction with the social world around them. They became important to public discourse precisely because they evolved to *become* important to it—and public discourse in turn evolved to accommodate their changing role.[41]

The development of self-regulatory norms and practices peculiar to each institution took place largely in the lifeworld, not in the law-world. This is not to say that law had nothing to do with it. The relationship between First Amendment institutions and First Amendment doctrine is complex and reciprocal. Just as these institutions became part of the infrastructure of public discourse,[42] so the infrastructure of the legal order influenced their development.[43] In addition, their own cultural and professional norms have influenced the path the law takes in regulating them.[44]

Accordingly, legal doctrine must not be shaped by the courts alone in a top-down fashion. Instead, we might think of the law as developing from *within* First Amendment institutions—from within their own norms and self-regulatory practices. First Amendment institutions ought to be genuine partners with the courts in shaping doctrine. The courts' approach in this area should operate "from the perspective of the lived experience of [the] institutional inhabitants."[45] Thus, the way the First Amendment develops *inside* the courts should in large measure be a function of the way public discourse develops *outside* the courts.

Finally, First Amendment institutionalism should carve up the world in functional and institutional ways. It should focus less on broad *legal* concepts and categories, such as whether something is a state actor or a public forum, and more on concepts, categories, and *institutions* that make up a prominent part of the lifeworld of free speech. The law's categories should be organized around discrete social and institutional practices, not abstract theories and principles. The word "library" should not just be a label for a particular entity that happens to be a plaintiff or defendant in First Amendment cases, and to which we strain to apply legal categories such as "public forum." It should be a legally relevant category in its own right, a category informed by the particular cultural role and institutional practices of the "library"— how it fits into our system of public discourse, what ends it serves, and what unique challenges it faces.

In particular, a functional and institutional approach to First Amendment institutions demands that we revisit our thinking about state actors and the public-private distinction. Instead of asking only whether an institution is public or private, we should ask what kind of institution it is. Is it a library, a journalist, a university, or some other institution central to public discourse that operates according to its own established norms and self-regulatory practices?

The institutionally agnostic and acontextual approach to First Amendment doctrine has landed us in a mess. If First Amendment doctrine is currently in crisis, we should not hesitate to explore other options. The institutional turn may not be perfect and it may not be the only option. But it is certainly worth exploring.

We have seen that the institutional turn's basic premises—responsiveness and reflexiveness—are supported by a broad range of theories and approaches drawn from several disciplines. This convergence around a common set of ideas—that law should be responsive to social context, and that it should view institutions and organizations as partners in lawmaking rather than as adversaries—does not demonstrate the truth of these ideas. But it does suggest an emerging awareness that law needs to find new ways of managing its relationship with the social world it regulates.

In keeping with the theme of this book, I will construct my justifications from the bottom up, not from the top down. We will see whether the institutional turn is justified by looking at how First Amendment institutionalism would operate, and whether it would offer a more responsive and reflexive solution to the problems of First Amendment jurisprudence than current doctrine does.

4

Institutions and Institutionalism

The case of *Jacobellis v. Ohio*[1] offers one of the most famous cop-outs in the history of Supreme Court decision-making. Nico Jacobellis, the manager of a movie theater in Cleveland Heights, Ohio, was convicted on two counts of possessing and exhibiting an obscene French art film. The Court reversed his conviction on First Amendment grounds.

Jacobellis was decided during an era in which the justices were forced to decide in case after case whether a particular film, magazine, or other speech material was obscene and therefore constitutionally proscribable, with each justice using a different standard.[2] Although some of us may be amused by the idea of nine old men convening to watch raunchy films somewhere in the bowels of the Supreme Court building,[3] the justices understandably found the practice wearisome.

That weariness showed in the concurring opinion filed by Justice Potter Stewart in *Jacobellis*. Stewart had concluded, he wrote, that criminal obscenity laws were "constitutionally limited to hard-core pornography." He went on: "I shall not today attempt further to define the kinds of material I understand to be embraced within that shorthand description; and perhaps I could never succeed in intelligibly doing so. But I know it when I see it, and the motion picture involved in this case is not that.[4]

"I know it when I see it" has become one of the best-known phrases in Supreme Court jurisprudence. It stands out because it seems to violate the idea that Supreme Court decisions should be based on "objective analysis" rather than "subjective will."[5] It seems, in other words, like a cop-out. But Stewart was on to something. Of course there are times when "we know it when we see it." Those intuitions do not emerge from nowhere, but neither do they emerge from a fully fleshed-out process of abstract reasoning. We "know it when we see it," even when we cannot fully explain *why* we know it, because we see something so often and understand it so implicitly. Our judgments on these matters can be fuzzy around the edges, but at the core they are often right on the mark.[6]

So it is with First Amendment institutions. We could spend ages attempting to construct an elaborate set of definitional criteria for such institutions, and a set of justifications for those criteria, and still fall short. Most of the time, though, and certainly for the most prominent First Amendment institutions, we needn't bother. In the lifeworld, at least, we know them when we see them.

Justice Stewart's words thus remind us how simple defining First Amendment institutions often is. Its supposed difficulty has led courts to tremble at the thought of taking the institutional turn, worried that doing so "would present practical and conceptual difficulties of a high order."[7] At the borders, it is true, defining First Amendment institutions can be difficult, and that concern will occupy us throughout Part Two. But many of those institutions, including the most important ones, are obvious to most of us.[8] Moreover, the practical and conceptual difficulties of maintaining an acontextual, institutionally agnostic First Amendment doctrine are no less great, and the results have not necessarily been any more impressive.

In this chapter I offer some basic thoughts on what defines "First Amendment institutions," focusing on two particular features: the central role they play in public discourse and their self-regulatory norms and practices. I then explore what the institutional turn means for First Amendment doctrine. I conclude that it counsels a bounded, but genuine, form of legal autonomy for these institutions—not so they may do whatever they wish, but so they may function as they should. As we will see, in some respects First Amendment doctrine has *already* taken the institutional turn, albeit not as forthrightly as it might.

Defining First Amendment Institutions

FIRST AMENDMENT INSTITUTIONS AS THE
INFRASTRUCTURE OF PUBLIC DISCOURSE

First Amendment institutions are those that play a central role in the forma-tion and dissemination of public discourse. They are the buttresses of what Jack Balkin has called the "infrastructure of free expression."[9] They are, as Rick Garnett eloquently puts it, "the scaffolding around which civil society is constructed, in which personal freedom is exercised, in which loyalties are formed and transmitted, and in which individuals flourish."[10]

To understand better the role that First Amendment institutions play in public discourse, we must first define public discourse itself. A promis-ing start is the definition offered by Robert Post, who describes public dis-course as "those speech acts and media of communication that are socially regarded as necessary and proper means of participating in the formation of public opinion."[11]

For Post, a crucial aspect of this definition is its link to the collective deci-sion-making that he places at the heart of democratic government, which depends for its legitimacy on the people's belief that they are "potential authors of [the] law." In order for them to maintain this belief, the people must be able to "participat[e] in the formation of public opinion." That pro-cess takes place through "communication in the public sphere." Public dis-course is thus defined as those communications in the public sphere, or media of communication within the public sphere, that contribute to the formation of public opinion, specifically about politics and democratic governance.[12]

I largely adopt Post's definition of public discourse here. But, particularly in light of the perceptive criticism his definition has received,[13] I emphasize that my take on public discourse has a somewhat different emphasis and a different goal, in three respects. First, Post's definition heavily emphasizes the *political* process and its legitimacy: the goal of public discourse is to pro-vide a site for "the formation of public opinion . . . *to the end of making govern-ment responsive to [the public's] views.*"[14] My understanding of public discourse is broader than that. Not all important public discourse sees politics, espe-cially electoral politics, as its endgame.[15] "Our interest in 'participating in the formation of public opinion,'" T. M. Scanlon writes, "is broader than our proper concern to be the authors of the laws to which we are subject."[16] It "includes an interest in participating in the shaping of *our shared culture.*"[17] Even when public discourse is on matters of what we sometimes call "public concern," those matters extend beyond politics and elections to include all the ways in which we form a common culture. Thus, "public discourse may serve not just as the primary source of democratic legitimacy but also as the primary medium by which the members of a modern heterogeneous society" form the very society itself.[18] Indeed, one of the central points of this book is that society is not just government. Instead, government is merely one strut in a broader infrastructure of which First Amendment institutions are a central feature. Some of the most important public discourse takes place in, through, and about these institutions too. Public discourse, in short, includes democratic deliberation—but also art, high and low culture, and all the elements of shared discussion that constitute a vital part of our social lives. And the institutions that serve as primary avenues of public discourse do not simply subtend the formal political process. They are not simply means to the end of making "government," or the state, responsive; they, and the culture of which they are a part, are an end in themselves.

Second, Post's use of public discourse (or so his critics charge) treats it as playing a gatekeeper role in First Amendment law. Speech that is not "public discourse" as Post defines it, such as commercial speech, may receive lesser First Amendment protection.[19] That raises the concern that if public discourse is defined too narrowly, it will leave a good deal of important speech poorly protected. My goal is different here, in two senses. First, the fact that First Amendment institutions are especially important to public discourse does not necessarily mean that speech by individuals or groups that fall outside this definition should receive reduced constitutional protection. The *kinds* of rules and categories that govern non–First Amendment institutions may be different, but that does not mean they should be left without protection. Second, public discourse serves a different role in this work. It is not a gatekeeper, but a guide. I use public discourse, broadly defined, not as a precondition for heightened constitutional protection in general, but specifically to help us locate and define First Amendment *institutions* in particular.

Finally, Post treats the definition and scope of public discourse as *constitutional* and *normative* questions.[20] That is, he treats public discourse as a *legal* concept within the body of constitutional law and theory, one whose boundaries are ultimately settled by asking whether particular speech acts serve "the value of democratic self-governance."[21] My focus is more social, or sociological, in nature. It shares with the philosopher John Searle the view that one of the "fundamental nature[s] and mode[s]" of human existence is its social and institutional quality.[22] My concern is thus not one of identifying a single normative value like "public discourse" that can help us order all of First Amendment law as it currently stands. Instead, it is to point out a fundamental reality—that life is social and institutional, that the infrastructure of society extends well beyond the state itself and includes a number of central institutions in which some of the most important speech and social interaction takes place—and make that reality a more important and more easily recognized part of First Amendment law.[23]

This broader understanding of public discourse, one that focuses more on social life in general than on the formal political process, clearly covers a great deal of territory. But it does not make every institution a First Amendment institution, as I use the term. Many of us spend more time in the workplace than we do anywhere else, and our identities are shaped as much by our jobs as they are by our participation in democratic institutions or political discussion. If "First Amendment institutions" simply meant those institutions in which our social lives are lived, the workplace would have as great a claim to be a First Amendment institution as the university or the church.

But workplaces do not share the fundamental *infrastructural* nature of First Amendment institutions. Our cars probably spend as much time in driveways and garages as they do on the road. For many purposes, however, we think of driveways and garages as incidental to transportation. The infrastructure of our transportation system, as we usually understand it, consists of things like highways, roads, and traffic laws and signals—things that are essential to our system of transportation, not its by-products. We could not imagine a transportation system without roads, but we could imagine it with a variety of ways of storing our vehicles: covered or uncovered driveways, parking garages, parking lots, and so on.

So it is with First Amendment institutions. They are not just *any* place in which social life occurs. They are those institutions that are foundational to our lives as social beings, as citizens and participants in our collective culture. They are the sites that equip us for social life and through which social life takes on much of its meaning. And here, to paraphrase Orwell, some institutions are more equal than others.

We can see this better by conducting a brief thought experiment. Imagine equipping a citizen for social life, much the way that a parent packs a child's duffel bag for summer camp. Just as the parent pictures the child's life at camp and fills her bag with the equipment she will need—insect repellent, swimsuit, extra underwear—so we can imagine outfitting a citizen for her life *as* a citizen. How would we fill her bag?

Some choices would be obvious. We expect a citizen to be capable of learning from and talking with others, so we might start with an education or a library card. We expect a citizen to be well informed about current events, so we might add news organs and communications media like newspapers, magazines, television stations, and the Internet. Many of us expect a citizen's social life to have a spiritual component or believe that the values we bring to our commitments as citizens rest on a religious foundation, so we would outfit her with a church. We might value our citizen's participation in the community, and thus include one or more associations, like the Girl Scouts, a soccer league, or the NAACP.

Other aspects of our lives, important as they may be, might not merit inclusion on the list of absolutely necessary items. Of course, we also expect our citizen to work, not only to provide the necessities of life but for the sake of being connected to and participating in the world around her. But many workplaces would do. Other items in the citizen's kitbag—an education, for example—are not so fungible. We would refuse to switch out education for some other item. Moreover, we would view such items—schooling, communications media, and so on—as essential ingredients for our citizen to find a job in the first place, let alone thrive at it. We would thus view some items as foundational and others, like a particular workplace, as secondary.

First Amendment institutions, then, are the institutions that are foundational or essential to our lives as citizens and participants in a common culture. In particular, they are the institutions that make especially important contributions to public discourse.[24] Other institutions are certainly important. We may pay more attention to what goes on at work than what is on the front page of the newspaper. But to say they are important is not to say that they are foundational. Most of us can imagine changing jobs, but we cannot effectively imagine ourselves as social beings without the basic equipment supplied by our First Amendment institutions. They form the infrastructure of our social lives.

First Amendment Institutions as
Self-Regulating Institutions

Another central feature that distinguishes First Amendment institutions from other institutions and justifies giving them special treatment under the law is their self-regulating quality. They operate according to a rich set of norms, practices, and rules—rules that are intrinsic to their identity, not just imposed by the courts or other regulatory authorities. Those norms and practices, by advancing the functional role these institutions play in our system of public discourse, ultimately serve our First Amendment values themselves. As we will see in Part Two, this feature also helps us resolve some (though certainly not all) of the boundary questions that First Amendment institutionalism raises; not all institutions, or even speech-centered institutions, have this functional self-regulating quality.

Consider universities. After centuries of development and tradition, universities are distinctive institutions whose basic features are readily identifiable. Their central role in the infrastructure of public discourse is relatively easy to define. It is an evolving role, to be sure, and there are continuing arguments about the part universities play in public discourse.[25] But those debates are less significant than the shared qualities that distinguish universities from other institutions. Universities are places of discovery, innovation, and heterodoxy. For students, they provide a basis for later intellectual, professional, cultural, and civic life. For professors, they provide resources, collegial support, and a haven for free and unfettered scholarship. For society at large, they increase our general knowledge base and the capacities of our citizens.

The traditions that make universities distinctive also make it possible to imagine incorporating them into the First Amendment in a reflexive or bottom-up way, one that learns from them rather than simply dictating to them. Universities are highly structured environments. Faculty members "live their professional lives within disciplinary constraints and norms,"[26] following a detailed set of internal norms that govern behavior within their institution.

These constraints make the university as an institution not only distinct, but self-regulating. Two aspects of its self-regulatory culture are especially important. First, self-regulatory practices are aspects of university culture itself. They emerge from historical developments that have made it the distinctive entity it is. They have developed in concert with the legal environment in which the university exists, but are also largely independent of the law. The maintenance of academic culture depends for the most part on the ways academics internalize that culture, not on what courts say or do.

Second, those self-regulatory practices are linked to the university's functions in public discourse: serving as a center for the advancement and dissemination of scholarly knowledge and educating students in the wider ideal of the acquisition of knowledge. Norms and practices such as the requirement that scholars demonstrate proficiency in their fields according to disciplinary standards serve the university's knowledge function. Norms and practices relating to the classroom, such as grading practices, serve its educational function. The norms and practices by which universities regulate themselves are thus intimately connected to the distinct contributions that universities make to public discourse.

This self-regulatory culture and the functional ends it serves show us why treating universities as First Amendment institutions has not only a responsive value, but a reflexive or bottom-up value. According these institutions some special status under the law is not contrary to the values the First Amendment serves; it *advances* those values. Universities self-regulate for reasons of their own, not just because the law requires them to do so. Culturally unique features such as academic freedom developed and existed long before the courts gave any thought to those concepts.[27] They would remain even if the courts denied that academic freedom existed, in a legal sense. Universities self-regulate because their norms and practices serve their goals. Those goals, in turn, contribute to public discourse.

Thus, the self-regulating internal norms of First Amendment institutions can substitute for the externally imposed, top-down model of judicial enforcement that currently animates First Amendment doctrine. Courts should not act as antagonists toward or supervisors of First Amendment institutions; they should treat them as *partners* in the process of shaping constitutional doctrine.

This working definition of First Amendment institutions helps distinguish them from other institutions. First, they play a distinctive infrastructural role in public discourse. They make public discourse as we currently understand it possible; without them we could not imagine public discourse as it is presently constituted. They provide us with the cultural and intellectual equipment to be citizens and social beings. Second, they are self-regulating. Their norms, practices, and traditions serve their particular values or ends, which in turn serve the broader ends of public discourse.

Variations of First Amendment Institutionalism: From Deference to Sovereignty

It is possible to imagine a range of versions of First Amendment institutionalism, along a spectrum from mild to radical. Here, I focus on some of the basic features that characterize these approaches. To varying degrees, they all involve concepts and labels, such as "deference," "autonomy," and "sovereignty," that are already widely used in the law. This has benefits and drawbacks. The main drawback is that these terms may have a life outside the law, but they are also legal constructs, efforts to give a degree of fixed legal meaning to a set of complex statuses and relationships. To speak in terms of the autonomy or sovereignty of First Amendment institutions can be descriptively useful and suggestive, but it can also be *too* suggestive, so redolent of existing meanings that it will confuse as much as it clarifies. Readers should treat the use of these terms here as approximations, as adaptations of existing concepts that may help us imagine how First Amendment institutions might be treated under a changed legal order, not as precise legal labels.

On the other hand, as we will see, the fact that these terms *do* fit fairly well suggests that First Amendment institutionalism is not as unprecedented as its detractors—or its supporters—might imagine. The seeds of the institutional turn have already been planted in every Supreme Court decision that ignores or modifies the acontextual, institutionally agnostic framework of current First Amendment doctrine in light of the Court's recognition of the importance and uniqueness of these institutions. Indeed, the aspects of institutionalism that are already present in First Amendment doctrine may help explain why that doctrine has managed to persist as long as it has without collapsing.

DEFERENCE

Deference occurs when a decision-maker, such as a court, follows a determination made by some other individual or institution that it might not have reached had it decided the same question independently. If a friend and I face a fork in the road and I am inclined to turn right, but instead I turn left at his behest, I am deferring to his decision.

Deference as a legal tool has been studied at high levels of abstraction by legal philosophers, and in detail in specific doctrinal areas, especially administrative law and national security law. But there has been much less study of deference as a general phenomenon in constitutional law.[28] This is surprising, because deference has been at the heart of our insecurities about judicial review for over a century.[29]

The two major justifications of judicial deference are epistemological and political.[30] The epistemological justification is that nonjudicial actors may have greater knowledge and expertise, so deferring will save time and lead to more correct outcomes. A classic statement of epistemologically based deference can be found in a key administrative law decision, *Chevron U.S.A., Inc. v. Natural Resources Defense Council, Inc.* There, the Supreme Court recommended deferring to administrative agencies' interpretations of their governing statutes both because those agencies possessed "more than ordinary knowledge respecting the matters subjected to agency regulations" and because judges might not be "experts in the field."[31]

The political justification for judicial deference focuses on the superior political legitimacy of nonjudicial institutions. Courts defer because the other party has a "constitutionally-prescribed authoritative status" as the sole or primary decision-maker in that area.[32] For example, the Constitution gives Congress the authority to provide and maintain the armed forces.[33] In that area, judicial deference is "at its apogee."[34] In other areas, the reason for deference might be a broader insecurity about the legitimacy of the unelected judicial branch as a decision-maker compared with the elected branches of government—a neurosis that constitutional lawyers dub the "countermajoritarian dilemma."[35] *Chevron* again states the point clearly: in such cases, "federal judges—who have no [political] constituency—have a duty to respect legitimate policy choices made by those who do."[36]

For such a central judicial device, deference is remarkably underexplored and underjustified. Justice Thurgood Marshall once complained that judicial pronouncements about deference often amount to "hollow shibboleths": rote invocations, unsupported by any serious explanation or justification.[37]

What explains the Court's failure to give serious attention to one of its primary jurisprudential devices? One possibility relates to our discussion of acontextuality. On the one hand, courts strive for a pure and acontextual system of law. On the other, they are routinely sucked in by the "gravitational pull of facts":[38] that is, they must somehow account for the differences in factual and social contexts that arise in different cases.

From this perspective, deference is the device by which courts negotiate the "tension between acontextual law and real-world factual diversity and complexity."[39] By deferring to institutional actors with more expertise and authority in particular areas, courts are able to bring in the expertise and knowledge about particular social contexts that their own acontextual approach denies them. Deference allows courts to bring responsiveness into the law by taking themselves *out* of the equation.

This explanation also tells us why courts have left deference so undertheorized. Deference can be something of a salvaging device for acontextualist judges. Like the exception and conservation strategies discussed earlier, it keeps the acontextualist mission going while quietly shoring itself up against its own flaws—against the need to acknowledge particular social contexts and institutions. If this is what courts are doing, it is no wonder they leave this area underexplained. A court employing deference is like the captain of a sinking ship who tries to patch it up and keep it afloat without alarming the passengers or crew—indeed, without undermining his *own* confidence in the vessel's seaworthiness. We can understand deference as a similar patchwork enterprise: a way of preserving acontextuality by plugging its holes while the ship is still at sea.

From the perspective of First Amendment institutionalism, deference thus serves to bring responsiveness and reflexiveness into First Amendment doctrine without, to belabor the metaphor, rocking the boat of acontextuality too much. Courts can retain the framework of acontextuality while using deference to give a greater interpretive role to institutions and decision-makers with more expertise and authority regarding particular factually complex social contexts. Courts should thus give real deference to the expertise and policy choices of First Amendment institutions. They should recognize that "context matters" and respect the institutions' own descriptions of and judgments about that context.[40]

Strikingly, in many First Amendment cases the courts already routinely acknowledge the special nature of First Amendment institutions. They are willing to ignore acontextual and inflexible rules where necessary to preserve these institutions' unique contributions to public discourse. We saw some examples in Chapter 2. In *American Library Association*, the Supreme Court recognized that instead of applying traditional public forum doctrine, it would have to consider the role of libraries in our system of public discourse. In *Forbes*, the Court treated a public broadcaster as a journalistic entity and not a garden-variety state actor. And in *Finley*, rather than rigidly following the rules concerning content-neutral versus content-based speech regulations, the Court decided the case in the shadow of the unique role played by institutions that make arts funding decisions.[41]

The courts have used deference in similar ways with other speech institutions. They have repeatedly deferred to core "academic" decisions made by universities, such as whether to deny tenure to a professor or discipline a student.[42] They have also deferred substantially to professional judgments made by public school educators and administrators.[43] In decisions involving the press, particularly under the law of defamation, courts frequently defer to the exercise of professional "editorial judgment."[44] These examples suggest that the courts have already admitted, if not embraced, some of the key precepts of First Amendment institutionalism.

The use of deference under current law, however, does not do as much as a more robust form of First Amendment institutionalism might. The amount of deference courts are willing to accord to speech institutions is still limited by their top-down understanding of constitutional law. For example, in *Grutter v. Bollinger,* a case involving affirmative action at a public law school, the Supreme Court deferred substantially to the "complex educational judgments" made by universities in shaping their own missions and selecting students, but warned that universities would receive deference only "within constitutionally prescribed limits."[45] It was willing to defer to the university's judgment, but only within the law's existing, and generally institutionally agnostic, doctrinal framework.[46] Similarly, in a variety of cases the Court has deferred broadly to the expertise of the military.[47] But some justices have emphasized that while the Court should hesitate to "strike down restrictions on individual liberties which could reasonably be justified as necessary to the military's vital function, we have never abdicated our obligation of judicial review."[48]

Although this is still a top-down vision of law, not a reflexive or bottom-up vision, the widespread but constrained use of judicial deference in existing First Amendment law suggests that the jump to a more robust form of institutionalism is smaller than we may imagine. As long as the courts continue to incorporate institutional concerns into their doctrine without reexamining their general doctrinal approach, however, they will have neither the full benefits of institutionalism—a genuinely responsive and bottom-up approach to the law—nor the full benefits of acontextuality.

Autonomy

Drawing on another common legal concept, some forms of institutionalism might focus on the *autonomy* of First Amendment institutions, treating them as entitled to a substantial "'right of self-government.'"[49] This perspective would, Frederick Schauer has written, "move the inquiry away from direct application of the underlying values of the First Amendment to the conduct at issue and towards the mediating determination of whether the conduct at issue was or was not the conduct of one of these institutions." For example, "If there is a reporter's privilege, . . . we might ask not whether this exercise of the privilege serves primary First Amendment purposes, but instead simply whether the person claiming the privilege is a reporter."[50]

Autonomy has limits, of course. Families are largely autonomous institutions, within which parents are free to make decisions for themselves and their children. But child neglect, abuse, and abandonment are not legitimate choices for families, and we allow state intervention when they occur.

Similarly, an autonomy-based form of First Amendment institutionalism might derive some limits from the functional nature of particular institutions. Imagine, for example, a newspaper called the *Daily Ronin*. Its reporters are self-serving rogues who gather information for their own profit and make or break promises of confidentiality at whim. If the press's autonomy were absolute, perhaps they could assert a right to act in this manner. But we could also ask, *are* these rogues "journalists"? *Are* they acting as a "newspaper," as the term is generally understood, both by the public and by the journalistic profession itself? We might conclude that they were not acting in a way that furthered the purposes for which we grant such institutions autonomy in the first place. Then they would be subject to the usual operation of the law.

Under autonomy-based institutionalism, in short, First Amendment institutions would have substantial scope for self-governance. But courts would still be empowered to ask whether an institution's actions fell "within the boundaries of behavior broadly consistent with the norms and practices of that institution, and whether those norms and practices serve the First Amendment values that are advanced by the role of that institution within the broader society."[51]

SOVEREIGNTY

If autonomy is about the right of persons or institutions to govern themselves, another common legal concept—sovereignty—is about power. A sovereign institution is "higher in authority than any other power, subject to no law, a law unto itself."[52] The United States can influence the affairs of Canada, but it does not *rule* over Canada, because the two are separate sovereigns. Similarly, the federal government of the United States cannot absolutely govern the affairs of individual states, nor can the states govern the affairs of the federal government, because the state and federal governments are dual sovereigns within our constitutional system.

We *could* think of First Amendment institutions as quasi-sovereign institutions—as a legal order unto themselves,[53] or as what Robert Cover famously called a *nomos*: a self-contained community that creates and regulates its own meaning.[54] We could treat them like sovereign states in a federal system: as simultaneously within the state and beyond its reach.

On this model, sovereignty resides in First Amendment institutions not for reasons of democratic pedigree—no one elects a newspaper—but because, in the structural architecture of our legal and social order, those institutions have evolved as the ones best suited to perform particular functions in public discourse. Within their proper sphere, in effect, *they,* not the state, are the institutions charged with creating legal meaning. Of course, there can be points of conflict between these sovereign orders, but we cannot settle those conflicts by simply declaring one institution the "winner." Rather, in complex ways, "constitutional law both arises from and in turn regulates culture."[55] In this sense, as in our federalist system of dual sovereignty, the Constitution itself, and its meaning, can be seen as the product of multiple sovereigns, sometimes contending and sometimes cooperating, but each fully entitled to exercise interpretive authority within its own realm.

Although sovereignty is a common legal concept, its use in the context of First Amendment institutions is somewhat novel and may at first glance seem radical. The concept suggests a degree of independence and freedom from state intrusion that we normally associate only with government entities, not private ones. But it is not true that these "sovereign" speech institutions are "subject to no law." They are institutions, not anarchies. Even when treated as subject to no legal authority outside themselves, they still constitute legal orders of their own. If they are not accountable to anyone else, they are still accountable to their own constituents and to their own cultural norms and practices, including the self-regulatory practices that are a defining characteristic of First Amendment institutions. When we say that they are entitled, in a sense, to take an important role in fashioning the meaning of the Constitution, we are not saying they will act just as they please.

Newspapers, for example, do not act utterly willy-nilly. They follow a deep set of norms and practices, all of which are ultimately related to their distinct contribution to public discourse. For a reporter to be accepted by her colleagues and editors, and for her newspaper to be accepted by the broader universe of journalists, each must follow the standards and practices of the profession. Churches, too, are accountable to their constituents and subject to competition from other churches, and thus face important incentives to self-regulate.[56]

This approach is not as radical as it may seem. The same focus on sovereignty has, in a messy fashion, characterized our constitutional system of federalism for more than two centuries. Nor is the idea of extending sovereignty beyond political jurisdictions to "non-state associations"[57] such as First Amendment institutions alien to western political thought. Ideas of this sort are commonplace in our political history, as we will see in Chapter 7, although they represent a minority view.

Finally, sovereignty is not necessarily an all-or-nothing proposition. Sovereigns have borders, and those borders are sometimes functional and conceptual rather than physical. Just as an autonomy-based understanding of First Amendment institutionalism could insist that the boundaries of institutional autonomy be closely connected to the particular roles and functions of the institutions, so a sovereignty-based understanding could insist that the sovereign boundaries of First Amendment institutions be drawn with reference to their functions and self-regulatory practices, and could acknowledge the courts' role in settling boundary disputes between these institutions and the rights and interests of others, including the state.[58]

Our discussion of these common concepts—deference, autonomy, sovereignty—suggests that there is room for diverse strategies within First Amendment institutionalism. Each has evident attractions and drawbacks, but together they represent a variety of possible paths out of the current institutionally agnostic approach to First Amendment doctrine. Some of these paths are more radical than others, but all of them are worth considering.

In my view, the best approach to First Amendment institutionalism is an intermediate one—partaking of all these concepts but emphasizing the middle way of institutional autonomy rather than a mild version of deference or a robust version of institutional sovereignty. Treating First Amendment institutions as autonomous—as largely entitled to regulate themselves, but within some functional limits—is responsive. It leads us away from the contortions that any rigidly acontextual doctrinal approach will inevitably engage in when confronting the lifeworld of public discourse. It recognizes the importance of First Amendment institutions to public discourse and is straightforward about the need to respect them. It is also reflexive. By giving these institutions substantial autonomy, it helps to make them part of our conversation about the meaning of the First Amendment and the contours of its doctrine. It allows doctrine to be formed in a relatively bottom-up manner that acknowledges the role of both courts and institutions in constitutional interpretation.

But the autonomy is still *bounded*. This approach insists that autonomy be related to the actual functions of the institutions and their contributions to public discourse. It thus leaves courts room to set *some* limits on their behavior. By focusing on institutional purpose and function, it also gives both courts and institutions something of a roadmap for thinking about the development of First Amendment doctrine.

Broader Constitutional Questions

Three final questions are worth addressing here. Each, in its own way, has implications not only for First Amendment institutionalism, but for constitutional law more generally.

ACONTEXTUALITY, CONTEXTUALISM, PARTICULARISM, AND INSTITUTIONALISM

Much of Part One has been about the existing tension in the law between what I call "acontextuality" and cases in which courts feel obliged to recognize that certain facts, contexts, and institutions are relevant to sound decision-making about the First Amendment and don't necessarily fit well within the existing acontextual and institutionally agnostic framework of current doctrine. Even if that description of our current situation is accurate, however, it raises difficult questions about how we might characterize First Amendment institutionalism. If it is not acontextual, what precisely is it?

As with our discussion of values such as autonomy or sovereignty, in answering this question we can draw on an existing store of terms in legal and constitutional theory that might help clarify the position of First Amendment institutionalism. As with the other terms, however, there is danger as well as promise in doing so: borrowing from those terms may help give a better idea of what First Amendment institutionalism is *for* as well as what it is against, but it may also end up importing tensions and controversies that already surround those borrowed terms.

If First Amendment institutionalism is not acontextual, we could think of it as adopting a *contextualist* approach to First Amendment law. For our purposes, we might think of the term as suggesting that it is impossible or inadvisable for the law to impose a structure of generally applicable laws and that law must necessarily confront and address, on their own terms, a series of individualized cases and contexts.[59] We might conclude on this basis, for example, that there is no such thing as the "plain meaning" of a statute, because "there is no such thing as 'acontextual meaning'": the meaning of a statute, like the application of an ostensibly generally applicable First Amendment rule, "will always already be situated within a framework of contextual information."[60] Legal questions, including constitutional questions, thus must be considered within their "real-world context."[61] This view is often closely associated with both legal and philosophical pragmatism.

First Amendment institutionalism clearly shares some of the basic intuitions of those who argue for contextualism in law. But arguments for contextualism have given rise to at least two potentially serious criticisms. First, it may be banal or unhelpful: no one truly thinks it is possible to utterly ignore context, but saying that we should be alive to context does not tell us enough about what contexts matter and why, and how we should deal with them.[62] Second, it leaves us with no law worthy of that label: deciding cases only with regard to context and without any overarching rules or theories leaves us with untrammeled discretion.

Those criticisms do not apply especially well to First Amendment institutionalism's championing of context and its elements of pragmatism, however.[63] As I discuss further below, a pragmatic approach need not abandon all formal rules in favor of formless case-by-case adjudication, and it need not ignore institutional and other constraints on judges.[64] First Amendment institutionalism opposes acontextuality, and favors some form of contextualism, in two respects. First, it believes the size, source, and nature of the general rules that currently govern First Amendment doctrine, at least where particular speech institutions are concerned, are the wrong ones. There is room for general rules and categories, but they must be drawn from the lifeworld of public discourse and must recognize the value of some real-world categories and institutions, such as universities or "journalism," rather than acontextual legal categories like the content distinction. Second, it believes the acontextual approach adopted by judges in First Amendment doctrine leaves too many decisions in the hands of judges. As a matter of comparative institutional competence and the allocation of institutional authority, it believes more responsibility for framing the rules and customs that govern First Amendment institutions should be left with those institutions themselves.[65]

First Amendment institutionalism, in short, *is* contextualist in orientation. But it is not an all-in contextualism that leaves courts with no general categories or concepts. Rather, it insists on a *different* set of categories and concepts, one drawn from the lifeworld rather than the law-world. And it insists that the institutions themselves, by virtue of their autonomous status, be given greater responsibility for working out the meaning of those categories, concepts, and practices rather than having courts impose a series of top-down rules on those institutions.

Another term drawn from legal theory that might seem to be a candidate to replace acontextualism is "particularism."[66] The term, for our purposes, can be taken to suggest that because general rules are too insensitive to particular facts and contexts in which decisions are made, the lawyer ought to avoid such general legal tools as "principles, rules, standards, policies, and tests."[67] Each case must be decided on its own merits, as if courts of law were to act purely as courts of equity.[68]

Again, that is clearly not what First Amendment institutionalism means or requires. Its starting point is Justice Holmes's reminder that we must think things and not words. But rather than making a sweeping metaphysical statement here, its point is much more basic and practical. As long as law's tendency to use purely *legal* categories, like "public forum" or "state actor," fails to recognize real-world contexts and categories—like newspapers or universities—that are profoundly important to our infrastructure of public discourse, it will fail to make First Amendment doctrine responsive to our needs. That does not mean First Amendment institutionalism rejects categories altogether. It simply means we ought to find a better set of categories, one that better reflects the real practices and architecture of public discourse.[69]

FORMALISM VS. FUNCTIONALISM

A closely related question is where First Amendment institutionalism falls in a common legal debate: the contest between formalism and functionalism. For constitutional theorists, the most important question in constitutional law often is not the *outcome* of particular cases, but the *methods* by which we reach them.[70] The list of competing methods of constitutional interpretation is long. The public dialogue on constitutional interpretation, which often reduces to a staged contest between those who champion interpreting the Constitution according to its "original meaning" or "original understanding" and those who favor a "living Constitution," barely scratches the surface.

Among the many contending positions is a prominent divide between those who argue that constitutional law ought to be "formalist" in orientation and those who believe it ought to be "functionalist." These simple terms often obscure more than they describe. In general, however, we can draw some basic distinctions between formalism and functionalism in constitutional law.

Formalist theories emphasize the value of strict, bright-line rules, while functionalist theorics believe that courts should apply more flexible standards. Formalism emphasizes the rule-of-law values we saw at work in acontextuality—stability, predictability, and generality—while functionalism emphasizes "pragmatic values like adaptability, efficiency, and justice."[71]

The institutional turn might seem to favor functionalism over formalism, and in some respects it unquestionably does.[72] But that is not always or necessarily the case. One of the leading First Amendment institutionalists, Frederick Schauer, is a card-carrying formalist.[73] His argument for the institutional turn is underwritten by formalism. An institutionalist approach, in his view, need not weigh the values and functions behind each institution on a case-by-case basis. If we treat institutions as a relevant category in constitutional adjudication, we can apply that category just as mechanically as we apply the kinds of legal categories we use today. Institutional categories will "serve as rules—as intermediating devices whose more or less rigid application will serve the values lying behind the rules more effectively than will direct application of those values on a more particularistic basis."[74] Schauer thus offers a functional, pragmatic argument for a formalist approach to the recognition of First Amendment institutions in constitutional law.

If Schauer is right, there is one less reason for formalists to resist the institutional turn in the First Amendment. They can have their cake—evenly sliced, of course!—and eat it too. Schauer's formalist approach might seem at first blush to be in tension with my own, which draws a link between institutionalism and contextualism. But that tension dissolves on closer examination. As we have seen, key institutionalist concepts, like "autonomy" and "sovereignty," are at least partly categorical: they treat the existence of First Amendment institutions as a pertinent fact that can help us *redraw,* rather than eliminate, the categories we employ in legal doctrine. Furthermore, Schauer's approach, although formalist in method, is functionalist in motivation. He advocates a formalist approach to institutionalism not because it will achieve some higher purity in the law, but because it "will serve the values lying behind the rules *more effectively*" than a case-by-case method.[75]

That said, it would be a mistake to be *too* formal in this area, at least if we want to remain true to the underlying premises of responsiveness and reflexiveness that justify the institutional turn. Even Schauer's more formal approach recognizes that institutional categories are not an end in themselves. Rather, his goal is to make First Amendment doctrine more responsive to the nature and structure of public discourse.

The institutional turn is also meant to encourage ongoing self-regulation: legal doctrine must be shaped in a bottom-up fashion that respects the fluid and evolving nature of First Amendment institutions. To fulfill that promise, it must be sensitive to the danger of freezing particular institutional boundaries along categorical lines. A "newspaper" is not a "newspaper" for *all* intents and purposes; moreover, the institution of "newspapers" has changed over time. Courts should give strong weight to the fact that a First Amendment institution *is* a First Amendment institution, giving it a wide berth of deference and autonomy. But they should not do so in too rigid a fashion. They should view themselves as partners with First Amendment institutions in an ongoing negotiation over their nature and practices, allowing constitutional meaning to emerge from that negotiation.[76]

The differences between Schauer's approach and my own are thus not so great. To the extent that we differ, I believe an institutional approach that is responsive and reflexive will be categorical *and* particularistic, formal *and* functional. It should avoid deciding cases in an overly particularistic fashion, but draw its categories broadly and loosely rather than imposing rigid categorical definitions on particular institutions.

State Action and the Public-Private Divide

A final puzzle concerns one of the key distinctions in constitutional law: the distinction between private action and public or state action. How we treat that distinction, and whether First Amendment institutionalism ought to recognize it at all, is an important question.

It is possible to take the institutional turn without eliminating state action doctrine or smashing the public-private divide to bits. Before we ask whether something is a First Amendment institution, we could first ask whether it is public or private, a private actor or a state actor, using our existing (and imperfect) doctrinal rules. We could, for example, say that only *private* broadcasters are First Amendment institutions and public broadcasters are not.

This approach has the advantage of parsimony. And, after all, there *is* something to be said for the public-private distinction. Maybe the fact that some institution is government-run means it should not fall within the category of First Amendment institutions. Where government speech institutions such as public broadcasters are concerned, maybe the primary means of guaranteeing their accountability should be the political process, not self-regulation.

These are good arguments, but not good enough. Even under current doctrine, the public-private distinction is not a bright line. This is most obvious in the field of race relations. In a famous decision involving the state action doctrine, *Shelley v. Kraemer,*[77] the Supreme Court held that *private* restrictive covenants banning the sale of real property to black families involved sufficient state action to trigger the Equal Protection Clause of the Fourteenth Amendment, because the covenants had the legal backing of the courts.

Shelley might best be understood as a case in which state action doctrine was contorted by the unique gravitational pull exerted by race in America, which required the courts to confront the ways in which racial discrimination linked public and private action together. The fact that the Court has neither extended this approach widely nor explained its failure to do so supports this explanation.[78] But the Court *has* taken the same approach in other cases. Significantly for our purposes, one of the most prominent examples involves the First Amendment. In *New York Times v. Sullivan,*[79] the Court held that the First Amendment applies to libel actions filed by public officials, in their personal capacity, against private citizens and corporations. It has also imposed stringent limitations on defamation actions brought by public *figures,* individuals prominent in matters of public concern, even when they are not government officials.[80] Although the Court has never really explained why these sorts of actions, and not other private lawsuits, meet the state action requirement, the underlying intuition seems to be that the First Amendment should apply in these cases because of their importance to public discourse, whether or not traditional state action is involved.

These are not the only cases in which courts have relaxed the apparent strictures of state action doctrine. Some of those cases involve First Amendment institutions. Public universities, for example, have been described as "unique state entit[ies]" that enjoy "federal constitutional rights against the state itself."[81] A line of lower court cases has similarly treated some state actors as institutions that enjoy First Amendment rights against the state.[82]

Where First Amendment institutions are involved, the public-private distinction has also been blurred by nonjudicial actors. Universities provide a key example. Some state constitutions treat public universities as distinct from the state for some purposes.[83] And state legislatures and courts have sometimes blurred the line from the other direction, treating private universities like state actors and requiring them to provide equal access to their property.[84]

None of this is meant to ignore the difficult questions that arise in the First Amendment area when we blur the distinction between public and private actors.[85] My goal is to examine and question state action doctrine, not to bury *or* praise it. That examination suggests state action doctrine is *already* less strict than the courts generally acknowledge. It already treats the institutional nature of some state actors, and the importance of public discourse, as a reason to loosen the usual strictures of state action doctrine in some cases.

From an institutionalist perspective, this is the right move. Even if state action doctrine makes sense, it is not always the *most* relevant or important inquiry. In cases involving First Amendment institutions, it may be less important to ask whether a particular institution is public or private than to ask what the *nature* of that institution is and what role it plays in public discourse.[86] Public broadcasters may have a different set of owners than private broadcasters. But the contribution they make to public discourse is the same, and they follow the same professional norms. If we must assign such an entity a "dominant characterization," it may make more sense to treat it as a "journalist" than as a "state actor."[87] In short, if we are resolved to think "things" and not "words," then we might be better off thinking about the *institutional* nature of First Amendment institutions than about their nominally public or private status.

The primary goal of this chapter has been to provide enough detail to demonstrate that the institutional turn is a *possible* path for the First Amendment. My secondary goal has been to show that, despite their professions of acontextuality, courts already exhibit many signs of having taken the institutional turn in First Amendment jurisprudence. In a number of cases, they have acknowledged the fundamental role played by speech institutions in public discourse, in the process creating tensions with current First

Amendment doctrine as a whole. Even fundamental aspects of constitutional law such as the public-private distinction are nowhere near as rigid as they purport to be; they already bend in order to accommodate institutional imperatives.

Two final points are worth emphasizing. First, to show that First Amendment institutionalism is a possibility—that it can be described and defined and its potential benefits explored—is not to make any claims for its perfection. This chapter has shown that courts *can* approach First Amendment institutions differently than they might under an acontextual doctrinal approach—indeed, that they already sometimes do. It has done so in the context of an argument, developed over the course of Part One, that there are good reasons, stemming from the inevitable imperfections of current doctrine, to imagine doing so. But I have not denied that this approach raises questions and problems of its own. We will explore those questions in greater depth in the chapters that follow, especially Chapter 11.

Second, in keeping with this book's general emphasis on responsive and reflexive law, and its insistence that top-down, acontextual legal rules will inevitably fail to properly acknowledge and accommodate the lived reality of public discourse and social life, it should be emphasized that First Amendment institutionalism cannot be reduced to a formula. It cannot be fully understood or developed without looking closely at the institutions themselves. The task of identifying First Amendment institutions and their boundaries, for example, cannot be worked out purely in the abstract; it must begin with a consideration of those institutions we can easily recognize as First Amendment institutions, and some of the variations on them that may present more difficult definitional issues. Our approach must, in short, be developed in large measure from the bottom up. That is the task of Part Two.

II

First Amendment Institutions in Practice

5

Where Ideas Begin:
Universities and Schools

On the list of obvious candidates for treatment as First Amendment institutions, universities are perhaps the most well-established. We have long associated their flourishing with the health of the American body politic. George Washington called education essential to "the security of a free constitution."[1] *Brown v. Board of Education,* the most famous Supreme Court decision of the last century, observed that public education has become "perhaps the most important function of state and local governments."[2] Educational institutions are fixtures in our social landscape. That is certainly true of universities, whose distinct nature has been a millennium in the making. It is also true, to a lesser extent, of primary and secondary, or "K-12," schools.

As entrenched as these vital infrastructural institutions are in American public discourse, however, they fit oddly within legal doctrine. Although universities can be crudely sorted as public or private, that distinction is often overshadowed by their shared traits and common practices.[3] Although K-12 public schools are wholly creatures of the state, the courts have never treated them quite like other government actors.

The distinct nature of these training grounds for public discourse would be better served by taking the institutional turn—that is, by treating them as unique institutions that have a special relationship with the First Amendment. In many respects this is what the courts already do. But the doctrine in this area will remain confused unless courts are willing to be forthright about what they are doing.

The Emergence of American Universities

By the Revolutionary War there were already nine colleges in the American colonies; the oldest, Harvard, was established in 1636. From the outset, these institutions were a blend of public and private. Both federally supported and state-founded universities arose soon after the founding of the United States; their number exploded after the Morrill Act of 1862 established the land-grant universities. Some were public (the University of California system began as a land-grant institution), some were private, such as MIT, and others were a mixture, such as Cornell.[4]

The modern research university that emerged in the mid-nineteenth century was the product of various changes in higher education that emphasized not only the university's teaching role but also its capacity to serve as a center for the production of knowledge and research.[5] One of the central influences on these developments was the experience of German universities, whose approach was imported to this country by American students and academics who had studied there.[6]

Three leading principles defined the more or less autonomous role of German universities. *Lehrfreiheit,* or "teaching freedom," distinguished German academics, who were civil servants, from other government employees, giving them freedom to pursue teaching and scholarship without the prior approval of state or religious authorities. *Lernfreiheit,* or "learning freedom," allowed students to determine their own courses of study and govern their own behavior. And *Freiheit der Wissenschaft,* or "academic freedom," allowed German universities to enjoy a right of self-governance. Although the state retained substantial control over appointments, universities were free to make their own decisions about internal matters under the direction of senior faculty.[7]

The transplantation was awkward. In Germany, universities were state controlled but faculty governed. In the United States, both public and private universities were under lay control, answerable to governing bodies of nonacademics. American universities thus faced two levels of potential interference: from the state itself and from lay governing boards.

Academic Freedom

What emerged from these circumstances was the concept of academic freedom, which remains one of the most definitive qualities of the contemporary American university. Louis Menand has called it "the philosophical key to the whole enterprise of higher education."[8] Academic freedom has installed itself somewhat uneasily within First Amendment doctrine, but it is, first and foremost, a professional or institutional norm.

The concept had its official origins in the establishment of the American Association of University Professors (AAUP) and the drafting in 1915 of its Declaration of Principles, which defined the university's fundamental task as the search for truth: to "promote inquiry and to advance the sum of human knowledge." The truth would thrive if researchers had "complete and unlimited freedom to pursue inquiry and publish its results." Although the university's truth-seeking function might contribute to the broader social good, its contribution to democracy was indirect. It was not to serve as a mirror *of* society, but as a resource *for* society, consisting of learned and disinterested experts.[9]

In contrast to the premodern American university's emphasis on instruction over scholarship, the AAUP saw the primary mission of the university as academic in nature and focused on professors. The Declaration thus emphasized "teaching freedom" over "learning freedom,"[10] and did not concern itself much with the university's institutional autonomy. That was more of a concern in Germany, where the threat to academic freedom came from the state. In American universities, however, with their lay governors eager to remove socialists and other pernicious influences, the threat often came from inside the university. Academic freedom was thus meant to govern professors' own behavior and serve as a bulwark against both internal and external interference.

Academic freedom was not a license for academics to say and write whatever they wanted on any issue. Although the Declaration sought to protect professors' extramural statements, it did so not because academics were entitled to say anything they pleased, but because academic freedom could not survive if academics were targeted for political views expressed outside the classroom. Significantly, the Declaration emphasized that "there are no rights without corresponding duties": "only those who carry on their work in the temper of the scientific inquirer" could properly invoke academic freedom.[11] Whether academics met that standard was to be judged by the members of their own disciplines, not by lay governors or the state.[12] But it *was* to be judged. Academics were free to teach, publish, and speak only insofar as they lived up to the professional standards of their disciplines.

Professional academic freedom is thus not coterminous with free speech. "Under the First Amendment," the Supreme Court has said, "there is no such thing as a false idea."[13] Under the professional concept of academic freedom, there *are* false ideas, or at least bad ideas and shoddy methods. Academic freedom would be hard to justify without a corresponding sense of academic obligation, including the obligation of a discipline to police its own members. Academic freedom, in short, constitutes a kind of implicit pact with the public: let us tend to our own affairs, and we will produce knowledge of lasting value to society.[14]

Constitutional Academic Freedom

In a culture in which the First Amendment has colonized thinking about public discourse, it was perhaps inevitable that the professional concept of academic freedom would eventually be absorbed into constitutional doctrine. Unfortunately, it was also inevitable that the courts, confronted by the difficulty of fitting an institutionally specific concept into an institutionally agnostic framework, would do a poor job of it. They opened a rift between the professional and constitutional concepts of academic freedom that persists to this day.[15]

The debut of constitutional academic freedom came with the Supreme Court's 1957 decision in *Sweezy v. New Hampshire*.[16] Paul Sweezy was subpoenaed and questioned by the state attorney general about lectures he had delivered at the University of New Hampshire. He refused to answer and was jailed for contempt. The Court overturned his conviction on narrow grounds that involved his due process rights under the Fourteenth Amendment, not his First Amendment rights. This turned out to be prophetic: most of the Court's pronouncements on academic freedom have been "rhetorical flourishes," not concrete holdings.[17] Nevertheless, what the Court had to say about academic freedom in *Sweezy* would set the tone for later decisions.

Writing for a plurality of the Court, Chief Justice Earl Warren asserted that the questions posed to Sweezy about his lectures threatened "an invasion of petitioner's liberties in the area of academic freedom and political expression—areas in which government should be extremely reticent to tread." Warren added unhelpfully: "The essentiality of freedom in the community of American universities is almost self-evident." His description of academic freedom, however, was a dog's breakfast: a mixture of the truth-seeking justifications offered by the AAUP and a broader set of justifications based on the supposedly democratic function of academic speech. He wrote: "Teachers and students must always remain free to inquire, to study and to evaluate, to gain new maturity and understanding." But he also emphasized "the vital role in a democracy that is played by those who guide and train our youth."[18]

That statement can be read as meaning nothing more than that the pursuit of knowledge for its own sake ultimately benefits society. But it can also be read as suggesting that the model of academic freedom should be a specifically *democratic* one, in which we value universities as rehearsals for the kinds of democratic discourse that citizens will engage in later in life. This is a departure from the model of scientific disinterestedness offered by the AAUP.

Justice Felix Frankfurter's concurring opinion focused squarely on the First Amendment. Frankfurter, a former Harvard law professor, emphasized the university's truth-seeking function, calling knowledge "its own end" in the university. Constitutional academic freedom formed a moat around the university, protecting it against state intrusion. He argued that "four essential freedoms" govern the life of a university: the freedom "to determine for itself on academic grounds who may teach, what may be taught, how it shall be taught, and who may be admitted to study." In short, Frankfurter viewed constitutional academic freedom as an *institutional* right belonging to the university as a corporate entity, not just to individual professors.[19]

Ten years later, a majority of the Supreme Court gave a ringing endorsement to constitutional academic freedom in its judgment in *Keyishian v. Board of Regents of the University of the State of New York*. "Our nation," wrote Justice William Brennan, "is deeply committed to safeguarding academic freedom, which is of transcendent value to all of us and not merely to the teachers concerned. That freedom is therefore a special concern of the First Amendment, which does not tolerate laws that cast a pall of orthodoxy over the classroom."[20]

Keyishian has been lauded as a powerful statement of the Supreme Court's allegiance to academic freedom.[21] From the perspective of the professional concept of academic freedom, however, the case is mixed. *Keyishian's* vision of academic freedom was not necessarily the same one that the Court recognized in *Sweezy,* or that the AAUP had advocated. Its decision turned on an analogy between the university and the broader democratic society. The classroom, the Court said, "is peculiarly the 'marketplace of ideas.'" The nation's future depends on "leaders trained through wide exposure to that robust exchange of ideas which discovers truth 'out of a multitude of tongues, [rather] than through any kind of authoritative selection.'"[22] This vision of academic freedom viewed it not in terms of the truth itself, but in terms of a free and unfettered process of discussion. The truth was a mere by-product; what really mattered was that students should be trained in the habit of democratic dialogue. *Keyishian* viewed the university as a miniature democracy subject to the rules of democratic discourse—a concept wholly foreign to the professional concept of academic freedom.

Almost from the beginning, then, two conflicts were apparent in the First Amendment doctrine of academic freedom. The first was the gap between academics' understanding of *professional* academic freedom and the courts' understanding of that freedom as a *constitutional* right. The second was the tension, within constitutional academic freedom, between its status as an *institutional* right and as an *individual* right. Converting a conception of institutional autonomy into a right of individual expression could not help but create tensions in the doctrine, especially when the broader drift of First Amendment doctrine was so individualistic and indifferent to institutions.

As long as the interests of academic institutions and individual academics coincided, that tension could be ignored. But it could not be ignored forever. Justice John Paul Stevens later described the conflict in these terms: "Academic freedom thrives not only on the independent and uninhibited exchange of ideas among teachers and students, but also, *and somewhat inconsistently,* on autonomous decision making by the university itself."[23]

Returning Constitutional Academic Freedom to Its Institutional Roots

Both of these tensions stem from the same broader problem in First Amendment law. They reflect the difficulty of fitting an institutionally oriented concept into a First Amendment framework that emphasizes struggles between the state and the individual speaker. Under this model, doctrinal tension is inevitable. Courts cannot respond to the unique qualities of universities, and the singular problems they face, unless their doctrine is capable of treating universities as unique institutions. If they treat them as miniature democracies and insist that the same doctrinal rules must apply in both realms, they will surely fail.

The solution is to return the constitutional concept of academic freedom to its institutional roots. Universities are not a free or unregulated marketplace of ideas, although the regulations are internal rather than external. They are laboratories *for* democracy, not laboratories *of* democracy: they contribute to democratic discourse, but not by following its rules.[24] They are an institution of their own, with their own norms, practices, and traditions. Public discourse will best be served in the long run by treating universities as self-regulating autonomous enterprises, not public forums.[25]

First Amendment institutionalism, I have argued, requires institutions that are both well established and governed by strong norms of self-regulation. Both features are present in the university. Academics "live their professional lives within disciplinary constraints and norms."[26] Everything academics do in their professional lives is jealously guarded by the gatekeepers of the profession, their own disciplinary colleagues.

This is a crucial difference between academic discourse and broader public discourse. In public discourse, the space taken up by matters of fact is smaller than that taken up by matters of opinion. In this realm it is generally assumed that each person is entitled to his or her own opinion. In academic discourse, by contrast, in order to be viewed as saying anything worth listening to, one's work must already have been certified by one's professional peers as sufficiently careful and perceptive to meet disciplinary standards. Popular supposition—and, sometimes, appearances—to the contrary, the academic profession does not suffer fools gladly. Public discourse welcomes them with open arms.

What does this mean for the institutional approach to universities? Above all else, it means courts should grant universities autonomy to make their own judgments on academic matters without interference from the state or from lay governing boards. The key is not to treat universities as miniature democracies, subject to all the First Amendment doctrines that apply elsewhere in public debate, but rather as largely autonomous realms.

Courts should step aside and allow universities to govern themselves. Where universities make proper academic judgments, judges should refuse to intervene.

The Supreme Court has often emphasized that courts owe deference to the "genuinely academic decisions" of university officials. It has said that courts are ill-equipped to deal with "the multitude of academic decisions that are made daily by faculty members of public educational institutions— decisions that require 'an expert evaluation of cumulative information and [are] not readily adapted to the procedural tools of judicial or administrative decisionmaking.'"[27] That is exactly how courts should deal with questions of university self-governance. The institutional turn reinforces this approach and helps point out some of the blind alleys the courts have gone down in the service of institutional agnosticism.

Among the most important of these is the question of whether the First Amendment protects the individual academic freedom of *professors* or the institutional autonomy of *universities*. Under an institutional approach, the relationship between the two becomes much clearer. Universities cannot serve their institutional mission unless they are treated as institutions— as separate realms operating under rules of their own. Courts lack a sufficient understanding of the academic enterprise to make judgments about what professional academic speech should be protected and what speech should be subject to regulation. As long as First Amendment doctrine follows the paradigm of the individual speaker against the restrictive state, legal interventions in this area are likely to be both overprotective of the speech of individual academics, even when they violate disciplinary norms, and underprotective of the obligation of university administrators to govern the enterprise according to its academic mission.

Judicial intervention, moreover, is not especially necessary. The very purpose of the university's traditions and self-regulatory practices is to protect individual professors in their capacity as researchers, writers, and teachers, to the extent that those protections are consistent with proper academic judgments. Any additional benefits of having the courts weigh in on behalf of individual professors are outweighed by the risk that judicial intervention will harm or distort academic speech. The judicial emphasis in academic freedom cases should be on *institutional* autonomy, not on the protection of individual professors.[28]

Similarly, an institutional focus on academic freedom clarifies the legal status of *students*. By and large, student speech within universities should be treated as falling outside the scope of academic freedom. The tools by which courts protect individual student speech are, broadly speaking, the same ones they use to protect individual speech in the public at large. Those are the wrong tools for the job. They succeed only at great cost to the autonomy and the value of universities. Free speech doctrine, we have seen, operates on the assumption that "there is no such thing as a false idea"[29]—that the government should be barred from making judgments about the value of particular speech acts based on the content of the speech. But this is exactly the job of universities: to *judge* student speech on its merits—and, often, to find it wanting.

Nor does it help for courts to turn to other institutionally agnostic doctrines, such as public forum doctrine. That doctrine fits poorly with universities, which must make content-based decisions about the speech that takes place within their gates.[30] Universities are not public forums. We only confuse things by straining to fit them within that framework. Student speech is important, and in appropriate cases may merit significant First Amendment protection. But it should not enjoy the *institutional* First Amendment protection to which universities themselves are entitled.

Finally, I must say something about what it means for a university to exercise professional academic judgment. Frederick Schauer has argued that rather than delve into these questions, courts should simply ask "whether the conduct at issue was or was not the conduct of one of these institutions."[31] But what does it mean to call something "the conduct of" an institution such as a university? It is not enough to simply say that a university has acted; we must decide whether it is *distinctly* the action of a university. Most administrative decisions taken with respect to university governance deserve to be treated as autonomous decisions under an institutional approach to the First Amendment. But a decision to engage in price fixing, or to shoot trespassers on sight, is not an *academic* decision, properly understood. It has no unique bearing on the academic life of the university. In fixing the boundaries of universities' institutional autonomy, we must protect what is unique to them as institutions, rather than treating everything they do as entitled to legal immunity.

We should, moreover, expect universities to make those decisions *as academic institutions*. However diverse our vision of the mission of the university may be, it is not unlimited. Universities may, for example, reasonably disagree about what constitutes plagiarism and what the penalty for plagiarism should be. But a rule stating that Prius owners are immune from charges of plagiarism and SUV owners are presumptively guilty has nothing to do with academic judgment. Whatever judicial role is appropriate in such cases, certainly this is not a case for judicial deference, any more than we would defer to golfers about the rules of football.

The trigger for the institutional autonomy of universities, then, is that they make "genuinely academic decision[s]." But what constitutes a genuinely academic decision can be a complicated question.[32] The courts have said that an academic decision is a professionally arrived at academic judgment that can only be judicially overridden if the university has engaged in such a "substantial departure from accepted academic norms as to demonstrate that the person or committee responsible did not actually exercise professional judgment."[33] This means that academic judgments must observe the norms, practices, and traditions that govern academic thinking and decision-making. Where those practices involve particular procedures, such as those surrounding tenure decisions, the procedures must be followed. Where they involve questions of expertise, experts must be consulted and deliver expert opinions. Decisions must be made on the basis of academic merits, not extrinsic factors.[34]

In a sense, this amounts to a kind of institutional due process. Courts should grant universities a wide scope of autonomy *if* it is reasonably clear that they have acted on an academic question and according to standard academic decision-making norms. Provided that the university has not simply acted on a lark, the courts should assume its decision falls within the scope of institutional autonomy.[35]

Guckenberger v. Boston University serves as an example. It involved Boston University's refusal to lift foreign language requirements for students who claimed an exemption under the Americans with Disabilities Act. The federal district court initially refused to dismiss the plaintiffs' action because the university administration had not engaged in "any form of reasoned deliberation" concerning whether modifying the requirement "would change the essential academic standards" of the university. The university subsequently did engage in careful deliberation over whether "the foreign language requirement is fundamental to the nature of the liberal arts degree at Boston

University." At that point, the court bowed out, holding that "the ADA does not authorize the courts to intervene even if a majority of other comparable academic institutions [would] disagree" in similar circumstances.[36]

Guckenberger is fairly instructive. A purely arbitrary decision taken by the university is not suitable for academic autonomy and judicial deference. But one that shows evidence of the exercise of academic judgment requires courts to defer to the university's institutional autonomy, even if other universities would decide differently. If the university has acted *as* a university, the court's inquiry should cease, absent extraordinary circumstances.[37]

We may add two more details to this approach. First, although the university's institutional autonomy is triggered by academic decisions, they need not be professorial decisions alone. Often, important decisions are made by university administrators, acting in the interests of the institution as a whole. Those judgments, too, are entitled to judicial deference. The key is that those decisions must be made not by courts or lay governors but by the professional apparatus of the university in accordance with institutional norms.[38]

Second, in keeping with the responsive and reflexive nature of the institutional turn, the boundaries of what counts as academic judgment ought to be loosely defined. The goal is not simply to replace one set of rigid categorical distinctions with another, especially if that rigidity comes at the cost of institutional pluralism.

In a contrasting view, Peter Byrne argues that constitutional academic freedom only extends to "the fundamental values of disinterested inquiry, reasoned and critical discourse, and liberal education."[39] Any definition of educational institutional autonomy that goes too far beyond this will "threaten to bring the entire right [of constitutional academic freedom] into disrepute."[40] But this approach risks reifying a particular legal definition of academic freedom, and of the university's mission. If that happens, courts will cease to be responsive or reflexive in evaluating whether that definition comports with shifting views within the university itself. As they have in the past, they will ultimately widen the gap between the professional and judicial concepts of academic freedom. Just as we should not encourage courts to believe that one set of doctrinal rules for the First Amendment can apply in the same way to every institution, so courts should not conclude that there is only *the* "university," narrowly defined according to some rigid and unchanging vision.

In practical terms, that means courts ought to be, so to speak, deferential about their deference: they ought to defer, not only to universities that exercise proper academic judgment, but to what universities say about the scope and boundaries of proper academic judgment. Courts should respect universities' own judgments about what their academic mission entails and what actions are needed to serve that mission, rather than evaluate those claims against a rigid, judicially imposed definition of the mission of the university.[41]

That gives universities broad discretion to describe their own mission and the scope of their institutional autonomy. But we can be reasonably sanguine about this, for several reasons. First, First Amendment institutionalism does not mean unfettered discretion. Universities' actions are embedded in a long, albeit evolving, tradition of cultural norms and self-regulatory practices. The proper norms and limits of their behavior have long been internalized by the universities themselves.[42] The constitutional autonomy of universities is the culmination of centuries of practices that demonstrate the university's trustworthiness as an independent and autonomous institution that makes important contributions to public discourse.

Second, courts are not the only—or even the most important—group to set limits on the boundaries of what constitutes a genuine academic mission or a proper academic judgment. The primary source of this limitation comes from the academics, students, and administrators who are the university's principal stakeholders. If a university departs significantly from what its stakeholders consider proper academic judgments, it will hear about it. As anyone who has sat through a faculty meeting is painfully aware, if academics know anything, it is how to complain. A university that engaged in flagrant racial discrimination in hiring, for example, would be resisted fiercely by its own stakeholders, on the grounds that "[p]rejudice is not an academic value."[43]

Third, even where a particular university departs from conventional academic norms, it will still be defining—and limiting—itself according to its own standards. Suppose a university declares that its mission requires it to impose restrictions on hate speech by students or faculty, on the grounds that the university ought to be a place of respectful discourse. That university is making a specific statement that can be used as a yardstick to measure the integrity of everything else it does. Even if the courts are obliged to let that university operate autonomously, it is still subject to examination and criticism by members of its own community and the academic community at large, who can disagree with that mission or ask what implications it holds for the university's other policies. Autonomy is a double-edged sword: it gives the university latitude to act, but also forces it to define and declare its actions, and thus give potential ammunition to critics within the academic community.

That sort of breathing room is necessary if doctrine is to be both responsive and reflexive, capable of taking into account both the particular problems faced by universities and the varied ways that universities address these problems. Universities evolve slowly, but they do evolve. As central as the truth-seeking idea of the 1915 Declaration remains for most universities, it cannot be fixed in amber. Universities will continue to debate what ought to drive the academic mission: truth-seeking, democracy, moral education, or something else. Those competing concepts suggest different values that universities might prize and different policies that might help achieve them. They involve subtle variations that might ultimately put different universities in very different places.

While insisting on our right as members of the academic community to debate vigorously whether some of these directions depart from the academic mission altogether, we can still allow room for institutional pluralism in terms of how universities see themselves and what policies they pursue. Those diverse experiments in university life will feed back into the academy's broader understanding about its own nature and about what policies support or undermine its enterprise. Whatever lessons the academy draws from those experiences may in turn feed back into the courts' understanding of what constitutes genuine academic judgment. In this way the law, rather than imposing a single vision of what *the* university is, will be part of a continuous feedback loop of experimentation and refinement.

No approach to the First Amendment status of universities will be perfect. The question is whether the institutional approach is better than the existing one. I think it is. It provides more candor about what courts are already doing: treating universities as unique communities that do not fit perfectly into general First Amendment doctrine, such as public forum doctrine. It is also less likely to fall into the kinds of inconsistencies that result when law tries to be institutionally agnostic. Those who raise concerns about according too much autonomy to universities have a point. But they should not wield those concerns as a veto without comparing the institutional turn frankly to the costs, benefits, and inconsistencies of current doctrine.

Boundary Questions

Before addressing specific questions about the legal treatment of universities as First Amendment institutions, it is worth returning to the question of boundaries—of what counts or doesn't count as a First Amendment institution. In the case of universities, the question is whether just any institution that calls itself a university qualifies for the kind of legal autonomy First Amendment institutionalism prescribes. Outside of the schools that everyone would accept as "universities," we can imagine two cases that test our intuitions for one reason or another. First, what about a for-profit institution, like DeVry University or Phoenix University, that might offer some of the basic services that other universities do but without providing all of the governance structures, potentially including tenure or faculty governance, that we associate with institutions of higher learning? Second, what about something that is even more nominally a "university," like Hamburger University, the "global center of excellence for McDonald's operations training and leadership development?"[44]

My sense, which certainly may be contested, is that simply presenting such examples suggests that these sorts of boundary questions will often be easier for courts to address sensibly than we might fear. In any event, these questions pose no greater difficulties than, say, those that confront courts under current doctrine when they are forced to say whether some institution is a "state actor" or not.

The answer to the question whether a for-profit educational institution should be treated as a "university" for purposes of First Amendment institutionalism is surely "it depends." But however that question is resolved in particular cases, it certainly should not depend on the mere fact that such an institution operates for profit. The real question is not *why* such institutions operate, but *how* they operate and what they do. Recall that the core of First Amendment institutionalism is that an institution serves a well-established function that forms part of the infrastructure of public discourse and that it operates as a substantially self-regulating institution. Recall, too, that

institutional autonomy is not boundless, but must be tied to the core function of that institution—its unique contribution to public discourse. For a
university to invoke institutional autonomy successfully, it must be seeking
the freedom to make its own *academic* decisions; it cannot invoke institutional autonomy to insulate *every* decision from judicial review.

Some for-profit educational institutions may barely resemble universities
at all: they may provide no tenure for faculty, no faculty role in institutional
governance, no support for research or publication, and so on. They may be
Hamburger University in all but name—and I cannot imagine any judge, or
anyone else, calling Hamburger University a university for First Amendment
purposes. But the less these institutions offer along academic lines, the less
likely it is that anyone, judges included, could possibly conclude that they
are making a uniquely academic contribution to public discourse, and the
less likely it is that they will have either a basis for calling the decisions they
do make "academic" or the need to invoke academic freedom. On the other
hand, some for-profit institutions mirror traditional universities much more
closely, both in terms of what they do and how they do it.[45] The more these
institutions seek to resemble traditional universities, whether to attract faculty or students or to receive the benefits of accreditation by academic organizations, the more they will commit themselves to the kinds of practices,
traditions, and internal constraints that make universities what they are.[46]

We should remember, in short, that First Amendment institutions and
their legal autonomy are defined both categorically and *functionally*. In the
case of universities, this means not only that a higher educational institution
must provide the kinds of contributions to public discourse that help define
our understanding of what universities are, but that only its *academic* decisions will be entitled to institutional autonomy. There will surely be boundary questions, but they will be less difficult than we might anticipate, and
no more difficult than the boundary questions the courts already confront
under current doctrine.

Cases and Controversies

In some cases regarding universities, the courts have reached more or less
the right result, if not always for clear and consistent reasons. In others,
the institutional turn demands different results. The institutional approach,

with its emphasis on self-regulation, leaves significant room to conclude that the courts ought to keep their hands off of particular disputes, while leaving the rest of us free to debate the merits of the actions that particular universities take.

WHO MAY TEACH

The deference shown by courts to university decisions about hiring, firing, and tenure offers strong evidence that the doctrine of constitutional academic freedom ultimately involves *institutional* autonomy, not just the rights of individual academics. The courts have made clear that decisions about "who may teach" must generally be free from judicial interference.[47] That deference applies to both public universities, where the First Amendment applies most directly, and private universities, where courts have interposed a deferential standard of review in statutory cases alleging discrimination in hiring.[48] Despite its critics,[49] this deferential approach is well established.

Institutionally oriented deference faces its sharpest conflict with institutionally agnostic doctrine in the case of employment discrimination laws, which generally recognize no relevant categorical distinctions between different kinds of employers.[50] From an institutionally agnostic perspective, there is no good reason that universities should be any freer than other employers to engage in employment discrimination. Congress recognized that when it amended the principal federal employment discrimination statute to remove a statutory exemption for universities.

From an institutional perspective, however, allowing "free-wheeling court supervision" of universities' employment decisions would allow courts to "seiz[e] control of [a university's] future identity and mission."[51] That concern is at its lowest ebb when a university acts in a straightforward invidiously discriminatory manner. But when a case involves a comparison of decisions to employ or promote one academic and not another, the courts intrude much further into the academic realm. Courts are better off treating these decisions as unreviewable, short of clear and convincing evidence that the university departed from proper academic standards.

An institutional approach would go a step further. One question in this area is whether universities, like some institutions and individuals, may resist being forced to disclose the content of their deliberations on hiring and tenure. In *EEOC v. University of Pennsylvania,* the Supreme Court held that they could not.[52] From an institutional perspective, the Court decided wrongly. Employment deliberations go to the heart of the university's autonomy: they involve genuinely academic peer review, in which members of a discipline professionally and, with the expectation of confidentiality, candidly assess the quality of a colleague's work. "Peer review certainly comes within the protection of institutional academic freedom if any university activity other than teaching and scholarship does."[53]

That does not mean university employment decisions must be utterly immune from judicial review. However broadly and deferentially the courts treat the category of genuinely academic decisions, some decisions will fall outside those boundaries. Even so, we must remember two important points. First, the scope of those boundaries must take into account the possibility of institutional pluralism within the wider realm of the university. Religious universities, for instance, may have strong reasons, closely tied to their unique mission, to take religion into account when making employment decisions.[54]

Second, it is worth reemphasizing that institutional autonomy removes only the *judicial* avenue for remedying all but the most obviously improper academic decisions. It does not eliminate *professional* avenues of criticism. Self-regulation should be the primary means of addressing universities' behavior. If we allow universities to debate how and on what basis employment decisions should be made, we may see the emergence of a *reflexive* approach to these issues. Courts, even as they defer broadly to universities' employment decisions, can identify emerging "best hiring practices" and treat those practices as a safe harbor in future cases. In short, even while carving out a broad scope of deference to the autonomous decision-making of universities, courts may also *learn* from them, creating a body of data about clearly permissible and clearly impermissible employment decisions and allowing universities to experiment and evolve within those rough boundaries.

What May Be Taught and How It Shall Be Taught

The questions of what university professors may teach and how they may teach it fall squarely within the scope of autonomous academic decision-making.[55] This is consistent with the 1915 Declaration, which places the responsibility for "curriculum, subject matter and methods of instruction" in the hands of the faculty as a collective body.[56]

Courts have been more conflicted about how to treat grading decisions, dividing over whether those decisions lie within the hands of individual faculty members or the faculty as a whole.[57] In this area, the institutional approach is the better one. Grading decisions are essential to the choices of individual faculty members, and arbitrary grade changes imposed from on high should be viewed with distrust. But more harm is done to the university as an institution by equating grading decisions with other speech acts by public employees. Treating grading decisions as individual expression, as one court has done,[58] ignores the fact that these decisions involve norms and practices driven by the faculty as a whole, not just individual professors engaging in unfettered "speech."

Indeed, decisions about what can be taught are just one of many important aspects of university life that occur within a distinctly institutional framework and thus require something other than the courts' institutionally agnostic and individually focused approach to First Amendment cases. The usual doctrine regarding speech by government employees, which turns on whether the speech is of "public concern" and whether it falls within the employee's "official duties," is ill-suited to academic speech, as the Supreme Court has conceded.[59] These tests do not adequately reflect the distinctive nature of universities, in which decisions about what and how to teach reside neither fully with individual professors nor fully with the faculty as a whole.[60]

All this suggests, again, that the university is a poor fit within institutionally agnostic First Amendment doctrine. Many of the decisions that individual professors make about what and how to teach must be theirs alone, if academic freedom is to mean anything. But individual professors cannot have the same liberty to make these decisions that an individual speaker has within public discourse. A philosophy professor who teaches the dialogues of Plato must have some leeway to decide which dialogues to teach and how to teach them. But she cannot decide to spend all her time in that class talking about astrology or the war in Iraq. A philosophy department, *as* a department, may not dictate the thoughts its members think, but it can insist that they teach philosophy. Professors have greater liberty than many other employees. But that liberty comes with a responsibility to observe the standards of their discipline. Their speech is free only insofar as it is also constrained.

Who May Be Admitted

When Justice Frankfurter spoke of the freedom of the university to determine who may be admitted to study, he had in mind a very different set of concerns from the ones that would later animate universities and courts. Frankfurter lived in an era in which universities had imposed quotas on the number of Jewish students[61] and in which students faced the threat of discipline or expulsion for their participation in leftist activities.[62] Frankfurter believed the university should admit anyone who met its meritocratic standards.

By the time the issue ripened, however, the question was whether universities could deliberately select students on the basis of race or other factors in order to remedy past discrimination in society and build a community of students that reflected the racial diversity of the population. In three cases decided twenty-five years apart, the Supreme Court held that universities could do so, although not for general remedial purposes and not by using race as an automatic basis for admission without engaging in individualized assessment of each applicant. Academic freedom featured prominently in these decisions, although it is not clear whether it really mattered or was a mere makeweight.

In *Regents of California v. Bakke,* a fractured Court struck down the medical school admissions policy of the University of California at Davis, which crudely reserved a certain number of spots for black students. The Court emphasized that the Constitution did not bar consideration of race as a "plus" factor in admissions decisions. In his pivotal opinion, Justice Lewis Powell rejected all the grounds advanced by the university for its policy save one: "the attainment of a diverse student body." That interest was linked directly to academic freedom, "a special concern of the First Amendment." A university that believed a "robust exchange of ideas" required a "diverse student body" should be given "wide discretion."[63] This First Amendment interest helped overcome the general strictures of the Equal Protection Clause, which might otherwise have barred universities from using race as a factor in admissions at all.

In 2003, in a pair of cases involving the University of Michigan, the Court reaffirmed universities' use of race as a plus factor in admissions, provided they did so as part of a sensitive evaluation of individual applicants. The Court struck down a cruder race-weighted admission system for undergraduates,[64] but in *Grutter v. Bollinger* it upheld an ostensibly more individualized admissions process for the law school. Again, academic freedom was at the heart of the Court's decision. Universities, Justice Sandra Day O'Connor wrote, "occupy a special niche" in the First Amendment and are entitled to substantial deference in making academic decisions, including the decision that "a diverse student body" is "essential to [the university's] academic mission."[65]

The vision of academic freedom and "educational autonomy"[66] in these cases is strikingly different from the traditional professional conception of academic freedom. In both *Bakke* and *Grutter,* the Court's vision of academic freedom is largely unmoored from the search for truth. Instead, it involves the need for robust debate within the university *(Bakke)* and the need for a healthy, legitimate democratic process and a diverse set of future leaders *(Grutter).* The Court speaks in terms of deference to universities' genuine academic decisions, including decisions about whom to admit. But its real thrust in both cases has less to do with deference than with its outright support of the use of race in university admissions, for reasons having more to do with the broader society than with the university itself.

Some scholars have doubted whether academic freedom was doing much work in these cases.[67] In many respects, the Supreme Court used academic freedom in *Bakke* and *Grutter* as an escape hatch. It allowed the Court to uphold race-conscious university admissions policies without having to reverse decisions that were far more skeptical of affirmative action in other contexts.[68]

There is good reason to be skeptical about what the Court really meant in its *Bakke* and *Grutter* decisions. But what it *said* provides powerful ammunition to supporters of the institutional First Amendment. The decisions are highly deferential to universities *as autonomous institutions,* speaking in terms of deferring to a university's own sense of its academic mission. Although the Court may have used the First Amendment as a vehicle here, it also recognized that universities have unique institutional needs, practices, and traditions, and should be trusted to make their own admissions decisions with minimal judicial interference.

REGULATING CAMPUS SPEECH

During the late 1980s and early 1990s, when political correctness was at its peak, a number of universities experimented with speech codes aimed at prohibiting hostile speech based on race, gender, sexual orientation, and so on.[69] The experiment was short-lived, partly because it provoked a negative reaction within the academic community and partly because the courts hastened to strike down the codes.[70]

Institutional autonomy had very little to do with this debate. To the contrary, one judge used the university's mission against it. In striking down a speech code at the University of Michigan on the basis of general First Amendment principles such as content neutrality, he argued that those general rules "acquire a special significance in the university setting, where free and unfettered interplay of competing views is essential to the institution's educational mission."[71] He later noted that he had avoided the phrase "academic freedom" in his opinion because his "concerns were directed to the [general] First Amendment implication of the code in action."[72] In short, the legal debate over campus speech codes, although nominally connected to the special mission of the university, proceeded as if the university was simply part of the broader community of public discourse and subject to the same rules.

From an institutional perspective, this was a mistake. Universities do not all share precisely the same sense of what their mission requires or how to achieve it. Some subscribe to the idea of a university as a miniature democracy. Others argue that some students are more vulnerable within the campus setting and therefore more in need of protection from insulting speech.[73] Still others contend that while the university is a place of fairly unfettered speech in general, it is entitled to regulate speech that does not contribute to its educational mission.[74]

The institutional turn rejects the idea that anyone, least of all the courts, must decide this issue once and for all. The United States is not short of universities. Courts should not assume that all of them place the search for truth at the heart of their mission, nor that the search for truth can only be served by the same free-for-all discourse that the First Amendment guarantees for public speech at large. Neither should they assume conversely that the university's proper mission is to provide a model of polite and respectful discourse. They should treat such decisions as what they are: matters of *academic judgment* which ought to be left to the universities themselves.[75] One need not approve of campus speech codes to prefer this approach; certainly I do not. But we ought to see the issue as one that lies within the realm of the university and outside the domain of the courts.[76]

Left to their own devices, I believe, the universities would have ended up rejecting these policies. That is, in fact, largely what happened.[77] The reasons the enthusiasm for campus hate codes dwindled are mostly independent of anything the courts did. It is doubtful that a few scattered court rulings did more to influence the short, unhappy life of the campus speech code than did the debate within the university community itself. If some universities wish to continue experimenting with these kinds of regulation, wisely or unwisely, they should be free to do so. That is a fair trade for the long-run benefits to public discourse created by university autonomy; and the sheer number of different universities would leave students free to opt out of the schools that insisted on maintaining and enforcing campus speech codes.

In the meantime, even if universities were free to experiment with different senses of their mission and what it entails for student speech, they would be forced to confront the *meaning* of that mission. A university that defined its mission in a way that allowed regulation of student speech might be able to muster reasonable arguments in support of that approach. But it might face both general scorn from the broader academic community and tough questions about whether it was acting consistently with its mission. It would certainly attract attention if it said one thing and did another; for example, if it said that minority students were uniquely vulnerable in some circumstances but treated them as free and autonomous agents in others.[78] The freedom of a university to define its own mission is also the freedom to hoist itself by its own petard.

ACADEMIC BILLS OF RIGHTS

The concern for institutional autonomy and institutional pluralism offers compelling reasons, quite apart from anything provided by conventional First Amendment doctrine, why legislative efforts to confine universities to the truth-seeking model of academic freedom must also fail. These efforts are generally referred to as the Academic Bill of Rights.[79]

Supporters of the Academic Bill of Rights argue that universities, by favoring liberal professors who engage in political indoctrination rather than disinterested inquiry, have abandoned their truth-seeking mission. Legislation is needed to protect "the intellectual independence of professors, researchers and students in the pursuit of knowledge and the expression of ideas from interference by legislators *or authorities within the institution itself."* Such legislation declares that neither hiring nor firing should be used to impose a "political, ideological or religious orthodoxy" on universities, which "should maintain a posture of organizational neutrality with respect to the substantive disagreements that divide researchers on questions within, or outside, their fields of inquiry."[80] It requires that "curricula and reading lists in the humanities and social sciences . . . provid[e] students with dissenting sources and viewpoints where appropriate."[81] Proposals to enact Academic Bills of Rights have moved through a variety of state legislatures and Congress, although without real success so far.

This all sounds innocuous enough. If anything, it brings the legal treatment of universities closer to the traditional professional conception of academic freedom. The legislation is written as an echo (or a parody) of prevailing First Amendment values. Just as the court that struck down the University of Michigan speech code treated the case as involving general First Amendment values rather than anything institutionally specific, so the Academic Bill of Rights tells universities, "You are obliged to do what your own mission demands, and what the First Amendment requires anyway: keep your thumb off the scales of public discourse within the university." For that reason, some scholars of academic freedom law have argued that these bills might survive a constitutional challenge.[82]

From an institutional perspective, however, an Academic Bill of Rights is a mistake. Let us assume that its proponents are both sincere and correct in their view that truth-seeking is the university's only permissible function. Even so, such legislation gravely misunderstands the truth-seeking value it purports to protect. Balance is not the same thing as truth. Holocaust deniers can (and should) be denied equal standing in history departments with those who affirm the Holocaust as historical fact. Stanley Fish puts it nicely: "it is precisely because the pursuit of truth is the cardinal value of the academy that the value (if it is one) of intellectual diversity should be rejected."[83]

Moreover, although these bills pay lip service to the university's unique institutional setting, they utterly ignore institutional autonomy. Whether a particular professor meets the standards of a discipline, and whether to include particular dissenting views in the curriculum, are questions for the considered judgment of academics themselves. Instead, an Academic Bill of Rights turns these questions over to legislatures and courts. In the guise of protecting the university's core values, it strikes at the heart of one of the university's most well-established traditions: self-governance. And it does so by transferring power from those best qualified to make these judgments to those least qualified to make them. We need not believe that universities are paragons of political neutrality and disinterestedness to fear that the cure would be worse than the disease.

Advocates of the Academic Bill of Rights also ignore institutional *pluralism,* brooking no variations in the definition of the academic mission. As we have seen, however, universities may have different views about their academic mission and how it is best served. Many favor a truth-seeking model; others favor a model more influenced by democratic or moral education. And even universities that do enshrine truth-seeking at the heart of their mission may not agree about what constitutes the truth, either generally or within a particular discipline, or about which policies best serve the search for truth. The Academic Bill of Rights freezes a particular notion of the university's mission in place. The best approach is not to legislate a specific definition of the university's mission, but to allow universities to formulate their own sense of mission, secure in their autonomy from outside interference but subject to substantial self-regulatory pressure. Doctrine in this area will be most responsive and reflexive if it allows for experimentation by the institutions, which are best suited to ask these questions and to engage in sensitive self-criticism of their own conclusions.

FUNDING WITH STRINGS

Law schools have for some time been obliged by their governing body, the Association of American Law Schools, to provide students with equal employment opportunities without regard to sexual orientation.[84] Schools are expected to limit the use of their facilities to prospective employers who abide by principles of equal opportunity. Until recently, however, the United States military discriminated against gays and lesbians.[85] The military was thus the target of protests and outright restrictions on its ability to engage in on-campus recruitment at law schools.[86]

Congress responded by passing the Solomon Amendment, which prohibits law schools from granting less access to the government for student recruiting than it gives any other employer.[87] The amendment uses government funding as both carrot and stick: the funding gives it a basis for imposing these regulations, and the failure to comply with them threatens the withdrawal of all Defense Department funding from the university as a whole, as well as a significant portion of nondefense federal funding from law schools.[88]

In *Rumsfeld v. Forum for Academic and Institutional Rights, Inc. ("FAIR")*, the Supreme Court unanimously upheld the Solomon Amendment in a forceful opinion written by Chief Justice John Roberts. An important aspect of the case was the fact that the Solomon Amendment involved a set of conditions on the recipients of government money. The plaintiffs wanted to take the government's money while rejecting its conditions. This was an element of the Court's opinion. But the Court was after bigger game. It wanted to show that even if Congress imposed the regulations *directly,* the amendment was still constitutional.

This is what the Court concluded, in a rather mechanical tour of conventional First Amendment doctrine. The law did not violate the First Amendment restriction against "compelled speech," the Court said, because the law schools were not being directed to engage in particular speech acts, but merely to provide equal access to military recruiters. It also rejected the argument that barring military recruiters amounted to protected expressive conduct by the law schools, pointing out that the schools remained free to protest the military's presence even if they were required to allow it on campus. Finally, it rejected the idea that law schools, as expressive associations, should be entitled to reject any visitors to campus who contradict their values. Military recruiters, it said, did not seek to join the law schools as members; moreover, since the schools remained free to protest the recruiters' presence, nothing about the Solomon Amendment made "group membership [in the law school] less desirable." The Court concluded with a gratuitous, if accurate, swipe at the plaintiffs for "attempting to stretch a number of First Amendment doctrines well beyond the sort of activities these doctrines protect."[89]

The decision in *FAIR* was a straightforward, unsurprising application of First Amendment doctrine.[90] Under current doctrine, the result was almost certainly correct, although the opinion left a surprising number of questions unanswered.[91] But that does not mean the Court's method of reaching it was right.

Consider some of the doctrinal questions left unanswered by *FAIR* and some of the questionable moves made by the Court in addressing its prior precedents. The Court began with the question whether the government's imposition of restrictions on the law schools tied to public funding represented an "unconstitutional condition." Although that doctrine purports to apply across the board, in prior cases the Court acknowledged that it might apply differently where a funding condition "would distort the usual functioning" of particular institutions as First Amendment speakers.[92] In one case, it noted in dicta that "the university is a traditional sphere of free expression so fundamental to the functioning of our society that the Government's ability to control speech within that sphere by means of conditions attached to the expenditure of Government funds" might be especially disfavored.[93]

These are difficult issues, but one finds no guidance on them in *FAIR*. The Court's opinion ignored these concerns altogether, engaging in a rote application of general First Amendment doctrine and concluding that, because the case ultimately raised no First Amendment problems, Congress could have "directly require[d] the schools to allow the military to recruit on campus."[94] In other words, government can, under threat of legal sanction, directly require universities to admit unwelcome guests to campus, even where *no* government funding is involved.[95] That position is more than insensitive to institutional context; it is destructive of the institutional autonomy of the university.

A more institutionally oriented approach to the *FAIR* case would place the autonomy of universities at the heart of the discussion. It would acknowledge that universities (including law schools) are entitled to shape their own missions, whether they emphasize the search for truth or equality. It would treat this choice as lying within the sphere of academic judgment, and defer substantially to some law schools' view that admitting military recruiters on campus on equal terms with nondiscriminating employers would harm their mission.

That does not mean the law schools should have won. *FAIR* involved more than one institution. It also involved the military's expert judgment that equal access to the law schools was necessary for its recruitment efforts to succeed, a consideration that also deserves substantial judicial deference.[96] But no hint of this conflict between competing claims to deference made it into the Court's opinion in *FAIR*. A genuinely institutional approach would have required the Court to acknowledge the competing claims. The Court *could* have concluded that the balance favored the right of law schools, as autonomous educational institutions, to decide what their mission meant for on-campus recruitment. Or it could have favored the military. Whatever the result, the conflict was there, and the Court should have addressed it.

There are two important caveats, however. First, we might ask whether it makes a difference that some of the plaintiffs were *public* law schools, and that even the private law schools were receiving at least some federal funding. If the government pays the fiddler, perhaps it should be allowed to call the tune. Somewhat ironically, the Court's own opinion in *FAIR* eased the sting of this rebuke. It made clear that the Court would have reached the same result even if no money had changed hands. That is a far more worrisome statement. It ought to concern anyone who values the independence of universities.

The Court probably did not mean what it said here. Surely its view that on-campus recruiting was not essential to the law school mission influenced its decision. It would almost certainly be unwilling to allow government, without even the fig leaf of funding, to impose a standardized grading curve, or to demand that all universities teach a core liberal arts curriculum. In other words, the Court's conclusions about the constitutionality of the Solomon Amendment *were* influenced by considerations of institutional context. We would be better off if the Court had been willing to say so. But if it had, it would be faced with the fact that those institutional judgments are precisely the kind that ought to rest with the university, not the courts.

Even if the Court's decision had relied solely on the fact that the Solomon Amendment was a condition imposed on the receipt of government funds rather than a direct regulation of the university, however, this line of inquiry asks the wrong questions. The questions the courts ought to be asking have less to do with whether universities are public or private, whether they accept government funds, and under what conditions, than about whether they *are universities*. If they are, they should be entitled to operate with a substantial degree of autonomy whether they take government money or not. It would be better if universities refused to accept any government money that conflicted with their mission as they understood it. Nevertheless, although the government is entitled to attach conditions to the funds it hands out, it is not free to impose conditions that undo our

First Amendment values—including our concern for the preservation of institutions, like universities, that are central to the infrastructure of public discourse.

This is, in effect, what government conditions like the Solomon Amendment seek to accomplish. Universities may be criticized for accepting government funds while bridling at the accompanying conditions, but the government too wants to have its cake and eat it. It values and subsidizes universities, because of their tradition of free inquiry, independence, and autonomy, but it balks when they actually *assert* their independence. It gets good value for its money from strong independent universities, but it expects subservience as well. It can't have both. Without institutional independence and decisional autonomy, universities are not universities, properly understood. From an institutional perspective, government ought not reap the benefits of universities if it is unwilling to recognize their independence.

The second caveat is this: to say the Court was wrong in *FAIR* is not to say that the law schools were right. The question of what the law schools' mission demands is one for the universities themselves, not for the legislature or the courts. But the schools were still open to criticism from inside and outside the academy. That the courts were, on the institutional view, obliged to defer to the law schools does not mean that their fellow academics were similarly obliged. Some academics, for instance, believe that the law schools' eagerness to bar the military threatens to widen the divide between the civilian and military worlds. If universities genuinely value open dialogue, they might be better off accepting the military presence on campus, even at some cost to their nondiscrimination policies. Equality-minded law students cannot assist in reforming the military from within, or even protesting its policies, if they never come into contact with it.[97]

More broadly, we might ask whether the law schools that resisted the presence of military recruiters were engaged in a genuinely academic judgment, let alone a sound one. If on-campus recruiting programs are truly central to a law school's academic mission, one might expect those programs to have substantial faculty involvement. In fact, faculty members pay little attention to them. This suggests that the schools' invocation of institutional autonomy in *FAIR* was merely strategic and not motivated by any abiding sense of academic mission.[98] One may question whether the law schools that opposed the presence of military recruiters made a serious effort to consider what their mission was at all, let alone whether it required imposing restrictions on the military.

In my view, the law schools were right to criticize the military's discriminatory policies and wrong to exclude it from on-campus recruitment. More important than this substantive issue, however, is that the schools ought to have made these decisions only after deep reflection about their academic mission. Had they engaged in such reflection, I think many of them would have concluded that limiting military access to students would do more harm than good to their mission. That is how self-regulation works, and it could have worked fine here without judicial intervention. Not all law schools need to share precisely the same sense of mission. Different law schools may reach different conclusions about equality and how best to secure it.[99] The problem with the Court's decision in FAIR is not that the law schools were right to deny the military full access to their employment programs; it is that the decision should have been theirs, not the government's.

DISCRIMINATION AND ANTIDISCRIMINATION

One area in which some defenders of academic freedom have been most willing to maintain constitutional limits on the university's behavior is discrimination. In theory, this should present no great conflict; most of the time, universities' own norms and traditions prohibit discrimination.[100] In practice, the conflict is greater. Some vocal advocates of academic freedom have argued for the widest possible scope of autonomy for universities, while seeking ways to avoid the ultimate implication of that argument: that universities might be freer than other entities to engage in discrimination, including racial discrimination. The law schools in FAIR, for example, relied heavily on the Supreme Court's decision in Boy Scouts of America v. Dale,[101] which if read vigorously would seem to allow universities to exclude students or professors on the grounds of traits, such as gender or race, that are otherwise legally forbidden grounds for discrimination. But the schools insisted that nothing about their reliance on Dale affected their obligation to obey the civil rights laws.[102] The more they denied that any conflict existed, the more glaringly obvious the conflict was.

An institutional approach to the First Amendment frames these issues differently. It sees the fundamental question here as having to do with jurisdiction, not moral justice. The question is not whether universities *should* discriminate, but whether those decisions are among the academic judgments that belong to the universities themselves, not legislatures or courts.

This approach can be seen in cases involving whether universities can impose their own antidiscrimination policies as well as in cases involving whether universities are wholly obliged to obey federal civil rights laws. I will suggest that the answers to these questions are, respectively, yes and no.

Begin with the universities' imposition of antidiscrimination policies. This was the subject of *Christian Legal Society Chapter of the University of California, Hastings College of the Law v. Martinez.* Hastings, a public law school, offered official recognition to student groups, including financial subsidies and other assistance as well as the right to use the law school's name and logo. Groups that sought recognition were obliged to abide by the school's policy prohibiting discrimination on the basis of race, religion, sexual orientation, and other forbidden categories. The student group that objected to this condition, the Hastings chapter of the Christian Legal Society (CLS), excluded anyone who did not subscribe to its religious tenets, including those who engaged in "unrepentant homosexual conduct," from full membership and leadership positions.[103]

The Supreme Court upheld the school's denial of recognition to the CLS. Central to its ruling was the litigation posture of the case, which treated Hastings's policy as a simple "accept all comers" policy. That made the case much easier to decide as a matter of existing constitutional doctrine. Rejecting the idea that the case presented two equal and conflicting lines of cases, one involving public forum doctrine and the other freedom of association, the Court decided that Hastings was best treated as a limited public forum. As in *FAIR,* the Court leaned on the school's public status, noting that the CLS, "in seeking what is effectively a state subsidy" through the school's sponsorship, "faces only indirect pressure to modify its membership policies; CLS may exclude any person for any reason if it foregoes the benefits of official recognition." The Court concluded that the "all comers" policy served legitimate governmental interests, such as encouraging "tolerance, cooperation, and learning among students," and did not discriminate on the basis of viewpoint.[104]

The Court's acceptance of the law school's interest in the policy was a curious mix of deference and refusal to defer. On the one hand, it asserted, "This Court is the final arbiter of the question whether a public university has exceeded constitutional constraints, and we owe no deference to the universities when we consider that question." On the other, it said that courts "lack the on-the-ground expertise and experience of school admin istrators," and cautioned courts "to resist 'substitut[ing] their own notions of sound educational policy for those of the school authorities which they review.'"[105] On its face, this view of institutional autonomy led the Court to accept Hastings's assertion that its interest in regulating its own affairs applied to extracurricular as well as classroom activities. In reality, it is not clear how much of a difference institutional autonomy made in this case, because the majority clearly approved of the law school's action.

The Court's decision in *CLS* has drawn criticism from those who believe it allows universities to disadvantage religious student groups because of their sincerely held beliefs. For these critics, it is no more untoward that the CLS might favor those who hold a particular religious doctrine than that a student chapter of the Sierra Club might favor environmentalists. In any event, they say, the special status of religious groups under the Constitution permits them to do so.

I am sympathetic to those arguments. But they are the wrong argu ments in the wrong place. The question is not whether the law school decided wisely, but whether it gets to decide for itself. From an institutional perspective, the decision belongs to the law schools, not the courts or leg islatures. Justice John Paul Stevens got this right in his concurring opinion. The campus is not the public square. It is "a world apart," one that serves "a distinctive role in a modern democratic society," and one that, "[l]ike all spe cialized government entities, . . . must make countless decisions about how to allocate resources in pursuit of [its] role." "As a general matter," he con cluded, "courts should respect universities' judgments and let them manage their own affairs."[106]

The outcome in *CLS* was thus arguably correct from an institutional perspective. But that is faint praise. The opinion itself is half-hearted in its institutionalism. Its application of doctrine is wooden and unconvincing. *Are* universities best treated as "limited public forums"? That phrase, like much of public forum doctrine, obscures universities' unique institutional context behind a neat and not especially descriptive label. It tells us what legal standard to apply, but it tells us little about the institution itself, or why the Court's broad conclusion that a "'governmental entity'" that qualifies as a limited public forum "'may impose restrictions on speech that are reasonable and viewpoint-neutral'"[107] is appropriate in this context.

This is thinking words, not things—or, put differently, it is thinking and talking in the wrong terms, in terms of pure legal categories rather than more responsive institutional ones. The Court lets labels do its work for it but does not really explain why universities deserve this label and not another. It certainly does not demonstrate that either reasonableness or viewpoint neutrality are useful or necessary tools in setting the limits of permissible university policy. *CLS* protects universities, but not in an institutionally oriented way. The only question should be whether the law school's policy was the product of a genuine academic judgment, broadly understood. If so, it must be upheld.

None of this means that the policy was a good one: there are ample reasons to criticize Hastings's view that excluding the CLS from official status would serve any serious academic value. But the institutional approach suggests that these are questions for self-regulation, not judicial involvement. That debate does not belong in a judicial forum. Nor need we come up with only one answer to this question. The lesson of institutional pluralism is that there is room for universities that welcome groups like the CLS and for universities that do not. One size need not fit all.

One reason the Court supported the law school's policy was its consistency with state antidiscrimination policies. "State law, of course, may not *command* that public universities take action impermissible under the First Amendment," it said. "But so long as a public university does not contravene constitutional limits, its choice to advance state-law goals through the school's educational endeavors stands on firm footing."[108] This raises the second question: Are universities obliged to abide by general legal policies forbidding discrimination, or should they be exempt from those requirements?

Most defenders of academic freedom and institutional autonomy balk here. That is understandable, because these questions touch on the third rail of American constitutional law and policy: race. If it is true that even a robust approach to institutional autonomy must remain within "constitutionally prescribed limits,"[109] this is a reasonable place to draw the line. Certainly that is what the Court appears to have done. It has made clear that even private schools may not restrict admission in order to create a racially exclusive body rather than a racially diverse one.[110] And it has not hesitated to look with disfavor on, say, a university that wishes to maintain its tax-exempt status while imposing campus rules against interracial dating.[111]

Those decisions are obviously important. But they are in tension with First Amendment doctrine. The tension was apparent in the *FAIR* litigation, in which the law schools relied on the Boy Scouts decision, which immunized an expressive association from the operation of a state civil rights law, while insisting that nothing about that argument rendered them immune from the civil rights laws. Properly read, *Dale does* cast doubt on whether universities ought to be subject to those laws, at least where they are willing to assert immunity from them. The law schools refused to admit this obvious fact.[112]

The tension is even more pronounced under an openly institutional approach. *Dale* raises serious questions about whether antidiscrimination laws ought to apply to universities that seek to avoid their application for *academic* reasons. These cases raise the other side of the question the Court confronted in *CLS:* Can universities seek to *defy,* rather than advance, government antidiscrimination policies?

If the universities are acting pursuant to their academic judgment, broadly defined, then the answer should be yes. Recall that the Court in *Grutter* allowed universities to engage in race-conscious decision-making with respect to student admissions as a matter of *academic judgment.* Such language implies that universities are entitled to substantial autonomy in this area, despite the usual rule that strict scrutiny should apply to race-conscious government decision-making. If *Grutter* is really about academic deference, then the same deference ought to apply when a university seeks, for academic reasons, to adopt admissions policies that *exclude.*

This is one area where defenders of academic freedom are likely to hesitate. But, with some important caveats, we ought to reconsider that hesitation. We value academic freedom and institutional autonomy because, on balance, we believe universities deserve broad autonomy where they are acting according to their own expertise and following their own well-settled norms and practices. If we are serious about an institutional approach to universities, we must allow the possibility that, just as it allows them to adopt affirmative action policies, it also allows them to discriminate. The wisdom of those policy choices is not at issue here; who gets to decide is.

Now for the caveats. First, this is an area in which institutional pluralism is likely to be especially important. Few universities are likely to pursue policies of exclusion. Even if an institutional approach allowed universities to discriminate, it is unlikely that many schools would do so. Second, a legal *ability* to discriminate for academic reasons is not an *obligation* to discriminate. Most universities agree that "[p]rejudice is not an academic value."[113] Schools that decided otherwise might be free to do so as a legal matter, but they would be subject to criticism, both from within their own walls and from the broader academic community and the public.

Finally, perhaps this is simply an area where the prescribed constitutional limits that the Court has spoken of should apply. Unless universities are treated as utterly sovereign realms, they will run up against *some* constitutional limits. This may be one of them. But our concern should be less with *what* limits apply than with *how* they apply. A key aspect of institutionalism is a reflexive approach to self-regulation, in which, as universities with different practices learn from one another, a set of best practices may emerge. Rather than impose a top-down antidiscrimination rule by fiat, courts might conclude that the view that prejudice is not an academic value is among the best practices of the university as an institution, one that has emerged as a general and universally binding academic value after experience and experimentation. This approach would lead to the same conclusion, but from a reflexive perspective.

Most universities would agree that the desire to exclude people according to classifications such as race or gender is simply not a proper academic judgment. Thus, we need not fear greatly the implications of an institutional approach where discrimination by universities is concerned. On the ground, little is likely to change. A few universities might take advantage of their legal autonomy to discriminate, but they would be exceptional and would face plenty of criticism from the academic community and the public. The specter of discrimination, serious as it may be, is not sufficient reason to reject the institutional turn.[114]

Summary

Universities are so well established and so bound by tradition that they serve as a paradigmatic example of a First Amendment institution. We have seen that an institutional approach to universities counsels a significant amount of autonomy for them, provided that they act within the proper sphere of their authority. Courts ought to read the scope of that autonomy broadly, not just because it lies outside their expertise but also because not all universities are the same. They exist within a universe of institutional pluralism, within which different universities may take different approaches to the same issues. In most cases, courts ought to allow this diversity of approaches to remain in place. In a few cases—and discrimination *may* be one of them—courts may find that a single best practice emerges from the universities themselves, and can then apply it systemically. But they should generally allow universities latitude for experimentation and diversity. This does not mean universities ought to be immune from criticism. But those debates belong with academics and citizens, not courts or legislatures.

We have also seen that our analysis does not turn much on whether universities are public or private. That distinction is not always helpful. Universities are far more united by their common attachment to academic goals, traditions, and practices than they are divided by their sources of funding. As long as universities adopt a diverse range of policies, we should focus on whether these decisions involve genuine academic functions, not whether they come from public or private schools.

A Borderline Case: Public Schools

Universities are not necessarily the most important educational institutions. That title may well belong to K-12 schools—particularly public schools, which, according to census figures, had some 49 million students in the United States in the late 1990s. Public education has long been deemed "perhaps the most important function of the state and local governments."[115] For almost as long, it has given rise to confusing and contradictory First Amendment doctrine.

Some selections from the case law tell the story. On the one hand, students do not "shed their constitutional rights to freedom of speech or expression at the schoolhouse gate." Public schools must respect the fact that students "in school as well as out of school are 'persons' under our Constitution." On the other hand, First Amendment rights must be "applied in light of the special characteristics of the school environment."[116] Public schools must "'inculcat[e] fundamental values necessary to the maintenance of a democratic political system.'"[117] Among other things, they may prohibit the use of offensive language in school, even if it would be permitted elsewhere.[118] These determinations will receive judicial deference as long as the schools' "actions are reasonably related to legitimate pedagogical concerns."[119]

These conflicting views have led to confusion on the part of public school administrators about the scope of their authority, although the trend is clearly toward greater authority and away from unbridled expression by students. This leads to a broader question: Are public schools First Amendment institutions, as universities are? And if so, what rules ought to apply to them? Public schools thus illustrate a recurring topic in this book: the ambiguous nature of the institutions that lie on the borderlands of First Amendment institutionalism.

The confusion stems from a couple of sources. First, the tradition of public schooling is less well established than that of university education. Compared with universities, which have had centuries to develop their traditions and practices, elementary and secondary schools are relatively recent innovations. It is hard to call something a First Amendment institution if its institutional roots are too shallow. Second, there have always been serious disputes about the mission of public schools. More so than universities, they are creatures of local control, and that leads to fierce debates over their role and purpose. Are they places "where community values are manifested," or where "overarching constitutional values must be enforced"?[120] If the former, *what* community values are essential to their mission, and who is responsible for shaping and implementing these values—local officials or educational professionals?[121]

This greatly complicates the institutional status of public schools for purposes of the First Amendment. If they are run according to the expert judgment of educators, applying fairly well-established self-regulatory norms and practices, it makes sense for courts to defer to them. If they are controlled by elected officials, however, a stronger judicial role can be expected. The question is whether public schools merit legal treatment as autonomous First Amendment institutions or whether they so clearly follow political rather than professional norms that granting them autonomy would be a mistake.

My tentative answer is mixed. In many respects, K-12 schools *do* deserve distinctive institutional treatment under the First Amendment. For the most part, they are professionally run and adhere to a reasonably identifiable and increasingly standardized set of educational practices. There is no doubt that K-12 education is a profession and follows many professional norms. It is also clear that public schools contribute profoundly to public discourse. Like universities, they are a vital part of our infrastructure of free expression. But their infrastructural role is very different from that of universities. We do not expect public schools to produce new ideas; we expect them to teach students how to read, write, speak, and think. They are not sites for the production of free speech, but sites for the production of the *capacity* for free speech.

All this points in somewhat conflicting directions, and in that sense the Supreme Court's confusion concerning public education mirrors the tensions that would arise under an institutional treatment of public schools. To the extent that they are professional and not just representative institutions, public schools deserve a degree of judicial deference. Educators ought to be free to make expert judgments about how to achieve the goal of preparing future citizens. If that means students shed some of their constitutional rights at the schoolyard gate, so be it.

In other respects, however, elementary and secondary schools deserve less judicial deference than universities. To the extent that their judgments are political rather than professional, those judgments lack the fully institutional, professionalized, and self-regulating character that entitles First Amendment institutions to substantial autonomy. When they involve public decisions by public representatives such as elected school boards, public schools are more like other government actors than like unique institutions. The decisions those officials make will be less hemmed in by professional constraints and should be subjected to more searching judicial scrutiny.

Furthermore, there may be less of a role for institutional diversity or pluralism in the public school than in the university. Given the voluntary nature of university attendance and the diverse nature of universities themselves, it is more feasible to imagine different universities—even public universities—adopting radically different approaches. But public schools share a more uniform sense of mission: to train students in basic thinking and learning, and to do so in a way that inculcates commonly held public values. Because public schools are relatively lacking in institutional diversity and pluralism, there is less need for the kind of experimental and deferential approach the institutional turn recommends for universities.

6

Where Information Is Gathered: The Press, Old and New

In 1974 Justice Potter Stewart, of "I know it when I see it" fame, gave a lecture at Yale Law School on "the role of the organized press—of the daily newspapers and other established media—in the system of government created by our Constitution."[1] That speech can be seen as a story about a path the law has not taken officially, but *has* taken more informally. It is also a story about paths Stewart could not then have imagined.

In First Amendment cases, Stewart said, the Supreme Court usually focused on "isolated individuals"—such as "the soapbox orator" and "the nonconformist pamphleteer"—confronting "governmental power." It was "seldom asked to define the rights and privileges, or the responsibilities, of the organized press."[2] But times had changed. The nation had just emerged from the Watergate era, in which public scrutiny of high government misconduct had been spearheaded by two young reporters, Carl Bernstein and Bob Woodward, and their newspaper, the *Washington Post*. The time had come, Stewart suggested, to reconsider the role of the press in our constitutional framework.

The First Amendment's guarantee of freedom of the press, Stewart argued, was, "in essence, a *structural* provision of the Constitution." It gave "protection to an institution." Indeed, it made the "publishing business . . . the only organized private business that is given explicit constitutional protection." The purpose of the Press Clause was to grant the press "institutional autonomy."[3]

In Stewart's view, the Press Clause established "a fourth institution outside the Government as an additional check on the three official branches." An institutional press was required to provide "organized, expert scrutiny of government." The press did not always act virtuously. It sometimes abused its power. But the balance between press freedom and press responsibilities must be maintained through "the tug and pull of the political forces in American society," not the courts.[4]

Doctrinally speaking, however, it was far from clear that Stewart was right, and it became even less clear as the years passed. Consider the concurring opinion of Chief Justice Warren Burger in *First National Bank of Boston v. Bellotti*.[5] The case involved a Massachusetts campaign finance law applied to business corporations. Burger wrote to answer what he called "a disquieting aspect" of the state's defense of the law: that it might "imping[e] on the First Amendment rights of those who employ the corporate form . . . to carry on the business of mass communications, particularly the large media conglomerates."[6]

It was almost impossible, Burger wrote, to distinguish, "either as a matter of fact or constitutional law, media corporations from [other] corporations." He rejected the argument that the Press Clause "somehow confer[s] special and extraordinary privileges or status on the 'institutional press.'" At most, he argued, the existence of separate clauses in the First Amendment applying to speech and the press reflected the distinction between expression and its dissemination. In practice, it meant even less: "there is no fundamental distinction between expression and dissemination."[7] For Burger, the Press Clause was now largely redundant, just an echo of the Speech Clause.

Defining the press, Burger noted, presented a "second fundamental difficulty with interpreting the Press Clause as conferring special status on a limited group." It would do more harm than good for the government or the courts to attempt to define the press. As a constitutional matter, the lone pamphleteer and the soapbox orator stood on the same ground as the *New York Times* or CBS. "The First Amendment does not 'belong' to any definable category of persons or entities," he concluded. "It belongs to all who exercise its freedoms."[8]

Burger's argument seems to have carried the day in First Amendment doctrine. We do not now recognize, as a constitutional matter, a special institutional status for the press. Even as Stewart insisted that the Court *had* accorded a special status to the press, it had already declined, albeit in a deeply fractured decision, to allow journalists to conceal the identify of their sources before a grand jury. Any effort to grant journalists a privilege against disclosure, the Court concluded in that case, "would present practical and conceptual difficulties of a high order." It declined to "embark . . . on a long and difficult journey to such an uncertain destination."[9]

That's the official story. But, as every journalist knows, that's rarely the whole story. Although Stewart's argument never won official recognition, in a more informal sense it is clear that the press *is* a First Amendment institution and has often been treated like one by the courts, albeit haltingly.[10] Various strands of First Amendment doctrine regarding the press gesture toward the institutional turn. The task of this chapter is to weave those strands together.

The task would be arduous enough if it only involved the "institutional press." But this is an era of new media: blogs, Twitter feeds, and other modes of expression unheard of in Stewart's day.[11] Their long-term impact on public discourse is still what journalists call a developing story.

The conventional wisdom on the new media is that they make the arguments for any special institutional status for the press increasingly untenable.[12] If it was difficult to distinguish between the institutional press and the lonely pamphleteer, the argument goes, it is even harder to distinguish between a newspaper and a blog. Whatever privileges attach to the institutional press should apply to everyone—or no one. Asked to choose between these alternatives, many would answer: Let it be no one. We would be back to the Press Clause as redundancy. That is the wrong way to frame the question. The question is not whether the new media are the "press," but whether they are their *own* institution, and if so, what rights, responsibilities, and limits they ought to have.

There are good reasons to treat the "old" press—including broadcast journalism—as a First Amendment institution. It is identifiable and long established; it is a major part of the infrastructure of public discourse; it follows its own norms, practices, and self-regulatory standards; and it is fully (if imperfectly) capable of acting autonomously. The new media are less well established. It is not yet clear whether they merit institutional autonomy, but they are surely moving in that direction. In many respects, their story shows us how emerging First Amendment institutions begin to develop their own norms and practices and their own ways of contributing to public discourse.

Taken together, the old and new press offer a valuable contrast between established First Amendment institutions and borderline or emerging ones, a contrast that may help us understand the nature and limits of First Amendment institutionalism. They provide a window on the role of self-regulation and reflexive or experimentalist techniques in the institutional First Amendment. And they show that evolving standards and practices may allow institutions to develop in ways that are consistent with First Amendment values—without much involvement by the courts.

The Old Media

THE RISE OF THE INSTITUTIONAL AND PROFESSIONAL PRESS

A standard argument against any special institutional treatment for the press under the First Amendment, despite the apparent textual specificity of the Press Clause, is that those who wrote and ratified it were talking about something entirely different from what we think of today as the institutional press. This view is represented by Chief Justice Burger's view, expressed in *Bellotti*, that the Press Clause covers much the some territory as the Speech Clause but was placed in the Constitution because of the Framers' experience with English censorship of the printing press and other technological innovations.[13] It is present in modern scholarship in a recent article by Eugene Volokh marshaling a variety of historical and other sources to argue that the Press Clause protects a universal individual right to the *technology* of the press rather than protecting the press, or journalism, as an "industry" or "institution".[14]

How much force that argument should have today is an open question. History, though relevant to our inquiry, may supply the beginning rather than the end of the question.[15] In any event, a deeper analysis, one focused on both the historical emergence of the press and its contemporary role, suggests that the position that the Press Clause simply refers to a particular technology doesn't cover all the relevant ground.

The press as an institution predates the American Constitution. Even before the advent of printing presses, networks for the dissemination of information were forming in Europe. These networks were interwoven with communications technology and policy—especially the postal system, whose growth, along with the rise of commercial trade, facilitated the spread of news. The networks, and the kinds of information they carried, expanded quickly. The first printed periodicals regularly reporting current events appeared around 1609, and others soon followed. By the end of that century, "journals with at least some independence of the state were beginning to assume an accepted, albeit restricted role in political communication."[16]

Newspapers played an important role in the American colonies up to and through the revolutionary era. One reason for this was the increasing number of readers: male literacy jumped from 60 percent in 1660 to 85 percent by the 1760s.[17] A major reason for that jump, in turn, was the rise of education, which points to the ways in which different First Amendment institutions complemented each other's development.

The role of the press took off during and after the Revolution. Newspapers were woven into both the constitutional framework of the new republic and its public infrastructure. Culturally, the rise of popular sovereignty and the notion that good republican citizens were obliged to be informed about the issues of the day encouraged the growth of newspapers, which became "the central venue of public discussion independent of government."[18] At an infrastructural level, the new federal government's decision to establish a postal system, and to effectively subsidize the postal delivery of newspapers, dramatically enhanced the papers' financial strength and expanded their reach. By the 1830s, Alexis de Tocqueville was marveling at the "astonishing circulation of letters and newspapers" in the "savage woods" of Kentucky and Tennessee.[19]

Many publishers believed "it was a part of their public duty to print materials on all sides of a question, even when they were counter to a particular publisher's own views."[20] On the whole, however, American journalism in its early days had "a bilious, disputatious, partisan tone,"[21] operating more on a partisan model than on a professional one.[22]

Even so, from the outset the builders of our constitutional system valued the press in distinctly institutional terms. The Continental Congress in 1774 pointed to its function in promoting "truth, science, morality, and arts in general" and its capacity to "shame or intimidate[ ]" government officers "into more honourable and just modes of conducting affairs."[23] Many early state constitutions provided explicit protection for freedom of the press even when they did not do so for freedom of speech; the Virginia Declaration of Rights, in 1776, called "freedom of the Press . . . one of the greatest bulwarks of liberty," and the Maryland constitution declared that "the liberty of the press ought to be inviolably preserved." Some of this language appeared in James Madison's initial draft of the First Amendment: "The people shall not be deprived or abridged of their right to speak, to write, or to publish their sentiments; and the freedom of the press, as one of the greatest bulwarks of liberty, shall be inviolable." Freedom of the press, in short, was seen as a "separate and distinct" right with an institutional flavor, one that if anything enjoyed priority over freedom of speech more generally.[24]

The citizens and leaders of the early United States had more than one contemporary model of the press to choose from in thinking about its role.[25] The first, which we might call the "free press" model, suggested that "the press should be free of state intervention so as to engage in criticism of government and thereby defend public liberty." It conceived of the press as an independent, autonomous institution carrying out a "watchdog" or "checking" function with respect to government. The second, the "open press" tradition, held that "all individuals have a right to disseminate their viewpoints for general consideration."[26] Rather than playing a specifically institutional role, the press was simply a medium for expression. it "convey[ed] the right to free expression to individuals, rather than to an institution."[27] The open press model may indeed have been more prominent in the early American understanding of the press's role in public discourse. But the free press model—the institutional watchdog model championed two centuries later by Justice Stewart—also contributed to that understanding.

Eventually, newspapers began to catch up with their aspirations to "impartiality and accessibility."[28] The nineteenth century saw the increasing professionalization of the press and an increasing focus on values such as impartiality, objectivity, independence from political parties, and the importance of gathering facts rather than simply propounding opinions.[29]

The reasons for this development involved both technology and economics. The advent of telegraphy helped journalism spread, but its cost put a premium on conveying information succinctly. An English newspaper

editor informed a war correspondent, "telegrams are for facts; appreciation and political comment can come by post."[30] Wire services distributed
stories to newspapers with diverse political affiliations, and thus had an
incentive to emphasize facts over opinions. These technological incentives
changed the structure of journalism in ways that would help form professional journalistic values. For example, the "inverted pyramid" structure
of news stories—giving the basic facts at the top and broadening the story
below, rather than telling the story in narrative form—was a response to
the need to provide basic information up front in case the telegraphic link
was broken in mid-transmission. The structure of the newsroom changed
too, incorporating a host of professional categories, such as copy editors and
assignment editors, as newspaper production became complex enough to
require a division of labor.[31]

Journalistic practices were influenced by social as well as technological changes, and they influenced social understandings of journalism in
turn. The culture of independent and impartial fact-gathering fit the scientific spirit of the times and the need for quick and reliable information
in the political and commercial environment. It also arguably comported
with economic imperatives: as newspapers became less dependent on political parties for their resources and more dependent on advertising, which in
turn encouraged them to write for a broader audience to maximize advertising revenue, those newspapers were more likely to adopt ideals of independence and impartiality.[32] Whatever the source of those changes, however,
the new norms quickly became embedded in both professional and public
culture. As the "idea of objectivity took root in the culture of journalism,"
the public "came to see the journalist's function in terms of independently
determined facts and independently formulated opinion."[33]

In the early twentieth century, the press adopted much of what was,
until recently, the modern structure of professional journalism, including
the formation of professional societies, the creation of journalism schools,
and, significantly, the development of codes of ethics.[34] These ethical codes
depended solely on self-restraint and were not "drafted and enforced by an
independent regulatory authority."[35] As with any professional code, their
values and precepts were contested, both within and beyond the profession.
Increasingly, however, journalism operated according to a professional self-
regulatory ideal, one that stressed the independent and impartial gathering

of facts according to standard methods of obtaining and disseminating information, subject to professional ethical constraints.

Summarizing the state of the profession around the turn of this century, Bill Kovach and Tom Rosenstiel identify several central principles, including the following: "Journalism's first obligation is to the truth. . . . Its essence is a discipline of verification. . . . Its practitioners must maintain an independence from those they cover. . . . It must provide a forum for public criticism and compromise." They define the purpose of journalism as giving citizens "the information they need to be free and self-governing."[36] These principles emphasize journalism's *infrastructural* role in public discourse: providing information in a clear and unobtrusive fashion to enable citizens to engage in informed discussions, decisions, and actions in social life. That its practices and principles are partly a by-product of technological change or economic imperatives is important but hardly unusual. Journalism is no different from railroads, highways, or any other aspect of infrastructure, physical or social. All of them involve a complicated relationship between technological resources and actual and perceived needs.[37]

JOURNALISM AND THE PRESS CLAUSE UNDER CURRENT LAW

Conventional wisdom holds that the First Amendment does not carve out a special role for the press. The *New York Times* is no different from the lonely pamphleteer or the soapbox orator. "For all of the plain differences between the institutional press and various other individual, organizational, and corporate speakers," writes Frederick Schauer, "the existing doctrine insists on ignoring those differences, and does so even at the cost of arguably rendering [the Press Clause] superfluous."[38]

Although there is support for that view, the whole picture is more complicated. On the one hand, as we saw in *Branzburg* and Chief Justice Burger's concurrence in *Bellotti*, the courts have shied away from treating the institutional press *as* an institution entitled to special treatment or legal autonomy. They have relied on general doctrinal categories and rules that apply to any speaker. The press, on this view, is not entitled to any special treatment under the First Amendment: the same case ought, in principle, to be decided the same way, regardless of whether a party is a lone speaker or a part of the institutional press. Conversely, if a law runs afoul of general First Amendment principles, such as the principle that government may not regulate speech on the basis of its content, it should be invalidated whether the speaker is a media conglomerate or a latter-day Tom Paine. All this is fully consistent with the lure of acontextuality in constitutional law.

On the other hand, in keeping with the courts' need to make exceptions to their generally acontextual approach where particular facts demand them, First Amendment law has evolved with the press in mind. What the courts cannot do explicitly without creating tension with the acontextual approach, they have sometimes done implicitly. In a host of cases, they have used the doctrinal escape hatch of judicial deference to make room for the institutional role of the press.

The clearest example can be found in the tort law doctrines regarding defamation and invasion of privacy. In principle, the Supreme Court has said that the same rules ought to apply to defamatory or invasive statements by media and nonmedia defendants; in defamation cases, for example, what matters is whether the speech involves a public figure, not the identity of the speaker.[39] In practice, however, the courts have woven the notion of the professional judgment of journalists into the fabric of the law itself. In doing so, they have moved a fair way toward the institutional turn, opening a space for both responsive and reflexive law within purportedly institutionally agnostic doctrine.

This phenomenon has been noted by Randall Bezanson, who dubs it "*Sullivan's* paradox"[40] after the Supreme Court's decision in *New York Times v. Sullivan.* That decision brought defamation law within the fold of the First Amendment by imposing an "actual malice" rule for libel involving public officials, subsequently extended to other public figures. The rule says that a libelous statement about such a person will not give rise to liability unless it was made "with knowledge that it was false or with reckless disregard of whether it was false or not."[41]

The purpose of the actual malice rule is to give members of the press, among other defendants, "breathing space" to do their work without undue fear of crippling liability.[42] Its result, however, has been somewhat unexpected. Because the rule has been treated as requiring an inquiry into whether the defendant—often a media defendant—knew or recklessly disregarded the possibility that a statement was false, it has led to "a de facto set of judge-made standards that covers all aspects of journalistic behavior," including "the use of sources, the quality of writing, the demand for corroboration, the duties of editorial supervision, and the use of quotations."[43] Thus, a judicial inquiry into whether a media defendant has acted within the "breathing space" provided by the rule turns on whether that defendant has followed professional journalistic standards. This is the seeming paradox: a rule intended to give the press breathing space potentially transfers a good deal of responsibility for press supervision to the courts.

How this works out in practice, however, is broadly consistent with the institutional turn. Courts in such cases "routinely defer to media judgments about newsworthiness."[44] They use the concept of professional editorial judgment as a set of functional criteria under which an action by the press may be treated as categorically entitled to judicial deference—as a question for the judgment of the press itself, not the courts.[45] Thus, in interesting but rarely complete or transparent ways, the courts have built into an ostensibly institutionally agnostic doctrinal system a mechanism by which press decisions are left largely to the press's own exercise of professional judgment, and that judgment is given judicial deference.

Some of the same tendencies are apparent elsewhere in the law affecting the press. The courts have held that the press has no right to violate generally applicable laws.[46] But they have also made clear that government measures that single out the press for differential treatment may be struck down where they risk "prevent[ing] such free and general discussion of public matters as seems absolutely essential to prepare the people for an intelligent exercise of their rights as citizens."[47] Although this approach is consistent with the institutional agnosticism of existing First Amendment doctrine, it also suggests a strong concern for the press as an institution.

More important still are what we might call "sub-constitutional" rules— statutes and policies without constitutional force that nevertheless have "constitutive" aspects in our system of public discourse—that recognize the infrastructural role played by the press.[48] Our vocabulary is replete with them: "The press pass, the press gallery, the press room, the press office, the press secretary (or public-information officer), the press bus or plane, and the press pool."[49]

Other press privileges involve a mix of judicially and legislatively created rights. Even though the Supreme Court has refused to grant journalists an explicit privilege to maintain the confidentiality of sources, many lower courts have recognized at least a qualified privilege; where they have not, the legislature has often stepped in to fill the gap. And many of the rights that the courts have described in institutionally agnostic terms have, in practice, been press rights. The public right of access to courtroom proceedings, for example, "as a practical matter . . . is more likely to mean press access," and the press will often receive preferential seating where courtroom space is limited.[50]

In sum, the courts have, despite their repeated denials, carved out a special role for the press and for its newsgathering techniques and editorial decisions. Through judicial deference, they have recognized that decisions by the institutional press contribute in important ways to public discourse and require professional judgments that the courts are loath to second guess.

The Press Clause after the Institutional Turn

What the courts have done haltingly and by half-measures, they should do more straightforwardly. When courts say one thing and do another, they leave legal doctrine open to uncertainty and incoherence. That uncertainty afflicts both the courts and the subjects of their rulings. Courts cannot frame clear doctrinal rules if they insist that their approach to the Press Clause is acontextual when it is not; journalists and newspapers cannot plan with confidence when they are told that they are no different from anyone else under the law, but are routinely deferred to when they make journalistic decisions. An openly institutional treatment of the press would lead to more doctrinal coherence for the Press Clause and more stability and predictability for the press.

An institutional treatment of the press would have both categorical and functional aspects. A court would be more willing to begin and end its inquiry categorically, simply by asking whether the institution at issue was "the press." When the answer was yes, it would begin with the assumption that the institution's decisions about how to gather the news and what to publish were insulated from further judicial scrutiny.

As for the functional aspect, just as universities are entitled to institutional autonomy for decisions reached on the basis of considered academic judgments, so an invocation of institutional autonomy by the press would be subject to inquiry into "both the reasons for having the privilege and the reasons for locating it in a particular institution."[51] Often, knowing that the institution was "the press" would satisfy the functional inquiry as well as the categorical one. Once the press was identified *as* the press, the court would not need to undertake an intrusive inquiry into whether a given action fulfilled its functional role of gathering and publishing newsworthy information.[52]

But a functional inquiry, whether implicit or explicit, would still help define the boundaries of the press's institutional autonomy. For the most part, the press does not act *as* the press, exercising its unique institutional role, when it deals with questions such as whether it must be subject to the same rules of collective bargaining that cover other unionized workplaces. But when a decision by the press implicates the core institutional functions that make it an important part of our social infrastructure, its institutional autonomy should be triggered.[53] Courts should decline to second-guess such decisions, even where generally applicable laws are at issue.

An institutional approach would strengthen the press's institutional autonomy, offering it more protection and greater leeway than it enjoys today across a range of journalistic activities. In particular, it would provide greater protection for journalism as an institutional *process*. Journalism is not simply the act of publishing the news; it is, centrally, the act of gathering it. News stories are the product of a complex process that includes finding and refining stories, amassing the information that goes into a story, and deciding what should get into print and what should be left out. As anyone who has worked in the institutional press knows, that process calls on a significant set of skills and traditions.[54]

Every step in the newsgathering process is guided by the experience, tools, and ethical norms that make journalism a profession. What makes these stories important contributions to public discourse is the process of newsgathering that goes into them. If the facts were readily available or apparent on the surface, newsgathering would be far less significant. But they are not. Most people lack the skills and resources to gather and collate information—to coax sources who would rather not speak, to collect bits and pieces of a story that only make full sense once they are combined, and so on.

This process is not a solitary one. Journalism is an institutional enterprise, one that depends on collaboration among reporters and between reporters and editors. Before a story is published, every line, every quote, every judgment call is subjected to checking and rechecking, debate and counter-debate, and institutional second-guessing. Good news stories— even average ones—are group productions.

An institutional approach to the press would grant significant autonomy to this newsgathering process. It would not treat freedom of the press as a mere echo of freedom of speech. It would recognize the infrastructural role of journalism's *process* and *function*—the "importance of press autonomy and the role of the press in the broader social-democratic architecture"[55]— and carve out a significant degree of legal autonomy for that process.[56]

That approach would result in some departures from current law. For example, depending on how one reads the Court's fractured decision in *Branzburg v. Hayes,* the press receives little or no institutional protection for the confidentiality of its sources.[57] The institutional approach recommends a strong constitutional privilege to preserve this confidentiality, which is a major part of journalism's contribution to public discourse: the revelation of information that is in the public interest and might otherwise be unobtainable.

We should not deny the potential for press abuse of this privilege, any more than we should overstate it.[58] All too often, reporters employ confidential sources when none are needed, thus depriving their readers of information that could help them judge the reliability of stories. Just as often, the press and its sources play a game to which the public is not privy. The source may be a high public official who wants to release information to engage in internecine warfare with a bureaucratic rival, or a political candidate who wants to keep her hands clean while tarring her opponent. A journalist may in turn cooperate with a source in order to be first with the scoop, knowing full well that the identity of the leaker is more newsworthy than the story itself.

The institutional approach is not blind to the possibility of abuse. But the primary responsibility for addressing abuse lies with the institutional press itself. Just as the primary guarantors for responsibility on the part of lawyers or doctors, who do enjoy a legal privilege of confidentiality, are the professionals themselves, so the primary guarantee of journalists' responsible use of confidential sources should be the ethical norms that guide them. The press regularly debates when and how to use confidential sources, and has come up with guidelines for their use.[59] These guidelines are no guarantee against abuse, but that risk is preferable to an acontextual approach that refuses to recognize the importance of newsgathering to public discourse.[60]

We must also consider the reflexive aspect of the institutional turn: its capacity to learn from and incorporate the experiences of the institution

itself, using them to help frame the outer boundaries of institutional autonomy. This kind of "rolling best practices" regime could help to establish a
standard for the use of confidential sources and modify that standard over
time as further experience suggests room for improvements.[61] The results
of this approach might not differ much in given cases from the lower courts'
current approach to the reporter's privilege, which requires courts to balance "the public's interest in the free dissemination of ideas and information
and the public's interest in effective law enforcement and the fair administration of justice."[62] But, while encouraging the evolution of higher standards, it
would leave the decisions primarily in the hands of the institutional experts.

Another area in which an institutional approach could depart from
current law is the application of civil and criminal laws to the newsgathering process.[63] Occasionally, journalists skirt or violate the laws that apply
to the rest of us. They receive and publish classified documents—the most
famous example being the publication of the government's secret history of
the conflict in Vietnam, the "Pentagon Papers."[64] They use newsgathering
techniques, such as hidden cameras, that arguably involve fraud or invasion
of privacy.[65] And they sometimes reveal the identity of confidential sources
in circumstances that lead the sources to consider the disclosure a breach of
promise.[66] In all these cases, the courts' response has been an acontextual
one: "generally applicable laws do not offend the First Amendment simply
because their enforcement against the press has incidental effects on its ability to gather and report the news."[67]

Although the fact that a law is one of general applicability may be
important, "[t]here is nothing talismanic" about it.[68] As with the rule of
content-neutrality, which can restrict more speech than a narrowly drawn
but content-specific restriction on speech, laws of general applicability can
"restrict First Amendment rights just as effectively as those directed specifically at speech itself."[69] As always, context matters.

Cohen v. Cowles Media, in which the Supreme Court held that a newspaper could be sued for breaching its promise of confidentiality to a source,
provides an example. That case involved a Republican operative's disclosure
of damaging information about the Democratic-Farmer-Labor candidate for
lieutenant governor of Minnesota in the 1982 election. The newspapers to
which the operative, Dan Cohen, had given the information decided, after
"consultation and debate," to publish Cohen's name.[70]

On these facts, the case involved a clear breach of promise, and Cohen suffered for it: he was immediately fired from his job. Under Minnesota law, however, a promise made under the legal theory advanced by Cohen is unenforceable unless "injustice can be avoided only by enforcing the promise."[71] The press's considered judgment that this information was necessary for the integrity of its communication with the electorate should have been relevant to the Supreme Court's decision. In asking whether injustice could be avoided only by enforcing the promise initially made by the newspapers, the Court could have balanced Cohen's asserted rights against "the importance of the information to public discourse," rather than mechanically asserting that the general applicability of the state law was all that mattered.[72] I am not saying the balance clearly favored the press over Cohen. But in striking that balance, the Court could have shown greater deference to the "consultation and debate" engaged in by the press defendants.

The institutional approach suggests that the choice in these cases is not between general application of the law and absolute press license to misbehave. That false dichotomy ignores the press's capacity for self-regulation. Since their heyday, deception, hidden cameras, and other unsavory journalistic techniques have abated considerably. Their decline has had as much to do with media self-criticism, which has led to the promulgation of new ethical norms limiting these practices, as with fear of civil liability. The institutional framework, traditions, and evolving norms of professional journalism do as much to restrain the press from improper actions as the blunt judicial invocation of the general applicability of laws.

Moreover, the scope of institutional autonomy for the press is broad but not infinite. Under a reflexive "rolling best practices" regime, the press would have a role in determining that scope. Such a regime would need to respect the institutional diversity of the press: there is room within journalism for advocacy as well as impartiality, for overamped broadcasters alongside the tweedy tones of PBS or NPR. The scope of press autonomy might be influenced more by the profession's most widely shared standards, those that form the basis of overwhelming professional consensus about what standards are absolutely necessary, than by its *highest* standards, which may be subject to continuing professional debate and refinement.

In sum, a contextual and institutional approach to the press takes greater advantage of both the institutional press's contributions to public discourse and its capacity for self-criticism and self-regulation. It grants the press more pronounced institutional autonomy, which includes not only the right to make its own judgments about what to publish but also a stronger privilege against government intrusion into newsgathering or the enforcement of generally applicable laws.

This approach runs contrary to the traditional acontextual view that everyone has the same obligations under the law, and may give rise to concerns that non-press speakers will be second-class citizens under the First Amendment. But the press's autonomy exists for a good reason, one that serves the needs of the public as much as the press: namely, the recognition that the courts can best serve public discourse by shoring up its infrastructure, which includes the institutional role played by the press in gathering and disseminating newsworthy information.

Nor does an independent and institutionally oriented Press Clause entail a lack of constitutional protection for non-press speakers. As I noted in Part One, First Amendment institutionalism is, for our purposes, a supplement to existing doctrine; it does not aim to wipe away the rest of First Amendment law. Individual speakers and groups that do not properly qualify as the "press" or other First Amendment institutions may not enjoy the particular brand of institutional autonomy that the institutional turn counsels, but they are still entitled to the usual panoply of speech protections under existing First Amendment law. The point of the institutional turn is to identify those infrastructural institutions that benefit public discourse for *all*, and protect their unique institutional functions—not to eliminate protection for other speech acts for which existing doctrine may be better suited.[73]

The courts have already assumed that context matters—that there must be at least some First Amendment protection for the press *as* the press. The institutional approach is simply more candid about doing what both the courts and the government have done on countless occasions: allowing the law of the Press Clause to be shaped by the press itself.

Is Institutional Autonomy for the Press Out of Place Today?

Public confidence in the press has plummeted since the Watergate era.[74] Much of the damage has been self-inflicted. The bill of indictments includes notorious examples such as the plagiarism and falsified reporting by Jayson

Blair at the *New York Times,* similar conduct by Stephen Glass at the *New Republic,* and the scandal in which the *Washington Post* had to return a Pulitzer Prize awarded for Janet Cooke's fabricated story about an 8-year-old heroin addict. In each of these cases, the self-monitoring and self-correction of these institutions, the layers of editors and (in the case of magazines) fact-checkers, failed badly.

Some of the distrust has to do with a public perception that the press has descended from "serious journalism" to "superficial journalism" focused on celebrities and meaningless scandals.[75] Some of it has to do with politics: people condemn the media for being politically biased without admitting it (a favorite criticism of the *Times* and many other mainstream papers) or for being openly biased while cynically claiming to be "fair and balanced" (a standard criticism of Fox News). And some of it has to do with the structure and economics of the news industry, in which shrinking budgets, corporate consolidation, and other factors have led to a downturn in coverage of serious news and a concern about the blurring line between the editorial and business sides of the press.[76] Finally, some of this distrust is part of a broader trend that raises larger problems for the institutional approach: a decline in public trust in *all* institutions.[77] These concerns will no doubt strike many readers as offering strong reasons to resist giving greater institutional autonomy to the press. Some journalists may agree, believing that changes both inside and outside the institution argue against establishing any kind of "journalistic caste system."[78]

The concerns are legitimate. It would be a mistake to base an institutional approach to the press on a utopian view of that institution. We lionize the press at our own peril. But the opposite response, a knee-jerk distrust of any institutional autonomy for the press, is also a mistake.

For one thing, the endless spate of critical views of the press is overstated. The press may be more embattled today than ever but, cynicism aside, it is also far more professional. Journalists have become better educated and more qualified.[79] Undergraduate and graduate journalism schools have proliferated, and although their value is questioned, there is little doubt that the result has been increased professionalism, if for no other reason than that they help inculcate in their students an allegiance to professional traditions, norms, and ethics.

For another, these debates are hardly new. It is wrong to compare the press of today, with all its faults, to some golden-age press of yesteryear, one that almost certainly never existed. The Framers themselves envisioned some kind of structural role for the press even though, as we have seen, it was then an amateur enterprise and far more rife with political agendas and outright falsehoods than it is today. The closest American journalism has come to a golden age was probably the mid-twentieth century, when high-level journalism became a serious enterprise and public confidence in elite institutions was high. But that era is unduly romanticized by those who focus on its highest exemplars instead of comparing its average reporter with the average reporter of today.[80] Even the debates about what press professionalism requires are not new, and are more seriously and routinely conducted within the profession today than they were a century ago.[81]

None of this excuses the press for its failings. But the institutional turn is not based on the myth that the press is perfect. Nor is it based on the idea that a single standard for press professionalism should apply across time and space. Rather, the institutional turn rests on a *comparative* assessment of who ought to regulate the press, and how. For that assessment to favor the press, we need only conclude that, all things considered, it deserves greater autonomy and a more substantial role in the regulatory process than it has been given so far.

There are good reasons to draw that conclusion. Although the press is imperfect, diverse in its values and approaches, and subject to ongoing debates about ethics and techniques, it is still essentially a professional enterprise. It brings to these debates a rich store of experience, expertise, and institutional self-knowledge. Through its expertise, the press makes significant contributions to the infrastructure of public discourse. It ought to have a greater role in shaping its own destiny under the Press Clause.

The judiciary is, for a couple of seemingly inconsistent reasons, at a comparative disadvantage. On the one hand, the courts' halting efforts to give the press some autonomy for newsgathering and editorial judgment suggest that the judiciary itself recognizes the press's comparative advantage in addressing these questions. The institutional turn is thus not a radical move away from what the courts already do. On the other hand, the blunt tools employed when the courts refuse to grant *any* institutional autonomy to the press or to recognize its unique status and function—the categorical invocations of "generally applicable laws"—suggest that the courts are unable to properly acknowledge and account for the press's contribution to public discourse, and that they know it. Judicial acontextuality and institutional agnosticism in this area, especially when honeycombed by exceptions, are less an assertion of confidence than an expression of insecurity.

An institutional approach to the press under the Press Clause does not require the courts to be wholly disengaged, but it does counsel a different role for them. Rather than acting as top-down regulators setting general standards for the press along with all other speakers, they should be coordinators and boundary-minders, granting the press substantial autonomy while allowing its self-identified best practices and professional norms to help shape the regulatory system. That core of professional values, along with the internal debates that arise from them, may be reason enough to grant the press greater autonomy under a far more institutionally specific model than we currently have. It is surely reason enough to *consider* experimenting with this approach.

The Old "New" Media

The "old media"—newspapers, magazines, and other print outlets—are not the only sources that disseminate news. For decades the most popular news providers, once known as the "new media," have been radio, broadcast television, and eventually cable television. This is the world of NBC, NPR, CBS, CNN, and other letters in our audio-visual alphabet soup.

Although more Americans rely on the broadcast media for news than on print media,[82] First Amendment theory and doctrine still pay more attention to print journalism than to radio and TV journalism.[83] Some of this has to do with tradition; some of it has to do with the assumption that First Amendment doctrines devised for the print media map easily onto the broadcast media; and some of it has to do with the complexity of the laws surrounding broadcast regulation, which scares off the generalists. All of these are good reasons; none of them is reason enough.

From the start, regulation of radio and television has been as much a product of accident as of intention. Radio, at first used mostly in ship traffic, became the province of military communication in World War I. After the war, U.S. policy, which could have dealt with the broadcast spectrum in any number of ways, from nationalizing it to turning it into a private regime of property rights, compromised by leaving the medium open to use by private broadcasters but controlling access to it.[84] These "early constitutive choices" would shape the regulation of the broadcast media long after the original justifications for those choices had withered away.[85]

The focus of this section is on the way we regulate broadcast *news*, not the broadcast media as a whole. But the way we regulate broadcast news is a product of those larger constitutive choices. We have ended up with what Lee Bollinger has called a system of "partial regulation" of the press, depending on the medium involved. The courts have left print journalism largely unregulated. With broadcast journalism, in contrast, they have engaged in "continuing experimentation with public regulation," in which choices about what news broadcasters present and how they present it have been subject to regulatory rules and pressures, including the threat of non-renewal of licenses.[86]

We encountered an example of this distinction in Chapter 1. In *Red Lion Broadcasting Co. v. FCC*, the Supreme Court upheld the broadcast media's obligation to provide a "right of reply" to those criticized in a story. Its decision was grounded on the view that "differences in the characteristics of new media justify differences in the First Amendment standards applied to them" and that it "is the right of the viewers and listeners, not the right of the broadcasters, which is paramount."[87] But a few years later, in *Miami Herald Publishing Co. v. Tornillo*, the Court rejected a right of reply for targets of newspaper stories. The autonomy model of the press, which was unavailing in *Red Lion*, proved decisive here. "A newspaper is more than a passive receptacle or conduit for news, comment, and advertising," Chief Justice Warren Burger wrote for the Court. "The choice of material to go into a newspaper, and the decisions made as to limitations on the size and content of the paper, and treatment of public issues and public officials—whether fair or unfair—constitute the exercise of editorial control and judgment." Any state regulation of this autonomous enterprise would be inconsistent with "First Amendment guarantees of a free press."[88]

It is now generally agreed that most of the justifications offered by the Court for the distinction between the print and broadcast media no longer work. One of the primary justifications was the scarcity of broadcast spectrum, which justified treating the airwaves as a public trust subject to heightened regulation. But nothing prevented the government from allocating spectrum under a different model, such as an auction, rather than regulating the content of the broadcast media on an ongoing basis.[89] In any event, technological changes in the medium, as well as the availability of alternative conduits such as cable, have largely eliminated the scarcity concern.[90]

Another justification for the distinction was broadcasting's "uniquely pervasive presence."[91] Broadcast's pervasive nature, in the Court's view, justified subjecting it to regulatory rules that would not have been countenanced for print, such as a ban on the use of seven "Filthy Words" at hours when children might be tuning in without parental supervision.[92] Here too, technological changes, including the advent of the V-chip and other parental control mechanisms, have sapped this justification of much of its strength.[93]

One may sympathize with the Court's struggles to keep pace with rapid technological developments in broadcasting. But its treatment of the broadcast media demonstrates the perils and, in the end, the unsustainability of an approach to the First Amendment based primarily on the "conduit," or the technological format by which speech is transmitted, rather than the nature of that speech. Context matters; but one must still find the *right* context.

We could argue for a different First Amendment model altogether, one that stresses the value of regulating speech, whether broadcast or print, in the public interest and in the service of public discourse. Some have advocated such a model, particularly for the broadcast media.[94] For a variety of reasons, it is difficult to understand why this model should apply to the broadcast media alone.[95]

Another possibility is the "partial regulation" model. Lee Bollinger argues that because "there are good First Amendment reasons for being both receptive to and wary of access regulation," we ought to split the difference. It is valuable, he suggests, to set aside at least one medium whose regulatory model "represent[s], or manifest[s], a principle of fairness." If the underlying reasons that broadcast was selected as that medium, such as the scarcity rationale, have withered away, that does not mean the experiment is not still worth trying; we should not be "intellectually crippled by the charge of inconsistency."[96]

One may agree with Bollinger that there ought to be room for experimentation within the First Amendment while rejecting his argument. Whatever the scope of permissible experimentation, it should not be arbitrary. The way we treat communications media ought to be based on "real differences in the methods of communication," differences that are "directly relevant to the interests the government seeks to further."[97] In the absence of real justifications for treating broadcast journalists differently from print journalists, such as scarcity or pervasiveness, we cannot justify an unequal regime for print and broadcast journalism.

With respect to the press or journalism aspect of broadcast media, I want to make two central points. First, an institutional approach would treat the press *as* the press. It would focus on whether a given entity was a journalistic entity engaging in the act of journalism, subject to the norms, traditions, and self-regulating practices that characterize the press. The fundamental practices and ethics of journalism do not vary according to whether a story is printed in a newspaper or aired on a network newscast or a cable news channel.[98] There are differences in presentation, of course: print stories allow for greater factual detail, permit viewers to shuffle between stories, and make it easier to run corrections; broadcast stories allow for greater visual detail and can be more visceral, but usually convey less factual content. Still, those distinctions don't alter the professional norms that govern both media. Whatever other distinctions may exist between broadcast and print, where the press is concerned the institutional approach applies equally to both.[99]

Second, for purposes of the institutional approach, little turns on whether the broadcaster is public or private. For one thing, few "public" news broadcasters are really public: they are structured to be free from government control over content.[100] More important, as the Supreme Court recognized in the *Forbes* decision discussed in Chapter 2, public broadcasters, when acting as press entities, do not act like "government" entities; they act like *journalists*, making "bona fide journalistic judgments."[101] Even public broadcasters are free, under the First Amendment, to "exercise 'the widest journalistic freedom consistent with their public [duties].'"[102]

None of this means that either public or private broadcasters, in their capacity as journalists, will always do the job we want them to do. But these complaints should lead to press self-criticism and the development of best practices, not a regulatory framework that arbitrarily distinguishes broadcast from print. The key category for courts to consider is neither the conduit through which journalistic speech takes place nor the broadcaster's public or private status, but the simple fact that it *is* journalism. Once that institutional identification is made, everything else should follow.

The New "New" Media

The rise of the Internet as a communications medium moves us from the well-settled precincts of First Amendment institutionalism to the white spaces on the map. It requires us to think about how the institutional approach to the First Amendment should respond to emerging institutions.

For most of us, talking about "the Internet" is an exercise in imprecision. We use the term to mean anything from the hardware and software that make communication between computers possible to the communication itself; it embraces everything from email to blogs. As with any capacious and ill-defined concept, when describing the Internet we fall back on metaphors: from "information superhighway" to the late Senator Ted Stevens's notorious phrase, "a series of tubes."[103]

It is no accident that much of the language we use to describe the Internet is architectural and infrastructural in nature. Recall our comparison, in Chapter 4, between the infrastructure of public discourse and that of transportation. Think of the old media as a city on an island, a communications Gotham, connected to surrounding areas by a finite number of bridges. The bridges are stupendous architectural achievements, but massively expensive ones. They provide access to the life within the city; but the routes are few, the tolls are fixed, and access can be limited by whoever owns or operates the bridges. Depending on a variety of factors, the traffic may flow much more easily in one direction than in the other.

The Internet, by contrast, is a network. Its nerves and filaments go in every direction. It grows as much by chance as by design. It was not built, at great expense, by a few for the limited use of many; instead, it *is* built, in an ongoing fashion and at relatively low marginal cost, *by* the many *for* the many.[104] Its traffic goes in every direction and encounters comparatively few tolls or bottlenecks. Its architectural or infrastructural nature is radically different from that of the old media, including the old "new" media, and it contributes to a radically different model of communication.

That romantic description has been challenged by scholars. (The Internet has no shortage of three things: porn, utopian champions of the networked future, and confirmed skeptics and dystopians.)[105] But it will do for purposes of contrast. The point made by Internet advocates is that this new network architecture poses a fundamental challenge to the old-media architecture.

One of the most eloquent champions of this view is Yochai Benkler, in his book *The Wealth of Networks*. The old communications media, he writes, required expensive up-front investments, and technological and economic factors required it to operate under a "one-way model," in which powerful media entities spoke *de haut en bas* to a dispersed and passive readership or viewership.[106] The salience and quality of the information those entities transmitted to their audience was managed internally, by a variety of professional norms and practices—the kinds we saw in our examination of the press. A relatively small, elite cadre of journalists would decide what was "news" and devote significant resources to gathering and disseminating it according to the rules of the profession; the audience would sit back and take what was given, secure in the authority of the journalistic "priestly class"[107] and bereft of efficient alternatives.

By contrast, in the networked media environment, information is gathered and shared by countless individuals and groups, using the Internet as a low-cost method of drawing together data and impressions from numerous sources. In Scott Gant's words, "We're all journalists now."[108] In the age of networked information, individuals "are free to take a more active role than was possible in the industrial information economy of the twentieth century." They are also "less susceptible to manipulation by a legally defined class of others—the owners of communications infrastructure and media." They are creating "a new public sphere . . . alongside the commercial, mass-media markets."[109]

Significantly, the networked media have routed around the old ways of certifying the relevance and accuracy of information, and in the process solved some of the problems of unreliability and information overload that afflict the networked environment. Benkler describes "widespread practices of mutual pointing, of peer review, of pointing to original sources of claims, and . . . the social practice that those who have some ability to evaluate the claims in fact do comment on them."[110] A famous example is the blogosphere's response to a report by Dan Rather of CBS News, who provided documents purporting to show that President George W. Bush had neglected his duties when he served in the Texas Air National Guard. Where Rather's authority would once have been taken on faith, or would have required other journalists to undertake laborious efforts to disprove his report, a legion of bloggers descended on the report, using aggregated information and expertise to argue that the documents were forged.[111] This is the Internet model of watchdog journalism—"peer review ex-post."[112]

The old and new media seem likely to coexist and intermix for the foreseeable future. The question is what Internet journalism does to the old institutional model of the press. Does it require us to abandon that model, or to adapt it? Are some components of the Internet, such as blogs, the "press"? If so, should the rules that govern the online press be the same ones that govern the traditional institutional press?

The answer is the lawyer's stock reply: "It's complicated." For one thing, the Internet is not a single thing: it is a congeries of platforms used for a variety of purposes. It is no more an institution, in the sense in which I use that word in this book, than the English language or the printed word is.[113] And much "Internet journalism" is just the old institutional press operating through a new delivery system. It makes little difference for these purposes whether you read the *New York Times* on paper or on your iPad, or whether you watch ABC News on television or on your laptop. Provided that those organizations are observing the usual institutional norms, the legal status of their traditional and online versions should be the same.

A number of other Internet activities, however, are taking on an institutional cast of their own. Sites like Wikipedia have adopted a peer-exchange method of providing the information we once got from printed encyclopedias; enterprises like the Gutenberg Project have developed functions analogous to those of libraries. Some blogs perform the same kinds of functions—gathering, disseminating, and commenting on the news—that old media like newspapers did. But they are also developing their own institutional practices: devising their own tools, harnessing and coordinating the actions of a multitude of individuals in a peer-to-peer rather than a top-down way, and so on.

The closest online counterpart of the institutional press is the blogosphere. We might thus think of blogs, or the blogosphere, as an emerging First Amendment institution, one suitable for treatment as a more or less autonomous institutional sphere along the lines of the institutional press.

"Along the lines of" does not mean "the same as." The institutional turn recommends that we shape the autonomy of each First Amendment institution in a way suitable to that particular institution—to its specific role in public discourse and the specific ways it fulfills that role. An institutional approach to blogs, whether under the Press Clause or under the First Amendment more generally, should define blogs' institutional autonomy in a way that is appropriate to the unique institutional features and practices of blogs. It would be a mistake to simply characterize blogs as "a new form of journalism,"[114] and extend to them the same institutional protections we give the traditional press. Instead, we should ask what protections are necessary given the purpose, value, and nature of blogs *as an institution*.

From this perspective, the most salient fact is that blogs form a *collective* and networked institution. Newspapers and broadcasters, as Benkler's description of them as "one-way" communicators suggests, are largely stand-alone enterprises. By contrast, it makes sense to say that there are no blogs—only the blogosphere. Blogging is a collective enterprise in which much of the value of the medium comes from the connections between blogs rather than the independent content of each individual blog.[115]

That element of collectivity makes a difference, both in considering blogs' suitability for treatment as an autonomous institution and in defining the scope and nature of their collective autonomy. Typically, we rely on newspapers to correct their own errors. We thus emphasize, through libel law, the importance of newspapers' acting according to proper institutional norms: reporting and editing without actual malice, exercising sound editorial judgment, and so on.[116] The relatively broad deference that courts give to these processes is both dependent on and, to some degree, formative of journalists' professional practices. We expect each individual newspaper or broadcaster operating under the old institutional model to have in place an adequate set of professional safeguards. That approach makes sense in an environment of "one-way" communication.

Blogs (at least the ones that are regularly updated and widely trafficked) operate differently. Their correction practices are collective, not singular. In the blogosphere, errors are disclosed and corrected through the exposure of mistakes and the airing of corrective views on many other blogs.[117] An individual blog or blog entry may be a horror-show of errors,[118] but the proper unit of evaluation is not any single blog or entry but what emerges from the blogosphere as a network. Most sensible blog readers (if that is not an oxymoron) know that individual blogs are unreliable and read them skeptically; the accuracy level of the blogosphere as a *collective* institution is much higher.

To be sure, this error-correction mechanism is not as institutionalized or generalized as the ethical codes and practices that govern the institutional press.[119] But an organic set of norms and practices *has* evolved in the blogosphere, and continues to evolve. Bloggers already seek to conform to a wide variety of relevant norms: linking to other sites; linking to the newspaper article or other source that forms the subject of a blog post; offering corrections to one's post once an error has been pointed out (usually while leaving the original error in place, to show how the discussion has evolved); and, most important, encouraging commenters, who also serve as error-correcting agents.[120] These practices have been institutionalized in the blogosphere, allowing the "watchdog function" to be "peer produced in the networked information economy."[121] And these bloggers' norms are matched by a corresponding set of *readers'* norms, such as that certain sites may be more trustworthy than others or that assertions made on any one site should not be credited unless and until they have been verified elsewhere. Indeed, the blogosphere is a networked collection of norms, including both producers *and* consumers of content, that bids fair to eliminate the distinction between the two.

This suggests two things. First, the blogosphere is developing the kinds of qualities—definable if evolving characteristics and a set of self-regulatory practices—that may entitle it to a degree of institutional autonomy for First Amendment purposes. Second, it says something about the nature and scope of that autonomy. Take the law of defamation. Libel law, once it had been colonized by the First Amendment, incorporated, through the actual malice standard, both the contributions that press coverage of public events makes to public discourse and the particular mechanisms that the institutional press uses to guard against false and damaging stories. It might proceed somewhat differently in the blogosphere,[122] extending the greatest protection to those blogs that actually make use of the Internet's collective error-correcting mechanisms, such as linking and commenting, as well as self-correction. In keeping with First Amendment institutionalism's emphasis on reflexive law, the courts would keep pace with the evolving norms of public discourse in the blogosphere, giving more legal cover to the blogs that make the greatest use of developing institutional best practices.

Other areas seem more problematic. For example, the profusion of bloggers makes it difficult to imagine granting bloggers the journalist's privilege to protect confidential sources or giving them equal access to statutory press credentials to cover the legislature and other public proceedings. Indeed, some argue that this sea change may portend an end to legal privileges for the press altogether, old and new.[123] For the time being, however, the problem is more apparent than real. Although many bloggers sneer at the mainstream media, most blogging is still parasitic on the reporting done by the established press.[124] In those cases, the issue will either not arise or will gain little purchase; one can't assert a privilege for a function—reporting—that one doesn't engage in.

But the question is primarily one of function, not of medium. If more bloggers engage in serious gathering and dissemination of news, their efforts should be rewarded by the same kinds of institutional privileges that ought to attach to the traditional press.[125] The contours of those privileges should be shaped by the institution's actual practices. Just as the networked media's error-correction mechanisms differ from those of the traditional media, so their newsgathering techniques may display increasingly distinctive characteristics. Or, as the recent collaboration between traditional news organizations and "networked" organizations to gather and report information, as in the "Wikileaks" episode, suggests, different kinds of organizations may converge around new forms of journalism or media, constituting a kind of "networked fourth estate."[126]

If we do see a profusion of emerging journalistic practices in the blogosphere or elsewhere on the Internet, and if greater numbers of citizens are in a position to claim some sort of institutional privilege in relevant circumstances, that should be cause for celebration, not concern. More is not always less. A perennial criticism of the traditional press is that it does not do enough serious reporting despite the privileges it enjoys.[127] If a new institution rises to the occasion and provides more serious and original contributions to public discourse, so much the better.[128]

Like most of the case studies in this book, the story of how the institutional turn in the First Amendment would affect the treatment of the press is not one of radical change. It is one of recognition and refinement—recognition of what the courts have already been doing, albeit haltingly, and refinement of the legal characterization of the press to make the courts' words match their deeds. The problem, again, is the tension between the courts' general reliance on acontextuality and their consistent, if episodic, awareness that context, including institutional context, matters. The institutional turn seeks to reinforce the latter tendency. In doing so, it can draw on ample resources within existing First Amendment jurisprudence.

For the traditional institutional press—the "old" media—this means that the courts should more wholeheartedly embrace the "central image" of the press that they have simultaneously extolled and resisted: that of an autonomous press, guided by evolving but genuine and substantial self-regulatory practices and professional norms.[129] They should identify the institutional press, or at least the institutional function of journalism; having identified it, they should largely step aside, allowing self-regulation to do its job. That autonomy should embrace legal privileges as well as immunities. It should be based on the function of the press, not its public or private status. It need not be absolute, but its scope should be broad and informed by the best practices of the institution itself. The goal should be autonomy of the press for the sake of the contributions the press as an institution makes to public discourse.

For the "new" media, the story should be much the same, although the details will necessarily change to fit their emerging institutional functions and practices. The question is not whether the new media should enjoy any autonomy at all; it is what shape this autonomy ought to take. The answer is necessarily incomplete, as the networked media continue to evolve. But they have been around long enough to develop some identifiable institutional practices, such as linking and commenting, that contribute to public discourse and allow for self-regulation. The precise institutional contours of the "new" press are still taking shape; the courts should allow them to do so, remaining vigilant but responsive.

This chapter carries one further lesson about the institutional First Amendment. Our story of the traditional press institutions and the emergence of new press institutions reveals the ways in which legal, economic, and technological forces have shaped the architecture of those institutions. Speech institutions, like all institutions, are always contingent: they depend on available social and technological resources.[130] The emergence of the networked media, which has only been possible in the last couple of decades, illuminates the ways in which the practices of the traditional media depended on and were shaped by the technology of printing presses and the broadcasting spectrum—as well as the public policies, such as reduced postal rates for newspapers, that made the spread of those media economically feasible. Speech institutions have always been partly organic and partly artificial, and they will continue to be so, even in an age when the architecture of the new media is so virtual as to be nearly invisible.

7

Where Souls Are Saved:
Churches

The First Amendment has long recognized what Ira Lupu and Robert Tuttle call "the distinctive place of religious entities in our constitutional order."[1] The Supreme Court has celebrated the power of religious organizations "to decide for themselves, free from state interference, matters of church government as well as those of faith and doctrine."[2] Despite the law's tendency to view religion as an individual matter, it has recognized the enduring importance of "the autonomy of religious organizations."[3] Given the prominent role that religious groups have played throughout our history, the long-established recognition of the "essential distinction between civil and religious functions,"[4] and the First Amendment's "singling out" of religion as a protected activity,[5] there are strong reasons to treat religious entities as autonomous First Amendment institutions.

That prospect raises a number of questions. *Are* religious entities readily identifiable and governed by strong self-regulatory practices? Can we expect them to use autonomy responsibly, given evidence of gross misconduct such as the clergy sex abuse scandal? Should the state keep its hands off the church when it comes to such matters as employment discrimination, or does the public interest in nondiscrimination require the state to intervene? A number of scholars have argued that we should limit church autonomy or eliminate it altogether,[6] while others have argued that whatever autonomy religious entities enjoy should not be based on their special status as *religious* entities.[7]

'Those practical questions are met by equally pressing theoretical ones. What does it say about our constitutional order, and about our social order more generally, to talk in terms of church autonomy? What does it mean for the infrastructure of public discourse to suggest that there are "two realms" or "two kingdoms" of social order—temporal and spiritual?[8] Does this concept reinforce the institutional turn in the First Amendment? Or is it a bygone idea, one that has lost its power as the reach of the state has extended across the whole range of human conduct?[9]

In this chapter I argue that there is a strong case for treating religious entities as First Amendment institutions and granting them a significant degree of legal autonomy. There are good reasons to believe that religious entities and their affairs constitute a separate "sphere": a sovereign realm that operates alongside the state and with which the state is substantially forbidden to interfere. Public discourse benefits from treating religious entities as sovereign spheres. The state has an important—but circumscribed—role to play in policing the boundaries of these institutions.

My use of suggestive terms like "sovereign" or "quasi-sovereign" in this chapter, along with my use of a broader set of sources in support of this chapter's arguments, including religious sources, marks something of a shift in language and tone compared with the last two chapters. That shift deserves some comment. In part, it is simply a function of the sources that naturally come into play here. It should be unsurprising that arguments about the infrastructural or institutional role of churches and other religious organizations within society have, both historically and today, been expressed in explicitly religious terms. It is also partly due to the nature of churches themselves: more so than universities or the press, churches are a part of the infrastructure of modern liberal society without necessarily being, or describing themselves as, "liberal" institutions. Even readers who agree that churches ought to be treated as First Amendment institutions may not embrace all the views or language that churches themselves would use in arguing for some form of legal autonomy. But they ought not be surprised at the difference in tone and emphasis that we are likely to find in the sources dealing with these questions.

For my purposes, there is both more *and* less to this shift in language and emphasis than initial appearances may suggest. One need not accept broad religious or metaphysical claims about the status of churches to agree that they ought to be classified as First Amendment institutions. From the perspective of the basic characteristics of such institutions set out in Part One, they are surely well-established, self-governing institutions with a longstanding infrastructural role in public discourse and a unique set of contributions to make to it. Those who resist the religious overtones implicit in calling the church a "sovereign sphere" may translate those terms easily enough into the less exalted language of First Amendment institutionalism, as I do frequently throughout this chapter.

But I think there is more to it than that. On a practical level, the terms I use here—the language of sovereign spheres, quasi-sovereignty, and so on—are not terribly significant. The kind of autonomy I argue for on behalf of churches in this chapter is still bounded; it still imposes limits on their legal autonomy as First Amendment institutions, just as there are limits on the autonomy of universities and the press. Yet there is surely *some* significance to the sheer richness of the language that is available to us here.

As a simple matter of history, at least, this language suggests just how ancient the contest between the authority of church and state is, and the degree to which the church, unlike newspapers and universities, was truly present at the creation—not only of our modern infrastructure of public discourse, but of our very social order. If it is now difficult for many readers to envision the church as a truly separate authority from the state, one with an equal—or superior—claim to authority, that was not always the case. The struggles between church and state for domination, cooperation, or accommodation are substantially responsible for the modern social order as we know it, including many of the features of the secular liberal state.[10] The language of those contests is of more than historical interest; its echoes are still heard today, even if they have mostly shifted to a more mundane register. Among other things, by helping to establish the general idea that the state may lack complete authority over other central social institutions, the churches helped to make room for the kinds of ideas that we have applied in varying ways to universities, the press, and other First Amendment institutions. In so doing, they continue to raise questions about the role and limits of the state.

In that sense, although a successful defense of the status of churches as First Amendment institutions can be made in the same terms we have seen in other chapters, there is a potential benefit to the richer, more evoca-tive—and surely more provocative—language and ideas we will see in this chapter. In an immediate sense, it raises questions about the endless contest between church and state that is embedded in the history and jurisprudence of the Religion Clauses of the First Amendment. Beyond this, however, it offers new and powerful ways of thinking about First Amendment insti-tutionalism itself, and its implications. It goes beyond arguments for the instrumental value of First Amendment institutionalism—its capacity to give us a more responsive, reflexive doctrine that contributes more usefully to modern public discourse—to ask more fundamental questions about the nature and limits of the state. It asks us to consider whether public discourse, and the institutions that support it, are just means to the end of democratic self-government—of making sure that *"governmental* decision making be somehow rendered accountable to public opinion"[11]—or whether they sug-gest something more: that "a true understanding" of our social order, and of human nature itself, must embrace "a multitude of different associations and communities," of which the state is just one among many.[12]

One certainly need not accept these ideas to accept First Amendment institutionalism; as the last two chapters have suggested, one may favor the institutional turn for purely instrumental purposes, seeing it as an improve-ment on the frailties of current First Amendment doctrine. It might be more prudent to leave things there. But I believe it is worth exploring these broader ideas too. The case of churches provides a fitting occasion to do so.

Sphere Sovereignty

Our story begins in an unexpected time and place—nineteenth-century Holland—with the neo-Calvinist theologian, journalist, and politician Abraham Kuyper. Kuyper's work has a surprising amount to teach us about the treatment of religious entities as First Amendment institutions, and about the theoretical justifications for the institutional approach to the First Amendment more generally.

Kuyper wrote in opposition to the dominant theories of sovereignty in his own day: popular sovereignty, which he feared would culminate in "the shackling of liberty in the irons of State-omnipotence,"[13] and state sov-ereignty, which he warned would lead to "state absolutism."[14] Drawing on

Calvinist theology, he envisioned three principal sovereigns: the state, society, and the church. He emphasized that these were *"separate spheres[,]* each with its own sovereignty,"[15] which should not lightly be interfered with by any other sovereign. The state must "honor and maintain every form of [social] life which grows independently in its own sacred autonomy." For Kuyper, this approach supplied the answer to "the deeply interesting question of our civil liberties."[16]

Kuyper calls the state "the sphere of spheres, which encircles the whole extent of human life."[17] Its role is to ensure that the other spheres operate harmoniously—a role that Kuyper sees as evidence that Calvinism "may be said to have generated constitutional public law." The state has three primary obligations: "1. Whenever different spheres clash, to compel mutual regard for the boundary-lines of each; 2. To defend individuals and the weak ones, in those spheres, against the abuse of power of the rest; and 3. To coerce all together to bear *personal* and *financial* burdens for the maintenance of the natural unity of the State."[18]

The state thus plays three central roles. The first involves the adjudication of what Richard Mouw has called *"inter*sphere boundary disputes": the state has the duty to ensure that each sphere is operating within its proper realm and not interfering with another. The second involves *"intra*sphere conflict": the state must ensure that the individual members of a social sphere are not abused within that sphere. Finally, the state may act for *"trans-*spherical purposes": it may provide public goods such as infrastructure or military protection.[19]

The state has a tendency "to invade social life, to subject it and mechanically to arrange it." Conversely, the social spheres tend to resist the state's authority. The proper resolution of this tension is to acknowledge the "independence [of each] in their own sphere and regulation of the relation between both, not by the executive, but under the law." The sovereign state must cooperate with the sovereign social sphere so that both can achieve their fated purposes.[20]

Kuyper envisions a vital role for churches, but he is adamant that no single church should dominate. The state cannot interfere with religious pluralism, because it is incompetent to make determinations about what constitutes the true church and because interference with the church falls outside its jurisdiction. Its role is that of a coordinator; it cannot choose a privileged sect from among the churches or resolve "spiritual questions."[21] Like the state, the church is limited in its jurisdiction and is obliged to remain within its own realm. Nor may it overreach within its own realm. If it does so, the state may intervene.

In sum, Kuyper's vision of sphere sovereignty is one of guided and divided pluralism. Each sphere has "its own unique set of functions and norms,"[22] and all of them are expressions of God's ultimate sovereignty. But each sphere, so long as it acts appropriately, remains sovereign—untouchable by church, state, or other institutions. Kent van Til offers a metaphor that captures Kuyper's vision:

> Imagine a prism that has refracted light into its multiple colors. These colors represent the various social spheres of human existence—family, business, academy, and so forth. On one side of the colored lights stand the churches—guiding their members in the knowledge of God, which informs (but does not dictate) the basic convictions of each believer. On the other side of the spectrum stands the state, regulating the interactions among the spheres, assuring that the weak are not trampled, and calling on all persons to contribute to the common good. Neither church nor state defines the role of each sphere; instead, each derives its legitimacy and its role from God.[23]

The resemblance between Kuyper's sphere sovereignty and the institutional turn in the First Amendment should be obvious. But to make a strong argument that this approach should inform our understanding of the American constitutional structure, we must see the ways in which Kuyper's vision is already immanent in the threads of American political and constitutional thought.

Those threads can be traced at least as far back as the writing of the sixteenth-century Calvinist philosopher Johannes Althusius.[24] For Althusius, the private association is an essential part of the organizing structure of society. Each association is fundamentally "responsible for its own self-government." The church is "a private voluntary association, whose members elect their own authorities and maintain their own internal doctrine and discipline, polity and property without state interference or support."[25]

Althusius does not rule out state regulation; the state can intervene where necessary to "defend the fundamental rights of every human being." But its fundamental role is to encourage conditions that "make it possible for participants of each association together to . . . form a community that orders the life of participants through just laws of their own making."[26]

Althusius lays the groundwork for Kuyperian sphere sovereignty. He offers a vision of "a civil society that is characterized by a variety of private associations and a horizontal social order." The state has an important role to play, but its power "is restricted with respect to nonstate associations on the basis of the latter's authority."[27]

On our shores, the influence of the Calvinist ideas that culminated in Kuyperian sphere sovereignty can be traced back to the Puritan colonists.[28] The Puritans' fundamental contribution to American constitutionalism was an understanding of rights and liberties based on the Calvinist doctrine of covenant, which led them to see church and state as "two separate covenantal associations, two coordinate seats of godly authority and power in authority." The preamble to the 1648 *Laws and Liberties of Massachusetts Bay,* for example, declared that "our churches and civil state have been planted, and grown up (like two twins)." Each was an "an instrument of godly authority," and each "did its part to establish and maintain the covenantal ideals of the community."[29] To be sure, the degree of mutual support between church and state was greater in the Puritan communities than it is under the modern understanding of American religious liberty.[30] Nevertheless, the parallels between Kuyper and the American Puritans—especially their view of church, state, and private associations as coordinate sovereigns entitled to substantial autonomy—are striking.

The Puritan influence is reflected in the thought of influential American revolutionary figures, and through them to some of our foundational accounts of religious liberty in the United States. John Adams admired the Puritans' creation of "a comprehensive system of ordered liberty and orderly pluralism within church, state, and society." He drew on their vision of religious autonomy in drafting the Massachusetts Constitution of 1780, which guaranteed churches the right to select ministers without state interference.[31] The same pattern of dual authority is apparent elsewhere in the early Republic. For the founding generation, "the jurisdiction of civil government and the authority of religion were frequently considered distinguishable."[32] In the antebellum period, for example, the Supreme Court's "key to resolving" church-state disputes "was to define a private sphere, protected against state interference by the vested rights doctrine and the separation of church and state."[33]

In short, we might see the Puritans, among others, as having infused American thought with some of the same ideas that would culminate in Kuyper's writings on sphere sovereignty. On this view, the American founders embarked on "a new experiment—one that decoupled religious and civil institutions. This new government would have no jurisdiction over religious matters, thus ensuring the autonomy of religious institutions and simultaneously depriving those institutions of any incentive to capture the organs of government to further their religious missions."[34] The traces of this line of thought remained in evidence well into the nineteenth century, when Alexis de Tocqueville commented on American society's "immense assemblage of associations."[35] That same pluralist spirit, it has been argued, continues to influence the Supreme Court's contemporary rulings on topics such as federalism, freedom of association, and freedom of religion.[36]

Evidence of a concern with the sovereignty or autonomy of non-state associations can also be found in a diverse array of other thinkers. They are not necessarily influential in the American worldview, but they hint at the broader appeal of sphere sovereignty as a middle ground between state absolutism and the atomistic individualism that so often characterizes American thought—one we have seen in the First Amendment trope of the soapbox speaker.

The British pluralists, for example, argued for a form of pluralism in which "self-governing associations" played a vital role in "organizing social life." They viewed the state as a sort of "society of societies, charged with the task of making the continued existence and mutual interaction of such associations possible through setting rules for their conduct."[37] Although the state might exercise regulatory power, it should do so in a manner "bounded by the behavior of other groups, with law emanating from several sources."[38] The state, they argued, was not the sole source of authority, and institutions such as churches did not owe their continued existence to its good graces. As David Nicholls writes, for pluralists like J. N. Figgis, "The state recognises groups because they exist; they do not derive their existence from being recognised."[39] Although Figgis understood that argument in explicitly religious terms, it need not be. From another perspective, one consonant with this book's argument that First Amendment law ought to be responsive to the lived reality of public discourse and social life, the law must recognize the importance of churches and other First Amendment institutions "because they exist as social facts."[40]

Although these ideas have never been dominant in American thought, they are present in the writing of American legal theorists like Robert Cover and Mark DeWolfe Howe.[41] Howe put the point simply and starkly: "The heart of the pluralistic thesis is the conviction that government must recognize that it is not the sole possessor of sovereignty, and that private groups within the community are entitled to lead their own free lives and exercise within the area of their competence an authority so effective as to justify labeling it a sovereign authority."[42]

Other writers, operating very much from within the American intellectual tradition, have argued for the importance of "mediating" or "intermediary" institutions, which stand "between the individual in his private life and the large institutions of public life." For these writers, mediating associations, including staples of Kuyperian thought such as "family, church, voluntary association, [and] neighborhood,"[43] help individuals to maintain their identities in the face of the crushing pressure of the state. The state should "protect and foster mediating structures," largely by leaving them alone and treating them as partners in shaping public policy rather than implementing it in a top-down manner.[44]

Finally, consider the Catholic doctrine of subsidiarity, which arose at about the same time as sphere sovereignty. It argues that the individual, rather than existing in isolation, "realizes his fulfillment in community with others." The state should not exercise its regulatory authority "to the point of absorbing or destroying [private associations], or preventing them from accomplishing what they can on their own."[45] It retains some regulatory authority over associations but should exercise it in a way that "protect[s] them from government interference, empowering them through limited but effective intervention, or coordinating their various pursuits."[46] As with Kuyperian sphere sovereignty, it would be a stretch to say that subsidiarity has directly influenced American political or constitutional thought. Still, the concept of subsidiarity, like that of sphere sovereignty, can surely be understood in ways that may help clarify and refine American constitutional doctrine in a wide variety of areas.

Religious Entities as First Amendment Institutions

Like First Amendment institutionalism, sphere sovereignty offers a vision of a legal order in which independent and substantially legally autonomous intermediary institutions, including the "church," are vital elements of a properly functioning society. In particular, it offers two lessons about the relationship between the state and intermediary institutions. First, although sphere sovereignty is respectful of the state, it does not treat it as an absolute good. It recognizes the state's fundamental importance, but views it as just one among many sovereigns, each constituting a legal order of its own. Again, Figgis puts the point powerfully: "The fact is, that to deny to smaller societies a real life and meaning, a personality, in fact, is not anti-clerical, or illiberal, or unwise, or oppressive—it is untrue."[47] Moreover, Kuyper values these mediating structures for their contributions to human well-being. Like Tocqueville, he recognizes that these institutions affect the individual on both a personal and a social level. They serve as a source of community in an egalitarian and commercial democratic republic that might otherwise render human life intolerably lonely.[48]

Second, sphere sovereignty assigns the state the vital but limited role of mediating between the various spheres and protecting the rights of the members of those spheres. Thus, sphere sovereignty does not ignore individual rights. Kuyper emphasized that each individual is "a sovereign in his own person" and stressed the importance of "liberty of conscience," "liberty of speech," and "liberty of worship." This is apparent in his description of the state's "right and duty" to "defend individuals and the weak ones, in [the various] spheres, against the abuse of power of the rest."[49]

This vision of sphere sovereignty is surprisingly consistent with aspects of our current constitutional order, such as the constitutional autonomy given to families[50] and our system of federalism.[51] More important for present purposes, however, it both offers a blueprint for First Amendment institutionalism and helps to legitimate it by giving it a deeper theoretical underpinning. It supplies a code of conduct for both institutions themselves and the state.

Thus, the concept of sphere sovereignty offers insight into some of the key questions raised by the institutional approach: When is state intervention in the affairs of First Amendment institutions appropriate, and how should that intervention proceed? It suggests that occasions for state intervention arise when there is a dispute *between* institutions, an intrusion on individual rights *within* a sphere, or a transspherical dispute involving public goods. The state may intrude on institutional autonomy or sphere sovereignty in such cases, but it should do so only when institutional self-regulation alone will not succeed, and only in a manner that respects the default position of institutional autonomy.

This approach is especially appropriate for the legal treatment of religious entities, which help form, shape, and propagate public discourse. The church is a well-established institution that predates the modern liberal democratic state and is firmly ensconced within its infrastructure, as the Religion Clauses themselves demonstrate. And many church entities are rich with self-regulatory norms and practices.

On this view, we should treat religious entities, like other First Amendment institutions, as substantially autonomous institutions. At the same time, precisely because churches are sovereign spheres, they must "live from their own strength on the voluntary principle." In the American version of sphere sovereignty, Kuyper's belief that the state lacks the authority to pronounce any sect to be the one true church suggests that some form of nonestablishment must be woven into the fabric of this approach.[52] What the treatment of religious entities as First Amendment institutions counsels, in short, is "a free Church, in a free State": substantially autonomous religious entities, operating according to their own purposes and within their own sphere, not entitled to state preferment but also substantially immune from state regulation.[53]

Some Applications

What does treating religious entities as First Amendment institutions—or sovereign spheres—mean for the jurisprudence of the Religion Clauses? In some cases it closely tracks what the courts already do; in others it requires a departure from current law. More important than the particulars, however, is the broader vision it offers of the relationship between the sovereign realms of church and state.

CHURCH AUTONOMY

Consider first the question of church autonomy, a capacious phrase that embraces a wide range of issues. One of the earliest constitutional discussions of church autonomy can be found in an 1871 Supreme Court case,

Watson v. Jones.[54] It dealt with the common phenomenon of church property disputes, in which warring factions within a church argue over who should be entitled to ownership of church property. In resolving one such dispute, the Court provided a number of fundamental principles that have influenced discussions of church autonomy ever since.

The Court began by asserting, "The law knows no heresy, and is committed to the support of no dogma, the establishment of no sect." It declined to adopt any approach to adjudicating church property disputes that would require the courts to determine whether a particular religious institution, or its leadership, had departed from established church doctrine. Instead, it laid down rules of conduct that varied according to the form of church polity in question. Disputes within congregationalist churches—churches that operate without any higher religious authority—would be decided "by the ordinary principles which govern voluntary associations."[55] Disputes within hierarchical religious organizations, such as the Roman Catholic Church, would be resolved by accepting as final the decision of the highest church adjudicator to address the question.[56]

Watson was followed by a series of Supreme Court cases that ratified a deferential approach to church disputes. The Court has held that under the Religion Clauses, "the civil courts [have] *no* role in determining ecclesiastical questions in the process of resolving property disputes" and may not resolve "underlying controversies over religious doctrine."[57] It has also said that "courts may not make a detailed assessment of relevant church rules and adjudicate between disputed understandings" of those rules, even if the underlying question is whether the ecclesiastical tribunal has acted consistently with its own law.[58] More recently, in *Jones v. Wolf,*[59] the Court said that state courts deciding church property disputes may continue to follow the rules laid down in *Watson,* or they may adopt a "neutral principles" approach, applying standard legal doctrine to interpret authoritative church documents and resolve property disputes, provided that those documents do not require the court to interpret *religious* doctrine.

These cases have generated a good deal of controversy, but we can bypass most of that here and focus on a few points. First, church property disputes strike at the very heart of what Kuyper would have considered the sovereign sphere of religious entities. In institutionalist terms, they involve issues that are fundamental to the functioning of religious entities. They should be dealt with primarily through the norms of self-governance that apply within a particular religious institution, not by judicial intervention.

Second, these disputes may require less boundary-policing than courts might engage in with respect to other First Amendment institutions. As we have seen, in dealing with institutions such as universities and the press, courts should be deferential toward professional best practices, allowing for some diversity of practices among institutions; but they may still have some role in setting a floor for appropriate institutional behavior. That approach would be more troubling for the resolution of internal church disputes, because it would embroil the courts in religious controversies they are not competent to resolve. Thus, under an institutionalist approach to church disputes, courts should avoid intervening even where a church appears to have departed from its own norms.[60]

Third, courts should not misunderstand the language of "neutral principles" that the Supreme Court used in *Jones v. Wolf.* The Court used deceptively similar language in its opinion in *Employment Division v. Smith,* which held that there is no constitutional right to a religious exemption from "neutral, generally applicable law[s]."[61] *Smith,* with its concerns for the "anarchy"[62] that would erupt if the courts had to weigh individual claims to religious exemptions from generally applicable laws, is a classic example of the Court's preference for acontextual rules.

Some writers have argued that the similarity between *Smith*'s language and the term "neutral principles" in *Jones* means we must reject any constitutional right to church autonomy.[63] This is a mistake. "Other than an unfortunate coincidence of language," Perry Dane argues, *Smith* and *Jones* "have little to do with each other and . . . cannot simply be strung together to suggest an erosion of religious institutional autonomy."[64] *Jones* simply recognizes the profound difficulty courts face in resolving what Richard Mouw would call "intrasphere" church disputes. The Court's response in *Jones*—giving religious entities the opportunity to structure their own governing documents with secular language that state courts can understand and enforce—offered churches a way to order their own "private rights and obligations" in an enforceable manner that could "accommodate all forms of religious organization and polity."[65] *Jones* was an effort to *accommodate* church autonomy, not to eliminate it.[66] Whatever the imperfections of the "neutral principles" approach, it does not undercut church autonomy.

Another issue involving church autonomy is the ministerial exception. Under Title VII of the Civil Rights Act, religious entities are immune from the operation of antidiscrimination law in cases concerning "the employment of individuals of a particular religion to perform work connected with the carrying on by such corporation, association, educational institution, or society of its activities."[67] Religious entities are free to discriminate against *any* employee, from ministers to janitors, on the basis of religion. The Supreme Court upheld this exception against an Establishment Clause challenge in *Corporation of Presiding Bishop of Church of Jesus Christ of Latter-day Saints v. Amos.* In a strongly institutionally oriented concurring opinion, Justice Brennan rhapsodized about religious entities as "organic entit[ies] not reducible to a mere aggregation of individuals" and argued that these entities required "autonomy in ordering their internal affairs" and "authority to engage in [a] process of self-definition," even if they would otherwise fall afoul of antidiscrimination laws.[68]

The statutory exemption for religious discrimination does not immunize churches from civil rights suits involving other protected categories such as race or sex.[69] The lower federal courts, however, have widely agreed that the Religion Clauses require a broader scope of immunity than the statute itself provides. They have concluded that religious freedom "bars *any* inquiry into a religious organization's underlying motivation for [a] contested employment decision" if the employee performs "particular spiritual functions."[70] In other words, churches are constitutionally immune from discrimination suits based on *any* protected category, including race or sex, provided that the plaintiff performs "ministerial" functions for the church.

In its recent decision in *Hosanna-Tabor Evangelical Lutheran Church and School v. EEOC,* the Supreme Court agreed with the lower courts, declaring firmly that the ministerial exception is a fundamental requirement of the Religion Clauses. To "impos[e] an unwanted minister" on a church, the Court held, would infringe the Free Exercise Clause by violating "a religious group's right to shape its own faith and mission through its appointments." And allowing courts to adjudicate the question of "which individuals will minister to the faithful" would also violate the Establishment Clause, because such decisions would constitute "government involvement in . . . ecclesiastical decisions."[71]

The Court's decision was quite right, and wholly consistent with the institutional turn. Read broadly, *Hosanna-Tabor* "implements our Constitution's recognition that the state is not the ultimate authority in all things"—that "some things are above or beyond the jurisdiction of the law precisely because the First Amendment stands as an affirmation of the penultimacy of the state." It recognizes that "civil authorities, including the courts, have 'a constitutionally prescribed sphere of action,' and [that] this civil sphere of authority is separate from the sphere of action reserved to religion."[72] If religious entities are to serve as a truly independent part of the infrastructure of public discourse and as proper intermediary institutions, they must have autonomy to make their own key decisions about whom they hire and fire. As Kuyper put it, "The Church may not be forced to tolerate as a member one whom she feels obliged to expel from her circle."[73]

One might argue that only employment decisions that are truly *religious* fall within the proper sphere of a religious entity's autonomy, while any decisions based on extrinsic factors such as race or sex fall within the state's purview.[74] That argument is mistaken. The activity itself—the hiring or firing of an employee of a religious organization—remains squarely within the core of the religious entity's sovereignty, whatever the reasons for that decision may be. Moreover, as Justice Samuel Alito pointed out in his concurring opinion in *Hosanna-Tabor,* asking whether the religious institution's basis for hiring or firing someone is truly extrinsic to its religious activities would require courts to make determinations they are not qualified to make.[75] Thus, an institutional approach supports church immunity with respect to employment decisions that involve the core decision to hire or fire "ministerial" employees. That immunity should be interpreted broadly, out of respect for both religious autonomy and institutional pluralism and diversity.[76]

If anything, an institutional approach to the ministerial exception favors the expansion of current doctrine. Under current law, Title VII permits religious entities to discriminate against any employee, but only for religious reasons. Conversely, the ministerial exception forbids courts to examine cases involving discrimination on any protected basis, but only where ministerial employees are concerned. A more robust version of First Amendment institutionalism might treat the question more categorically. Churches, *qua* churches, might be entitled to substantial decision-making autonomy with respect to membership and employment matters, regardless of the nature of the employee or the grounds of discrimination.

That does not mean, however, that religious entities should be immune from criticism and moral influence in these cases. *Hosanna-Tabor* affirmed the ministerial exception, but it did not and could not affirm that the church employer in that case acted properly.[77] Even if the courts must not intervene in those decisions, that does not mean that others—especially co-religionists, but others as well—may not criticize them, or that this internal or public dialogue will yield no results. Bob Jones University, for example, prohibited interracial dating for decades, even *after* it lost a constitutional challenge to the tax penalties it suffered as a result of its policy. It ultimately changed the policy as a result of public criticism and self-reflection, not regulatory pressure.[78] Just as universities are unlikely to take advantage of their autonomy to discriminate and will face significant internal criticism if they do, so religious entities that discriminate on questionable grounds can and should expect criticism. But these disputes should be primarily a matter for self-regulation, not legal intervention.

<h2>Sexual Abuse and Clergy Malpractice</h2>

The most controversial issue involving church autonomy concerns sexual abuse by members of the clergy and church cover-ups of that abuse. These scandals have spawned an enormous amount of litigation, resulting in significant settlements and bankruptcies while causing some traditional legal defenses to buckle under the sheer weight of social disapproval. It has also sparked some of the most vehement opposition to the general idea of church autonomy.[79] I cannot do justice to the complexity of this issue here.[80] But the controversy helps us see that with religious entities, as with other First Amendment institutions, there are limits to the scope of legal autonomy. Most defenders of church autonomy already agree on this point,[81] but it is worth stressing, lest critics of church autonomy use the sexual abuse scandal unfairly as a cudgel.[82]

Whether we use the language of sphere sovereignty or First Amendment institutionalism, it is clear that state intervention is appropriate when an institution abuses its own members. Neither sphere sovereignty nor First Amendment institutionalism entails church immunity from liability for the sexual victimization of minors or adults. Immunizing religious entities in such cases, far from contributing to public discourse, would imprison their victims behind a wall of silence. However robust the form of First

Amendment institutionalism that applies to churches, it does not include immunity for conduct that is obviously harmful in and of itself, and that would be considered harmful regardless of whether the injured party was or was not a member of the church.[83]

But the institutional turn may influence *how* we intervene in these cases. We should be cautious, preventing judges and juries from deciding issues that lie further afield from the abuse itself and closer to the church's religious mission—issues such as broad questions of entity responsibility, the manner of selecting or monitoring church officials, and questions of church structure in the context of bankruptcy. Claims based on "clergy malpractice" have been widely rejected, for instance, because they require courts to "articulate and apply objective standards of care for the communicative content of clergy counseling," embroiling courts in questions they lack the competence or authority to resolve.[84]

Drawing on the libel cases we saw in Chapter 6, Ira Lupu and Robert Tuttle argue that courts should apply a version of the Supreme Court's "actual malice" test to civil suits against religious entities for religious misconduct. Courts should reject any regime of tort liability that "imposes on religious entities a duty to inquire into the psychological makeup of clergy aspirants," lest these institutions fall into a form of "self-censorship[ ] that is inconsistent with the freedom protected by ecclesiastical immunity from official inquiry into the selection of religious leaders." Church officials should not be liable for abuse committed by individual clergy members, unless the institution "had actual knowledge of [its] employees' propensity to commit misconduct." Such a rule would give "religious organizations 'breathing space' within which to organize their own policies, select their own leaders, and preach their own creeds."[85] That approach is consistent with First Amendment institutionalism. Even as quasi-sovereign spheres, churches do not lie beyond the state's regulatory reach altogether. Still, regulatory efforts should be shaped in a way that allows churches to participate in defining and regulating themselves.

There is a difference between leaving open a limited scope for the immunity of religious entities and arguing that they ought to be free to do whatever they wish. Churches and other First Amendment institutions are subject to significant internal critique and reform, nonlegal public pressure, and reputational forces. Those forces have all been brought to bear in the clergy sexual abuse cases, and rightly so. Certainly churches have strong incentives to engage in self-regulation—not least, the religious values that shape them as communities.[86] As long as those pressures and incentives exist, a constrained form of immunity should not deter religious entities from voluntarily seeking to avoid sexual misconduct and harm to church members.

THE ESTABLISHMENT CLAUSE

The Establishment Clause of the First Amendment forbids any laws respecting an establishment of religion. Some writers have argued that current Establishment Clause doctrine is in serious tension with sphere sovereignty— and, by extension, with an institutional account of religious freedom. Johan Van der Vyver, for example, asserts that the doctrine wrongly assumes that "church and state, and law and religion, can . . . be isolated from one another in watertight compartments." To the contrary, he asserts, sphere sovereignty is based on the "intertwinement" of church and state. Nicholas Wolterstorff argues that Kuyper would view those aspects of Establishment Clause doctrine that forbid government funds from passing to religious entities as "founded on untenable assumptions and hopelessly confused."[87]

In my view, it is not clear that a sphere sovereignty or First Amendment institutionalist account of religious freedom requires a radical shift away from current Establishment Clause doctrine. We can best see this by dividing Establishment Clause cases into two categories: those involving equal funding and equal access to the public sphere for religious entities, and those involving symbolic support for religious entities.[88]

Kuyper was most concerned with maintaining equal funding and equal access, especially for religious schools.[89] Contrary to his views, one could argue that a sphere sovereigntist approach forbids state support of any kind for religion, because churches are supposed to "live from their own strength on the voluntary principle."[90] But the church is only one among a multitude of sovereign spheres, and the key principle that should guide these cases is equality. So long as the other spheres are entitled to share in the state's largesse, religious entities should be as well.[91]

The law is already moving in this direction. Current doctrine suggests that government funds *may* flow to religious organizations, provided that aid is apportioned on an equal basis with aid to secular organizations and that the decision whether to accept this aid is the product of "true private choice."[92] Similarly, the Court has emphasized that religious entities are as entitled as secular entities to engage in speech in the public square, including the use of public fora such as after-hours public school programs.[93] On the aid issue, then, current law is not as far away from the sphere sovereignty approach as its critics suppose.

The other major battleground in Establishment Clause doctrine concerns religious symbolism: cases in which government's endorsement is sought for a variety of religious practices, such as the invocation of God in public schools or the erection of public displays such as the Ten Commandments. The best approach here is a strict one. The separate sovereign spheres of state and church are mutually limiting, and both are harmed when they intermix. From an institutionalist perspective, granting religious entities legal autonomy is necessary in part because these entities can serve as an independent source of ideas and arguments in public discourse.[94] If First Amendment institutionalism's goal is to preserve a set of institutions that contribute *independently* to public discourse, it would be inconsistent with that goal to allow the state to openly favor (or disfavor) particular forms of religious speech. Kuyper might have viewed things differently. The best reading of his ideas in the *American* context, however, is that sphere sovereignty and First Amendment institutionalism support a strict reading of the Establishment Clause in cases involving government-supported religious speech.

If any institution is a candidate for treatment as a First Amendment institution, it is the church. Religious entities not only predate the modern state; the modern state is in large measure a product of the existence of the church.[95] Much of Western political history has been a footnote to the effort to reconcile the sovereign spheres of church and state.[96]

On less abstract grounds, too, churches can lay a strong claim to treatment as First Amendment institutions. They play a vital role in our social infrastructure. They nurture some of the most significant elements of the human capacity for engagement with society. They are places for the development of the whole person: social and individual, spiritual and political. They are sources of political ideas, arguments, and commitments.[97] Churches, in short, ought to be substantially autonomous institutions, free to operate and evolve with minimal state involvement. The state, and the courts, will necessarily be involved in policing some of the boundaries of churches' conduct toward their own members and toward others. But that involvement should be sensitive, deferential, and limited.

Though the state's regulatory role should be limited, there are other ways of addressing church misbehavior. Not least among these is the role of churches themselves: their capacity for self-critique, internal dialogue, and self-regulatory norms.[98] Nor are they immune from public criticism; the significant public attention and criticism sparked by the clergy sex abuse scandal, and the churches' responses to this criticism—some productive, some less so—bear witness to that. Given the profound importance of churches to our social infrastructure and their long tradition of self-regulation, we should hesitate before concluding that a top-down strategy of state regulation is the best response to church misconduct.

The role of churches as First Amendment institutions also sheds light on the institutional turn itself. Kuyper's notion of sphere sovereignty serves as a valuable reminder that the state is not all there is. There are other spheres—other sovereign realms of human activity, individual and social—that offer rich and important sources of meaning. To say this is not to disparage the state's coordinating role as "sphere of spheres." But it is to identify the state *as* a sphere, and a limited one at that. The state, like churches and other First Amendment institutions, has "a proper role" and "a certain sphere of responsibility." But it "comprises only a part of the overall society, not the whole of society or even most of the public aspects of modern society."[99] For our society to function and evolve in a way that does full justice to the richness of our social infrastructure, the state must recognize that there are other sovereigns.

In his classic article on these other sovereigns, which he called "nomic communities," and their relationship to the law, Robert Cover wrote, "[J]ust as constitutionalism is part of what may legitimize the state, so constitutionalism may legitimize, within a different framework, communities and movements. Legal meaning is a challenging enrichment of social life, a potential restraint on arbitrary power and violence. We ought to stop circumscribing the *nomos;* we ought to invite new worlds."[100] Cover's advice holds true for religious entities as well as for other First Amendment institutions. In thinking about these institutions as sovereign spheres, we encounter limits on the state's power to circumscribe. We invite new worlds.

8

Where Ideas Reside: Libraries

Most of the First Amendment institutions we have examined so far contribute actively and *vocally* to public discourse. Libraries, the subject of this chapter, are somewhat different. They are places where views are shaped and changed, not expressed. The atmosphere of the library is not "the tumult of the public square" but the silence of the monastery.[1]

When it comes to libraries, the courts outdo themselves in their propensity to rhapsodize.[2] Libraries are "hallowed place[s]," locations "dedicated to quiet, to knowledge, and to beauty."[3] They "pursue the worthy missions of facilitating learning and cultural enrichment."[4] The courts agree that libraries are vital institutions in a democratic state.

That is about the only thing about libraries they *do* agree on. The Supreme Court has decided few relevant cases about libraries, and those few decisions are badly splintered. They provide little guidance for the lower courts that deal more often with cases involving libraries. Nor have scholars filled the gaps left by the courts.

One reason for the gaps in this area is the lure of acontextuality. Courts have long sought to assimilate libraries into the generally applicable, institutionally agnostic framework of First Amendment law, without much success.[5] In particular, they have debated whether the public library is a public forum and what kind of public forum it is.[6] *Private* libraries are free to act as they wish. But public libraries are the face of American library culture,[7] and they are subject to all the intricacies of acontextual legal doctrine. The courts' efforts to categorize libraries in legal rather than institutional terms have rendered the law in this area a mess, beyond the ability of the most subtle and puissant librarian to organize.

These legal issues have gotten more complicated just when the limits on libraries' ability to select and store information—and hence the need for librarians to make tough choices about what to include or remove—have decreased dramatically. The rise of the Internet, which the Supreme Court has likened to a "vast library,"[8] has raised questions about what Internet content public libraries can refuse to make accessible and whether that decision belongs to the libraries or the government.

The Supreme Court has conceded the difficulty of fitting libraries into an acontextual framework, recognizing that their constitutional status depends on "the role of libraries in our society."[9] That question can be complex. Like other First Amendment institutions, libraries have occasioned debates over their proper role and function. By any measure, however, the Supreme Court has done a poor job of responding to the modern role of the library. An examination of libraries from an institutionalist perspective may help clean up the mess the Court has made of these questions.

Examining libraries as First Amendment institutions also illuminates broader issues raised by the institutional turn, particularly the complexities of First Amendment institutionalism on the public side of the public-private divide. Public libraries are unquestionably government institutions. But they are a particular *kind* of government institution. Their identities owe as much or more to their status as libraries as to their status as publicly funded bodies. Libraries are not whatever governments declare them to be: they are a particular institution, dedicated to public use but constrained by their nature *as* libraries. Libraries are useful, then, in helping us to think about the limits of government control over First Amendment institutions—even when those institutions are publicly funded.

The case of libraries also carries one further lesson for First Amendment institutionalism, and a more hopeful one at that. Outside one major new issue—the role of laws requiring libraries to provide Internet filters—and some fairly subsidiary issues, there are relatively few lower court cases dealing squarely with libraries' core functioning, and thus with their potential rights as First Amendment institutions.[10] Part of the reason for this may be that the Supreme Court has provided so little guidance that litigants don't wish to throw the dice by pursuing litigation. But a major part of the reason is more encouraging: lawmakers and public officials, outside the messy context of school libraries, may generally respect libraries' professionalism and expertise and recognize the fundamental contribution libraries make to public discourse, and so may seek to interfere relatively rarely.[11]

The treatment of libraries as First Amendment institutions thus offers another broad implication for First Amendment institutionalism in general. The relative *lack* of conflict here suggests that the institutional turn may be achievable without undue practical difficulties. Not every move toward institutionalism raises insuperable questions about definitions, boundaries, or limits. In some areas, at least, lawmakers and public officials may already demonstrate respect for the unique infrastructural contributions that these institutions make to our system of public discourse, and for the most part are willing to leave them alone, even when they are publicly funded.

History, Values, and Professionalism

Libraries are closely related to two of the oldest First Amendment institutions: universities and churches. Many of civilization's earliest record-keeping efforts involved religious documents, and some ancient libraries operated along what we might think of as an academic model.

The library has long been a fundamental part of the American social landscape. The central figures of the early American Republic who championed the press and the university also championed the library. The eighteenth century saw a proliferation of libraries.[12] The movement to create genuinely "public" libraries, run by the government for the use of everyone, exploded in the late nineteenth and early twentieth centuries.

Libraries were consistently linked to the health of American democracy. Benjamin Franklin, who helped establish one such institution in 1731, argued that libraries helped make "the common tradesman and farmer as intelligent as most gentlemen from other countries, and perhaps contributed to the stand so generally made throughout the colonies in defense of their privileges."[13] Vartan Gregorian, the head of the New York Public Library in the 1980s, spoke for this idea when he called the library "a critical element in the

free exchange of information at the heart of our democracy."[14] Public libraries were also a major force in the assimilation of immigrants, bringing them
into literacy, citizenship, and appreciation for the "American way of life."[15]
One such immigrant was Justice Felix Frankfurter, who "learned English by
reading newspapers in the New York Public Library."[16] Thus, libraries served
both democratic development and individual self-fulfillment.

Like the press, libraries were literally infrastructural, encoded in American law.[17] Copyright law's "fair use" doctrine has long permitted libraries to
copy and disseminate reading materials. And assumptions about the institutional role of the library in public discourse were woven into the "communications infrastructure," forging a close link between the library's social
and legal meaning.[18]

None of this means the library has been static. Libraries have long
debated their own role. One such debate was over whether the library should
serve as a "distillation" of the finest books or should collect as many books
as possible.[19] Another concerned the role of librarians: should the librarian
be a neutral facilitator, helping readers find anything they want, or a moral
instructor, steering them only to what is edifying?

These tensions manifested themselves in internal struggles among
librarians as their work became increasingly professionalized.[20] When
the American Library Association (ALA) was founded in 1876, its leaders
"endorsed the librarian as moral censor."[21] That same year, a report from a
graduate school of library science declared that public libraries must always
work "in the direction of moral and social improvement." On the other side,
librarians increasingly advocated a competing model, sometimes called the
"universal model," which viewed the library's role as exposing readers to a
"multitude of differing opinions."[22] The librarian should facilitate readers'
own explorations, not substitute a particular moral vision on their behalf.

Despite this tension, the fundamental debate was over what role the
librarian should play, not the state. Neither side necessarily sought government intervention; both focused on professional *self*-regulation. In short,
the debate was over what librarians should do as professionals, not what the
government should do to libraries. For proponents of both the moral and
the universal models, primary responsibility lay with librarians, who knew
best how to address the library's needs and were guided by developing professional norms. Their work was considered a "science," as indicated by the

establishment of schools of "library and information science" in universities. And it was increasingly seen as the work of professionals, not amateur curators.[23]

The universalists won the debate. The librarian's task was to develop "more perfect ways" of organizing information "so that the researcher would have the best possible chance of finding what was desired."[24] This professional self-conception was well established by the time the ALA, in its Library Bill of Rights in 1939, emphasized the "special institutional role of the library in providing both the substance of intellectual materials to read as well as a space in which to do it safely."[25] The fundamental tenets of the librarian's role became the professionalization of methods of selecting and classifying library materials[26] and opposition to public or private censorship.[27] In sum, libraries have long been recognized as a fundamental part of the social infrastructure of public discourse, characterized by professional norms and self-regulation.

Libraries and the Supreme Court

The courts have long recognized libraries' vital role in the infrastructure of public discourse, but when confronted directly by such cases they have done a poor job of capturing what that role entails. Consider, for example, Chief Justice William Rehnquist's plurality opinion for the Court in *United States v. American Library Association*. In describing the "role of libraries in our society," Rehnquist cited the argument of a book published in 1930— almost a decade before the drafting of the Library Bill of Rights—that the librarian's aim is "to give the public, not everything it wants, but the best that it will read or use to advantage."[28] This is like citing the Stamp Act of 1765 to explain the rights and liberties of American citizens, without mentioning the Declaration of Independence.

Two key Supreme Court decisions discuss the relationship between libraries and the First Amendment. Both are worth examining, although neither provides much guidance.

The first, *Board of Education, Island Trees Union Free School District No. 26 v. Pico*, involved a school library, and so raised issues that are imperfectly applicable to freestanding libraries. Several members of a local school board attended a conference sponsored by a group called Parents of New York

United, at which they were given lists of "objectionable" books. Back home, they ordered the removal of several books from school libraries in the district, colorfully calling them "anti-American, anti-Christian, anti-Sem[i]tic, and just plain filthy." After controversy ensued, the board appointed a committee of parents and school staff to review the books. The committee recommended retaining some, removing others, and making one available only with parental approval. The board overrode the committee and decided instead to remove most of the books altogether.[29] A group of students sued.

There was no majority opinion for the Court. The plurality opinion, written by Justice William Brennan, stressed the narrow ground of the opinion: it dealt only with the *removal* from school libraries of books originally placed there by the school authorities, or without objection from them," not the *acquisition* of books. Brennan acknowledged that courts should generally refrain from interfering in the decisions of local school officials, but said this deference has its limits. Although "all First Amendment rights accorded to students must be construed 'in light of the special characteristics of the school environment,'" those rights carry more weight in the context of "the special characteristics of the school *library*."[30]

In that context, Justice Brennan wrote, "the First Amendment rights of students may be directly and sharply implicated by the removal of books from the shelves of a school library," not least because the First Amendment guarantees not only the right to speak but, in some contexts, "'the right to receive information and ideas.'" While schools must have freedom to make choices about the curriculum, that near-absolute discretion cannot extend "into the school library and the regime of voluntary inquiry that there holds sway." School boards enjoy "significant discretion to determine the content of their school libraries," especially with regard to the *acquisition* of books, but cannot exercise their discretion to *remove* books "simply because they dislike the ideas contained in those books." On the facts, and in light of the board's departure from any "established, regular, and facially unbiased procedures for the review of controversial materials," the plurality refused to dismiss the case in favor of the board.[31]

Justice Harry Blackmun partly concurred with the plurality judgment, but wrote separately to explain his "somewhat different perspective on the nature of the First Amendment right involved." In his view, the case turned solely on the principle that "the State may not . . . deny access to an idea simply because state officials disapprove of that idea for partisan or political reasons." The lure of acontextuality influenced his view. He did not believe any right at issue in the case was "somehow associated with the peculiar nature of the school library." Rather, the principle that should apply here, as in any other free speech dispute, was the institutionally agnostic one that government action "calculated to suppress novel ideas or concepts is fundamentally antithetical to the values of the First Amendment."[32]

Four justices dissented, and each wrote an opinion. Justice Lewis Powell saw the case as a school case, not a library case, emphasizing that local school officials "should have the responsibility for determining the educational policy of the public schools." Likewise, Justice Sandra Day O'Connor argued, "If the school board can set the curriculum, select teachers, and determine initially what books to purchase for the school library, it surely can decide which books to discontinue or remove from the school library."[33]

Chief Justice Warren Burger wrote that the plurality's argument for a right to receive information had no natural stopping point and would lead just as easily to "a constitutional 'right' of the people to have public libraries," a prospect he found absurd. He scoffed at the distinction between acquisition and removal decisions, which, he wrote, turned "a coincidence of timing" into "the basis of a constitutional holding." Burger, like Powell, saw *Pico* as a school case, not a library case; he saw public schools not as a professional enterprise but as a political one—a "democracy in a microcosm."[34] He would have left the decision entirely in the hands of the school board.[35]

Justice Rehnquist, in his dissenting opinion, "cheerfully concede[d] that it would be unconstitutional for a school board to remove books for "narrowly partisan" reasons. But this was not such an extreme case. Rather, it involved "the role of government as educator, as compared with the role of government as sovereign." In its role as educator, the government necessarily made content-based speech distinctions, which should not be second-guessed by judges. Rehnquist rejected the notion that government's role as educator might be different in the context of the school library, arguing that libraries, like any other aspect of public schools, are "not designed for freewheeling inquiry," but rather serve an "inculcative role" that lies within the discretion of the school board.[36]

Pico leaves libraries with no clear guidance. The only common ground is that government regulations involving "blatant political orthodoxy" will face strict scrutiny.[37] But that conclusion does not depend on any special qualities of the library as such. It is an acontextual rule, a general principle affecting government regulation in all its forms. On its own, it does little to help us resolve cases in which acquisition or removal decisions are made by librarians themselves for professional reasons.[38]

If we focus on the plurality opinion, we find slightly more guidance: book acquisition decisions are entitled to broad discretion, while book removal decisions will be scrutinized more carefully by the courts. But Justice Brennan offers little justification for that distinction. As I explain below, there *are* stronger justifications for this distinction, but they remain at best half-glimpsed in Brennan's opinion. For the most part, *Pico* is, rightly or wrongly, far more about schools than about libraries. Although Brennan stresses "the special characteristics of the school *library*,"[39] for most of the justices, *Pico* is about the *school* library. Any guidance it offers to libraries as such is incidental.

The Supreme Court's 2003 decision in *United States v. American Library Association* addressed the role and legal status of public libraries more directly. As with *Pico*, however, the Court's decision was fractured, and its clarity on the First Amendment rights of public libraries was rendered more uncertain, largely due to the doctrinal posture of the case. In part because of the acontextual rules that framed the case, involving unconstitutional conditions and public forums, *ALA* ended up presenting a refracted and distorted image of the library, not a clear and direct one.

ALA involved the Children's Internet Protection Act (CIPA), legislation designed to "address the problems associated with the availability of Internet pornography in public libraries." Congress, which had provided funding intended to enhance public libraries' access to the Internet, became concerned that this funding was "facilitating access to illegal and harmful pornography." CIPA required any public library receiving the funding to install filtering technology designed to prevent library patrons' access to obscene images and child pornography (both of which may be proscribed under the First Amendment) and to limit minors' access to "harmful" images.[40] These conditions were challenged by the American Library Association and by one public library.

Chief Justice Rehnquist's plurality opinion began by summarizing unconstitutional condition doctrine: Congress is free to attach conditions to its spending programs, but it cannot "induce the recipient to engage in activities that would themselves be unconstitutional." Accordingly, he focused on whether public libraries *themselves* could choose to use filtering software. This led to his call to examine "the role of libraries in our society." That role, he said, "has never been to provide universal coverage. Instead, public libraries seek to provide materials that would be of the greatest direct benefit or interest to the community." Libraries must be *selective.* Their choices require the exercise of the "discretion that public libraries must have to fulfill their traditional mission."[41]

The plurality put that conclusion to surprising use. Focusing on whether librarians could voluntarily impose filtering conditions, rather than on whether the government could impose conditions *on* libraries, ended up hurting the libraries' case. Rehnquist argued that in some contexts, "the government has broad discretion to make content-based judgments in deciding what private speech to make available to the public." The word "government" is crucial here. For the plurality, public libraries may serve a special function, but they are still the "government." Indeed, because they are government entities, it is not even clear they have *any* First Amendment rights. All Congress was doing with its funding restrictions was ensuring that these public bodies "fulfill their traditional role of obtaining material of requisite and appropriate quality for educational and informational purposes."[42] It was helping libraries to do what they would do of their own accord. CIPA thus did not impose an unconstitutional condition.

Two arguments stood in the plurality's way, and it made short work of them. The first was the idea that the public library might be treated as a public forum, one in which the people have an interest in the free flow of information. To the plurality, however, public forum doctrine was "out of place in the context of this case." Libraries do not "encourage a diversity of views from private speakers"; they furnish only "materials of requisite and appropriate quality." Since the library was not a public forum, the filtering requirement could not violate public forum doctrine. Second, there was the *Pico*-like suggestion that the imposition of Internet filters is more like a removal decision than an acquisition decision and that public libraries have "less discretion in deciding which Internet materials to make available than in making book selections." The plurality flatly rejected this argument.[43]

Two justices concurred in the judgment. For Justice Anthony Kennedy, the case turned on the uncontested fact that an adult patron could, consistently with the law, request the library to unblock the filtered material.[44] For Justice Stephen Breyer, the filtering condition paralleled the kinds of "editing" functions that libraries perform as a matter of course. He would have applied "intermediate scrutiny" to such decisions, asking "whether the harm to speech-related interests is disproportionate in light of both the justifications and the potential alternatives." As long as adults were able to request libraries to unblock Internet filters, he concluded, any burden on First Amendment rights was "comparatively small" and proportionate, given the important government aim of restricting access to materials that were illegal or harmful to minors.[45]

For Justice David Souter, who dissented, the key question was "whether a local library could itself constitutionally impose [similar] conditions on the content otherwise available to an adult patron through an Internet connection, at a library terminal provided for public use." In Souter's view, such a requirement would be an impermissible content-based restriction on speech; it would "simply be censorship." He rejected the plurality's effort to equate those restrictions with the kinds of selection decisions libraries inevitably make. Although libraries make selective acquisition decisions, they do so because they have limited resources: "[t]here is only so much money and so much shelf space." But the use of Internet filters "defies comparison to the process of acquisition."[46] The library's single, initial "acquisition" decision is the choice to make access to the *whole* Internet available. Once it has Internet access, its resources are unlimited and it need not make further selection decisions with respect to the available material.

Nor did Justice Souter agree with the plurality that these restrictions were consistent with the library's traditional mission. If anything, he wrote, the "[i]nstitutional history of public libraries in America discloses an evolution toward a general rule, now firmly rooted, that any adult entitled to use the library has access to any of its holdings." Contrary to the plurality's view that libraries did not exist to provide universal coverage, Souter argued that the profession itself understood the library's job as one of providing "all people . . . access to all ideas." Thus, there was "no support for [Internet filters] in the historical development of library practice." Beyond this, he stated bluntly, "we can smell a rat when a library blocks material already in its control. . . . Content-based blocking and removal tell us something that mere absence [of a book] from the shelves does not." Acquisition choices, at least in a universe of finite resources, involve complex decisions that the courts should not second-guess. But the "difference between choices to keep out and choices to throw out is . . . enormous." Souter would have affirmed *Pico*'s distinction between book acquisitions and removals, classified the filtering condition as a removal, and subjected it to strict scrutiny as "the censorship it presumptively is."[47]

Justice John Paul Stevens also dissented. Like the plurality, he agreed that libraries could "experiment with filtering software as a means of curtailing children's access to Internet Web sites displaying sexually explicit images." For Stevens, however, it was a wholly different question whether the federal government could "*impose* that requirement" on the nation's libraries.[48] In his view, it could not.

Part of Stevens's dissent consisted of standard, institutionally agnostic doctrinal analysis. The second half of his analysis, however, focused on libraries themselves. Stevens likened libraries to universities, suggesting that both require autonomy to make basic decisions in light of their mission.[49] A statute directly imposing limits on that autonomy would be unconstitutional, he argued, and it was "equally clear that the First Amendment protects libraries from being denied funds for refusing to comply with an identical rule." He acknowledged that unconstitutional conditions doctrine generally does not prevent the government from constraining its employees' official speech, but he saw public libraries as "an important medium of communication," not merely a sector of government speech designed to "foster or transmit any particular governmental message." CIPA's funding restrictions would "distort[ ] that medium."[50]

ALA produced five opinions and no majority. Unlike *Pico*, it directly addresses libraries. But *ALA* is distorted by unconstitutional conditions doctrine, which ends up producing a Bizarro version of the library. The guidance *ALA* provides about the First Amendment status of libraries is ultimately not much better than what we get from *Pico*.

Nevertheless, *ALA* does offer substantial consensus on one point, namely that library cases turn, "in the first instance, on what a library is and how it is understood to function"—that is, on "how the Court characterizes the social meaning of libraries."[51] Both the plurality and the dissenters agreed that libraries function in unique ways and that their job necessarily involves the use of discretion in deciding what materials to make available. For the plurality, however, libraries serve something like a moral function, akin to the nineteenth-century model of the library: they exercise discretion not just because of their limited resources, but because their mission involves selecting the most "appropriate" material. For Justice Souter, in contrast, libraries' role is to provide access to as much information as possible. Where scarce resources are not at issue, as is the case where the Internet is involved, any decision to place limits on access to materials is contrary to the library's mission and amounts to censorship.[52]

The justices also disagreed on the precise status of the library as a First Amendment actor. For the plurality, libraries are simply the government.[53] The filtering condition is thus an unexceptional instance of government imposing limits on its own speech. Indeed, for the plurality, it is not clear that public libraries have any First Amendment rights at all. But for Justices Souter and Stevens, libraries are distinct institutions—a distinct "medium of communication"—that must be understood in their own unique terms. To impose restrictions on information beyond those the libraries voluntarily put in place would distort the functioning of those institutions.

So there is *some* agreement in *ALA:* libraries must be considered in light of their own professional function. Beyond that, there is chaos. The question is whether the institutional turn can bring greater clarity to this area.

Libraries as First Amendment Institutions

Most legal scholars who have examined the role and rights of libraries have converged on roughly the same idea: Courts should defer to libraries as *professional* entities. We should treat them much the same way we treat universities, whose professional judgments are protected by academic freedom and entitled to substantial legal autonomy.

This idea was advanced well before *Pico* and *ALA*. In 1975, Robert O'Neil proposed a concept of "library freedom," similar to that of academic freedom, which would include "all the elements vital to the exercise of a librarian's professional judgment and responsibility."[54] In 1993, a decade before *ALA*, Rodney Smolla argued that cases involving libraries should be driven by a "professionalism principle," under which "decisions concerning the content of speech in institutions such as libraries" should be committed to "the sound discretion of professionals in the field," who would select or remove books according to "the professional criteria that have evolved within their areas of expertise."[55]

More recently, Jim Chen has argued for the importance of treating "the law of librarianship as a branch of First Amendment jurisprudence." Courts should favor the universalist model of the library over the selective, morally inculcative model. They should respect the "subtle and complex craft" of "librarianship" and provide "[a]ggressive protection against political interference in library management."[56] And Marc Jonathan Blitz has argued that libraries, like universities, "may need [to] be assured significant operational autonomy from the majoritarian institutions that create and fund them."[57] Blitz agrees that libraries' First Amendment rights cannot be properly addressed by public forum doctrine, but observes that this "tells us only that libraries cannot have precisely the same kind of protection as parks; it does not tell us what kinds of protections they *should* have." His principle of "library autonomy," like O'Neil's "library freedom," analogizes libraries to universities in order to create a space in which libraries are free to follow their own professional principles.[58]

That is essentially the view taken by First Amendment institutionalism. Libraries are "(relatively) easily identifiable and play a special role in knowledge acquisition."[59] They play an evolving and complex, but not unbounded or unfamiliar, role in our infrastructure of public discourse. Like all institutions, libraries evolve, but the broad outlines of their purpose and function have remained fairly stable through the ages. They are efforts to store and organize the records of human experience and make them accessible to others. The library is a "ritual representation of collective wisdom."[60] It makes the public discourse of the present and the future possible by gathering together the public discourse of the past and the present.

Libraries share another quality of First Amendment institutions: the capacity for self-regulation. They have undergone the same process of professionalization, the same development of norms, practices, and ethics, as universities and other First Amendment institutions. Librarians have always argued about what to include and exclude and how to organize and collect materials. But their debates have become increasingly *professional,* subject to the evolution and enforcement of professional norms. These factors make libraries strong candidates for the kind of autonomous status championed by First Amendment institutionalism.

At the level of legal doctrine, treating libraries as First Amendment institutions means treating library decisions as professional decisions to be made within the institution itself, according to professional principles and in keeping with the institution's role and traditions.[61] The role of government and the courts should essentially be one of abstention and noninterference.

This institutional approach does a better job than traditional doctrine of explaining the distinction between acquisition and removal, although it ultimately insulates both kinds of decision from political control or judicial review. As Justice Souter observed in *ALA*, libraries have "only so much money and so much shelf space," and their acquisition decisions are therefore both "necessary and complex."[62] It is impossible for any single library to acquire every book that exists. Even the libraries with the greatest resources and the most capacious storage capacities are still holding out teacups in a deluge to catch what drops they can. Libraries have responded by professionalizing decisions about what information to acquire, turning these decisions into something halfway between a science and an art—a very apt description of professionalism. Those decisions require the exercise of professional judgment. They necessarily involve distinctions based on content, and thus defy the usual First Amendment doctrinal categories.[63] Absent an obvious departure from professional procedures, these decisions should not be second-guessed by courts.

Removal questions, too, are bounded by professional considerations.[64] If they differ from acquisition decisions, the difference is that the boundaries between sound and unsound decisions to remove books are easier for the courts to police. Once a book is acquired, there are fewer legitimate reasons to remove it or make it inaccessible. As Justice Souter wrote, "we can smell a rat" when a library "removes books from its shelves for reasons having nothing to do with wear and tear, obsolescence, or lack of demand. Content-based blocking and removal tell us something that mere absence from the shelves does not."[65]

My point is not that we should impose a binary rule like that of *Pico*, subjecting acquisition decisions to rational basis review and removal decisions to strict scrutiny. That sort of distinction is helpful, but it still relies on a crude doctrinal rule of thumb instead of respecting libraries as institutions. On an institutional view, both acquisition and removal decisions should largely be left to the autonomy of the library. As we have seen, however, the autonomy of First Amendment institutions is not absolute. Courts operating in a responsive and reflexive fashion should at least ensure that removal decisions are made according to the professional judgments of librarians and that they follow the institution's established procedural and professional norms.

A corollary point is that such policy decisions should be made by libraries themselves. That may seem obvious, but it is not. Public libraries are professionally run, but publicly funded and responsible to elected bodies. Regulation and judicial scrutiny in this area thus involve a potential tension between "[professional] insulation and political accountability."[66] That tension is evident in the plurality opinion in *ALA*, which on the one hand argues that it is important to "examine the role of libraries in our society" and on the other subsumes libraries within the broad category of government speakers.[67] It is exacerbated by the generally acontextual bent of First Amendment doctrine, which lumps the "government," or "government speakers," into a fairly undifferentiated category.

The institutional turn rejects that broad and clumsy categorization. It suggests that respecting libraries as First Amendment institutions requires insulating library practices and decisions from political control. Library decisions may be entitled to judicial deference when they have been "made by a certain cadre of professionals"—namely, librarians—but not when there has been "external influence in this process by non-professionals," such as elected library boards or city officials.[68] What entitles public libraries' decisions to judicial deference and legal autonomy is not that they are *government* decisions, but that they are *library* decisions—decisions made according to the professional norms of the institution and for the end of furthering the library's place within our infrastructure of public discourse.

Libraries deal with a host of issues other than acquisition and removal, from the inclusion or exclusion of particular patrons to policies involving public meeting rooms. Those decisions, too, should more or less be left to the discretion of libraries in their institutional capacity. It is more understandable that courts have decided such cases under public forum doctrine,[69] since these cases involve the library as a gathering place, not a professional enterprise. But that is still the wrong approach. The question in these cases should not be whether a public library is a public forum, let alone what type of public forum it is; rather, it should be whether the libraries are exercising sound professional discretion, according to the standard norms of the profession, in making these decisions. Those standards already track what the courts would say anyway.[70] Absent special cause for concern, libraries should be left to make these judgments for themselves.

The Public-Private Divide

Private libraries enjoy nearly absolute First Amendment protections under current doctrine and so do not depend strongly on institutional considerations.[71] Public libraries are different. They fall on the "public" side of the "public-private" divide. To give them a special right to institutional autonomy *against* the government actors that support them raises difficult questions that the Supreme Court has not yet resolved.[72] Our discussion of libraries as First Amendment institutions thus helps to illuminate a broader issue: the relationship between First Amendment institutionalism and the public-private distinction.

The best way to address that issue is to emphasize the *institutional* nature of a First Amendment institution, not its source of funding. From this perspective, the question of whether public libraries have a First Amendment right to institutional autonomy despite their status as creatures of the government is less troubling than it sounds.[73] The public-private distinction is a crude sorting device, designed to distinguish institutions that are primarily subject to political control from institutions that are entitled to assert their own constitutional rights. It may have value, but it is still only a crude mechanism, and it is simply out of place in some contexts.

Libraries are one such context. I say "libraries," not "public libraries," because for our purposes public and private libraries are largely indistinguishable. Both serve the same ends, are informed by the same traditions, and observe the same professional norms. Would-be librarians do not choose between attending schools of "private library and information science" or schools of "public library and information science." Both types of libraries largely play the same fundamental role in public discourse, a role that has little to do with their public or private status.

Is this unfair to the government? Is it wrong to tell the government that, while it is not constitutionally required to establish any public libraries, if it does so its ability to regulate them will be limited? Might that have the perverse effect of discouraging governments from establishing public librar-ies at all? That possibility is remote, for reasons that demonstrate why the institutional approach does not unfairly limit the government. Public librar-ies exist because there is a long tradition of valuing libraries, for the unfet-tered access to reading materials they offer to patrons who wish to prepare themselves for citizenship, to arm themselves for participation in public dis-course, or just to "quietly and briefly expos[e] themselves to unfamiliar ideas in a library's shelves."[74] Public libraries exist because the *public* recognizes their vital infrastructural role and is willing to support it.

That is what the government "buys," so to speak, when it establishes a public library: public access to an *institution*. It does not buy just any "gov-ernment speaker"; it buys a particular kind of institution, with a particular institutional role and a specific set of institutional practices and professional constraints. Laws that inhibit public libraries, as an institution, from mak-ing the kinds of decisions that are "central to their own role in the market-place of ideas" are rightly suspect.[75] The government, having committed to the support of a library, cannot radically alter the conditions under which libraries operate, including conditions of professionalism and autonomy. Governments need not fund public libraries at all, and they may decide to close them down. But as long as the library doors are open, the government must accept them *as* libraries and treat them as such. As I noted at the begin-ning of the chapter, there are relatively few cases in which public authorities seek to intervene directly in the operation of libraries. Perhaps that fact, in addition to suggesting that lawmakers are capable of recognizing and respecting some of the key precepts of First Amendment institutionalism, also suggests that the government generally accepts this bargain.

In short, libraries, like universities, "occupy a special niche in our consti-tutional tradition" and are entitled to a proper measure of autonomy.[76] Just as the government cannot tell a public university precisely what and how to teach, so it cannot operate a public library without respecting the autonomy of the library as an institution.

9

Where People and Ideas Meet: Associations

Americans are prodigious joiners. There are hundreds of thousands of associations in the United States. Some 79 percent of Americans belong to one or more of them.[1] Although it has become common to lament the declining participation in civic and other associations,[2] they are far from an endangered species. Their importance should not be ignored.

Neither should their complexity. Researchers have distinguished between primary, secondary, and tertiary associations, depending on the nature of the personal contacts involved.[3] Courts and legal scholars have distinguished between "intimate," "expressive," and "non-expressive" associations,[4] and commercial and noncommercial associations.[5]

In recent years freedom of association has received growing attention from legal scholars. Much of the renewed interest dates back to the Supreme Court's 2000 decision in *Boy Scouts of America v. Dale*,[6] upholding the Boy Scouts' expulsion of a gay assistant scoutmaster despite a state antidiscrimination law. *Christian Legal Society v. Martinez*,[7] a 2010 case in which the Court upheld the right of a public law school to deny official status to a student group that excluded actively gay members, encouraged still more interest.

That both cases involved issues of gay rights is not a coincidence.[8] The expansion of equality of citizenship has been one of the central narratives of the American constitutional experience.[9] As Martin Luther King, Jr. put it, borrowing a maxim from the nineteenth-century abolitionist Theodore Parker, "The moral arc of the universe is long, but it bends toward justice."[10] Parker's words have become equally canonical in the equal rights struggle for gays and lesbians.[11] The conflict between freedom of association and civil rights does not mean that advocates of civil rights for particular groups necessarily oppose freedom of association: associations have been at the forefront of the gay rights movement, just as they were in the earlier civil rights movement. But it does show that freedom of association can involve tension between the constitutional values of equality and liberty.

The tension will be greatest in cases regarding the scope and limits of state sovereignty. To say that associations have the power to resist the authority of the state is to contest the limits of state power. This chapter's discussion of associations and their role within the institutional First Amendment is thus ultimately a meditation on the nature and number of sovereigns in our society and the limits of their sovereignty. As with our discussion of churches as First Amendment institutions in Chapter 7, one can support an institutional turn within freedom of association for largely instrumental purposes without accepting all of these ideas and their implications. But the larger questions raised here are still worth exploring and may provide some insights into broader questions involved by the institutional turn, such as the nature and status of the state, the deeper structure of our social order, and the reasons why proper definitions of public discourse should not focus narrowly on formal democratic self-government alone.

Two more things may be said by way of introduction. First, as I have emphasized before, the institutional turn in the First Amendment is not an unqualified good. Freedom of association has benefits, but it also has a dark side—namely, the ways in which associations can resist the state's ability to vindicate equality and other important social goods. To conclude that the benefits outweigh the costs does not require us to deny that there are costs. But the courts' current approach in this area is deeply problematic. Simultaneously acontextual in theory and context-driven in practice, it is riddled with inconsistency. The institutional approach may at least lay a firmer foundation for freedom of association and make some of the contradictions in current doctrine more visible.

Second, focusing on associations as First Amendment institutions helps us to explore some of the broader practical questions raised by First

Amendment institutionalism. It offers further guidance on the central question of how to define First Amendment institutions and their limits. It also helps us consider the comparative role of the courts and the institutions themselves in policing those limits. Finally, it sheds light on how we should address conflicts *between* First Amendment institutions: cases in which the interests of different First Amendment institutions are at odds with one another.

History and Theory

American social thought notes our propensity to join groups, but it also celebrates our "rugged individualism." Although "our most basic myths" lean in favor of individualism, both are longstanding traits and the tension between them is not new.[12]

The centrality of associations to our country's social infrastructure has been recognized from the beginning. Associations exploded in number and importance in the period around the birth of the American Republic.[13] Many celebrated them; others feared them. George Washington, in his farewell address to Congress, denounced "all combinations and Associations" that sought "to direct, controul, counteract, or awe the regular deliberation of the Constituted authorities." These groups, he argued, threatened to "make the public administration the Mirror of the ill concerted and incongruous projects of faction, rather than the organ of consistent and wholesome plans digested by common councils and modified by mutual interests." James Madison took a more nuanced view, fearing political factions but arguing that their power should be constrained by diffusing them across an extended republic rather than suppressing them.[14]

A generation or so later, Alexis de Tocqueville wrote, "In no country in the world has the principle of association been more successfully used or applied to a greater multitude of objects than in America." He noted that "Americans of all ages, all conditions, and all dispositions constantly form associations. . . . Wherever at the head of some new undertaking you see the government in France, or a man of rank in England, in the United States you will be sure to find an association."[15]

That last sentence contains the core of Tocqueville's insight into the profusion of associations in America. Modern writers view freedom of association as being in conflict with equality.[16] But for Tocqueville, associations were both a product of American equality and a necessary counterpart to it. In the absence of an aristocratic caste, associations were necessary "to prevent the despotism of faction or the arbitrary power of a prince." Without the habit of associating for common purposes, citizens of democratic states might lapse into passivity or even "barbarism." Through their involvement in associations, Americans learned "the art of rendering the dangers of freedom less formidable."[17]

The British pluralists, whom I mentioned in Chapter 7, have much to teach us about freedom of association and its relationship to the institutional turn.[18] The legal historian and early pluralist Frederic Maitland, drawing on the work of the German scholar Otto von Gierke, emphasized "the ubiquitous reality and vital importance of group entities." Maitland described a "line of advance" in legal thought that was "no longer from status to contract but through contract to something that contract cannot explain, and for which our best, if an inadequate, name is the personality of the organized group."[19] Rather than a single sovereign bearing the label of the state, "there were in fact many sovereignties operating in a parallel way in any given society." For the pluralists, modern society was "a network of associations," a collection of multiple sovereigns. It was a mistake to treat these associations as if they existed at the sufferance of the state.[20]

That was so for more or less practical reasons. To be sure, there was a metaphysical air to some of the pluralists' writings, owing in part to the religious concerns that animated writers like J. N. Figgis.[21] But their point was also wholly practical and broadly consistent with the institutional turn. In arguing that the law should recognize the existence of non-state associations and that the regulatory power of the state cannot be permitted to extinguish them, they were also making the same point we saw in Part One of this book: that law should not become too unrooted from social fact and from the reality of public discourse as we actually experience it—including our experience of public discourse in and through institutions and associations. The law, they suggested, "must recognise reality if it is to be an effective instrument of social control."[22] And a central aspect of our social reality is that groups exist, have a life of their own, and play a substantial role in individual and social life. These are not metaphysical assertions but "social facts."[23] These facts must "become the basis of our laws, as . . . of our life."[24]

In short, if law is to be responsive to "the life that surrounds it," if it is to "close[ ] the gap between the world described in law and the world in which men live," it must be able to acknowledge and accommodate the role played by associations in social life and public discourse, rather than leaving those entities completely at the mercy of the state.[25]

The pluralists had their opponents, whose criticisms we will take up in due course. For now, our point is simply that the argument that associations are not merely lesser subjects of the state is hardly novel, although it has usually been a minority view.

"Between the I's"

Almost 70 years ago, in *Thomas v. Collins*, Justice Wiley Rutledge wrote: "It was not by accident or coincidence that the rights to freedom in speech and press were coupled in a single guaranty with the rights of the people peaceably to assemble and to petition for redress of grievances. All these, though not identical, are inseparable. They are cognate rights, and therefore united in the First [Amendment's] assurance."[26] Aviam Soifer calls Rutledge's opinion "rich in dynamic, relational language" and significant for adopting a "structural approach to First Amendment rights" in which association is not a mere by-product of freedom of speech but an independent right. He also observes that it is "nearly forgotten today." Instead, Soifer writes, modern freedom of association law is caught "between the 'i's'": limited to instances of "*intimate* or *instrumentally* expressive association."[27]

Consider an influential Supreme Court decision from 1984, *Roberts v. United States Jaycees*.[28] The Jaycees, a large voluntary association devoted to networking and training for young businessmen, admitted women in some capacities but not as full members. The Minnesota Department of Human Rights sued them under state human rights legislation that forbade discrimination in "places of public accommodation."

Writing for the Court, Justice William Brennan upheld the application of the law to the Jaycees. Brennan distinguished two categories of freedom of association. The first was "intimate association": the freedom to "enter into and maintain certain intimate human relationships" such as marriage. Brennan treated intimate association as part of the right to privacy shoehorned into the Due Process Clause of the Fourteenth Amendment. The second category was "freedom of expressive association": the "right to associate for the purpose of engaging in those activities protected by the First Amendment—speech, assembly, petition for the redress of grievances, and the exercise of religion." This right, he wrote, was important but not unlimited.[29]

In particular, Brennan focused on whether the forced inclusion of women would significantly affect the Jaycees' *expressive* interests. The human rights law, he said, reflected "the State's strong historical commitment to eliminating discrimination" and was "unrelated to the suppression of expression." He concluded that the record did not show that "admission of women as full voting members will impede the organization's ability to . . . disseminate its preferred views."[30]

Justice Sandra Day O'Connor wrote separately to emphasize her view that the majority's approach "accords insufficient protection to expressive associations and places inappropriate burdens on groups claiming the protection of the First Amendment." For O'Connor, the Court's decision should have turned on a dichotomy between "commercial associations," which she would have accorded minimal protection, and "expressive associations," which should enjoy "complete control over [their] membership." She saw the Jaycees as a commercial association, not an expressive one.[31]

Roberts has two central implications. First, freedom of association is valued not for its own sake, but for its contribution to *speech*. This strain runs through Brennan's whole opinion. He writes: "There can be no clearer example of an intrusion into the internal structure or affairs of an association than a regulation that forces the group to accept members it does not desire." But his primary concern is that such regulations "may impair the ability of the original members to *express* . . . those views that brought them together."[32] To borrow Marshall McLuhan's terminology, the association is merely a medium, a way of transmitting a message. The message is what matters.

Second, the full measure of constitutional protection is offered to associations only if they are "expressive associations," with the implication that courts get to decide whether the group is an expressive association or not. Even then, *Roberts* invites courts to determine the "preferred views" of the association and whether forcing it to include unwanted members will "impair" the dissemination of those views.[33]

Andrew Koppelman has ably summarized the message of *Roberts*: "if an association is organized to express a viewpoint, then constitutional difficulties are raised by a statute that requires it to accept unwanted members *if* that requirement would impair its ability to convey *its message*."³⁴ To extend Soifer's play on letters, judicial power resides in the "i's"—in the courts' power to decide *if* an association is organized to express a viewpoint, what *its* message is, and *if* the forced inclusion of unwanted members will impair that message. This allows Justice Brennan to conclude in a strained fashion that because the Jaycees' predominant "message" is the advancement of young businesspeople, forcing the group to include women will not impair its message. He is concerned only with whether the state can force an association to include "individuals with ideologies or philosophies different from those of its existing members,"³⁵ not with whether changing the makeup of the group will alter the association itself. Only the heaping on of judicial discretion to second-guess the Jaycees' message allows the *Roberts* majority to evade the obvious conclusion that the Jaycees' "voice" has been "undeniably altered" by the law.³⁶

Judicial Deference

Roberts was followed by other cases upholding the application of antidiscrimination laws to membership organizations.³⁷ But indications of a shift in the Court's approach surfaced a few years later, when the Court upheld the right of the organizers of a St. Patrick's Day parade in Boston to exclude a group whose members identified as gay, lesbian, and bisexual descendants of Irish immigrants.

The case, *Hurley v. Irish-American Gay, Lesbian and Bisexual Group of Boston,* was only a small step away from *Roberts.* If anything is an inherently expressive association, it is a parade. But the tone of the Court's opinion, written by Justice David Souter, was strikingly different. Souter forthrightly stated that an association need not assert "a narrow, succinctly articulable message [as] a condition of constitutional protection," lest the First Amendment fail to shield "the unquestionably shielded painting of Jackson Pollock, music of Arnold Schönberg, or Jabberwocky verse of Lewis Carroll." Furthermore, the parade organizers could not be deprived of protection simply because they had been "rather lenient in admitting [other] participants" to the parade while excluding the gay, lesbian, and bisexual group: "A private speaker does not forfeit constitutional protection simply by combining multifarious voices, or by failing to edit their themes to isolate an exact message as the exclusive subject matter of the speech." Quoting an earlier case, he added that "'*all* speech inherently involves choices of what to say and what to leave unsaid.'" The niceties of selection extend not only to the composition of a message, but also to what one refuses to say.[38]

Justice Souter's deference to the parade organizers *as* speakers—his willingness to give them leeway to "select the expressive units of the parade from potential participants," even where those units "may not produce a particularized message"—is significant. Just as significant is that the Court viewed that message from the *organizers'* perspective[39] and acknowledged the association's discretion to shape its message.

The Supreme Court's willingness to defer to "expressive associations" leapt to the forefront in *Boy Scouts of America v. Dale,* the most important decision on freedom of association in recent years. James Dale, an assistant scoutmaster, was expelled from the Boy Scouts of America when he came out as gay and was pictured in a local newspaper discussing his work on issues facing lesbian and gay youths. The letter explaining the revocation of his membership stated that the Scouts "specifically forbid membership to homosexuals."[40] Dale sued under a New Jersey antidiscrimination statute.

In a 5-4 decision, the Court upheld Dale's exclusion. Chief Justice William Rehnquist phrased the question as "whether applying New Jersey's public accommodations law in this way violates the Boy Scouts' First Amendment right of expressive association." The Court viewed the case as requiring it to determine whether the Boy Scouts was an expressive association, what views that association took on homosexuality, and whether requiring it to include Dale would "significantly affect the Boy Scouts' ability to advocate public or private viewpoints."[41]

Judicial deference strongly drove the decision. It took little work to conclude that because the Boy Scouts "seeks to transmit . . . a system of values," it was expressive.[42] The Court was equally deferential on the question of what those values were. The Boy Scouts says little publicly about homosexuality, and what little it says is not terribly clear.[43] For the majority, however, it was enough that the Boy Scouts had stated during the litigation that homosexuality was inconsistent with leadership in the Scouts.

On whether Dale's forced inclusion would impair the Boy Scouts' message, the Court was equally forthright: "As we give deference to an association's assertions regarding the nature of its expression, we must also give deference to an association's views of what would impair its expression." It emphasized that an association cannot avoid the application of antidiscrimination laws "simply by asserting that mere acceptance of a member from a particular group would impair its message." But in practice, given the Court's deference to the association, little more was needed. Because Dale was a "gay rights activist," his presence "would, at the very least, force the organization to send a message . . . that the Boy Scouts accepts homosexual conduct as a legitimate form of behavior." It would somehow "propound a point of view contrary to [the Boy Scouts'] beliefs."[44]

The majority curtly rejected the New Jersey Supreme Court's conclusion that the Boy Scouts' "message" had little to do with homosexuality, and thus would not be impaired by Dale's inclusion. The Scouts should not be forced to identify a highly particularized message. Even if the group mostly avoided speaking on sexual issues, it was still entitled to choose a "method of expression" that excluded openly gay leaders. Nor did it matter if there was internal dissent over the policy, as long as the leadership had staked out a position on the issue: "The fact that an organization does not trumpet its views from the housetops, or that it tolerates dissent within its ranks, does not mean that its views receive no First Amendment protection." That protection should be strong, even in the face of the state's interest in combating discrimination. The Court did not say it was applying strict scrutiny, but it appeared to do just that, summarily concluding, "The state interests embodied in New Jersey's public accommodations law do not justify such a severe intrusion on the Boy Scouts' rights to freedom of expressive association."[45]

Justice John Paul Stevens filed a furious dissent, plainly driven as much by his distaste for the Boy Scouts' policies as by his differences with the majority.[46] New Jersey's antidiscrimination statute, he wrote, by placing the state "in the vanguard in the fight to eradicate the cancer of unlawful discrimination of all types from our society," was "designed to replace prejudice with principle." The majority had failed to "accord this courageous State the respect that is its due."[47]

Stevens lambasted the majority for showing excessive deference to the group's description of its expressive message and its assertion that requiring the inclusion of gay scoutmasters would impair that message, emphasizing that the Court ought to engage in *independent inquiry* on these questions.

An organization making a claim of freedom of expressive association "must *at least* show it has adopted and advocated an *unequivocal* position inconsistent with a position advocated or epitomized by the person whom the organization seeks to exclude." Absent a searching and independent judicial inquiry on this point, "there would be no way to mark the proper boundary between genuine exercises of the right to associate . . . and sham claims that are simply attempts to insulate nonexpressive private discrimination." The majority's approach, Stevens warned, threatened to turn antidiscrimination law into "a nullity."[48]

With no trace of deference to the group, Stevens scrutinized its views and policies on homosexuality and concluded, "It is entirely clear that [the Boy Scouts] in fact expresses no clear, unequivocal message." He said the group might have a First Amendment right to "refrain from including debate and dialogue about homosexuality as part of its mission." But, like the *Roberts* Court, Stevens rejected the idea that including Dale would prevent it from discussing, or refusing to discuss, that subject. Dale's inclusion, he wrote, "sends no cognizable message to the Scouts or to the world." Stevens's conclusion was blunt: the Boy Scouts' desire to exclude Dale reflected an "atavistic" view about gays and lesbians, one "nourished by sectarian doctrine"; the Court's willingness to allow the group's desires to trump the state's antidiscrimination law would "'erect our prejudices into legal principles.'"[49]

The Value of Associations

Dale has elicited volumes of scholarly criticism and some fervent defenses, along with other commentaries that support the result but question its foundation, or that roughly favor the Court's approach but think the Boy Scouts should have lost for other reasons. The critics' most powerful charge is that *Dale,* if taken seriously, is limitless. Its near-total deference to associations threatens to undermine the entire structure of antidiscrimination law. Critics taking this line insist that any group making such a claim must at least demonstrate that it has a *clear* public message that could be *clearly* impaired by the forced inclusion of members.[50]

Any approach to freedom of association, to be sure, must confront the question of its limits. But we cannot assess its limits, or evaluate its costs and benefits, without understanding what associations contribute to society.

Their value extends beyond the communication of messages. Associations are important to our infrastructure of public discourse, but they are not important simply because they *involve* public discourse. Associations matter as much for the fact of belonging to them as they do for whatever messages they happen to express. We must move beyond the association as message and focus on the association as medium.

Associations serve many functions besides communicating messages. First and foremost, they are places where individual identities are formed: places of "soul-making," in Richard Garnett's words.[51] They are places where we find and make ourselves in relation with others. Like the "intimate" relationships that Justice Brennan lauded in *Roberts,* social relationships can be central to the formation of our identities.[52] Members who find value in the identity-forming aspect of an association may not care whether that association sends a message to anyone else.

Of course, the identity-forming aspects of associations generally do involve communication. But most of that communication is *within* the association, not between the association and the public. Members may begin from shared premises—an abiding interest in the literary works of Stephenie Meyer, say—and find consensus or disagreement within those shared premises (Team Edward or Team Jacob?). Through discussion with other members they may modify their views or become more strongly confirmed in them. They may find meaning in submitting to organizational authority, or in dissenting from within and trying to alter the group's direction. Indeed, even the act of *leaving* a group can be a powerful identity-forming move. In a sense, none of this is directly *public* discourse—it would be important to its members even if kept strictly confidential—but it is essential to it nonetheless. Associations are vital to the formation of individual citizens regardless of whether they engage in expressive activity toward the public.

We can add more layers to this. For one thing, it is a mistake to treat associations severally: to ask whether a person will benefit from being, say, a Boy Scout, or whether he will be crushed by being excluded. Most people belong to a variety of groups. Our identities are formed as much by our negotiations between these different aspects of our selves as they are by any one single group.[53]

Moreover, as Tocqueville observed, associations serve as training grounds for citizenship. They are not rigid and inflexible in their views.

Their views *evolve,* through constant negotiation among members and leadership. They are sites for potential cooperation and collective action, and for potential disagreement and dissent. Whether or not the association "speaks," its *members* are likely to learn how to speak by participating in the group, whether in agreement or disagreement. It is a mistake to assume that associations are most important when they speak with one voice. Often, what matters most is the compromises they make.[54]

Finally, associations serve a complex but essential *structural* role.[55] Like the other institutions we have examined, they form a fundamental part of the infrastructure of public discourse. Like those institutions, they do so by being in creative tension with their own members, with other institutions, and with the state. Thus, it is less important that associations convey a particular *message to others* than that they serve as a source of *meaning to their members,* and that this meaning is not dictated by the state. A healthy society depends upon both common and differing values. Associations serve as refuges from the state's encompassing tendencies and unifying values. They are sources of resistance and social change—potential "breakwaters, albeit irregular and ill-constructed, against the omnipotence of the state."[56] They are sources of values that might not otherwise be formed or heard, both challenging and refreshing the state and public discourse.[57]

The state should not be too imperial: it should not seek to make every sector of public and private life a reflection of its own values and procedures.[58] This is true for both instrumental and intrinsic reasons. Practically speaking, a state that imposes values on every corner of its realm risks becoming brittle, disconnected, and nonadaptive. Beyond this, though, lurks a broader point: the state's reach is not absolute. Just as we are multiple selves, formed by a host of associations—ideological, ethnic, religious, linguistic, social, cultural—so the state is ultimately only one among many sovereigns, one among a contending set of associations that offer independent sources of meaning.[59] Instrumentally, the state impoverishes itself when it seeks a monopoly over loyalty and meaning. Intrinsically, the state lacks the *right* to such a monopoly. It must acknowledge and respect the "norm-generating autonomy" of its fellow sovereign, the association.[60] Associations thus serve a structural role both within sovereignty and between different "sovereigns."

This means it is a mistake to focus too narrowly on the expressive role of associations, as Justice Brennan did in *Roberts.*[61] Associations serve too complex a role in the infrastructure of public discourse to be reduced to mere megaphones. They are formative as well as expressive. To require an association to send a clear and articulable message, or to impose the kind of intrusive scrutiny about its purpose and message that Justice Stevens recommended in his dissent in *Dale,* is to miss the point. It slights the essential sovereignty of associations themselves and the contributions they make to both self-sovereignty and popular or state sovereignty.

The Dark Side of Freedom of Association

If the message-based understanding of freedom of association is so flawed or incomplete, why do so many insist upon it? Why do some go even further and assert that the state may impose stringent limits even on genuinely expressive associations?[62]

One reason is the concern that a non-message-based approach to freedom of association, let alone one that treats associations as sovereigns, will undo important legal goals such as the elimination of invidious discrimination. This concern is valid. But it is a mistake to shape freedom of association law with only this single dilemma in mind. Doing so purports to solve the conflict between freedom of association and civil rights, but it does so only by failing to appreciate the full measure and meaning of human association. Reducing freedom of association to a form of speech may be an effective form of prophylaxis, but so is castration. It is not a genuinely *responsive* strategy, in the sense in which I have used that word.

More broadly, the resistance to a robust version of freedom of association arises from a fear of associations themselves. It stems from a fear that illiberal groups will use freedom of association to shield beliefs that run contrary to our liberal tradition and favor exclusion over inclusion.[63] It often involves the worry that associations will mistreat some of their own members and deny their own autonomy as individuals.[64]

Above all, these fears reflect the long shadow cast on the nation by race. They reflect both our long history of public and private subordination of African-Americans and other racial minorities, and the use of freedom of association to defend this subordination. These fears extend beyond race to include other minorities, particularly gays and lesbians. They lead to the suspicion that any strong defense of freedom of association is really just a "cover for bigotry."[65] That suspicion is evident in the connection that Andrew Koppelman draws between freedom of association and a "libertarian right to exclude" that he calls "racist to the core."[66] Defenders of freedom of association will understandably blanch at the accusation.

Judges have an additional concern. They are the voice of the state, and specifically the voice of generally applicable and institutionally agnostic principles. Associations defy easy incorporation into the acontextual architecture of judicial decision-making. They seem to involve nothing *but* context. Judges who are entranced by the lure of acontextuality will naturally resist their claims.

In particular, as guardians of state sovereignty, judges will resist the association's invocation of its own "sovereignty." Even though judicial doctrine sometimes celebrates the role of units smaller than the national government, such as the state governments enshrined in our system of federalism, it remains strongly attached to the idea that the formal sovereignty of governments constitutes the "definitional limit" of constitutionally recognized power.[67] Courts sometimes speak in terms that seem protective of associations, but for reasons that betray indifference to their actual nature and importance.[68]

We ought to reconsider these fears about freedom of association, and especially the judicial assertion of the imperial reach of the sovereign state. The concern that freedom of association will create "pathologies of decentralization"[69] has arguably become a pathology of its own. Kuyper was right: the state must not become "an octopus, which stifles the whole of life."[70] If liberalism is to mean anything, it cannot mean liberalism all the way down.[71] The liberal state must leave room for multiple groups, divided loyalties, and new sources of meaning. It must resist the temptation to "circumscrib[e] the nomos."[72]

Associations as First Amendment Institutions

Associations fit, albeit imperfectly, into the institutional matrix we explored in Part One. They contribute to the infrastructure of public discourse in ways that extend far beyond the content of any particular communication, or even the intention to communicate a particular message. They are places in which speech is formed and identities are shaped, in which citizens rehearse for public discourse, find modes of resistance to the state, and seek refuge from the pressures of public life. Like other First Amendment institutions, they are both dangerous and necessary.

An institutional approach to the First Amendment, one that "sees speech as embedded in and formed by a set of social practices" embodied in an array of infrastructural institutions rather than mechanical legal rules,[73] must find a place for associations. And it must do so at a structural level, not just on a case-by-case basis. Rather than focusing on whether an association in a given case is expressing a clearly articulated message, we should ask whether it *is* an association: an entity marked out for categorical treatment as a First Amendment institution.[74] Our concern should be with associational autonomy, not associational expression. That autonomy should include, as it did in the academic freedom cases discussed in Chapter 5, the right to exclude unwanted members.

Once the association is identified as a First Amendment institution, the reach of the state, and of the courts, is sharply reduced. The role switches from a directly regulatory function, in which the state is entitled to balance an association's right to liberty against competing constitutional values such as equality, to one of responsiveness, cooperation, and deference. As *Dale* suggests, the state should defer to "an association's assertions regarding the nature of its expression" and to its "view of what would impair its expression."[75]

If anything, the problem with *Dale*'s language is not its deference, but its emphasis on *expressive* association. The value of associations lies as much in "private conversation and joint *doing*" as it does in speech directed at others.[76] Courts should recognize that an association can be "expressive" in important ways whether its expression is public or private, externally or internally directed. The risk that this approach will give too much latitude to associations' own assertions about their purposes is outweighed by the need to control "the state's tendencies to dominate and control [associations] through the interpretations and meanings it assigns to a group's activities."[77] Judicial deference to an association's interpretation of its activities and needs is necessary to tame those tendencies. Courts should respect the idea that the state is not the only institution capable of creating meaning in our society.

Identifying and Limiting Associations

A major problem—perhaps the central problem—with freedom of association is the question of definition. How do we determine whether a particular association is entitled to freedom of association? The more robust that freedom is, the more important defining associations becomes. If we broadly protect freedom of association, we risk either granting too much freedom to too many groups or watering down that protection altogether.[78] If we are too narrow in defining associations, or in our understanding of what freedom of association entails, we risk sapping associations of their ability to serve an infrastructural role in public discourse.[79] We need to know whether the Ku Klux Klan is just like the NAACP for purposes of freedom of association, and whether either is just like AT&T, a law firm, or a local social club.

These definitional concerns arise with other First Amendment institutions as well. That is why courts have hesitated to grant the institutional press any special constitutional rights and why they have struggled to define the scope of the ministerial exception for religious institutions. But the problem is more pronounced with associations. The other institutions can be identified, more or less, through intuition and social knowledge. Associations are less clear-cut and more varied, embracing "expressive" and "non-expressive" associations, advocacy groups and corporations, bowling leagues and political parties. In considering freedom of association, we thus range beyond the core of First Amendment institutionalism and into its borderlands.

This raises a broader concern about the application of the institutional turn to freedom of association. One of the key factors supporting the autonomy of First Amendment institutions is their capacity for self-regulation. Given associations' diversity, it is difficult to point to their self-regulatory capacity with any assurance. Some have ample self-regulatory practices and traditions; others do not. Treating associations as First Amendment institutions thus raises the question of what role self-regulation should play in defining these institutions.

Courts and scholars have struggled to find a limiting principle for defining those associations that are entitled to heightened constitutional protection. The principle that prevailed in *Roberts* was the distinction between expressive and non-expressive associations. As we have seen, that distinction won't do. A competing approach has been that of Justice O'Connor, who focused on the distinction between commercial and noncommercial associations. That distinction, too, raises difficult questions.[80] Critics point out that many expressive associations, such as newspapers, are commercial enterprises, and not all noncommercial associations (say, bowling leagues) are genuinely expressive.[81] Nevertheless, a number of scholars consider this the best available approach to defining associations for purposes of the right to exclude members. They admit that no "comprehensive algorithm" exists to distinguish between "social and commercial associations," but they say this distinction is the best we can do.[82]

The institutional approach takes a middle way. It focuses less on categorical distinctions between associations and more on autonomy and self-regulation. It asks what role self-regulation plays in the social context in which particular associations operate. Even if we are initially deferential toward the autonomy of associations of all kinds, some associations are more likely to *assert* that autonomy and to self-regulate in a way that serves their infrastructural value to public discourse. Others—especially commercial associations—are less likely to do so, and more likely to accept or even welcome regulation by the state.

Take private law firms. Of course some of them discriminate against women. But they do not, as a general rule, treat this behavior as a "message" they seek to convey to others or as a meaningful principle that guides their internal relations. They "do not endorse any religious or moral doctrine according to which they have a duty not to hire women as lawyers."[83] We might say that their internal norm is one of equality and openness of membership, even if that norm is violated in particular cases. Or we might say they operate according to the norm of the market rather than that of the *nomos*.

That is not true of all associations. The Catholic Church in the West currently suffers from a shortage of men who are willing to serve as priests. From a market perspective, it might benefit from opening the priesthood to women. At least for the present, however, it is unlikely to do so. That is because it inhabits a genuinely separate *nomos*, a normative universe in which strong reasons of religious doctrine and conscience require limiting the priesthood to men. It will do so even if it suffer market disadvantages as a result—if, say, more people are likely to join a church that ordains women.

Whether we agree with that normative decision or not, it deserves protection. It strongly defines the worldview of the church's members and not just its hierarchy, and is a fundamental part of the way members understand themselves within the group and in relation to others. It defines the Church, not so much as being opposed to the state and its liberalizing norms, but as falling outside those norms. This meaning-creating capacity serves a vital infrastructural role in public discourse. Any change in Church policy should be for its own reasons, not at the state's insistence.

Thus, in attempting to distinguish between associations that are entitled to strong legal autonomy and those that are not, we should focus less on categories such as commercial or noncommercial and more on whether they live by the rules of the market and the state or by those of an independent *nomos*. Courts should allow associations to make this choice independently rather than forcing it on them.

Even under this regime, many associations will prefer to be counted as part of the liberal state and subject to its rules. Justice O'Connor was almost right to say that an "association must choose its market."[84] More precisely, associations inevitably *do* choose their markets. As a matter of self-definition, they choose whether to come within the state and its norms or to remain outside it. Even a private firm that discriminates against women is unlikely, for reasons of both market competition and self-image, to celebrate that fact or to publicly invoke freedom of association in order to escape liability. The cost, both economically and in terms of self-respect, would be too high.[85] Other associations, such as churches, will make a different choice. But they will all make a choice. That choice deserves respect.

That still leaves the question of what limits should apply, even to an association that is willing to openly assert its autonomy as an independent *nomos*. My answer draws on the general principles of First Amendment institutionalism and sphere sovereignty. Courts should approach the limits of freedom of association in a responsive and reflexive fashion, leaving associations room to evolve and not imposing top-down solutions on them. Courts should see state intervention as appropriate primarily to resolve disputes *between* spheres and to ensure against the abuse of members *within* the associational sphere.

The basic considerations here are third-party harm, exit, and voice. None of these three concepts should be read too broadly. Take third-party harm. Associational autonomy includes the right to exclude would-be members and to set the terms of membership. Individuals who are excluded from such an association, or who chafe at its terms, suffer harms only insofar as they wish to become or remain members; they are not genuine third parties. African-Americans who wish to join the Ku Klux Klan and are denied membership, or Catholic women who wish to become priests but cannot, may feel keenly injured. But they are only injured *as members,* or potential members, of the association, not because the association imposes a harm on them beyond the circle of membership.[86] Those harms should find no legal traction. On the other hand, an association should not be able to harm genuine third parties with impunity. It makes little difference whether the car that runs you over is owned by Joe Smith or the Red Cross. Injuries imposed on true bystanders have nothing to do with freedom of association.

The second consideration, the right of exit, is the most important safeguard against abuse of members.[87] Exit is the principle that allows a member to "voluntarily leave 'the effective jurisdiction of the group' if she so desires."[88] A member of an association who wants to leave it must be free to do so.

The institutional approach rejects efforts to redefine exit in a sweeping manner that threatens associations' institutional autonomy. Andrew Koppelman, for example, argues that meaningful exit from the Boy Scouts is not possible because a member who departs or is exiled "must still live in a society in which the only boys' organization with quasi-official status publicly stands for the proposition that gay people are inherently defective and contaminating." Madhavi Sunder asserts that in a case like that of the Boy Scouts, courts should protect the right of members to remain within the organization as dissenters. Others have suggested that the exit option is unavailable or diminished when a member is ignorant of other options, socialized to prefer the group, or economically dependent or subordinate.[89]

We must not use these legitimate concerns as an excuse to eviscerate associational autonomy. Some bedrock level of education, access to information, and economic independence may be necessary for citizens to be meaningful rights-holders; indeed, First Amendment institutions like libraries and schools provide precisely these resources. But those basic conditions do not require each association to serve as a mirror of the liberal state. To say otherwise would drastically alter the nature of associations. It would cripple their ability to serve as a space outside the state in which meanings other than those of the state can be formed. It would deny the possibility that individuals may find sustenance in experiencing different ways of life—including ways of life that involve submerging oneself in the values and strictures of a community or group.[90] The right of exit necessarily involves complex negotiations. There may be room for courts to intervene in extraordinary cases or for the state to ensure that individuals have enough education and resources to be voluntary members of associations. As long as their membership *is* voluntary, however, the state should be reluctant to intrude.[91]

The third safeguard against associational abuse is voice: the possibility of challenging, criticizing, and resisting an association's norms, values, and rules. Voice is related to exit in complex ways. A strong voice option may minimize the likelihood of exit from an association; conversely, a strong exit option may minimize the exercise of voice.[92]

Like the other two concepts, the idea of voice should not be read too broadly. If Nancy Rosenblum is right that associations need not "mirror liberal democratic principles and practices,"[93] then we should not expect associations to observe the standard liberal rules concerning the exercise of voice. A Catholic dissenter to the exclusion of women from the priesthood may criticize the Church from outside, and from inside insofar as its rules permit it. But the rules of internal dialogue that apply should be those of the association itself, not those of the liberal regime.

Even on those terms, voice can be a meaningful safeguard against abuse of associational autonomy. Associations are subject to internal debate over values and rules, and may change their policies after deliberation. The Jaycees, the subject of *Roberts,* provide an example. As Judge Richard Arnold noted in his opinion for the Eighth Circuit in that case, the question whether to include women as full members of the Jaycees was "vigorously debated within the organization. On three occasions a resolution favoring the admission of women [was] defeated, but each time a larger minority . . . voted for it."[94] In other words, the state, and the Court, did not need to override the Jaycees' own processes. The system would have worked on its own—slowly, but surely.

Conversely, if an association suppresses its own dissenters, it will be subject to criticism and influence from sources other than the state or the group itself. It may suffer a drop in membership; Boy Scout membership declined, for example, after the group insisted on excluding homosexuals.[95] In short, the exercise of voice by the *public* may influence an association's decision about whether to exclude certain individuals.[96] That will in turn affect the desirability of the exit option for members, who may choose to leave an organization because of public criticism.

Finally, it is important to remember that associations can criticize *one another.* Judicial oversight "is not the only—or even necessarily the most effective—means of countering the detrimental impact of [discriminatory] associations. . . . Often, the best weapon against the corrosive mediating function of one association is the mediating function of another association."[97] For every Ku Klux Klan or Jaycees, there is an NAACP or a NOW. Indeed, the very act of challenging the policies of one association may reinforce bonds within another, thus encouraging both groups to participate in public debate and teaching their members a valuable lesson about public discourse.

In short, voice and exit serve as important limiting factors. Those who worry that a robust freedom of association will allow illiberal associations to swallow up our civic space are mistaken. Associations—even powerful ones—come and go. The Moral Majority, for example, was once seen by some as a major threat to liberal democratic society; today it is the answer to a Trivial Pursuit question.[98] Critics of exclusionary or illiberal groups see them as endlessly expanding forces. But as the Moral Majority (or the real estate market) demonstrates, bubbles also burst. Courts should therefore not use the voice or exit options to restrict associations unduly. Rather, they should interpret them in a way that leaves associations free to flourish—or die.

Associations against the State and the Problem of Race

With associations, as with other First Amendment institutions, institutional autonomy sometimes conflicts with the legitimate needs of the state. Under current doctrine, we deal with this problem through balancing. We ask whether there is a "compelling state interest" that can outweigh associational freedom. Institutional autonomy is not absolute: even a robust form of institutionalism may allow courts to ensure that institutions remain within "constitutionally prescribed limits."[99] Still, an approach that emphasizes the autonomy of particular institutions will deemphasize balancing, giving courts less leeway to weigh state interests against institutional rights.

In the case of freedom of association, that concern is raised most sharply by the question of race. The elimination of racial prejudice and discrimination is among the most compelling of state interests. Some critics worry that freedom of association will allow groups and businesses to discriminate against historically disadvantaged groups and reverse the gains of the civil rights movement.[100]

In a series of cases between the mid-1960s and mid-1970s, the Supreme Court rejected this tactic, which was used by a variety of groups attempting to beat back the application of antidiscrimination laws. The most important decision is *Runyon v. McCrary*.[101] Two Virginia private schools were sued under the civil rights laws for denying admission to black students and invoked freedom of association in response. The Court held that the schools were subject to suit.

Justice Potter Stewart emphasized that the case involved only the question whether the civil rights statute "prohibits private, commercially operated, nonsectarian schools from denying admission to prospective students because they are Negroes, and, if so, whether that federal law is constitutional as so applied." He declined to address whether the law would apply to similar practices by "private social organization[s]" or private religious schools. The Court summarily rejected the schools' freedom of association claims. Parents might have a First Amendment right to send children to schools "that promote the belief that racial segregation is desirable." But that did not mean "the practice of excluding racial minorities from such institutions is also protected by the same principle." There had been "'no showing that discontinuance of (the) discriminatory admission practices would inhibit in any way the teaching in these schools of any ideas or dogma.'"[102] The schools could *teach* the desirability of racial segregation, but they could not tailor their admissions policies to reflect that belief.

Runyon is a case of questionable reasoning in support of a sympathetic result. As John Inazu notes, it is "implausible to claim that forcing a school to abandon its racially discriminatory admissions policy would not inhibit its teaching of racist ideas and dogma."[103] This is particularly true if, as the institutional approach does, we reject a message-based approach and conclude instead that an association's choice to include or exclude particular members is an integral part of that association.[104]

That does not mean *Runyon* is wrong, and even those who think its reasoning questionable may be quite content to live with its result. But it suggests a failure to resolve, or even acknowledge, deep tensions in the law of freedom of association. Any meaningful discussion of that freedom must confront *Runyon*. Yet many scholars and courts ignore it—the majority opinion in *Dale* never mentions the case—or invoke it only for rhetorical purposes.[105] When they do confront it more directly, they are unconvincing. This was especially evident in the litigation over the Solomon Amendment, which we discussed in Chapter 5. There the plaintiffs argued that *Dale* supported their right to exclude military recruiters, while maintaining that this position did not undermine the vitality of *Runyon*. But, of course, it did.[106] This tension is a prime illustration of the snares of acontextuality. It shows the failure of an acontextual approach to capture the diverse contexts in which a constitutional right like freedom of association arises.

The best answer to the *Runyon* dilemma may ultimately be a contextual one. Perhaps *Runyon* is best understood in terms of the complex connections between public law and private conduct where race is concerned. Many private schools' decision to segregate on the basis of race was part of a broader public program of "massive resistance" to the desegregation of public schools following the 1954 ruling in *Brown v. Board of Education*. As Evelyn Brody tells the story, "Forced to desegregate their public schools by *Brown*, Southern States took drastic action, financially starving their public schools and providing funds to or for the benefit of whites-only private schools." In this sense, the discriminatory private academies were not a genuine product of the meaningful pluralism that underlies freedom of association; they were a public-private partnership aimed at perpetuating "America's gravest and longest-running failure of pluralism."[107]

On this view, the decisions in *Runyon* and other freedom of association cases involving race can best be justified as interventions that were necessary to preserve the integrity of the infrastructure of public discourse. Society had to ensure that the sovereign sphere of private association was open to *everyone* before it could justify a robust freedom of association for *anyone*. This position is basically consistent with the institutional turn, which permits state intervention to ensure that our system of sovereign spheres is operating as it should.

This answer eases the tension between the treatment of associations as First Amendment institutions and the broader concern with the American tragedy of race. But it does not resolve it completely. It may be that *Runyon* is now more symbolically important than doctrinally significant.[108] It may be that as race relations in America improve, there will be greater scope for a robust form of freedom of association even where race is involved.[109] Not everyone who is deeply interested in racial equality opposes this prospect.[110] But it will offer cold comfort to others—not least the members of other disadvantaged groups, such as gays and lesbians, who face continued discrimination without the special solicitude the Supreme Court has shown for race. Even die-hard First Amendment institutionalists must acknowledge the tension that remains.

To be clear, I am not arguing that *Runyon* is good law or bad law from the institutionalist perspective, only that there are serious questions about its coherence. Even so mild a conclusion may be disturbing to some.[111] Nevertheless, we must acknowledge the tension, under current doctrine, between freedom of association—including the freedom championed by the plaintiffs in the Solomon Amendment litigation, supporters of the *Dale* decision, and others—and cases like *Runyon*. We must acknowledge the tension between law's aspiration to acontextuality and the actual contexts in which particular constitutional cases arise. We must face our demons more squarely.

On this issue, the institutionalists may have an uneasy time. But that uneasiness is preferable to what we have now: the quiet but naïve slumber of those who pretend that we can have both freedom of association and *Runyon,* both the exclusion of military recruiters and the use of civil rights laws to prohibit racially discriminatory private schools. We need more honesty and clarity here, even if we sleep less soundly as a result.

Nested Institutions

Some disputes involve First Amendment institutions nested *within* other First Amendment institutions. In particular, they involve associations found within universities. Because private universities can generally control the terms of their own environment, such disputes raise no significant legal issues there. In public universities, however, given the courts' difficulty in reconciling the principle of university autonomy with their usual acontextual treatment of government bodies, cases dealing with the rights of associations such as student clubs raise greater constitutional concerns.

These issues came to the fore in a case discussed briefly in Chapter 5, *Christian Legal Society v. Martinez*.[112] Recall that the Hastings College of the Law designated some student groups as Registered Student Organizations (RSOs). RSOs were entitled to seek financial assistance from the law school, to take advantage of various channels of communication it provided, and to use its name and logo. The Hastings chapter of the Christian Legal Society (CLS) sought RSO status in 2004. Hastings believed the group's bylaws violated the school's nondiscrimination policy, which forbids RSOs to discriminate on the basis of sexual orientation. According to Hastings, its policy required RSOs to "allow any student to participate, become a member, or seek leadership positions in the organization, regardless of [her] status and beliefs." Because the CLS excluded from member or officer status those who accept or engage in "unrepentant homosexual conduct," Hastings denied it RSO status, but allowed it to operate without the school's official sponsorship. The group sued, alleging, among other things, a violation of freedom of association.[113]

A crucial premise of the majority's decision, written by Justice Ruth Bader Ginsburg, was that the parties had stipulated that the nondiscrimination policy required acceptance of all comers. The majority took that stipulation as obligating it to consider "only whether conditioning access to a student-organization forum on compliance with an all-comers policy violates the Constitution."[114] I take that premise as a given here.

The majority opinion was an exercise in slotting. It saw the question before it as whether the case should be resolved under public forum doctrine or freedom of association doctrine. Justice Ginsburg held that Hastings was best dealt with as a limited public forum.[115] That classification turned the decision into a foregone conclusion. All that was required in such a forum was that the policy neither discriminate on the basis of viewpoint nor impose unreasonable restrictions. In considering the latter question, the Court emphasized the deference it owed to university officials. Given that deference, it easily upheld the all-comers policy as reasonable. The policy ensured equal access to "the leadership, educational, and social opportunities" offered by RSOs. The broad all-comers approach made it easier for

Hastings to enforce its policy without inquiring too closely into groups' motivations for exclusionary polices. Hastings reasonably believed the all-comers policy "encourages tolerance, cooperation, and learning among students." Finally, it was reasonable for the law school to refuse to subsidize groups that might violate the antidiscrimination policies of California law. In sum, the policy presented a reasonable compromise. Hastings was entitled to "draw a line in the sand permitting *all* organizations to express what they wish but *no* group to discriminate in membership."[116]

Justice Stevens concurred. His opinion focused directly on the nature of universities. "The campus," he wrote, "is a world apart from the public square in numerous respects, and religious organizations, as well as all other organizations, must abide by certain norms of conduct when they enter an academic community." Because public universities "serve a distinctive role in a modern democratic society" that requires them to make a host of decisions about how to allocate their resources, "courts should respect universities' judgments and let them manage their own affairs." Justice Stevens would have upheld the policy as written, not just the "all-comers" version. "A free society must tolerate" groups that discriminate in membership, he concluded. "It need not subsidize them."[117]

What is most striking about this hotly disputed and highly anticipated case is that so little is striking about it.[118] Justice Ginsburg is a skilled doctrinalist, and *CLS* is a dryly technical decision. Although it pays lip service to the idea of deferring to universities, it is really driven by broad, acontextual doctrinal categories.[119] By treating Hastings as a limited public forum, the majority equates the university with all other limited public forums; by treating the question as whether or not CLS was entitled to government subsidies, it shows little concern for the deep nature of associations and their needs and aims. *CLS* can be criticized for its treatment of the facts or its application of existing doctrinal categories. But this misses the point. The broader lesson of the case lies not in how well it manipulates existing doctrine, but in how ill-suited that doctrine is to the resolution of conflicts between different First Amendment institutions.[120]

If the Court had examined *CLS* through a genuinely institutional lens, the outcome might not have been different. But the language would have been, and so would the ensuing public conversation. It is a mistake to view this sort of conflict through too narrowly doctrinal a lens, and particularly to view a law school or university as if it were just any government actor. Doing so fails to capture the nature of both the law school and the CLS as First Amendment institutions.

Reasonable people may differ concerning the proper result under an institutionalist reading of *CLS*. In my view, for reasons similar to those offered by Justice Stevens, Hastings probably should have won. Universities "serve a distinctive role in a modern democratic society." Their role is crucial to the infrastructure of public discourse. That role depends on their own sense of mission and their own interpretation of university practices and traditions. It is a mistake to equate them with other government actors: to see them as limited public forums, grantors or withholders of public subsidies, or any other broad doctrinal categorization of "the government." Their *institutional* status requires legislative and judicial deference. Hastings should have been free to take the position that its mission required it to exclude discriminatory groups.

Stevens errs, however, in assuming that all universities have the same mission, and that this mission *necessarily* requires religious and other groups to "abide by certain norms of conduct when they enter an academic community."[121] That view is inconsistent with institutional pluralism—with the ways in which institutions such as universities or newspapers vary in understanding their mission and what it requires. Universities need not emphasize equal access and nondiscrimination, any more than newspapers *must* be neutral rather than partisan. A university should be equally free to adopt a mission favoring broad access to its resources for a variety of groups, including groups that exclude some potential members.

Whichever path it chooses, the university, as the primary institution involved, should be able to make that choice for itself. In a heated dissent, Justice Samuel Alito charged that the majority believed there should be "no freedom for expression that offends prevailing standards of political correctness in our country's institutions of higher learning."[122] Even if Alito was right about the majority's motives, his broadside is still off the mark. As First Amendment institutions, universities, consistent with their own sense of what their mission demands, should have the choice to be "politically correct" *or* "politically incorrect"—provided they do so *as* universities. The university's right to sponsor groups like the CLS, or to exclude them altogether, trumps the nested rights of the associations in question.

This is only the beginning of the discussion. It can and should continue within universities, in the broader academic community, and in the public at large. Those who believe that we lose more than we gain by excluding groups such as the CLS and that universities ought to be home to a variety of associations, including those inhabiting a separate *nomos,* are free to press this argument. But the battle should not be fought within the courts. It cannot be settled once and for all by some court's wooden characterization of a university as a public forum or as a government body doling out subsidies. A true victory for diversity and pluralism in *CLS* would have involved neither demanding that student groups include all comers nor insisting that universities cannot tell them to do so. It would have involved adopting a robust institutional framework that would help us see that there is room for universities to reach different decisions on this question—and that the law should have little to do with it.

Freedom of association is something of a stepchild of the First Amendment, not as well loved as the freedom of speech or religion. It produces both fear and awkwardness: the fear that associations will use their freedom to resist the movement toward equality for all citizens, and the awkwardness with which associations fit into a constitutional framework that emphasizes state sovereignty.

Associations have a strong claim to be treated as a First Amendment institution. They serve a vital function in our social infrastructure. They are places in which identities are formed and in which individuals can speak to one another, and to the state as well, while remaining in some sense outside the state's grasp. In that respect, associations *are* a threat to the state: they are a site of resistance and a visible reminder of the limits of government. But without them, both the state and its citizens would lose an important source of meaning and independence; without them, life within the state would be far more intolerable. They are worth valuing and preserving, even when we disagree with their choices.

10

The Borderlands of Institutionalism

Having examined some of the most obvious First Amend-
ment institutions, we arrive at the borderlands of First Amendment institutionalism: the more uncharted territories of the institutional turn. These
territories are not uncharted because they are unfamiliar; they are all well-
known institutions. They are borderline cases for two other reasons. First,
they raise questions about the definition of First Amendment institutions
and the scope of their autonomy. Second, they have not been entirely com-
fortably situated within the law of the First Amendment. Each of them has
posed vexing questions for the courts, which have been caught between the
desire for acontextual doctrine and the awareness that these institutions
present a strong case for the importance of context.

I will begin with the smallest of these institutions, the family, and then
consider the corporation, professional speech, and politics. These are rich
subjects, and I cannot do them full justice here. Rather, I will survey each
of these institutions and use them to raise broader questions about First
Amendment institutionalism.

The Family

For most of us, the family is the most familiar institution and the germ of
every other institutional attachment. From cradle to grave, it shapes our identities and allows us to shape the identities of others, especially our children.

The family is often seen as possessing many of the characteristics that define First Amendment institutions. It has been called "a deeply rooted, fundamental social institution, a basic unit undergirding the social and political order," a "seedbed of civic virtue."[1] It is, in short, an essential element of the infrastructure of public discourse.

Families have long enjoyed a certain degree of autonomy in constitutional law.[2] That autonomy is a rare holdover from the early twentieth century, the first era in which the Supreme Court found a host of substantive rights within the Due Process Clause of the Fourteenth Amendment. Two such cases, *Meyer v. Nebraska* and *Pierce v. Society of Sisters*,[3] together suggested that the Due Process Clause protects the substantive right "to marry, establish a home and bring up children."[4] The link between family rights and other individual and institutional constitutional rights, such as religious freedom, has been aptly labeled a right to "free exercise of the family."[5]

Many constitutional cases involving family rights have "a fairly straightforward First Amendment dimension."[6] Scholars have compared family rights to the First Amendment rights of free exercise[7] and freedom of association.[8] On that view, the family is the ur-association: one of the first and most important places in which we engage in self-formation, group identity, and "message formation and communication,"[9] whose autonomy from the state is needed if families are to maintain their own meanings, values, and traditions.[10]

The analogy between families and our core First Amendment institutions has considerable strength. Family is a fluid concept, one that has undergone centuries of change and evolution;[11] despite or because of these changes, it remains an essential part of our social framework. As with voluntary associations, the family's contribution to public discourse is not just expressive. Besides serving as a bulwark against the state, it is a site in which identities are formed, minds are educated, and personalities are prepared to contribute to civic and social life. The broad range of court decisions supporting a degree of autonomy for the family, even in the absence of a clear textual source in the Constitution, offers evidence that the courts, clumsily but confidently, agree that families should function largely unhindered by the state's desire to impose particular meanings and messages on them. For supporters of the institutional turn, none of this is surprising.

One question that arises in exploring the family as a First Amendment institution is whether recognizing some degree of family autonomy threatens the state's ability to function—especially if courts are obliged to defer to any "family" describing itself as such, just as the Supreme Court deferred to the Boy Scouts' description of their own message in *Dale*. Any broad collection of intimate groups, from communes to polygamous compounds, might assert rights against state interference in the name of the family.[12]

A related question has to do with the areas in which family rights might be invoked. One might worry that the occasions when families invoke institutional rights mark precisely those times when state regulation is most needed. Families, even more than associations, are potential breeding grounds for inequality and abuse. Children in particular, but women as well, may be subjected to economic and social inequalities that make both voice and exit difficult if not impossible.

These concerns have led some scholars to question the value of parental rights or family autonomy. But some of their arguments go beyond a fear of abuse, to a fear of the family's potential illiberalism and a belief that the liberal state must have broad power to intervene in family life. Thus, James Dwyer has argued that the state must be free to intercede in family decisions, including questions of religious education, in order to replicate traditional liberal values within the family and to guard against illiberal views.[13] And Kimberly Yuracko, emphasizing a fear of "anti-secular separatism" and a desire to bring families within "the liberal fold," has argued that states "must"—not may—"check rampant forms of sexism in homeschooling so as to prevent the severe under-education of girls by parents who believe in female subordination."[14]

In a sense, this entire book is a response to such concerns. Those who see the state's liberal values as having an imperial reach, and any separate institution as posing a threat to that reach, are unlikely to be satisfied by any answers I can provide. But that does not mean there are no answers at all.

First, critics who argue against family autonomy are swimming against the tide. Even though the family fits awkwardly into First Amendment jurisprudence and constitutional law more generally, the courts have not hesitated to treat it as a "private realm . . . which the state cannot enter."[15] The tradition of treating families as substantially autonomous units predates any particular effort to locate their autonomy in a specific constitutional right.[16] Although the burden in this book has generally been on the institutional turn to demonstrate that any departures from current doctrine are justified, here the burden shifts to those who would so radically alter current doctrine.

Moreover, whether under current doctrine or the institutional approach, the family is hardly immune from regulation. To the contrary, it is hedged round by legal regulation and obligation, from the definition of family itself and the law concerning the formation and dissolution of marriages, to the many legal protections for children, to the complex web of tax and other family-related laws.

Although the institutional turn might redraw this regulatory framework in some cases, it does not require a turn away from regulation altogether. Recall Kuyper's reminder that even under a strong vision of sphere sovereignty the state has an obligation to "defend individuals and the weak ones, in those [sovereign] spheres, against the abuse of power of the rest."[17] The institutional turn does not demand that the state be disarmed, left completely unable to guard against abuses. What it requires is sensitivity and deference. Law's role is to preserve the family's contributions to our social infrastructure. The institutional turn rejects an approach that uses the coercive power of the law to replicate the values of the state within the sphere of the family. To that extent, it is incompatible with militantly liberal arguments that the state should regulate sexism, religious fundamentalism, and other illiberal tendencies within the family. But it hardly requires the state to ignore cases of serious abuse.

Finally, the relatively unrooted constitutional status of family autonomy—its failure to find a secure, textually specific place within any particular constitutional provision—speaks to a broader point. The concept of "First Amendment institutions," although it is a step forward in our way of carving up the world, is an imperfect label, given in this book to particular institutions because of their close relationship to public discourse and its infrastructure.

But the institutional turn is ultimately about institutions themselves, not the constitutional categories into which we slot them. Once we focus on those institutions, we see that their infrastructural role in our social firmament stretches beyond any particular constitutional categorization.[18] This book is focused on public discourse and the First Amendment alone; that project is sizable enough. But one could imagine future efforts to imagine and limn the contours, not of "First Amendment institutionalism," but of *"constitutional* institutionalism." The prospect of treating the family as an institution worthy of broad constitutional protection is thus both promising and dangerous: promising because it focuses our attention on a social context that is far more salient to most of us than any particular legal or constitutional category, and dangerous precisely because of its broad potential scope.

The Corporation

Any consideration of institutions would be incomplete without a discussion of corporations, which have become a "dominant form of social organization."[19] Not only are corporations profoundly influential in speaking and selling to citizens as well as lobbying politicians; they are also places where we speak to *one another.* Our conversations may be influenced by schools and universities, the press, and churches, but they frequently occur in the workplace. Cynthia Estlund has aptly labeled the workplace a "satellite domain" of public discourse: "a domain that lies outside the core of public discourse but contributes to that discourse in unique and important ways."[20] It is a site where we often discuss matters having little to do with our jobs: politics, faith, culture. (Where else but in the office do we discuss last night's episode of "The Office"?)

Of course, many First Amendment institutions can take the corporate form. The *Washington Post* is a publicly traded company, much of whose income derives from its ownership of Kaplan, Inc., an educational test preparation company. Harvard University, one of the first chartered private corporations in the United States, has an endowment in the billions of dollars. The Boy Scouts of America is a huge nonprofit corporation directly authorized by the United States Congress.

As far as corporate law is concerned, the rights and obligations of these entities are no different from those of other companies. Our concern in this book, however, is with the institutional nature of particular entities, not the specific organizational form they adopt. The question is whether the corporation *as an institution* should carry some legal significance for purposes of constitutional law. It has to do, in short, with one of the recurring questions of this book: the boundaries of First Amendment institutionalism. Is *any* institution a "First Amendment institution"? Do corporations qualify as

First Amendment institutions simply because they take the corporate form or by virtue of their prominence in our daily lives?

The answer is both no and yes. Wal-Mart is an institution of sorts, and it may play a bigger role in the lives of its customers and employees than most newspapers or voluntary associations. Its business necessarily involves speech; most corporate activity takes place through the written and spoken word. Nor is there any doubt that corporations affect and engage in public discourse. Every dialogue on major matters of public concern eventually touches on corporations, and corporations may participate in this dialogue as well.

Corporations and similar entities are thus relevant to public discourse. But that does not make them a fundamental part of its *infrastructure*. Certain entities—churches, newspapers, libraries, and so on—are clearly vital parts of that infrastructure. Corporations as such are less essential to public discourse. The same water-cooler conversations can take place between employees at Wal-Mart, the Metropolitan Museum of Art, or Joe's House of Bait and Fried Chicken.

It is true that we may prefer to work for or buy from one company rather than another. Our choice of employer may be far more important to us than our choice of newspaper. The decision to change employers may occasion more soul-searching than the decision whether to join a church down the street or one a little farther away. These kinds of choices can be of great personal moment. But they are less significant from the structural or infrastructural perspective of public discourse. The corporate form is just a form. To be sure, speech by or within corporations is hardly irrelevant. Issues such as gender- or race-based harassment in the workplace and whether a company is free to engage in unfettered commercial or political speech are obviously First Amendment concerns. But that does not make corporations central to public discourse from an *institutional* standpoint. Corporations may still enjoy First Amendment rights, and the courts should approach corporate speech cases with sensitivity to the particular context in which they arise. But First Amendment institutionalism is not a tool for every occasion.

Unsurprisingly, given the ongoing judicial struggle between recognizing and abjuring context in First Amendment law, the doctrine of commercial speech, including commercial speech by corporations, is somewhat muddled. The Supreme Court has taken an increasingly protective view of commercial speech, roughly defined as "speech proposing a commercial transaction."[21] But that protection is not absolute. False or misleading commercial speech receives no First Amendment protection. Even accurate commercial speech may be regulated if the law passes intermediate scrutiny, a less demanding test than the strict scrutiny applied to most content-based regulation of speech.[22]

The Court's justification for protecting commercial speech strikes a familiar note, in two respects. First, it equates commercial speech with most other speech. Just as citizens need unhindered access to political facts and opinions, so they have "a strong interest in the free flow of commercial information."[23] Its approach is also rooted in a broad distrust of government speech regulation. Second and somewhat contradictorily, however, the Court remains convinced that context does matter in commercial speech cases and that the government ought to have a greater degree of latitude to regulate it than it does with, say, political speech.[24] In short, while refusing to treat commercial speech as an institutionally unique form of speech, the Court has recognized some value in protecting it while cautioning that this value does not preclude *all* regulation.

In other words, commercial speech doctrine exemplifies both the lure of acontextuality and the courts' inevitable recognition that an acontextual approach may fail to recognize morally or socially relevant distinctions between different institutions within public discourse. The problem is not that the courts have failed to recognize that context matters *at all* where commercial speech is concerned, but that, in part because of the acontextual nature of their default rules, they have failed to identify useful contexts or categories.

Despite the difficulties of distinguishing between commercial and other forms of speech, we should not be surprised that the courts have been willing to extend greater protection to *political* speech, even when engaged in by commercial enterprises such as corporations. Although the Supreme Court has dodged the issue, it would likely hold that laws inhibiting corporations from engaging in speech on matters of public concern should receive heightened scrutiny.[25] The Court has also made clear that corporations, like individual speakers, are entitled to engage in political speech in the context of elections and that campaign finance laws targeting corporate speech as such are doomed. In *Citizens United v. Federal Elections Commission,* Justice

Anthony Kennedy put the point simply: "the First Amendment does not allow political speech restrictions based on a speaker's corporate identity."[26]

But the Court's defense of corporate political speech is not based on the belief that corporate speech is unique. To the contrary, its decisions have been driven by a desire to *eliminate* any consideration of context. Consider *Citizens United*'s treatment of a provision in the campaign finance law that exempted media corporations. Kennedy wrote that the regulation of corporate political speech could "produce the dangerous, and unacceptable, consequence that Congress could ban [the] political speech of media corporations" such as newspapers. Yet he rejected the exemption itself, arguing that Congress cannot "distinguish between corporations which are deemed to be exempt as media corporations and those which are not."[27] Thus, in a striking example of acontextualism, *Citizens United* says that *any* law regulating press speech on political issues deserves strict scrutiny, but *no* law may single out the press for protection for this reason.[28] As I wrote earlier, given the Court's acontextual bent, sometimes the only way to save the village is to burn it.

One last area of corporate speech worth mentioning is speech *within* corporations—the kinds of exchanges between employees that lead Cynthia Estlund to call the workplace a satellite domain of public discourse. Workplace speech is governed by a host of laws governing such matters as sexual or racial harassment. By and large, the courts have not treated these cases as raising significant First Amendment concerns. We might understand the courts' relative disregard for the First Amendment issues raised by workplace harassment laws as an effort to treat the workplace as a "managerial domain," in which "an image of dialogue among autonomous self-governing citizens would be patently out of place."[29]

There are good reasons to question whether that description of the workplace really captures the amount of public discourse that takes place there.[30] From an institutionalist perspective, however, the kinds of distinctions the courts have drawn make sense. Although public discourse may occur at work, that does not make the workplace a primary element of the infrastructure of public discourse. Conversations in the workplace—including loose sexual and racial speech, and sometimes harassment—are incidental to that structure.

We ought to be concerned about the First Amendment implications of workplace harassment laws, to be sure. But we should not treat corporations and other workplaces as having a unique institutional status that prevents government from regulating this conduct at all. Our approach should be relatively responsive and bottom-up, allowing some sensitivity to the diversity of workplace contexts while leaving employers room to form best practices in this area.[31] But it should not absolutely preclude the regulation of workplace speech.

This brief discussion suggests two conclusions. First, although the speech of corporations and other commercial entities has institutional implications, it is not the speech of a First Amendment institution properly understood. Corporate speech as such is not sufficiently central to the infrastructure of public discourse to merit the distinctive autonomy that applies to First Amendment institutions.

But the institutional turn is not altogether irrelevant to corporations. The idea that context matters still applies here, even if it does not lead to a robust form of institutional autonomy. The Supreme Court, in its treatment of corporations and corporate speech, which is sometimes strongly protective and at other times allows for more government regulation than might apply to other speakers, has muddled toward the same conclusion. That it has done so in a decidedly uncertain fashion is evidence of both the lures and the snares of acontextuality.[32]

Professional Speech

An additional candidate for treatment as a First Amendment institution is professional speech. Like some of the other institutions we have examined, it is difficult to define precisely but easy to understand intuitively. James Brundage has defined a profession as "a line of work that . . . claims to promote the interests of the whole community as well as the individual worker," that "requires mastery of a substantial body of esoteric knowledge," and that is closely bounded by "a body of ethical rules different from and more demanding than those incumbent on all respectable members" of society.[33] The standard examples are law and medicine.

The courts have struggled to come up with a coherent picture of the relationship between the First Amendment and professional speech.[34] Much of their difficulty stems from the categories with which the law carves up the world. The standard conception of First Amendment speech is that of the lone soapbox speaker confronting the massive power of the government. The goal of First Amendment doctrine, from this perspective, is to give the greatest possible latitude to individual speech and to hedge in the government, especially by forbidding it to engage in content-based speech regulation.

This picture is woefully incomplete. It is shorn of any social context—indeed, it is *meant* to be shorn of social context, lest judges be left with too much discretion—save for faith in the individual speaker and distrust of the state.[35] It does not tell us what to do with speech that "fulfills a more defined social role," in a relationship between professional and client that "runs far deeper than the relationship between pedestrians and soapbox orators."[36] Nor does it tell us how First Amendment doctrine, which generally treats the truth as just "another opinion,"[37] ought to deal with realms such as professional speech, where expertise based on a body of specialized knowledge is the very basis of the value and legitimacy of the speech.

There is good reason for professional speech to find a home in the institutional First Amendment. It meets the basic definitional criteria for First Amendment institutions. Like newspapers and universities, the professions are venerable institutions.[38] They are replete with professional practices, norms, and ethical obligations that are mostly a matter of self-regulation.[39]

The harder question is whether professional speech serves the same infrastructural role in public discourse as the other institutions we have discussed. Professionals help clients to make *"personal* choices based on the cumulative knowledge of the profession."[40] Drawing up a will is important to the client but not necessarily to public discussion; a proctological exam is not the same as a political debate (although some would beg to differ). Above all, while our general picture of public discourse is of "uninhibited, robust, and wide-open" debate,[41] professional speech is highly constrained.

Still, a strong case can be made for the infrastructural role of professional speech in public discourse. Much of the speech that is central to the formation and progress of public discourse is equally constrained. Universities, newspapers, libraries, and other institutions are valuable to public discourse precisely *because* they are constrained: they contribute to public discussion through professional, self-regulated speech.

More broadly, professional speech is both individual *and* social. It assists individuals in making personal choices, but does so against the backdrop of public-mindedness that characterizes professional values and functions. The balance between private needs and public concerns is woven into the fabric of professional speech. Drawing up a will may be a profoundly personal matter, but the lawyer's advice on how to do so is bounded by the requirement that she assist the client in carrying out his intentions *within the law,* under a set of legal and ethical constraints designed to protect both the client and the public good. Although lawyers are expected to be zealous advocates on behalf of clients, that advocacy is constrained by their obligations as officers of the court, which may limit the kinds of arguments they can make on a client's behalf. Similarly, the American Medical Association's Principles of Medical Ethics emphasize that physicians must treat their responsibility to patients as paramount, but must also consider their obligations "to society, to other health professionals, and to self."[42]

Professional advice thus contributes to public discourse in two ways. To the extent that it champions the autonomy of the individual client or patient, it serves many of the values—identity formation, knowledge, individual autonomy, self-realization, and so on—that enable citizens to function *as* citizens, and that form the core of the standard justifications for free speech.[43] In addition, it helps shape and preserve public discourse. A lawyer's work on behalf of a client, for example, may require her to challenge the state's official account, to insist that the state justify the use of force, and to challenge the constitutionality of particular government actions. In this way, professional speech is one of the "institutions that play a central role in the public and private dialogues through which we constitute ourselves as a community."[44]

Treating professional speech as a First Amendment institution thus makes a good deal of sense. Doing so may help the courts reach a fuller understanding of the contexts in which public discourse takes place and the contributions that the professions make to that discourse.

Consider some examples. Some dentists believe that dental amalgams, which use both silver and mercury to fill cavities, are dangerous because mercury may leach into the patient's body.[45] The American Dental Association considers amalgams safe and prohibits dentists from advising patients to have them removed. But a dentist with contrary views is free to express them to the public at large.[46] The speech is the same in both cases. Yet one can be regulated and the other cannot. Standard First Amendment doctrine cannot easily account for the difference.

The institutional turn has less difficulty dealing with this conundrum. A dentist caring for a patient is acting in the context of a professional relationship, one characterized by the expectation that the dentist's advice represents the current state of professional knowledge. It is a fiduciary relationship: the patient, owing to the inequality of knowledge between him and the dentist, is entitled to expect competent professional advice, not just the dentist's personal opinion.[47] Dentists offering advice to patients, in short, are supposed to provide the best views *of the profession.* They may be free to offer dissenting views outside that context—indeed, if professional knowledge is to advance, professionals must be able to challenge the boundaries of received professional opinion—but they are constrained in what they can say within the fiduciary relationship.

Similarly, there is a difference between offering professional investment advice to individual clients and offering opinions about investments to the general public. The latter type of speech takes place within general public discourse, in which opinions are freely offered and just as freely ignored. The situation is different where a professional "takes the affairs of a client personally in hand and purports to exercise judgment on behalf of the client in the light of the client's individual need and circumstances."[48] This is no longer simply individual speech; it is *professional* speech, one in which both the professional and the client have specialized roles and expectations that can be backed by regulatory force.

That conclusion can cut in favor of government regulation or against it. One of the major debates about regulation of physicians' professional speech has concerned abortion, where opponents of abortion rights have sought to limit what they cannot ban outright. In 2005, the South Dakota legislature enacted a bill setting out requirements for obtaining informed consent for an abortion. Among other things, it required physicians to give their patients a written statement warning that "the abortion will terminate the life of a whole, separate, unique, living human being."[49] In the ensuing litigation, the U.S. Court of Appeals for the Eighth Circuit denied a preliminary injunction against the enforcement of the statute. "While the State cannot compel an individual simply to speak the State's ideological message," it said, "it can use its regulatory authority to require a physician to provide truthful, non-misleading information relevant to a patient's decision to have an abortion." The court relied on the Supreme Court's statement in *Planned Parenthood v.*

Casey that physicians' speech rights are limited by "the practice of medicine, subject to reasonable licensing and regulation by the State."[50]

The Eighth Circuit cannot be blamed for following what it saw as governing doctrine. But the doctrine itself can be faulted. The state's power to regulate the professions is not absolute. The delegation of power between the government and professional regulatory bodies is a two-way street. The government must respect the proper institutional boundaries of the profession. The limited nature of this delegation is epistemic: it relies on the government's awareness that the profession has superior knowledge about what rules are required. But it runs deeper than that: it recognizes that, even where the coercive power exercised by the profession is on loan from the state, the profession is still an institution that exists apart from the state.

In short, if the professions are to retain the qualities that make their contributions to public discourse so fundamental, the state's power to intervene cannot interfere with the essential qualities that make a profession what it is. Within its proper sphere, professional speech must remain free from the exercise of state authority—even, somewhat paradoxically, where the profession's enforcement power draws on the state. South Dakota's law, by requiring doctors to follow a state-dictated script that did not necessarily reflect the views and best practices of the medical profession, broke the state's side of the bargain. If professional speech were treated as a First Amendment institution, the law would have been struck down.[51]

The institutional turn also helps us to make better sense of one of the most difficult First Amendment areas: the relationship between professional speech and government-funded speech, which is governed by the doctrine of unconstitutional conditions. The general assumption is that if the government pays the piper, it ought to be able to call the tune. But there are limits. The government cannot condition its funding on the recipient's surrender of constitutional rights, at least where they lie "beyond the scope of the benefit" received.[52] The state may insist that the recipient of a grant for scientific research not spend the money at the racetrack, but it may not condition the same grant on her willingness to surrender her membership in the NAACP or the Republican Party.

This still leaves a lot up for grabs. Unconstitutional conditions doctrine is "too crude and too general to provide help in dealing with contested cases."[53] The doctrine offers little help in determining whether a funding recipient is acting within the domain of his own constitutional rights or is only a mouthpiece for the government. Acontextual and institutionally agnostic First Amendment doctrine cannot answer that question by itself; only a consideration of the social and institutional context in which particular speech occurs can. Once again, First Amendment doctrine may resist context but finally cannot do without it.

The Supreme Court has recognized that the institutional domain of particular speech may set limits on government's ability to use funding conditions to have its own way. The key case is *Rust v. Sullivan,* which involved a challenge by physicians who received federal funds to provide family planning services. The relevant legislation barred funds from being used in programs "where abortion is a method of family planning." The regulations implementing the legislation forbade physicians receiving the funds to counsel patients concerning abortion, refer them to abortion providers, or "encourage, promote, or advocate abortion as a method of family planning."[54]

The Court upheld the regulations. But it warned that government funding would not be "invariably sufficient to justify Government control over the content of expression." It offered a pertinent example: "[W]e have recognized that the university is a traditional sphere of free expression so fundamental to the functioning of our society that the Government's ability to control speech within that sphere by means of conditions attached to the expenditure of Government funds is restricted by the vagueness and overbreadth doctrines of the First Amendment. . . . It could be argued by analogy that traditional relationships such as that between doctor and patient should enjoy protection under the First Amendment from Government regulation, even when subsidized by the Government." The Court held, however, that the constraints on the recipients of family planning funds did not "significantly impinge upon the doctor-patient relationship," both because the program itself did not "justify an expectation on the part of the patient of comprehensive medical advice" and because the doctors who received funding were not required to present the government's views as their own.[55]

This suggests that the government is not *completely* free to use its purse strings to alter the nature of certain kinds of discourse. It may have some power to call the tune, but it cannot turn a violinist into a tuba player, or a doctor into something else. In the language of sphere sovereignty, the state may be the "sphere of spheres," but it cannot use its power and money to alter the very nature of the other spheres. In certain realms, "government should be required to afford a degree of independence to institutions and speakers notwithstanding the presence of government funding, toward the end of ensuring a vigorous public debate."[56] It can direct the speech of its own employees or those recipients of funds who are so closely identified with the government that no one risks mistaking them for independent professionals. But when "funding a bounded speech institution" such as the medical or legal profession, "the government will be held to funding the entire institution unless it extracts the actors sufficiently from their traditional roles."[57] It can choose to subsidize professional speech or not, but cannot distort it beyond recognition.

The Court applied this principle in *Legal Services Corporation v. Velazquez*, a case involving restrictions imposed on the federally funded Legal Services Corporation, which provides legal assistance to indigent clients. The restrictions prevented the recipients of funds from making "effort[s] to amend or otherwise challenge existing welfare law."[58] Technically, the Court's decision turned on whether the speech at issue could be characterized as "government speech," and thus whether the case could be distinguished from *Rust v. Sullivan*. But answering that question required it to consider what it meant for this speech to be "government" speech, which in turn required the Court to say something about the nature of the professional speech involved: the provision of legal services on behalf of private clients.

To the Court, the government's actions, which prevented legal aid lawyers from offering the kinds of advice they would normally provide, sought "to use *an existing medium of expression* and to control it . . . in ways which distort its usual functioning." The government could have chosen not to enter the field at all. Once it did, however, its options were constrained. It could not use funding restrictions "to exclude certain vital theories and ideas" without altering the attorneys' "traditional role."[59]

The Court in *Rust* and *Velazquez* has the right idea about professional speech, but it lacks proper language with which to express it. Absent a more socially and institutionally sensitive account of what is at stake in these cases and a more responsive set of doctrinal tools, its decisions in this field will remain inconsistent and underdeveloped. Unless it can properly take the measure of professional speech and its importance to public discourse, it will not be able to put its rulings on a sound footing. First Amendment institutionalism offers a better, finer-edged, more sensible set of tools for dealing with professional speech than the ones currently available to the courts.[60]

Politics

The last area in our tour of the borderlands of First Amendment institutionalism is different from the others; it is broader, focusing on an entire *system* as a social institution, rather than on a particular "institution" in the more organizational sense that I have generally emphasized. This domain is the area of electoral politics. Election law scholars point out that democratic politics is "a product of specific institutional structures and legal rules."[61] At an institutional level, the system of politics involves far more than just a variety of instances of freestanding political speech, as the courts understand the term. Instead, politics is a distinct social institution with its own structures, regulatory norms, and informal practices.[62] In all its aspects—from laws regulating third parties, to restrictions on campaign spending and financing, to the social norms that have grown up around party politics in the United States, to balloting and redistricting—it can be viewed as a single interlocking entity. Scholars arguing in this vein, who come mostly from the field of election law, maintain that "democratic politics must be treated as a distinct domain for constitutional purposes" and that it should be "understood as a special area of the law requiring its own, unique set of legal paradigms."[63]

In many respects, this is more a negative prescription than a positive one. To say that elections are their own institution does not tell us much about the function of that institution or how the law can best serve that function. I cannot answer those questions here. Indeed, I am not wholly persuaded that election law *should* be considered a First Amendment institution. Nor am I convinced that treating it as one would lead to the kinds of results that many of its advocates urge, which generally favor broad government authority to regulate campaign speech. But I can still make some general points.

First, results aside, it is possible to recognize the merit in the basic argument. Although the Supreme Court has gradually constitutionalized the field of democratic politics since it entered that "thicket" in the Warren Court era,[64] the result has not been the domestication of election law *within* the Constitution, but its gradual estrangement from the rest of constitutional law. Election law is a complex field. Its structures, laws, regulations, and elephantine judicial decisions are largely unfamiliar to constitutional law scholars, even those who work in the First Amendment. The relationship between election law and conventional First Amendment jurisprudence is about as close as that between a stereo installation manual and the sonnets of Shakespeare.

Second, the shape the law has taken in this area—meandering, under-theorized, and inconsistent with much of First Amendment law—is evidence that some recognition of the institutional nature of electoral politics might be a good thing. Not only in the First Amendment but across constitutional law, there are electoral cases that do not fit squarely into surrounding doctrine.[65] That inconsistency does not tell us whether election law ought to conform more closely to conventional First Amendment doctrine or instead should strike out in radical new directions. Where the First Amendment is concerned, the Supreme Court seems increasingly inclined to follow the former course.[66] Either way, however, if the Court is going to enter this thicket, it ought to know what the effects of its actions will be. General principles alone will not answer those questions very well. A more institutionally oriented approach might.

Third, the institutional turn is not a grant of unbounded autonomy. It insists that the law must reflect the broader purposes of the social institution in question. Where autonomy and institutional self-regulation will best serve those purposes, they are what we should have; where more state regulation is required—or where such regulation is part of the institutional structure itself, as some have argued with respect to campaign finance laws—the institutional turn should allow it.

In either case, my point is not that the "institution" of "politics" ought to be allowed to do whatever it wants, or that the state, as a participant in that institution, ought to be able to regulate it at will. It is that it may be time to rethink our categories. The law, rather than prizing its own purity above all else, should be responsive to and reflective of our social practices. Some have argued that the values underlying the First Amendment would be better served if we allowed more regulation of the political process instead of subjecting such laws to strict scrutiny.[67] I reserve judgment on that question. But an institutional understanding of politics at least reminds us that the fundamental goal of First Amendment institutionalism is to have better doctrinal categories, not simply to immunize certain institutions from regulation altogether.

Finally, a strong institutional approach to electoral speech would carry costs as well as benefits. Increased government discretion to regulate elections and electoral speech might well lead to abuse. The idea of the state as a dangerous censor is a caricature, but it is not unfounded. The principal argument against government regulation of campaign finance and other forms of electoral "speech"—namely, that elected officials will use the law in a self-serving fashion to protect incumbents and hurt challengers—has force. As John Hart Ely put it, "Courts must police inhibitions on expression . . . because we cannot trust elected officials to do so: ins have a way of wanting to make sure the outs stay out."[68] We might hesitate before giving government too much regulatory power in this area, even in the name of institutionalism. *Citizens United* might be a problematic decision, insofar as it displays a lack of clarity or realism about the social and institutional facts involved, while still remaining more or less the right outcome.[69]

Moreover, because the Supreme Court has moved in the direction of applying strict scrutiny to laws that regulate campaign finance and other aspects of electoral speech, there would be significant costs involved in transitioning to a more deferential regime. The question Robert Post asked more than a decade ago still applies: "what constitutionally would be gained, and what lost, by demarcating elections as a separate domain of First Amendment doctrine?" We cannot answer that question without doing what institutionalists demand: inquiring into the social and constitutional values "inherent in particular social structures, rather than communication per se."[70] The institutional turn should certainly influence the shape of First Amendment doctrine in the field of electoral speech. But that still tells us little about where the doctrine should go.

Our tour of the borderlands of First Amendment institutionalism closes on an open-ended note, if not a positively gloomy one. That is deliberate. The more clearly defined and essential to the infrastructure of public discourse an institution is, and the more capable of self-regulation, the easier it is to imagine taking the institutional turn. Most of Part Two has focused on those central institutions. They offer the strongest case for an institutional approach in place of a doctrine that struggles, sometimes against itself, to remain acontextual. But our path grows less certain the further away from that core we move. In the borderlands, answers are necessarily more tentative.

The broader lessons of the institutional turn are valuable, however, even for borderline institutions like corporate, commercial, and electoral speech. Whether at the core or at the periphery, we cannot make sense of current doctrine without paying careful attention to the social and institutional context of the speech in question.

III

Problems and Prospects

II

Critiques of First Amendment Institutionalism

The institutional turn is important, but it is not everything. As I have observed elsewhere in this book, it is not meant to be the
sole guide for First Amendment doctrine. It is a supplement, not a substitu-
tion. The soapbox speaker, as we have seen, does not constitute the whole
of public discourse.[1] Still, the soapbox speaker does exist, and she represents
a multitude of individual speakers for whom existing doctrine continues to
serve a valuable purpose. Current doctrine is weakest where its broad rules
do not adequately account for the importance of particular institutions and
their self-regulatory practices to the infrastructure of public discourse; in
such areas, I have argued, the institutional turn might greatly improve First
Amendment law. But current doctrine may function more productively in
other areas.[2] The institutional turn ought to be an important part of the
edifice of First Amendment law, not its entirety. Individual speakers, as well
as groups that do not constitute First Amendment institutions, should continue to be protected.

Moreover, even if First Amendment institutionalism is valuable, that
hardly means it is perfect. Reshaping First Amendment doctrine around
social and institutional categories can help make it more responsive to
the real world of public discourse and less top-down in its approach to the
regulation of public discourse. Even so, context will inevitably outstrip the
efforts of doctrine to account for it.

In this chapter, rather than make a strong positive argument for First Amendment institutionalism, I pause to examine some of the arguments against it. Only a few scholars, as yet, have raised questions about the costs and benefits of First Amendment institutionalism.[3] Others support the institutional turn but have acknowledged some of the questions it raises.[4] There have been few sustained critiques of the institutional turn in the First Amendment, however. The critics deserve their own turn at bat. Here, I summarize the best of these critiques and offer some of my own.

Substantive Critiques

DISTRUST OF GOVERNMENT

The standard justifications for freedom of speech include democratic self-government, individual autonomy, and self-fulfillment. Lurking behind all of these justifications, however, is something more: an overarching distrust of government.[5]

Distrust of government is pervasive in American history and culture.[6] John Hart Ely, who titled his classic contribution to American constitutional theory *Democracy and Distrust,* wrote that "a distrust of the self-serving motives of those in power significantly animates the entire enterprise" of judicial review. Erwin Chemerinsky has noted, "The conventional wisdom about the Constitution emphasizes the Framers' distrust in government, as reflected in their desire for separation of powers, federalism, and ultimately a bill of rights."[7] The conventional wisdom may not be entirely accurate, but clearly distrust of government is a primordial and perennial concern in American society.

Nowhere is this distrust more apparent than in First Amendment law. A "deep[ ] distrust of governmental power" infuses First Amendment law.[8] It has long been "immanent though unarticulated in the Court's basic approach to free speech."[9]

In many respects, distrust of government explains First Amendment doctrine better than the other standard justifications of free speech.[10] If we valued democratic self-government above all, we might ask of a law regulating speech only whether it enhances or diminishes our capacity for self-government. Many speech-restrictive laws, such as those regulating nonpolitical expression like art, might be treated as irrelevant to this inquiry; others might be upheld on the grounds that some restrictions on speech, such as campaign finance laws, *enhance* democratic self-governance.[11] Similarly, if we valued autonomy or self-fulfillment above all else, we might ask *in each case* whether the challenged law directly furthered those values or not.[12]

But we don't. "The rules implementing the First Amendment," Richard Fallon writes, "seldom direct that cases should be resolved on the basis of an all-things-considered assessment of what would be best in light of underlying values" such as autonomy, democracy, or self-fulfillment. Such an approach would be desirable in theory but perilous in fact. It would require government decision-makers to make those assessments, and we do not trust them to do so fairly and competently. That distrust leads us to craft rules that put government officials and judges at one remove from those kinds of determinations.[13]

The central rule of the modern First Amendment—content neutrality—is a strong example. It is best understood as a mechanism for keeping substantive decisions about the merits of speech out of the hands of legislatures and courts alike.[14] Starting from the assumption that government restrictions on speech should not be trusted, the courts "presume improper motivation" when the government aims its regulatory power at the content of speech.[15]

Distrust of government forms a powerful basis for criticizing First Amendment institutionalism. The criticism is twofold. First, our primary concern should be with the state and the dangers it poses to public discourse, not with various speech institutions. Second, institutionalism will give the state too much power to play favorites. Courts will single out for protection those "traditional" institutions favored by the elite.[16] Both arguments have their virtues, but both are flawed.

The first argument—that we should focus on the state rather than speech institutions—is valid enough. It has not escaped notice that its application is highly inconsistent: we distrust government's ability to single out certain kinds of hate speech for regulation, for instance,[17] but not to enforce speech-centered criminal laws such as those involving threats or conspiracies. Still, that inconsistency does not make the argument invalid.[18]

But this argument has other problems. Government actors who are dangerous enough to warrant the kinds of rigid tests applied by the courts in First Amendment cases are surely crafty enough to find ways of getting around those tests. Indeed, in some ways, the more rigid the doctrine, the easier it is to circumvent. (And the more necessary. Even if we assume the purest of motives on the part of the government, one lesson of this book is that the contexts in which speech arises are so various that judges *must* bend the law to take away its sting in particular circumstances.) Courts routinely characterize content-neutral laws as content-specific, and vice versa, in order to achieve a particular outcome. Even where laws are content-neutral, the government retains power to regulate a substantial amount of speech.[19] So the argument from distrust of government is just as applicable to existing doctrine as it is to the institutional turn.

Of course, no approach can restrain government perfectly. Even a better mousetrap can't catch every mouse. The point of current doctrine is not to eliminate the possibility of government abuse but to *constrain* it. So we might still have reason to favor current doctrine over the institutional approach. But we must weigh the alternatives fairly. Current doctrine is far from perfect. Inconsistency of application makes it an uncertain hedge against government abuse. Conversely, the institutional approach is not blind to the dangers of government discretion. It simply adopts another set of rules to guard against it—rules based on institutional rather than doctrinal categories.[20]

All I am arguing here is that we have less reason to fear the institutional turn from the perspective of distrust of government than we might assume, and less assurance that current doctrine is a guarantee of safety. Against the possible costs of the institutional approach, we must weigh the imperfections of current doctrine. The balance is close enough that we can at least consider taking the institutional turn—especially when we keep in mind that its reach is limited to First Amendment institutions, leaving current doctrine in place for other areas.[21]

We must also consider the underinclusiveness of current doctrine. One of the principal goals of the institutional turn is to make First Amendment doctrine responsive to the actual social roles and practices of particular speech institutions. Current doctrine has failed, in cases involving newsgathering, libraries, and other institutions, to provide full protection for the kinds of activities we value in these institutions. Indeed, distrust of government, which results in broad and acontextual doctrinal rules, sometimes results in *less* protection for these institutions.[22] That is not to say current doctrine offers them *no* protection. But it is unclear whether it is ultimately any more speech-protective than the institutional turn would be.

The second argument from distrust of government is that courts would play favorites. Like the first argument, it does not sufficiently distinguish itself from current doctrine. In theory, courts operating under the present doctrine ought to treat a university the same as a fishmonger. In practice, that is not the case. Courts may be insufficiently attentive to institutional context, but they are hardly blind to it.[23] No court has said that fishmongers, like universities, "occupy a special niche in constitutional tradition."[24] What current doctrine lacks is not *any* protections for important speech institutions, but consistency and coherence in the justification and application of those protections. That incoherent state is far more fertile ground for abuse than an openly institutional approach would be.

It *is* possible that under the institutional turn judges would be slow to recognize new speech institutions and quicker to protect "traditional" elite institutions. But that possibility should not be fatal. For one thing, the institutional turn does not require the abandonment of current doctrinal rules where "First Amendment institutions" are not involved. If a court rejected the claim that some emerging institution was entitled to autonomy as a First Amendment institution, it could still fall back on standard First Amendment doctrine.

Moreover, this conservatism has a purpose. We single out First Amendment institutions for autonomy because they are well-established central elements of the infrastructure of public discourse and because they have a substantial tradition of self-regulation. Where those conditions don't clearly apply, there is less reason to grant them institutional autonomy. That does not mean emerging institutions cannot eventually win some autonomy, as we saw with the case of the new media in Chapter 6. But if courts are slow to identify those institutions, there may be some wisdom in that.

Last but not least, we should remember two central aspects of First Amendment institutionalism. First, although it seeks a more responsive, reflexive approach to the conduct of First Amendment institutions, in order to respect the insfrastructural value of these institutions within public discourse and to make law better reflect our actual social practices, First Amendment institutionalism does not seek the kind of all-in, case-by-case contextualism that might make it easier for courts to play favorites. It operates more categorically than that, singling out general kinds of institutions—newspapers, churches, and so on—and deferring to them as long as they act within proper (but broadly defined) institutional bounds. A court would thus not be in a ready position to recognize the institutional autonomy of one newspaper and reject, on arbitrary grounds, the similar status of another.

Second, recall from our discussion of sphere sovereignty, the British pluralists, and other sources that one of the basic concepts at work in First Amendment institutionalism is the idea that the state is but one part of our infrastructure of public discourse and social life, and that other institutions—associations, churches, universities, and others—are equally vital and legitimate parts of our social order. In asserting that our social and political system is not simply "a matter of the individual and the state," and emphasizing the importance and independence of a "multitude of different associations and communities," especially First Amendment institutions, the institutional turn may serve as another, and perhaps a better, means of restraining government.[25]

In short, the arguments from distrust of government have some weight. But they are not strong enough to justify current doctrine, especially given its imperfections in guarding against the very abuse by government that it is supposed to rein in. Nor are these concerns left entirely unaddressed by the institutional turn itself.

Furthermore, distrust of government is not the end of the story. It tells us we ought to be wary of the government, but it says nothing about what institutions we ought to *trust* enough to grant them heightened constitutional protection. If our concern is with what institutions best serve First Amendment values and guard against abusive government action, we need a full comparative institutional analysis, one that includes significant speech institutions.[26]

Once we take that full picture into account, the calculus grows more complicated. Many people may distrust "government" in bulk, for example, but trust public universities. The question is not whether government ought to be reined in by doctrinal tools such as content neutrality. It is whether we are better off taking that route than taking the institutional turn, which gives substantial autonomy to *some* speech institutions, private or public, fettering government in some ways but liberating it in others—not because it is the "government," but because some public entities have an important *institutional* status.

DISTRUST OF INSTITUTIONS

Of course, not everyone trusts institutions. In keeping with the traditional First Amendment focus on the soapbox speaker, along with Americans' traditional ambivalence toward large institutions, many First Amendment scholars are inclined to distrust them. They deride the institutional press as a slow-moving Goliath set against an army of individual Davids, each wielding a blog instead of a slingshot.[27] They wonder whether the modern university still deserves academic freedom.[28] They question whether churches, which are capable of profound abuses, ought to be any less subject to the law than anyone else.[29] They view the Boy Scouts of America as a corporate behemoth,[30] and argue more broadly that private institutions, no less than the government, pose a potential threat to individual rights.[31]

Institutions—all institutions, the government included—*are* imperfect. The institutional turn carries costs and risks as well as benefits and possibilities. Even institutions that are capable of self-regulation are not capable of *perfect* self-regulation. Churches have betrayed their members' trust, in ways ranging from sexual abuse to the dismissal of ministerial employees for illegitimate reasons. Newspapers have printed inaccuracies, some carelessly and some maliciously; what may be worse, they have failed to work hard enough at ferreting out the truth. Libraries have blundered and censored. Universities have abused their professional discretion. Voluntary associations can make entry, exit, and the exercise of voice difficult. In an imperfect world, both individuals and associations, public or private, will sometimes misuse their freedoms. First Amendment institutionalism does not pretend otherwise.

But that is not the question. The issue is whether an approach that takes seriously the institutions that contribute to the infrastructure of public discourse might, on balance, improve First Amendment law, even when the less than ideal conduct of individual First Amendment institutions has been factored in. It is, in short, a matter for comparative analysis. Critics who argue from distrust of institutions cannot win the argument by asserting what we already know—that institutions are capable of harm as well as good. They can prevail only by showing that, all else being equal, current doctrine does a better job than institutionalism of reining in institutional abuse *and* harnessing institutional benefits.

Critics of First Amendment institutionalism have not yet attempted such a task.[32] I doubt they could succeed if they did. At most, the case for this argument will be marginal. Acontextuality is a double-edged sword. It hems in government abuse by limiting the occasions on which government can regulate speech as speech, but it hems in institutions by treating them all the same. Such a crude tool works clumsily at best. Because it is aimed primarily at *governmental* abuse, it will not prevent every instance of institutional abuse. And because, if applied consistently, it prohibits government from tailoring its regulations and exemptions in a way that serves the underlying value of these institutions, it may do a poor job of *advancing* these institutions in situations where they actually *enhance* public discourse.

Looming behind all of this is the fact that current doctrine is hardly as crisp as this description suggests. The courts' statement that generally applicable laws apply to religious claimants as much as anyone else has not prevented them from carving out constitutional exemptions for religious institutions that discriminate in hiring, for example. Current doctrine sometimes underprotects institutions and sometimes exempts them from regulation—but without any clarity or consistency as to when or why. The courts, trapped by their scorn for "the law of the churn," lack the doctrinal tools to justify or reconcile this state of affairs.

First Amendment institutionalism is no guarantee of good behavior by First Amendment institutions. But its emphasis on bounded autonomy, self-regulation, institutional evolution and pluralism, and a bottom-up approach to judicial review *may* do better than current doctrine at restraining the bad and encouraging the good in those institutions. In emphasizing bounded autonomy and treating these institutions as entitled to substantial judicial deference when following their own best practices, the institutional turn seeks to harness both the virtues of these institutions and their capacity for self-regulation. It leaves room for them to evolve. And by emphasizing that evolving best practices will be a safe harbor against government regulation or judicial review, it encourages them to live up to their own ideals and learn from one another.

The institutional turn may also do a better job of unleashing the potential of First Amendment institutions. It does so by being *responsive* rather than indifferent to them. Its focus on their contributions and capacities invites the courts to encourage and protect their positive aspects, such as press newsgathering, rather than treating the First Amendment solely as a negative device aimed at restraining government. Its focus on *institutional* character means that courts will be less blinkered by the public-private distinction and more capable of treating some public institutions, such as libraries and universities, as First Amendment institutions rather than perceiving only the monolithic state.

This is speculative, to be sure. But it answers one piece of the argument from distrust of institutions: that any approach that emphasizes the autonomy of First Amendment institutions runs the risk of doing greater harm than good. That is true. As Justice Holmes taught us, all constitutional law is an experiment. But the institutional approach might not be so perilous an experiment after all; it has its own ways of restraining the worst in institutions and bringing out the best. Moreover, current doctrine has not succeeded spectacularly at achieving the same goals.

This will not satisfy those who believe that every institution is a threat—that the "mainstream media" have failed us completely, or that the Boy Scouts and the churches are leviathans. I think their fears are overstated. The potential for rich, inclusive, and productive public discourse is greater *with* these core speech institutions in our midst than without them. And institutional self-regulation can be as powerful a force for restraint as state regulation or heightened judicial scrutiny. To say that regulators and courts should not second-guess these institutions is not to say that either their members or the broader public cannot criticize them. Institutions evolve precisely through this mechanism of internal debate and external criticism. The mechanism will not stop working just because we recognize the limits of *state* intervention into these separate spheres. Indeed, to the extent that the institutional turn, by placing more responsibility in the hands of the institutions themselves and of the public, encourages more institutional self-examination and greater public scrutiny of and engagement with these institutions, it may lead to a better, richer, more productive and effective public discourse as a result.

Nor should we forget the importance of institutional pluralism. The *New York Times* is a powerful newspaper, but it is not the only model of journalism, and the more powerful it becomes, the more competitors it attracts.

The Boy Scouts is a large association, but not the only one; and its public positions, such as its views on homosexuality, may provoke both internal debate and the rise of substitute groups. The Roman Catholic Church is a powerful entity, but it does not lack internal debate. As long as voice and exit remain part of the picture, and as long as any given institution exists within a diverse ecology of competing institutions, we should not turn the fear of institutions into a legal principle that threatens to hinder more than help.

INDIVIDUALISM

Another objection to the institutional turn is that it runs contrary to a long tradition of individualism in First Amendment discourse and doctrine. On this view, the First Amendment's function is "to sponsor the individualism, the rebelliousness, the antiauthoritarianism, the spirit of nonconformity within all of us."[33] The mere suggestion that this tradition ought to be tempered may occasion resistance.

Whatever sympathy I have with that position[34] is not enough to make me favor building an impregnable wall around current First Amendment doctrine. For one thing, that view gives too much credit to current doctrine's ability to serve the individualist ideal. The First Amendment today has more to do with distrust of government than with trust in individuals. Doctrinal tools such as the distinction between content-neutral and content-based regulations of speech serve to restrain the state, not to enhance speech; they may sometimes even have the net effect of reducing the total amount of individual speech.[35] It is a mistake to see current doctrine as a perfect guarantor of individual self-expression.

More important, any argument from individualism that is indifferent to speech institutions—to what I have called the infrastructure of public discourse—will be incomplete. If we value individualism we must value institutions as well, because of what they mean for individual self-development and self-expression. We humans do not emerge from the womb with our identities fully formed. We are social beings. Just as one cannot be "an orchestra musician without an orchestra,"[36] so one cannot find meaning and identity without a community in which to forge that identity.[37] Even the most silent monks have religious brothers; even the most introverted individuals find solace and connection in social groups. What are large sectors of social life on the Internet if not gathering places of individuals who feel otherwise disconnected from society—a kind of online island of misfit toys, finding fellowship at last?

Institutions are just as vital for self-expression as for self-formation. The Tom Paine of First Amendment tradition is just as much a creature of institutions as of romantic individualism. He is formed by education, made infamous by newspapers, sustained or railed against by churches, and remembered by libraries. Individuals become a public and monologues become dialogues because of the institutions that knit them together. To genuinely value individuals is to value the institutions that form, connect, and advance them. The First Amendment need not deny the importance of individualism in order to recognize the centrality of institutions to public discourse.

EQUALITY

Much of modern First Amendment doctrine is meant to hold legislatures and courts to the principle of equality: that government "may not use its regulatory power to increase [or decrease] the ability of unpopular or minority voices to reach their audience. All points of view must be treated the same."[38]

Concern with equality looms large in judicial and scholarly resistance to the institutional turn. One major reason courts have refused to endow the Press Clause with any independent force—and why some journalists themselves agree with this position—is that it could enshrine the press as an elite group. The same impulse underlies resistance to the notion of institutional privileges for churches. Similarly, although courts often treat universities differently from other institutions, a concern for equality underlies the refusal to grant them any special privileges against the disclosure of confidential deliberations in antidiscrimination litigation.[39] Arguments from equality are shot through with suspicion of efforts to give "special rights" to some institutions.[40]

The equality objection to the institutional turn has both principled and pragmatic aspects. At the level of principle, the argument is that according special treatment to any particular speaker or speech institution violates the basic tenet that all speakers are equal. At the pragmatic level, it has more to do with the incompetence of government officials and judges to make distinctions between more or less important or deserving institutions. Better to treat all speakers and speech institutions the same than to do a bad job of sorting them out.

The argument from equality has some traction. But its rhetorical appeal is stronger than the argument itself. Pragmatically, it is not true that current doctrine is genuinely impartial to different speakers or institutions. Even under the spell of acontextuality, courts regularly make qualitative distinctions between speakers and speech situations on the basis of context—often in areas where there is little reason to think they are competent to do so.[41] If the First Amendment is to have much meaning at all, courts will have to make distinctions, or to defer when government officials make them, as in the case of the vast array of nonconstitutional press privileges. As one critic of institutionalism has observed, "the fact that a First Amendment theory calls for line drawing is not a sufficient objection to that theory. Line drawing is both inevitable and desirable in First Amendment doctrine."[42]

That current doctrine already draws such distinctions is not an argument *for* the institutional turn. But it suggests the weakness of the pragmatic version of the argument from equality. Indeed, the fact that the institutional turn openly contemplates treating institutions "unequally," while current doctrine professes equality without practicing it, suggests that the institutional turn might ultimately do a *better* job of respecting equality. Institutionalism at least offers an *argument* for the preferential treatment of certain institutions, a basis for defining those institutions, and a reflexive approach designed to ensure that institutions remain consistent with their function and mission. By contrast, the inconsistency of current doctrine is as likely to produce confusion as equality.

The argument from equality is flawed at the level of principle as well. There is an equality of sorts in treating a soapbox speaker the same as a newspaper. But equality—as "Sesame Street" and Aristotle tell us—ultimately consists in treating like things alike and different things differently; and not all speech acts or speech institutions are alike. Much depends on the baseline we adopt.[43] For some purposes, a broad range of speakers and speech institutions may be alike; especially where content regulation is concerned, there may be good reasons to require the state to treat all speech the same. But even here, current doctrine does not always do so, as we saw in Chapter 1 with the distinction between "high-value" and "low-value" speech. At other times, however, we *do* distinguish between different speech acts and speech institutions. And so we should. Some institutions play especially important roles in public discourse. These institutions are worth valuing, not just in themselves, but for what they contribute at both an individual and a social level to identity formation, speech, and democratic participation. These contributions arguably demand special treatment—sometimes more expansive freedom and sometimes, as with the rigorous, content-specific disciplinary standards of evaluation for academic speech, tighter constraints. Institutions require different treatment because they make distinct contributions to public discourse. This impulse is the essence of equality, not its negation.

This is not the only possible baseline, although it is a good one, and one that the courts often implicitly adopt. The argument from distrust of government provides reasons why we might opt for a baseline that treats all speech equally. My goal is not to claim an absolute victory for the institutional turn. It is simply to point out that the arguments against it are not as strong as they may seem. It is not clear that current doctrine truly serves the principle of equality; it is not clear that granting "special rights" or "privileges" to central speech institutions truly undermines that principle. There is ample room to imagine carving up First Amendment doctrine in a more institutionally sensitive way without sacrificing substantive equality.

Standards and Balancing versus Rules and Categories

Another objection falls between the substantive and procedural critiques of the institutional turn. It forms part of an endless conversation in law: the debate between rules and standards. Should law focus on broad categorical rules that can be applied mechanically, such as a rule that no vehicle may exceed fifty-five miles per hour on a highway with that posted speed? Or should it focus instead on broader standards more closely keyed to the goal of the particular law, such as a statute that forbids driving at an unsafe speed?

In First Amendment doctrine, this debate is often phrased in terms of balancing versus categoricalism. The categorical approach to the First Amendment, somewhat like the rule-based approach to law, asks whether a given case "falls within certain predetermined, outcome-determinative lines." In theory, once something has been slotted into a particular category—high- or low-value speech, content-neutral or content-discriminatory regulation, and so on—"all the important work in litigation is done." Balancing, by contrast, requires the judge in a First Amendment case to "place competing rights and interests on a scale and weigh them against each other."[44] The result of that exercise rests on factors such as the importance of the asserted right and the strength of the government's asserted interest.

Advocates of both balancing and categoricalism will each have their own concerns with the institutional turn. Those who favor categoricalism may fear that an institutionally sensitive and openly contextual approach will lead to ad hoc balancing, in which the courts engage in an unprincipled form of all-things-considered decision-making.[45] Advocates of balancing may fear that, by singling out institutions for a general presumption of autonomy, the First Amendment inquiry will be overinclusive, protecting those institutions even where core speech values are not implicated.[46]

There is something sterile about this whole debate. In theory, these approaches are distinct; in practice, they tend to converge.[47] Rules and categories will tend to proliferate and loosen; the more rigid they are, the more likely they are to end up riddled with exceptions. Standards and balancing approaches will morph into increasingly rigid rules and categories, as judges reach a consensus about which contexts should generally yield the same result in every case.[48]

In any event, neither approach is necessarily inconsistent with the institutional turn. Rather, the institutional turn uses both. To the extent that it makes the identification of central speech institutions a linchpin of its analysis and accords them substantial autonomy, it is somewhat categorical in nature. To the extent that it allows courts to ask, albeit deferentially, whether the practices of a given institution align with that institution's mission, self-regulatory role, and contribution to public discourse, it allows for some balancing.

One thing the institutional turn is *not,* however, is a recipe for ad hoc balancing. If anything, it is about the proper allocation of institutional responsibility for decisions, a concern that looms large in constitutional law but, as we have seen, is not always dealt with well by current First Amendment doctrine, with its preference for general, institutionally agnostic rules. Institutionally minded courts will not engage in an unweighted, all-things-considered balancing of factors. Rather, their first and most important task will be to identify First Amendment institutions and defer to them. To the extent that they are called on to determine whether an institution is acting outside the bounds of its autonomy, the inquiry will not be ad hoc. Rather, the courts will weigh particular institutional practices against the broader backdrop of public discourse, the norms and traditions of the institution, and what the ongoing experience of those institutions teaches about those institutions' best practices. The constraints on balancing under this approach will use different "categories" from those found today, to be sure. But there will still be categories and constraints. There is room for debate over the precise mixture of rules and standards, categories and balancing, that ought to comprise the institutional approach. Those general concerns will inevitably remain part of the discussion under the institutional turn. But they neither contradict it nor offer any reason to worry more over this approach than about current doctrine.

Procedural Critiques

Another set of criticisms of First Amendment institutionalism is more focused on procedure. It concerns the practical difficulties and costs of adopting a more institutionally sensitive framework. As law students quickly learn, the line between substance and procedure is blurry. But "procedural" is a useful term here; it captures the idea that even those who see the institutional turn as substantively attractive may believe there are strong procedural or second-order arguments against it. I consider a few representative concerns here.

DEFINITIONAL PROBLEMS

The central question for courts contemplating some version of the institutional turn is how to define the relevant institutions. The classic example is the Supreme Court's refusal to grant strong privileges to journalists under the Press Clause because of the difficulty of figuring out who would qualify.[49] Likewise, some scholars fear that courts' definitions of First Amendment institutions will be flawed, suspect, or boundless.[50]

These arguments have some merit. It *is* hard to identify a First Amendment institution with precision, particularly a new or emerging one. At the same time, some institutions *are* relatively easy to discern. It may be tough to distinguish the *New York Times* from a local penny-saver in theory, but it is much easier in practice.

Even at the borderlands of First Amendment institutionalism, the definitional questions are not insurmountable. We are not asking whether something is an institution *tout court,* but whether it is a *First Amendment* institution: whether it is central to the infrastructure of public discourse, well established by custom, and capable of meaningful self-regulation consistent with its function. The answers to those questions may be hard to get exactly right, but it is possible to do a pretty fair job.

Nor is the definitional inquiry any more troubling than the kinds of questions courts already ask. Courts routinely draw lines in First Amendment doctrine. It is true that under the institutional turn those lines will be more influenced by the lifeworld—the lived experience of public discourse—than the conceptual lines that lawyers currently draw. But even though courts today talk in terms of conceptual categories, they often smuggle in contextual and social definitions. As long as they are caught between the lure of acontextuality and the call of context, any lines they draw may be blurrier than anything the institutional turn would produce. Like the other arguments against institutionalism, the definitional argument is reason for caution, not opposition.

Setting Limits

Another procedural question asks whether courts will grant First Amendment institutions too much (or too little) autonomy. This concern is especially pertinent for those who resist the institutional turn because they distrust institutions, worrying that courts will defer too broadly to these institutions and allow them to run roughshod over individual rights. We have already discussed this argument, and I hope this book has at least demonstrated that there are still grounds to consider taking the institutional turn. But I am trying to begin the debate, not end it.

At a procedural level, the concern is less grave. Every system of rights is also a system of limits.[51] Whether we think of constitutional law in terms of rules or standards ultimately makes little difference. Courts and other government bodies will either balance different rights against different interests on a case-by-case basis or engage in a similar calculus at the front end, when they frame the categorical rule and its exceptions. There is simply no getting around this necessity. Nor is there any reason to think that that the current doctrinal approach is any better at eliminating it than the institutional turn would be

Indeed, the institutional turn might do better. Current First Amendment jurisprudence is so caught between the desire to craft acontextual doctrine and the need to make allowances for context that it can do neither coherently. The institutional turn at least offers a clear and relatively well-grounded set of justifications for the limits it imposes on institutional autonomy. It asks whether a particular institution is acting within the scope of its proper mission and functional contribution to public discourse, and it does so in a bottom-up manner that is capable of respecting institutions' capacity for self-regulation and encouraging their best practices. It makes central speech institutions partners with the courts in implementing the First Amendment, while allowing the courts to retain an important, if chastened, role as monitors and coordinators of institutional practices.

Neither the courts nor the institutions themselves will always get the balance right. But we should not assume they will always fail at the task. The path of doctrinal development under the institutional turn will have its own twists and turns, as all doctrinal development does. But it *will* have standards—standards that are responsive to the real world of public discourse rather than tethered to the judicial obsession with doctrinal purity.

Moreover, the institutional turn is not meant to be the whole of First Amendment law. Outside the institutional setting, current doctrine will still apply. The question, therefore, is whether a mixed system, which allows for some responsiveness to key speech institutions while providing a back-stop of standard doctrine for other speakers, would make us better off than a doctrinal system that emphasizes only acontextuality, and thus cannot make sense of its own frequent and inevitable recognition of contextual specificity. That question cannot be answered definitively. But when properly understood, it is closer to equipoise than defenders of current doctrine might suppose.

TRANSITION COSTS

The strongest procedural or systemic argument against the institutional turn involves transition costs.[52] Every move from one legal regime to another creates a host of difficulties as people adapt. Expectations must be adjusted; those who live under the new rules must alter their behavior; those who apply them must reeducate themselves. If transition costs are too large, it may not make sense to change, even for a new regime that is superior to the old one.[53] Despite the possibility that the institutional turn represents an advance in First Amendment doctrine, then, the question remains whether it is worth taking. Answering this question requires us to consider both the benefits of the change and the costs of making it.

I believe the costs would be relatively small. First, the institutional turn signifies a partial change in First Amendment doctrine, not a total makeover. While it requires a modification of the way courts treat some speech institutions, it does not demand that all of First Amendment doctrine be scrapped.

Second, as we saw in Part One, the problem with current doctrine is not that it utterly rejects an institutionally sensitive approach, but that it contradicts itself. Sometimes courts insist on acontextuality; sometimes they consider institutional context. The point of the institutional turn is to make the courts more candid and consistent about the role and value of particular speech institutions. But it does not require us to start with a blank slate. Its seeds already exist in current doctrine, however inconsistent and undertheorized the courts' respect for institutional context may be. Given the degree of concern for context that is present, albeit submerged, in current doctrine, we should not exaggerate the costs of shifting to a more institutionally sensitive doctrine.

So much for the costs. We must also ask about the benefits of doctrinal change. As Dale Carpenter has pointed out, "Every time we 'carve up' the First Amendment we run . . . risks." He argues that none of the potential benefits of the institutional turn are "compelling enough at this stage to run the risks created by a newly institution-conscious First Amendment," especially given the extent to which current doctrine already, if inconsistently, accommodates institutions.[54]

This is a double-edged argument. If courts and government officials already grant some autonomy to First Amendment institutions, then the benefits of the institutional turn are reduced, and even minor costs may deter us from making the switch. On the other hand, if the courts are *already* institutionally sensitive at times, then the risks Carpenter worries about must perforce be relatively small and the benefits need not be so great to justify taking the institutional turn.

I think the benefits outweigh the costs. In some cases, our central speech institutions are hampered by current doctrine. For example, although there is some legal protection for newsgathering and other activities by journalistic enterprises, there could be more still. We might benefit from the increase in original reporting this would encourage.

Moreover, we must also factor in the costs of current doctrine. First Amendment law today is caught between doctrinal purity and institutional sensitivity. It is at war with itself, and that leads to inconsistency and uncertainty. Current doctrine may tilt closer to acontextuality, at a cost to the independence of crucial speech institutions, or it may drift further away from it, thus undermining the benefits of generality and the predictability it purports to offer. Either way, we may be at a point of crisis, a juncture at which change is both necessary and inevitable.[55] It is at times like these, with the old doctrinal order foundering, that the possible benefits of doctrinal change are most attractive.

Candor, consistency, and stability in First Amendment doctrine are no small things. They are exactly what current doctrine promises—but fails—to provide. An institutionally sensitive First Amendment may, in the long run, offer more of these goods than the current approach can. It is *possible*, at least, that the benefits of moving to a more institutionally responsive vision of the First Amendment will outweigh the costs.

12

Institutionalism Beyond The First Amendment?

My concluding chapter is about connections. Through most of the book, my focus has been close to the ground. In Part One, I presented some problems with current First Amendment doctrine and argued that the institutional turn represents a potentially feasible solution. Both the problems and the solution are closely related and practically oriented. The First Amendment and the values it serves involve much more than a contest between a single individual speaker and a single sovereign state. As the pragmatist philosopher John Dewey observed, "[p]eople are creatures of social context."[1] One crucial piece of this context is that the speech that makes up public discourse, and the values of the people who engage in it, are often formed and communicated in and through certain institutions, which form as central a part of our social order, and of what I call the infrastructure of public discourse, as the state itself. A doctrine that is too "institutionally agnostic," too driven by the categories of the law-world to take proper account of "the differentiated institutions that together comprise a society,"[2] will fail to give us the kind of responsive, reflexive, institutionally aware approach that could make First Amendment law, and public discourse itself, all it should be.

In Part Two, by looking closely at those institutions themselves, we saw that it is possible and potentially beneficial to take an institutional turn in the First Amendment, and saw how courts often do just that, despite the continued obeisance they pay to acontextual legal rules. The institutional turn could make better sense of the doctrine we have now, with its profusion of exceptions, qualifications, and seemingly ad hoc decisions, while pointing it in new and better directions.

Here, though, I do not want to conclude by way of summation, but instead to look outward: to move in some ways beyond First Amendment institutionalism itself, in order to better understand its place within constitutional theory. I will draw together a variety of emerging ideas in constitutional law and theory, ideas that may seem distant from the project of First Amendment institutionalism and, sometimes, even from one another. Each has been subject to external criticism and internal debate, and each has its differences from the other. But my goal here is to lump, not to split. Ultimately, all of these seemingly disparate ideas support the institutional turn in the First Amendment and point to something larger.

Drawing these connections has two payoffs for a turn toward institutionalism and away from the lure of acontextuality. First, there is substantial common ground among the many scholars who are dissatisfied with the state of constitutional law, and specifically with the state of First Amendment law. They find a widening gap between what the law says and what it does, between its promises and capacities, between the law-world and the lifeworld. They have sought to put constitutional law on a sounder and more responsive footing. The institutional turn in the First Amendment is a natural ally of this movement.

Second, by pointing out the surprising degree of common ground in these constitutional reform efforts, I hope to show that First Amendment institutionalism, and the institutional turn in constitutional law more generally, deserves greater attention. Given its consistency with a broad range of emerging approaches in constitutional law and theory, the institutional turn in the First Amendment may draw legitimacy and strength from those projects. In turn, it may offer them a greater degree of detail and clarity. Taken together, these emerging ideas about constitutional law and governance, and the kinship they exhibit, offer one more reason that we should at least imagine taking the institutional turn, in the First Amendment and elsewhere.

Rethinking Doctrine

The central debate in constitutional law and theory is over the "meaning" of the Constitution. The standard approach seeks, in fairly Olympian terms, the "true" meaning of the Constitution, and suggests in turn that the answer to that question will tell us how the Constitution ought to apply in concrete cases. The discussion often focuses on which interpretive methods might enable judges, in particular, to apply the Constitution *legitimately*. It is an important debate, but tends to become tedious and intractable.

In recent years, a number of scholars have turned their attention away from what we might call the "inputs" of constitutional meaning—text, history, structure, and so on—and focused instead on the "judicial *outputs* that feature in the enterprise of constitutional adjudication."[3] They argue that an inevitable gap exists between "the meaning of constitutional guarantees, on the one hand, and judicially enforceable rights, on the other."[4] The gap arises because courts are institutional actors, hemmed in by imperfect knowledge of the "pure" meaning of the Constitution, of the facts of actual cases, or both. Moreover, discovering and applying "pure" constitutional meaning— if it even exists—is not their only task. They must also find ways of doing constitutional law that can be applied by courts, lawyers, and other actors.[5] They are administrators, not oracles. Thus, it is more productive to focus on "what the court *does*" than on what the law, in some abstract sense, "is."[6] This emerging body of constitutional scholarship has been variously labeled "constitutional implementation theory," "constitutional decision rules theory," "metadoctrinalism," and the "new doctrinalism."

This approach has its critics. Daryl Levinson has argued that the distinction between constitutional meaning and constitutional doctrine is misleading. There can be no two-step movement from pure constitutional meaning to constitutional implementation, because the two are inextricably intertwined. Similarly, Rick Hills asserts that no "gap exists between 'pure' constitutional meaning and implementing doctrine," because "the meaning of a constitutional provision *is* its implementation."[7]

For our lumper's purposes, however, there is a good deal of common ground between decision-rules theorists and critics like Levinson and Hills. Both believe that "forward-looking, empirical, and all-things-considered analyses" should "pervade constitutional adjudication," in contrast with attempts to understand the Constitution solely in light of historical meaning or "principle."[8] And both agree that "implementation of the law has critical importance for constitutional doctrine," although some see a meaningful distinction between meaning and doctrine while others do not.[9]

This line of scholarship offers support for the institutional First Amendment, and in turn may be strengthened by the arguments I offer in this book. To begin with, we agree on the general diagnosis of what ails constitutional law, although we use somewhat different language. The problem is what Kermit Roosevelt calls "constitutional calcification." Constitutional doctrine may be simple enough at first. Over time, however, as the Supreme Court encounters a variety of cases presenting different factual contexts, and as background factual or legal understandings change, "doctrine becomes more complex."[10] The Court is then faced with a number of equally imperfect choices. It can abandon or reform its doctrine in particular areas, but this may only create greater inconsistency within constitutional law as a whole. It can attempt to make broader doctrinal changes, but with similar risks. In the end, the Court may end up warping constitutional doctrine in the very act of trying to preserve it.

This argument is strikingly similar to my own in Part One. Constitutional calcification is, from this perspective, a description of courts caught between the lure of acontextuality and the need to implement law in a way that is responsive to factual and institutional context. The result is inconsistency and instability, as judges either fail to respond to relevant facts or attempt to maintain the supposed purity and generality of doctrine through legal subterfuge.[11]

Both First Amendment institutionalism and the "rethinking doctrine" movement prescribe roughly the same cure for this disease. The cure is not to forswear doctrine but to be more conscious of its role and function, and to narrow the gap between thinking "words" and thinking "things." Recall Justice Holmes's advice that we "must constantly translate our words into the facts for which they stand, if we are to keep to the real and the true."[12] That is our goal. Constitutional doctrine does not exist to celebrate its own purity. Law takes shape meaningfully only in application. The way to avoid constitutional calcification is to concentrate on how legal rules function in practice.

Thus, "rethinking doctrine" scholarship reinforces the diagnoses and prescriptions offered by the institutional turn. But the benefits run both ways.[13] First Amendment institutionalism deepens our understanding of one of the most valuable tools for the implementation of constitutional doctrine: judicial deference. By demonstrating the central role of deference as a doctrinal tool for constitutional implementation, institutionalism offers valuable details concerning how we actually go about implementing doctrine. Scholars involved in rethinking constitutional doctrine should view First Amendment institutionalism as a kindred spirit.

Rethinking Governance

Another important set of ideas in contemporary legal scholarship has been variously called "democratic experimentalism" and "new governance," previously discussed in Chapter 3. Its approach to law, emphasizing "decentralized yet centrally monitored government,"[14] focuses on problem-solving and collaborative learning among institutions and stakeholders rather than top-down regulation. This approach has been called "the most promising candidate for a theory of government activity in the [current] constitutional order."[15]

Both this approach and First Amendment institutionalism emphasize structuring constitutional law in a way that "responds to the conditions of modern life."[16] Few constitutional thinkers are indifferent to those conditions, of course. But these approaches share a sense of *how* to achieve the goal. They emphasize the value of non-state as well as state institutions, and they encourage those institutions to elaborate and revise their activities as circumstances change. They argue for a bottom-up rather than a top-down legal regime, one that devolves decision-making authority to the relevant institutions rather than concentrating it in the government. They urge regulators to foster "a system of experimentation, rather than[ ]—or at least in addition to—laying down specific rules."[17]

The new governance theorists have said less about the role of the courts—understandably, since their focus is on governance in general, not judicial review. What they *have* said, however, is consistent with First Amendment institutionalism.[18] Joanne Scott and Susan Sturm, for example, describe courts in the new governance regime as "catalysts." Courts and the institutions whose actions they review have a "dynamic and reciprocal" relationship: "courts both draw upon the practice of governance in their construction of the criteria they apply to their judgments and provide an incentive structure for participation, transparency, principled decision-making, and accountability which in turn shapes, directly and indirectly, the political and deliberative process." Courts should collaborate with institutions in crafting public norms, rather than serving as "unilateral interpreters and enforcers of legal rules."[19]

The kind of collaborative role that these scholars envision for the courts broadly resembles what I have said about the judicial role in First Amendment institutionalism. It is one in which courts learn from and defer to the norms and practices of institutions that are part of the infrastructure of public discourse, while encouraging those institutions to employ the best practices available to them given their own (potentially diverse) sense of mission.

The rethinking governance movement has its critics, to be sure.[20] Some of their criticisms resonate with the critiques of the institutional turn surveyed in Chapter 11—for example, that surrendering authority to local government bodies or private institutions will end up "deferring or compromising" the "liberal values of justice and democracy" and thus "put vulnerable people at risk."[21] Nevertheless, it is worth pointing out the common ties between First Amendment institutionalism and new governance. Those common ties reinforce the claims of this book, and give new governance theorists an additional reason to explore the implications of their work for First Amendment law.

Rethinking Sovereignty

The institutional turn offers a departure from the conventional view of the state as the sole source of power and interpretive authority. It argues that we might view First Amendment institutions as sovereign spheres of their own, partners rather than servants in the formation of constitutional meaning. Given the permeable nature of the border between "constitutional law" and "constitutional culture,"[22] this argument is not as novel or radical as it may seem. Even in current legal culture, with its urge toward acontextuality, First Amendment law is inevitably influenced by the central speech institutions that it governs. Still, we should not downplay the change from current thinking that this approach represents.

Stirrings of a parallel movement in constitutional theory are present in the work of Heather Gerken, who advocates a new way of thinking about the allocation of power across a range of governmental institutions. Gerken argues that our attachment to conventional notions of sovereignty, in which the sovereign exercises absolute power within its sphere, has led us to neglect the importance of a variety of "special purpose institutions"—"juries, zoning commissions, local school boards, locally elected prosecutors' offices, state administrative agencies, and the like." Paying closer attention to these institutions "would expand our understanding of how the center and periphery interact, helping us to develop an account of the power of the servant to compete with our existing account of the power of the sovereign."[23]

Gerken's focus is on governmental entities, not private ones. She is interested in questioning the nature of sovereignty rather than expanding the number of sovereigns. Although she argues that neither federalism scholars nor First Amendment scholars have fully considered the lessons each might have for the other, she concentrates not on the speech institutions we have focused on here, but on limited-purpose *public* entities, such as the jury, in which minorities can express themselves through the use of government power rather than resorting to dissent from outside government.[24]

That said, there are intriguing points of overlap between First Amendment institutionalism and Gerken's "rethinking sovereignty" project. They suggest a shared dissatisfaction with the ways in which we carve up the world under current doctrine, as well as a common set of recommendations for reform. Both are skeptical of accounts that overemphasize the power of the central government to impose public norms and open to the idea that legal meaning may reside in various entities. Both emphasize the structural nature of the First Amendment, not just the individualist view captured in the image of the soapbox orator. And both share the same fear: namely, that once power is devolved away from the central government, institutions may be able to "insulat[e] local decisions from reversal even when they fly in the face of deeply held national norms," a concern that is influenced by "the tragic history of slavery and Jim Crow."[25]

Neither account can justify the other; both may be wrong. Still, it is worth noting that they proceed from the same concerns and point to some of the same solutions—and that similar ideas show up in the "rethinking governance" literature as well. When so many people identify the same problem with the current approach and propose similar solutions, we might conclude that that there *is* a genuine problem, and the beginnings of a critical mass favoring a particular solution.

Other scholars have taken a pluralistic approach to sovereignty that resembles First Amendment institutionalism even more closely.[26] Following in the footsteps of Robert Cover and the legal pluralists of an earlier era, they reject the idea of "the state as an omnicompetent sovereign." They argue that "the government is only one of a bewildering array of overlapping and competing authorities,"[27] and that it is time to attempt "to articulate the normative jurisprudence that might flow from [this] observation[ ]."[28] They believe the law ought to leave more "space for variations and experimentation" by a variety of institutions, including the speech institutions that have been the focus of this book.[29]

Again, their common ties do not make these arguments correct. But the degree of overlap between these independent arguments about the possibility of expanding our understanding of sovereignty to include a variety of local or non-state actors is powerful evidence in support of the institutional turn.

Rethinking the Judicial Role

A key lesson of the institutional turn is that the meaning of the First Amendment is not the sole province of judges. When judges defer to the self-regulatory norms and practices of First Amendment institutions, they are not just making a statement about their own epistemic limitations. Nor are they ceding all authority to those institutions. Rather, they are accepting these institutions as *partners* in the shaping of constitutional meaning. Self-regulating institutions like churches and the press mostly cultivate their own goals and evolving traditions; they do not simply slavishly follow judicial instructions about the meaning of the First Amendment. In a sense, what they do, by virtue of their infrastructural role in public discourse, *is* the "meaning" of the First Amendment.

A similar line of thought can be found in a variety of writings on what has been called "the Constitution outside the courts." The general theme is that courts are not the only place in which constitutional meaning is fixed. We should recognize the role of other actors in constitutional interpretation: nonjudicial government institutions such as the executive and legislative branches, popular movements of citizens, and other public and private actors.

This general description obscures some important differences. Some writers have essentially argued that ridding ourselves of judicial review altogether would encourage a richer and less judicially straitened politics.[30] Some have advocated a form of "popular constitutionalism" in which "the people themselves" are the ultimate constitutional authority.[31]

That approach has recently inspired others, most notably Reva Siegel and Robert Post, to assert that the "pendulum" in constitutional theory "has swung too far, from excessive confidence in courts to excessive despair." They want to show that courts and social movements cooperate, sometimes peacefully and sometimes with considerable tension, in shaping constitutional meaning. From this perspective, "adjudication is embedded in a constitutional order that regularly invites exchange between officials and citizens over questions of constitutional meaning."[32] Courts play a vital role "in using professional reason to interpret the Constitution"; at the same time, "judgments based on professional legal reason can acquire democratic legitimacy only if professional reason is rooted in popular values and ideals."[33] When judicial pronouncements diverge significantly from the popular understanding, then the people, through a variety of popular movements, will attempt to "persuad[e] others—and therefore ultimately the Court—to embrace their views about constitutional meaning."[34]

These approaches focus on individuals and popular social movements, and their aim is to encourage a more democratically legitimate politics. There is a decidedly politically progressive tilt to much of this work.[35] By contrast, First Amendment institutionalism is more concerned with strengthening the structural role played by central speech institutions in our infrastructure of public discourse. It is largely indifferent to ideology or popular movements. It seeks, not to encourage better "left" or "right" politics, but to reinforce the institutional structures that are central to public discourse. Its goal is a more structurally sound public discourse, not a more just world as such.

But our common ground is just as important. We share a sense that judicial review, especially along a conventional top-down model, is not all there is. We refuse to treat actors and events outside the courts as mere "inputs" for judicial review and view nonjudicial actors—whether popular movements or established institutions—as partners with the judiciary in shaping constitutional meaning.[36]

Connections

Of course, there are dangers in "lumping" rather than "splitting."[37] But there are also benefits to bringing these approaches together and connecting them to First Amendment institutionalism. The first is diagnostic. An increasing number of legal scholars not only see problems with constitutional law and theory; they agree on what those problems are. In different ways, they share the basic insight of this book: that the courts' attachment to the lawyer's way of carving up the world, and our insistence on the primacy of the courts in declaring the legal meaning of the Constitution, has caused a slippage between what the courts say and what they actually do.

The second benefit is prescriptive and practical. All these lines of inquiry share a basic reform agenda. They all focus, in different ways, on "the pluralization of forms of public [and private] action" and on "institutional architecture and the relationships among private and public actors." They agree on the value of a bottom-up approach to regulation and adjudication.[38] They all focus in different ways on the notion that constitutional doctrine is not simply laid down by the courts but involves collaboration with others. This suggests significant common ground about how we might make constitutional law and doctrine more responsive to the lifeworld.

Finally, there is what we might call an imaginative payoff. My primary goal in this book has been to make the institutional turn *imaginable,* in part by showing that the kinds of moves it requires are already immanent in current doctrine. The more common ground we find concerning the problems with current constitutional and First Amendment law, and the more agreement there is about possible paths of reform, the less threatening and the more promising this imaginative leap ought to be.

This book began with a grim diagnosis. Many of us who study the First Amendment see the crisis quite clearly: First Amendment doctrine has become "striking chiefly for its superficiality, its internal incoherence, [and] its distressing failure to facilitate constructive judicial engagement with significant contemporary social issues connected with freedom of speech."[39]

This crisis extends beyond First Amendment law. It is a broader crisis of acontextuality: a nagging conflict between judges' desire for pure, generally applicable legal doctrines, based on a lawyerly way of carving up the world, and their inevitable recognition that the contexts and institutions that come before them in different cases defy those general categories.

Judges may succeed for a time in trying to serve both ends. As long as they succumb to the lure of acontextuality, however, reconciliation will prove impossible. For First Amendment law in particular, the gap between the law-world and the lifeworld shows no signs of narrowing.

The institutional turn is one way out of this dilemma. It tells the courts, and the state, that they are not the only authorities on constitutional meaning. It reminds them that the First Amendment is not just a contest between the soapbox speaker and the censorious state. It is embedded in a structure of public discourse. Like any such structure, it involves an infrastructure, one composed in particular of institutions, each of which contributes to public discourse in specific ways.

By deferring to these institutions—the press, churches, libraries, voluntary associations, universities, and perhaps others—the courts will improve First Amendment law and enhance public discourse. They will retain a key role in policing the boundaries of institutional autonomy, but invite First Amendment institutions to act as their partners in shaping and protecting our discourse.

The institutional turn will demand different results, in some cases, than those provided by current doctrine. More important, it will demand changes in how we think about the relationship between public discourse and constitutional theory and doctrine. Rethinking the way we carve up the world of the First Amendment may lead to a more coherent, productive, and *sustainable* legal regime. Reshaping First Amendment law in a more openly contextual, institutionally sensitive, bottom-up fashion may help free the First Amendment from its increasingly ossified doctrinal state and give it room to breathe.

This book is not the first word on the subject. I hope it will not be the last. It is, rather, a bridge between the first stirrings of the institutional turn and its unknown future. What the institutional First Amendment will look like if it reaches maturity is an open question. Although I have sought to provide practical guidance in this book and to suggest that the institutional turn in the First Amendment *is* practical, there is no doubt that the institutional turn is also an imaginative exercise, and we cannot know entirely where it will lead.

If there has, at times, been a tension between the on-the-ground discussions of First Amendment institutions offered in this book and some of its broader explorations—musings on the potentially limited role of the state and on the possible status of other institutions as "sovereign spheres" or on the notion that ours is "a society of societies, each and all with rights, liberty and life of their own"[40]—that tension can be productive and generative. On a mundane and immediate level, the basic building blocks of First Amendment institutionalism are already immanent in current doctrine. To take further steps in that direction does not demand too much of us. But there is room, too, as Robert Cover once urged us, to imagine and "invite new worlds."[41] As Larry Kramer puts the point, using language that is strikingly consistent with this work, "[P]aying careful attention to constitutional visions generated outside the official organs of the state is important, if for no other reason than the certainty that our own sense of the good will be improved by a more catholic sense of the possible."[42] That is more than reason enough for a little intrepidity: to begin imagining where the institutional turn in the First Amendment might take us.

Much of the answer to that question will not depend on courts and scholars alone. It will rest in the hands of our First Amendment institutions themselves. That is as it should be.

Notes

Introduction

1. *See Hosanna-Tabor Evangelical Lutheran Church & Sch. v. EEOC,* 132 S. Ct. 694 (2012).
2. *See* John H. Cushman Jr., *Religious Groups Greet Ruling with Satisfaction,* New York Times, Jan. 12, 2012 (online version) (quoting Prof. Rick Garnett).
3. *See, e.g., Billionaire Foster Friess Discusses Campaign Finance,* NPR, *All Things Considered,* Jan. 19, 2012.
4. *See, e.g., Arkansas Educ. Television Comm'n v. Forbes,* 523 U.S. 666 (1998).
5. *See, e.g.,* David Hinckley, *Williams Nails NPR, But Hails Its Reporters,* New York Daily News, April 5, 2011, at 69.
6. *See, e.g., Bethel Sch. Dist. No. 403 v. Fraser,* 478 U.S. 675 (1986).
7. *See, e.g., United States v. American Library Association, Inc.,* 539 U.S. 194 (2003).
8. *See, e.g., Parate v. Isibor,* 868 F.2d 821 (6th Cir. 1989); *Lovelace v. Southeastern Mass. Univ.,* 793 F.2d 419 (1st Cir. 1986).
9. *See, e.g., New York Times v. Sullivan,* 376 U.S. 254 (1964).
10. *See, e.g.,* Dennis Hale, *ADR and the Minnesota News Council on Libel,* Dispute Resolution J., June 1994, at 77, 78.
11. *See, e.g., Baltimore Sun Co. v. Ehrlich,* 437 F.3d 410 (4th Cir. 2006).
12. Jack M. Balkin, *The Future of Free Expression in a Digital Age,* 36 Pepperdine L. Rev. 427, 432 (2009); Richard W. Garnett, *The Story of Henry Adams's Soul: Education and the Expression of Associations,* 85 Minn. L. Rev. 1841, 1854 (2001).
13. Richard W. Garnett, *Do Churches Matter?: Towards an Institutional Understanding of the Religion Clauses,* 53 Vill. L. Rev. 273, 274–275 (2008).

14. *Federal Election Comm'n v. Nat'l Conservative Political Action Comm.*, 470 U.S. 480, 493 (1985); *see also* Owen Fiss, *Liberalism Divided: Freedom of Speech and the Many Uses of State Power* 12 (1996) ("For the most part, the free speech tradition can be understood as a protection of the street corner speaker").

15. Frederick Schauer, *Principles, Institutions, and the First Amendment*, 112 Harv. L. Rev. 84, 107 (1998).

16. Dale Carpenter, *The Value of Institutions and the Values of Free Speech*, 89 Minn. L. Rev. 1407, 1411 (2005).

17. *Branzburg v. Hayes*, 408 U.S. 665, 704, 703 (1972).

18. *American Library Ass'n*, 539 U.S. at 203, 205.

19. *See generally* Robert C. Post, *Recuperating First Amendment Doctrine*, 47 Stan. L. Rev. 1249 (1995).

20. *See, e.g., American Legal Realism* (William W. Fisher III, Morton J. Horwitz, & Thomas A. Reed eds., 1993).

21. Victoria Nourse & Gregory Shaffer, *Varieties of New Legal Realism: Can a New World Order Prompt a New Legal Theory?*, 95 Cornell L. Rev. 61, 136–137 (2009).

22. *See* Antonin Scalia, *The Rule of Law as a Law of Rules*, 56 U. Chi. L. Rev. 1175 (1989); Stephen Breyer, *Our Democratic Constitution*, 77 N.Y.U. L. Rev. 245, 252–255 (2002).

23. Mark DeWolfe Howe, *Foreword: Political Theory and the Nature of Liberty*, 67 Harv. L. Rev. 91, 91 (1953).

24. *See, e.g.,* Frederick Schauer, *Institutions as Legal and Constitutional Categories*, 54 UCLA L. Rev. 1747, 1764 (2007).

25. *See, e.g.,* Frederick Schauer, *Hohfeld's First Amendment*, 76 Geo. Wash. L. Rev. 914 (2008); Frederick Schauer, *Is There a Right to Academic Freedom?*, 77 U. Colo. L. Rev. 907 (2006); Frederick Schauer, *Towards an Institutional First Amendment*, 89 Minn. L. Rev. 1256 (2005); Frederick Schauer & Richard H. Pildes, *Electoral Exceptionalism and the First Amendment*, 77 Tex. L. Rev. 1803 (1999).

26. Post, *supra* note 19, at 1280–1281.

27. *See, e.g.,* Richard H. Fallon, Jr., *Judicially Manageable Standards and Constitutional Meaning*, 119 Harv. L. Rev. 1274 (2006); David Chang, *Structuring Constitutional Doctrine: Principles, Proof, and the Functions of Judicial Review*, 58 Rutgers L. Rev. 777 (2006); Kermit Roosevelt III, *Constitutional Calcification: How the Law Becomes What the Court Does*, 91 Va. L. Rev. 1649 (2005); Mitchell N. Berman, *Constitutional Decision Rules*, 90 Va. L. Rev. 1 (2004); Richard H. Fallon, Jr., *Implementing the Constitution* (2001); Lawrence Gene Sager, *Fair Measure: The Legal Status of Underenforced Constitutional Norms*, 91 Harv. L. Rev. 1212 (1978).

28. *See, e.g.,* Christopher K. Ansell, *Pragmatist Democracy: Evolutionary Learning as Public Philosophy* (2011); *Law and New Governance in the EU and the US* (Gráinne de Búrca & Joanne Scott eds., 2006); Charles F. Sabel & William H. Simon,

Destabilization Rights: How Public Law Litigation Succeeds, 117 Harv. L. Rev. 1015 (2004); Orly Lobel, *The Renew Deal: The Fall of Regulation and the Rise of Governance in Contemporary Legal Thought,* 89 Minn. L. Rev. 342 (2004); James S. Liebman & Charles F. Sabel, *A Public Laboratory Dewey Barely Imagined: The Emerging Model of School Governance and Legal Reform,* 28 N.Y.U. Rev. L. & Soc. Change 183 (2003); Susan P. Sturm, *Second Generation Employment Discrimination: A Structural Approach,* 101 Colum. L. Rev. 458 (2001); Michael C. Dorf & Charles F. Sabel, *A Constitution of Democratic Experimentalism,* 98 Colum. L. Rev. 267 (1998).

29. Douglass C. North, *Economic Performance through Time,* 84 Am. Econ. Rev. 359, 360 (1994).

30. Joseph Blocher, *Institutions in the Marketplace of Ideas,* 57 Duke L.J. 821, 840 (2008).

31. I thus elide, for some purposes (but not others), the distinction between, say, "academia, which is an institution, and Duke University, which is an organization." Blocher, *id.,* at 842.

32. Paul Horwitz, *Grutter's First Amendment,* 46 B.C. L. Rev. 461, 589 (2005).

33. Robert Post, *Participatory Democracy and Free Speech,* 97 Va. L. Rev. 477, 483 (2011). James Weinstein takes a similar approach, writing: "Public discourse consists of speech on matters of public concern, or, largely without respect to its subject matter, of expression in settings dedicated or essential to democratic self-governance, such as books, magazines, films, the internet, or in public forums such as the speaker's corner of the park." James Weinstein, *Participatory Democracy as the Central Value of Free Speech Doctrine,* 97 Va. L. Rev. 491, 493 (2011). Note that both writers' definitions, with their singling out of particular "media of communication" and "essential settings," already take us a good deal of the way down the institutional path.

34. Post, *supra* note 33, at 482–483.

35. *Id.* at 484 (emphasis added).

36. *Id.* (emphasis added).

37. Richard M. Cook, *Alfred Kazin: A Biography* 54 (2008).

38. Indeed, the metaphorical balance may now favor First Amendment institutions over physical infrastructure. *See* Richard Florida, *The Rise of the Creative Class: And How It's Transforming Work, Leisure, Community and Everyday Life* 222 (2002) (noting research finding that "investments in higher education infrastructure predict subsequent [urban and regional] growth far better than investments in physical infrastructure like canals, railroads or highways").

39. *Cf.* Ronald Dworkin, *Law's Empire* (1986).

40. For more on this point, *see* Paul Horwitz, *Churches as First Amendment Institutions: Of Sovereignty and Spheres,* 44 Harv. C.R.-C.L. L. Rev. 79 (2009); *see also* Robert M. Cover, *Foreword: Nomos and Narrative,* 97 Harv. L. Rev. 4 (1983).

41. *See, e.g.,* Erwin Chemerinsky, *Rethinking State Action,* 80 Nw. U. L. Rev. 503 (1985).

42. *See, e.g.,* Gregory P. Magarian, *The First Amendment, The Public-Private Distinction, and Nongovernmental Suppression of Wartime Political Debate,* 73 Geo. Wash. L. Rev. 101 (2004).

43. *See, e.g.,* William P. Marshall, *Diluting Constitutional Rights: Rethinking "Rethinking State Action,"* 80 Nw. U. L. Rev. 558 (1985).

44. *American Library Ass'n,* 539 U.S. at 203.

45. *See, e.g.,* Mark Tushnet, *Taking the Constitution Away from the Courts* (1999).

46. Cover, *supra* note 40, at 28.

47. *See* Paul Horwitz, *Three Faces of Deference,* 83 Notre Dame L. Rev. 1061, 1073–1078 (2008).

48. *See, e.g.,* John H. Garvey, *Institutional Pluralism,* AALS News, March 2008, available at http://www.aals.org/documents/newsletter/march2008.pdf.

49. *See, e.g.,* Carpenter, *supra* note 16.

50. *See, e.g., Thomas v. Review Bd.,* 450 U.S. 707 (1981); *Presbyterian Church in U.S. v. Mary Elizabeth Blue Hull Memorial Presbyterian Church,* 393 U.S. 440, 445–446 (1969).

51. *See* Paul Horwitz, *Act III of the Ministerial Exception,* 106 Nw. U. L. Rev. 973 (2012).

52. *See, e.g.,* Post, *supra* note 19.

1. The Conventional First Amendment

1. Often, but not always. Others argue that no single value or justification can ground First Amendment values such as free speech. *See, e.g.,* Steven Shiffrin, *Dissent, Democratic Participation, and First Amendment Methodology,* 97 Va. L. Rev. 559, 559 (2011); Steven Shiffrin, *The First Amendment and Economic Regulation: Away from a General Theory of the First Amendment,* 78 Nw. U. L. Rev. 1212 (1984).

2. I omit here the justifications for freedom of religion, although freedom of religion plays a central role in Chapter 7. For a discussion of those justifications, *see* Paul Horwitz, *The Agnostic Age: Law, Religion, and the Constitution* (2011).

3. John Milton, *Areopagitica* (1644).

4. Kent Greenawalt, *Free Speech: A Philosophical Enquiry* 130 (1982); *see generally* John Stuart Mill, *On Liberty,* in *Selected Writings of John Stuart Mill* 121 (Maurice Cowling ed., 1968) (1st ed. 1859).

5. Some developments in First Amendment law did occur earlier. *See, e.g.,* David M. Rabban, *Free Speech in Its Forgotten Years* (1997).

6. *United States v. Abrams,* 250 U.S. 616, 628, 630 (1919) (Holmes, J., dissenting).

7. *See, e.g.*, Stanley Ingber, *The Marketplace of Ideas: A Legitimizing Myth*, 1984 Duke L.J. 1.

8. *See, e.g.*, *Citizens United v. Federal Election Comm'n*, 130 S. Ct. 876 (2010).

9. *See, e.g.*, William P. Marshall, *In Defense of the Search for Truth as a First Amendment Justification*, 30 Ga. L. Rev. 1 (1995).

10. *United States v. Schwimmer*, 279 U.S. 644, 655 (1929) (Holmes, J., dissenting).

11. Alexander Meiklejohn, *Political Freedom: The Constitutional Powers of the People* 25, 26 (1960) (emphasis added).

12. Frederick Schauer, *Free Speech: A Philosophical Enquiry* 38 (1982).

13. Meiklejohn, *supra* note 11, at 37-41.

14. *See, e.g.*, Martin H. Redish & Abby Marie Mollen, *Understanding Post's and Meiklejohn's Mistakes: The Central Role of Adversary Democracy in the Theory of Free Expression*, 103 Nw. U. L. Rev. 1303 (2009); Robert C. Post, *Meiklejohn's Mistake: Individual Autonomy and the Reform of Public Discourse*, 64 U. Colo. L. Rev. 1109, 1114 (1993).

15. *See, e.g.*, Cass R. Sunstein, *Democracy and the Problem of Free Speech* (1993); Owen M. Fiss, *The Irony of Free Speech* (1996); Owen M. Fiss, *Liberalism Divided: Freedom of Speech and the Many Uses of State Power* (1996).

16. *See, e.g.*, Robert Post, *Participatory Democracy as a Theory of Free Speech: A Reply*, 97 Va. L. Rev. 617, 620 (2011) ("I . . . consider art as deserving constitutional protection because of its connection to public opinion formation in a democracy").

17. *See, e.g.*, Robert H. Bork, *Neutral Principles and Some First Amendment Problems*, 47 Ind. L.J. 1 (1971).

18. Sunstein, *supra* note 15, at 134.

19. 376 U.S. 254 (1964).

20. *Id.* at 273, 270.

21. *See, e.g.*, *Citizens United v. Federal Election Comm'n*, 130 S. Ct. 876 (2010); *see also Morse v. Frederick*, 551 U.S. 393, 403 (2007) ("Political speech is, of course, at the core of what the First Amendment is designed to protect") (quotations and citation omitted).

22. Kent Greenawalt, *Free Speech Justifications*, 89 Colum. L. Rev. 119, 143 (1989). *See also* Thomas I. Emerson, *Toward a General Theory of the First Amendment* (1966); C. Edwin Baker, *Human Liberty and Freedom of Speech* (1989); Martin H. Redish, *The Value of Free Speech*, 130 U. Pa. L. Rev. 591 (1982).

23. Although I lump these justifications together under the same rubric for purposes of this general discussion, some would resist doing so. For recent and sophisticated arguments offering more specific descriptions of these approaches, *see* Symposium, *Individual Autonomy and Free Speech*, 27 Const. Comment. 251 (2011).

24. 403 U.S. 15 (1971).

25. *Id.* at 15, 25 (citing *Winters v. New York*, 333 U.S. 507, 528 (1948) (Frankfurter, J., dissenting) (alterations omitted)).

26. Baker, *supra* note 22, at 5.

27. Redish, *supra* note 22, at 593.

28. Greenawalt, *supra* note 4, at 146–147. *See, e.g.,* Lee C. Bollinger, *The Tolerant Society* (1986); Vincent Blasi, *The First Amendment and the Ideal of Civic Courage: The Brandeis Opinion in* Whitney v. California, 29 Wm. & Mary L. Rev. 653 (1988).

29. Bollinger, *supra* note 28, at 10.

30. 274 U.S. 357 (1927).

31. *Id.* at 377 (Brandeis, J., concurring).

32. *Id.* at 375, 376.

33. *See, e.g., Brandenburg v. Ohio*, 395 U.S. 444 (1969).

34. Vincent Blasi, *The Checking Value in First Amendment Theory*, 3 Am. B. Found. Res. J. 521 (1977); Greenawalt, *supra* note 4, at 143.

35. Dale Carpenter, *The Value of Institutions and the Values of Free Speech*, 89 Minn. L. Rev. 1407, 1410 (2005).

36. *Ward v. Rock Against Racism*, 491 U.S. 781, 791 (1989).

37. Lee C. Bollinger & Geoffrey R. Stone, *Dialogue, in Eternally Vigilant: Free Speech in the Modern Era* 1, 9 (Lee C. Bollinger & Geoffrey R. Stone eds., 2002). One could argue that the real first question of First Amendment doctrine is whether speech has occurred at all, but I leave that question to one side here. For analysis, *see, e.g.,* John Greenman, *On Communication*, 106 Mich. L. Rev. 1337 (2008); Robert Post, *Recuperating First Amendment Doctrine*, 47 Stan. L. Rev. 1249 (1995). *See also Spence v. Washington*, 418 U.S. 405 (1974).

38. *See, e.g.,* Geoffrey R. Stone, *Free Speech in the Twenty-First Century: Ten Lessons From the Twentieth Century*, 36 Pepperdine L. Rev. 273, 282 (2009) (observing that, with certain "significant exceptions," the Supreme Court "has not upheld a single content-based restriction of speech . . . in half a century"). A recent exception is *Holder v. Humanitarian Law Project*, 130 S. Ct. 2705 (2010).

39. *Police Department v. Mosley*, 408 U.S. 92, 95 (1972).

40. Geoffrey R. Stone, *Content Regulation and the First Amendment*, 25 Wm. & Mary L. Rev. 189, 189 (1983); *see also* Susan H. Williams, *Content Discrimination and the First Amendment*, 139 U. Pa. L. Rev. 615 (1991); Geoffrey R. Stone, *Content-Neutral Restrictions*, 54 U. Chi. L. Rev. 46 (1987).

41. Thus, James Weinstein has argued that despite its seemingly sweeping nature, the content-neutrality rule does far less than is often assumed. *See* James Weinstein, *Hate Speech, Pornography, and the Radical Attack on Free Speech Doctrine* 40–43 (1999).

42. *See, e.g.,* Erwin Chemerinsky, *Content Neutrality as a Central Problem of Freedom of Speech: Problems in the Supreme Court's Application*, 74 S. Cal. L. Rev. 49 (2000);

Martin H. Redish, *The Content Distinction in First Amendment Doctrine,* 34 Stan. L. Rev. 113 (1981).

43. *Hill v. Colorado,* 530 U.S. 703, 707 (2000).

44. *Id.* at 719.

45. *Id.* at 735 (Souter, J., concurring).

46. *Id.* at 748 (Scalia, J., dissenting).

47. *See, e.g., R.A.V. v. City of St. Paul,* 505 U.S. 377 (1992).

48. *See, e.g.,* Barry P. McDonald, *Speech and Distrust: Rethinking the Content Approach to Protecting the Freedom of Expression,* 81 Notre Dame L. Rev. 1347 (2006).

49. *Dun & Bradstreet, Inc. v. Greenmoss Builders, Inc.,* 472 U.S. 749, 758 (1985).

50. *See, e.g., Young v. American Mini Theatres, Inc.,* 427 U.S. 50, 61 (1976).

51. *Chaplinsky v. New Hampshire,* 315 U.S. 568, 571–572 (1942).

52. In what follows, I treat low- and no-value speech together.

53. *See* Stone, *supra* note 38, at 284.

54. *See R.A.V.,* 505 U.S. at 382–386.

55. *U.S. v. Stevens,* 130 S. Ct. 1577, 1584 (2010) (quotations and citations omitted). *See also Brown v. Entertainment Merchants Ass'n,* 131 S. Ct. 2729 (2011).

56. *See Marsh v. Alabama,* 326 U.S. 501 (1946).

57. *See, e.g., Hudgens v. NLRB,* 424 U.S. 507 (1976); *Lloyd Corp. v. Tanner,* 407 U.S. 551 (1972).

58. *See, e.g., Brentwood Academy v. Tenn. Secondary Sch. Athletic Ass'n,* 531 U.S. 288 (2001).

59. *See, e.g., New York Times v. Sullivan,* 376 U.S. 254 (1964).

60. *See* Robert C. Post, *Constitutional Domains: Democracy, Community, Management* 240 (1995). I omit here a further complication, which will be addressed in various ways in subsequent chapters: the status of speech by government *employees. See, e.g., Garcetti v. Ceballos,* 547 U.S. 410 (2006); *San Diego v. Roe,* 543 U.S. 77 (2004); *Connick v. Myers,* 461 U.S. 138 (1983).

61. *See, e.g., Pleasant Grove City, Utah v. Summum,* 129 S. Ct. 1125 (2009); *Johanns v. Livestock Marketing Ass'n,* 544 U.S. 550 (2005). For general discussion, *see, e.g.,* Symposium, *Government Speech: The Government's Ability to Compel and Restrict Speech,* 61 Case W. Res. L. Rev. 1081 (2011); Symposium, *Government Speech,* 87 Denv. U. L. Rev. 809 (2010).

62. In such cases the remedy is political. If voters don't like particular statements made by the government—say, that immigrants are welcome, or unwelcome—they can elect a government that will say something else.

63. *Citizens United,* 130 S. Ct. at 900 (quoting *First Nat'l Bank of Boston v. Bellotti,* 435 U.S. 765, 776 (1978)).

64. For a useful summary of public forum doctrine and criticisms of that doctrine, *see* Lyrissa Lidsky, *Public Forum 2.0,* 91 B.U. L. Rev. 1975 (2011).

65. 307 U.S. 496, 515 (1939).

66. *Perry Educ. Ass'n v. Perry Local Educators Ass'n,* 460 U.S. 37, 45 (1983).

67. *See id.* at 45–46, 46 n.7.

68. *Id.* at 46.

69. *Red Lion Broadcasting Co. v. FCC,* 395 U.S. 367, 392 (1969).

70. *Miami Herald Publishing Co. v. Tornillo,* 418 U.S. 241 (1974).

71. *In re Complaint of Syracuse Peace Council against Television Station WTVH Syracuse, New York,* 2 F.C.C.R. 5043 ¶ 2 (1987).

72. *See, e.g., United States v. Playboy Entertainment Group,* 529 U.S. 803 (2000).

73. *See, e.g., Denver Area Educ. Telecomm. Consortium, Inc. v. FCC,* 518 U.S. 727, 777–778 (1996) (Souter, J., concurring); Stuart Minor Benjamin, *Stepping into the Same River Twice: Rapidly Changing Facts and the Appellate Process,* 78 Tex. L. Rev. 269 (1999).

74. Bollinger & Stone, *supra* note 37, at 14.

75. *See, e.g., Reno v. ACLU,* 521 U.S. 844 (1997).

76. *Kovacs v. Cooper,* 336 U.S. 77, 97 (1949) (Jackson, J., concurring).

77. *Metromedia, Inc. v. City of San Diego,* 453 U.S. 490, 501 (1981). For criticisms of this approach, *see, e.g.,* Laurence H. Tribe & Michael C. Dorf, *Levels of Generality in the Definition of Rights,* 57 U. Chi. L. Rev. 1057, 1070–1071 (1990).

78. *Simon & Schuster, Inc. v. Members of New York State Crime Victims Bd.,* 502 U.S. 105, 118 (1991) (quotation and citation omitted).

79. *See, e.g., id.* at 124–128 (Kennedy, J., concurring in the judgment).

80. *Ward,* 491 U.S. at 791 (quotations and citations omitted).

81. *See, e.g., Hill,* 530 U.S. 703; *Heffron v. Int'l Soc'y for Krishna Consciousness,* 452 U.S. 640 (1981); Ashutosh Bhagwat, *The Test That Ate Everything: Intermediate Scrutiny in First Amendment Jurisprudence,* 2007 U. Ill. L. Rev. 783, 787.

82. 391 U.S. 367 (1968).

83. *See Texas v. Johnson,* 491 U.S. 397 (1989). I have not discussed a third standard of review in constitutional law, the rational basis standard, which upholds any law that is reasonably related to a legitimate governmental interest. Rational basis scrutiny is an important part of constitutional law generally, but it is not an especially important part of judicial review in First Amendment cases. *See* Bhagwat, *supra* note 81, at 787.

84. This is probably more true of the Supreme Court than the lower courts, in fairness. Those courts, after all, are confronted with many more specific speech contexts than the Supreme Court, and must perforce struggle to figure out where those cases fit within the broad strokes of First Amendment doctrine. Still, while this kind of consideration may proliferate at the lower court level, when the Supreme Court takes these cases it tends to prune rather than expand.

2. The Lures and Snares of Acontextuality

1. Oliver Wendell Holmes, *The Path of the Law*, 10 Harv. L. Rev. 457, 474, 474–475 (1897).

2. Benjamin C. Zipursky, *Minimalism, Perfectionism, and Common Law Constitutionalism: Reflections on Sunstein's and Fleming's Efforts to Find the Sweet Spot in Constitutional Theory*, 75 Fordham L. Rev. 2297, 3008 (2007).

3. Michael Moore, *Theories of Areas of Law*, 37 San Diego L. Rev. 731, 734 (2000).

4. Jeremy Waldron, *The Concept and the Rule of Law*, 43 Ga. L. Rev. 1, 7 (2008); *see also* Richard H. Fallon, Jr., *The "Rule of Law" as a Concept in Constitutional Discourse*, 97 Colum. L. Rev. 1, 7–9 (1997).

5. Oliver Wendell Holmes, *Law in Science and Science in Law*, 12 Harv. L. Rev. 443, 460 (1899).

6. Robert C. Post, *Recuperating First Amendment Doctrine*, 47 Stan. L. Rev. 1249, 1250 (1995).

7. Anita Bernstein, *Engendered by Technologies*, 80 N.C. L. Rev. 1, 82 (2001).

8. *See* Frederick Schauer, *The Dilemma of Ignorance: PGA Tour, Inc. v. Casey Martin*, 2001 Sup. Ct. Rev. 267.

9. *See generally* Frederick Schauer, *Prediction and Particularity*, 78 B.U. L. Rev. 773 (1998).

10. *See, e.g.*, Ernest J. Weinrib, *Legal Formalism: On the Immanent Rationality of Law*, 97 Yale L.J. 949 (1988).

11. Brian Leiter, *Heidegger and the Theory of Adjudication*, 106 Yale L.J. 253, 273 (1996).

12. *See, e.g.*, Frederick Schauer, *Thinking Like a Lawyer: A New Introduction to Legal Reasoning*, ch. 2 (2009).

13. Frank H. Easterbrook, *Cyberspace and the Law of the Horse*, 1996 U. Chi. Legal F. 207.

14. *See* Lawrence Lessig, *The Law of the Horse: What Cyberlaw Might Teach*, 113 Harv. L. Rev. 501 (1999).

15. *See, e.g.*, Richard A. Epstein, *Simple Rules for a Complex World* (1995); Henry J. Friendly, Book Review, *Air Law*, 77 Harv. L. Rev. 582 (1964).

16. Frederick Schauer, *Principles, Institutions, and the First Amendment*, 112 Harv. L. Rev. 84, 112 (1998). *See, e.g.*, Ronald Dworkin, *Law's Empire* 178–184 (1986); Ronald Dworkin, *A Matter of Principle* 72–103 (1985).

17. *See, e.g.*, Antonin Scalia, *The Rule of Law as a Law of Rules*, 56 U. Chi. L. Rev. 1175 (1989).

18. Roderick M. Hills, Jr., *The Pragmatist's View of Constitutional Implementation and Constitutional Meaning*, 119 Harv. L. Rev. F. 173, 174 (2006).

19. *See* Paul Horwitz, *Three Faces of Deference,* 83 Notre Dame L. Rev. 1061 (2008); Paul Horwitz, *Universities as First Amendment Institutions: Some Easy Answers and Hard Questions,* 54 UCLA L. Rev. 1497 (2007).

20. *See* Martha Minow, *Stripped Down Like a Runner or Enriched by Experience: Bias and Impartiality of Judges and Jurors,* 33 Wm. & Mary L. Rev. 1201 (1992).

21. *See* Isaiah Berlin, *The Roots of Romanticism* 24–25 (Henry Hardy ed., 1999).

22. Moore, *supra* note 3, at 734.

23. 376 U.S. 254, 270 (1964).

24. Leiter, *supra* note 11, at 274–275.

25. Post, *supra* note 6, at 1271, 1272.

26. Scalia, *supra* note 17.

27. Which is not to say that it carries no costs with it, or that it is impossible to envision other ways of thinking about the rule of law, including versions that are broadly consistent with the general themes of this book. *See, e.g.,* Martin Krygier, *Philip Selznick, Normative Theory, and the Rule of Law,* in *Legality and Community: On the Intellectual Legacy of Philip Selznick* 19, 38–41 (Robert A. Kagan, Martin Krygier, & Kenneth Winston eds., 2002).

28. *Chaplinsky v. New Hampshire,* 315 U.S. 568, 572 (1942).

29. *See Valentine v. Christensen,* 316 U.S. 52 (1942).

30. *Morse v. Frederick,* 551 U.S. 393, 403 (2007); *see also Snyder v. Phelps,* 131 S. Ct. 1207, 1215 (2011) ("[S]peech on public issues occupies the highest rung of the hierarchy of First Amendment values") (quotations and citation omitted).

31. Daniel A. Farber, *The Categorical Approach to Protecting Speech in American Constitutional Law,* 84 Ind. L.J. 917, 935 (2009).

32. The leading case is *Miller v. California,* 413 U.S. 15 (1973).

33. *See, e.g., Ashcroft v. Free Speech Coalition,* 535 U.S. 234 (2002); *Reno v. ACLU,* 521 U.S. 844 (1997).

34. *See FCC v. Pacifica Foundation,* 438 U.S. 726 (1978).

35. *See, e.g., FCC v. Fox Television Stations, Inc.,* 129 S. Ct. 1800, 1819–1822 (2009) (Thomas, J., concurring); *id.* at 1826–1828 (Stevens, J., dissenting).

36. *See, e.g., Cohen v. California,* 403 U.S. 15 (1971).

37. *See, e.g., R.A.V. v. City of St. Paul,* 505 U.S. 377 (1992).

38. *See, e.g., Thompson v. Western States Medical Center,* 535 U.S. 357 (2002); *Lorillard Tobacco Co. v. Reilly,* 533 U.S. 525 (2001).

39. *See, e.g., Milavetz, Gallop & Milavetz, P.A. v. U.S.,* 130 S. Ct. 1324, 1342–1343 (2010) (Thomas, J., concurring in part and concurring in the judgment).

40. To be sure, it has not disappeared altogether. Although the categories discussed in *Chaplinsky* have come much further under the umbrella of First Amendment protection, the Court continues from time to time to insist that some forms of speech deserve protection, but not *full* protection. In particular,

government may continue to regulate speech on the basis of its "secondary effects," as long as the regulation is not aimed at the speech as such. *See, e.g., City of Los Angeles v. Alameda Books, Inc.,* 535 U.S. 425 (2002) (upholding a zoning restriction on multiple "adult entertainment" businesses operating in the same building, on the basis of studies associating those enterprises with higher crime rates in the surrounding area). Even here, however, the speech itself is not wholly unprotected; the regulation must be content-neutral, must serve a substantial government interest, and must leave open "reasonable alternative avenues for communication." *City of Renton v. Playtime Theatres, Inc.,* 475 U.S. 41, 50 (1986).

Moreover, although the scope of "low-value" or "no-value" speech has decreased, it is still true that many kinds of speech, such as securities fraud or speech constituting a combination in restraint of trade, are generally viewed as falling outside the "boundaries of the First Amendment" altogether. Frederick Schauer, *The Boundaries of the First Amendment: A Preliminary Exploration of Constitutional Salience,* 117 Harv. L. Rev. 1765, 1767 (2004). As we will see in later chapters, however, this gap tends to support, rather than rebut, both my point about the lures of acontextuality and the institutional approach I explore in this book. As a matter of conventional First Amendment theory and doctrine, it is widely agreed that these boundary questions have been underexplored and difficult to justify. *See id.* at 1768 ("[I]t may . . . be the case that less of the First Amendment can be explained by the [conventional] tools of legal and constitutional analysis than we have formerly recognized"). On the other hand, once we recognize that First Amendment doctrine is regularly, if uncomfortably, based on a host of "political, social, cultural, historical, psychological, rhetorical, . . . economic"—and *institutional*—"forces," *id.,* then we have taken a step away from legal acontextuality and toward a form of law that is responsive to "things" in the world.

41. Larry Alexander, *Free Speech and Speaker's Intent,* 12 Const. Comment. 21, 22 (1995). *See also* Eugene Volokh, *The Trouble with "Public Discourse" as a Limitation on Free Speech Rights,* 97 Va. L. Rev. 567 (2011) (arguing for what he calls a "presumptive all-inclusive approach" under which "all speech is presumptively protected against content-based restrictions imposed by the government," and implying that different degrees of protection will be based on the government's interest in particular cases rather than on categories of high-value or low-value speech as such); Robert Post, *Participatory Democracy as a Theory of Free Speech: A Reply,* 97 Va. L. Rev. 617, 628–629 (2011) (interpreting Volokh's argument as suggesting that differences in the treatment of different forms of speech "are best explained by differences in the governmental interests that are at stake").

42. *See, e.g.,* Wilson Ray Huhn, *Assessing the Constitutionality of Laws That Are Both Content-Based and Content-Neutral: The Emerging Constitutional Calculus,* 79 Ind. L.J. 801, 804 (2005).

43. *See, e.g.,* Harry T. Edwards & Mitchell N. Berman, *Regulating Violence on Television,* 89 Nw. U. L. Rev. 1487, 1529 n.199 (1995).

44. *See, e.g., U.S. v. Stevens,* 130 S. Ct. 1577, 1585 (2010).

45. The "if" is important here. As Frederick Schauer has noted, a large number of speech acts, such as the speech covered by federal securities laws, are uncontroversially excluded from First Amendment coverage. *See* Schauer, *supra* note 40. And yet the Court typically *talks* as if there are few meaningful distinctions between different kinds of speech for First Amendment purposes.

46. *Pac. Gas & Elec. Co. v. Pub. Utils.Comm'n,* 475 U.S. 1, 8 (1986).

47. *See, e.g., Va. State Bd. of Pharmacy v. Va. Citizens Consumer Council,* 425 U.S. 748, 761–762 (1976).

48. *See, e.g., Citizens United v. FEC,* 130 S. Ct. 876, 899–903 (2010).

49. *But see* Eugene Volokh, *Freedom of the Press as an Industry, or for the Press as a Technology?: From the Framing to Today,* 160 U. Pa. L. Rev. 459 (2012) (arguing that the Press Clause is best understood, according to the usual sources of interpretation, as providing a univeral "right to publish using mass technology" rather than as protecting the press as an "industry").

50. *First Nat'l Bank of Boston v. Bellotti,* 435 U.S. 765, 801, 802 (1978) (Burger, C.J., concurring).

51. 408 U.S. 665, 704 (1972).

52. *See, e.g., Richmond Newspapers, Inc. v. Virginia,* 448 U.S. 555 (1980); *Pell v. Procunier,* 417 U.S. 817 (1974).

53. *See, e.g., Dun & Bradstreet, Inc. v. Greenmoss Builders, Inc.,* 472 U.S. 749 (1985); *Garrison v. Louisiana,* 379 U.S. 64 (1964).

54. *See Cohen v. Cowles Media Co.,* 501 U.S. 663 (1991).

55. David Fagundes has argued, however, that some of what the courts have done in this area *is* in tension with the text of the First Amendment, which does not single out the state for better or worse treatment than other speakers. *See* David Fagundes, *State Actors as First Amendment Speakers,* 100 Nw. U. L. Rev. 1637, 1648 (2006).

56. Elsewhere I have argued that in some ways it may make sense to be stricter when enforcing the Establishment Clause against state and local governments than when enforcing it against the federal government, notwithstanding the text's singling out of an establishment of religion by "Congress." *See* Paul Horwitz, *Demographics and Distrust: The Eleventh Circuit on School Prayer in* Adler v. Duval County, 63 U. Miami L. Rev. 835 (2009).

57. *See, e.g.,* Frederick Schauer, *Towards an Institutional First Amendment*, 89 Minn. L. Rev. 1256, 1262–1263 (2005); Schauer, *supra* note 16, at 117.

58. *See, e.g., Pleasant Grove City, Utah v. Summum*, 129 S. Ct. 1125 (2009); *Johanns v. Livestock Marketing Ass'n*, 544 U.S. 550 (2005).

59. *See, e.g.,* Martin H. Redish, *The Content Distinction in First Amendment Analysis*, 34 Stan. L. Rev. 113, 128 (1981).

60. *Whitney v. California*, 274 U.S. 357, 377 (1927) (Brandeis, J., concurring).

61. Geoffrey R. Stone, *Content-Neutral Restrictions*, 54 U. Chi. L. Rev. 46, 54, 57 (1987).

62. *See generally* John Hart Ely, *Democracy and Distrust: A Theory of Judicial Review* (1980).

63. Morton J. Horwitz, *Foreword: The Constitution of Change: Legal Fundamentality Without Fundamentalism*, 107 Harv. L. Rev. 30, 99, 100 (1993).

64. *See* Kathleen M. Sullivan, *Post-Liberal Judging: The Roles of Categorization and Balancing*, 63 U. Colo. L. Rev. 293, 293 (1992).

65. Horwitz, *supra* note 63, at 100.

66. *See, e.g., Adderley v. State of Fla.*, 385 U.S. 39, 47 (1966) ("The State, no less than a private owner of property, has the power to preserve the property under its control for the use to which it is lawfully dedicated").

67. *See generally* Robert C. Post, *Between Management and Governance: The History and Theory of the Public Forum*, 34 UCLA L. Rev. 1713 (1987).

68. Laurence H. Tribe, *American Constitutional Law* § 12-24, at 987 (2d ed. 1988).

69. Stone, *supra* note 61, at 93.

70. Or, to put it differently, "In its current form, the state action doctrine exhibits the transformed element of classical legal thought—neoformalism." *Developments in the Law—State Action and the Public/Private Distinction: The Evolution of the State Action Doctrine and the Current Debate*, 123 Harv. L. Rev 1255, 1262 (2010).

71. Frederick Schauer, *Institutions as Legal and Constitutional Categories*, 54 UCLA L. Rev. 1747, 1756 (2007).

72. *Id.* at 1759, 1761.

73. *See, e.g.,* Mark Tushnet & Gary Peller, *State Action and a New Birth of Freedom*, 92 Geo. L.J. 779 (2004); Erwin Chemerinsky, *Rethinking State Action*, 80 Nw. U. L. Rev. 503 (1985); Duncan Kennedy, *The Stages of the Decline of the Public/Private Distinction*, 130 U. Pa. L. Rev. 1349 (1982).

74. *See, e.g.,* Larry Alexander, *The Public/Private Distinction and Constitutional Limits on State Power*, 10 Const. Comment. 361, 361–362 (1993).

75. Richard S. Kay, *The State Action Doctrine, the Public-Private Distinction, and the Independence of Constitutional Law*, 10 Const. Comment. 329, 330 (1993).

76. *Grutter v. Bollinger,* 539 U.S. 306, 307 (2003).

77. *See, e.g.,* Adrian Vermeule, *Instrumentalisms,* 120 Harv. L. Rev. 2113, 2116 (2007); Richard A. Posner, *The Role of the Judge in the Twenty-First Century,* 86 B.U. L. Rev. 1049, 1053 (2006); Cass R. Sunstein & Adrian Vermeule, *Interpretation and Institutions,* 101 Mich. L. Rev. 885, 887–888 (2003); Richard A. Posner, *Pragmatism versus Purposivism in First Amendment Analysis,* 54 Stan. L. Rev. 737, 738 (2002); Steven D. Smith, *The Pursuit of Pragmatism,* 100 Yale L.J. 409, 428 (1990). It bears pointing out that some formalists or "acontextualists" would view a pragmatic defense of formalism or acontextualism with horror.

78. 523 U.S. 666, 670 (1998) (quotation and citation omitted).

79. *Forbes v. Arkansas Educational Television Communication Network Foundation,* 22 F.3d 1423, 1428 (8th Cir. 1994) (en banc).

80. *Forbes,* 523 U.S. at 671–672.

81. *Forbes v. Arkansas Educational Television Commission,* 93 F.3d 497, 505 (8th Cir. 1996).

82. *Id.* at 504.

83. *Forbes,* 523 U.S. at 672–673, 674.

84. *Id.* at 676 (emphasis added).

85. Schauer, *supra* note 15, at 90, 91.

86. 20 U.S.C. § 954(d)(1).

87. *See Nat'l Endowment for the Arts v. Finley,* 524 U.S. 569, 577–578 (1998).

88. It may still be relevant in one limited context, that of broadcasting indecent speech during hours when children may be likely to hear it. *See FCC v. Pacifica Found.,* 438 U.S. 726 (1978). Even that limited exception to the general rule that indecent speech is fully covered by the First Amendment is in question as of this writing.

89. *Finley,* 524 U.S. at 585, 585–587 (quoting *Advocates for the Arts v. Thomson,* 532 F.2d 792, 795–796 (1st Cir. 1976)).

90. *Id.* at 595–598, 599 (Scalia, J., concurring in the judgment).

91. *Id.* at 616.

92. Schauer, *supra* note 16, at 97.

93. *See id.* at 96.

94. 539 U.S. 194 (2003).

95. *See, e.g., Rust v. Sullivan,* 500 U.S. 173 (1991); *Speiser v. Randall,* 357 U.S. 513 (1958).

96. *American Library Association,* 539 U.S. at 205, 203.

97. Lillian R. BeVier, *United States v. American Library Association: Whither First Amendment Doctrine,* 55 Sup. Ct. Rev. 163, 165 (2003).

98. *Id.* at 166.

99. The phrase is Lord Mansfield's. *See Omychund v. Barker,* 26 Eng. Rep. 15, 33 (K.B. 1744).

100. Frederick Schauer, *Exceptions*, 58 U. Chi. L. Rev. 871, 872 (1991).

101. *Id.*

102. *See, e.g.*, Ashutosh Bhagwat, *Hard Cases and the (D)evolution of Constitutional Doctrine*, 30 Conn. L. Rev. 961, 962 (1998).

103. *American Library Association*, 539 U.S. at 205.

104. I discuss this dilemma, in different language, in Paul Horwitz, *Law's Expression: The Promise and Perils of Judicial Opinion Writing in Canadian Constitutional Law*, 38 Osgoode Hall L.J. 101 (2000).

105. *See, e.g.*, Philippe Nonet & Philip Selznick, *Law and Society in Transition* 73 (2d ed. 2001).

106. Oona A. Hathaway, *Path Dependence in the Law: The Course and Pattern of Legal Change in a Common Law System*, 86 Iowa L. Rev. 601, 641 (2001).

107. Post, *supra note 6*, at 1270, 1275.

108. Schauer, *supra* note 16, at 86–87.

3. Taking the Institutional Turn

1. Victoria Nourse & Gregory Shaffer, *Varieties of New Legal Realism: Can a New World Order Prompt a New Legal Theory?*, 95 Cornell L. Rev. 61, 113 (2009).

2. *See, e.g.*, Philippe Nonet & Philip Selznick, *Law and Society in Transition: Toward Responsive Law* 64 (2001) ("Legality, understood as close accountability to rules, is the promise of autonomous law; legalism is its affliction. A focus on rules tends to narrow the range of legally relevant facts, thereby detaching legal thought from social reality.").

3. Robert A. Kagan, *Introduction to the Transaction Edition*, in Nonet & Selznick, *id.*, at vii, xxiv.

4. *See* Jürgen Habermas, *Between Facts and Norms* (William Rehg trans., 1996); Jürgen Habermas, 1 *The Theory of Communicative Action: Reason and the Rationalization of Society* (Thomas McCarthy trans., 1984); Jürgen Habermas, 2 *The Theory of Communicative Action: Lifeworld and System: A Critique of Functionalist Reason* (Thomas McCarthy trans., 1987). For a general guide to Habermas and the law, *see* Hugh Baxter, *Habermas: The Discourse Theory of Law and Democracy* (2011). As I note in the text, I borrow loosely from Habermas, adapting his language to my own purposes. As screenwriting credits sometimes say, this discussion should be seen as "inspired by" Habermas rather than as a strictly faithful use of his concepts.

5. William E. Forbath, *Habermas's Constitution: A History, Guide, and Critique*, 23 L. & Soc. Inquiry 969, 987 (1998).

6. Lawrence B. Solum, *Freedom of Communicative Action: A Theory of the First Amendment Freedom of Speech*, 83 Nw. U. L. Rev. 54, 105 (1989).

7. Forbath, *supra* note 5, at 988.

8. Robert C. Post, *Law and Cultural Conflict*, 78 Chi.-Kent L. Rev. 485, 488 (2003).

9. Philippe Nonet & Philip Selznick, *Law and Society in Transition: Toward Responsive Law* 76–77 (1978).

10. Brian Z. Tamanaha, *The Tension between Legal Instrumentalism and the Rule of Law*, 33 Syracuse J. Int'l L. & Com. 131, 149 (2005).

11. Robert Post, *The Supreme Court Opinion as Institutional Practice: Dissent, Legal Scholarship, and Decisionmaking in the Taft Court*, 85 Minn. L. Rev. 1267, 1381 (2001).

12. Kagan, *supra* note 2, at xi.

13. Ronen Shamir, *Professionalism and Monopoly of Expertise: Lawyers and Administrative Law, 1933–1937* 361, 383 (1993).

14. *See, e.g.,* Nonet & Selznick, *supra* note 9, at 82–83, 115–118.

15. *See, e.g.,* Robert Post, *Reconciling Theory and Doctrine in First Amendment Jurisprudence*, 88 Cal. L. Rev. 2353, 2355 (2000) (observing that despite the "chaotic collection of methods and theories" in First Amendment jurisprudence, "those fluent in the law of free speech can predict with reasonable accuracy the outcomes of most constitutional cases," due largely to basic agreement about the sensible ordering of "communication within our society").

16. Bradley C. Karkkainen, *"New Governance" in Legal Thought and in the World: Some Splitting as an Antidote to Overzealous Lumping*, 89 Minn. L. Rev. 471, 474 (2004).

17. This approach is most closely associated with the work of Gunther Teubner, who builds on the work of Niklas Luhmann. *See, e.g.,* Niklas Luhmann, *Law as a Social System* (Klaus A. Ziegert trans., Fatima Kastner *et al.* eds., 2004); Gunther Teubner, *Law as an Autopoietic System* (1993).

18. *See, e.g.,* Eric W. Orts, *Reflexive Environmental Law*, 89 Nw. U. L. Rev. 1227, 1232 (1995).

19. William E. Scheuerman, *Reflexive Law and the Challenges of Globalization*, 9 J. Pol. Phil. 81, 84 (2001).

20. Michael C. Dorf & Charles F. Sabel, *A Constitution of Democratic Experimentalism*, 98 Colum. L. Rev. 267, 283 (1998). For a helpful, example-filled treatment of democratic experimentalism as a governance mechanism, *see* Christopher K. Ansell, *Pragmatist Democracy: Evolutionary Learning as Public Philosophy* (2011).

21. *See* Jamison E. Colburn, *"Democratic Experimentalism": A Separation of Powers for Our Time?*, 37 Suffolk U. L. Rev. 287, 289 (2004).

22. Jason M. Solomon, *Law and Governance in the 21st Century Regulatory State*, 86 Tex. L. Rev. 819, 834 (2008).

23. Orly Lobel, *Lawyering Loyalties: Speech Rights and Duties Within Twenty-First-Century New Governance*, 77 Fordham L. Rev. 1245, 1247 (2009).

24. John Braithwaite & Peter Drahos, *Global Business Regulation* 28 (2000) (quoted in Lobel, *id.* at 1247).

25. *Oncale v. Sundowner Offshore Servs., Inc.*, 523 U.S. 75, 81–82 (1998).

26. *See Faragher v. City of Boca Raton*, 524 U.S. 775, 805 (1998).

27. *See* Susan Sturm, *Second Generation Employment Discrimination: A Structural Approach*, 101 Colum. L. Rev. 458, 480–489 (2001).

28. Orts, *supra* note 18, at 1264.

29. *Id.*

30. Christine Parker, *The Pluralization of Regulation*, 9 Theoretical Inquiries L. 349, 368 (2008).

31. *See, e.g., New Institutionalism: Theory and Analysis* (André Lecours ed., 2005); B. Guy Peters, *Institutional Theory in Political Science: The "New Institutionalism"* (1999); W. Richard Scott, *Institutions and Organizations* (1995); *The New Institutionalism in Organizational Analysis* (Walter W. Powell & Paul J. DiMaggio eds., 1991); James G. March & Johan P. Olsen, *Rediscovering Institutions: The Organizational Basis of Politics* (1989).

32. Thorstein B. Veblen, *The Limitations of Marginal Utility*, 17 J. Pol. Econ. 235, 245 (1909) (quoted in Scott, *supra* note 31, at 3).

33. Edward L. Rubin, *The New Legal Process, the Synthesis of Discourse, and the Microanalysis of Institutions*, 109 Harv. L. Rev. 1393, 1413, 1414 (1996).

34. *Id.* at 1414.

35. Michael R. Siebecker, *Building a "New Institutional" Approach to Corporate Speech*, 59 Ala. L. Rev. 247, 261, 265 (2008).

36. Edward L. Rubin, *Law and the Methodology of Law*, 1997 Wis. L. Rev. 521, 556.

37. *See, e.g.,* Cassandra Burke Robertson, *Judgment, Identity, and Independence*, 42 Conn. L. Rev. 1 (2009); Rakesh Khurana, *The Social Nature of Boards*, 70 Brook. L. Rev. 1259 (2005); Jody Freeman, *Collaborative Governance in the Administrative State*, 45 UCLA L. Rev. 1 (1997).

38. Norman W. Spaulding, *Reinterpreting Professional Identity*, 74 U. Colo. L. Rev. 1, 10 (2003).

39. *See, e.g.,* Ansell, *supra* note 20, at 27 ("Pragmatist institutionalism emphasizes the dynamism of institutional change").

40. *See, e.g.,* Alex S. Jones, *Losing the News: The Future of the News That Feeds Democracy* (2009).

41. *See generally* Jürgen Habermas, *The Structural Transformation of the Public Sphere: An Inquiry into a Category of Bourgeois Society* (Thomas Burger trans., 1991) (1962).

42. *See, e.g.,* Jack M. Balkin, *Digital Speech and Democratic Culture: A Theory of Freedom of Expression for the Information Society*, 79 N.Y.U. L. Rev. 1 (2004).

43. *See, e.g.,* Anuj C. Desai, *Wiretapping before the Wires: The Post Office and the Birth of Communications Privacy*, 60 Stan. L. Rev. 553 (2007); Anuj C. Desai, *The*

Transformation of Statutes into Constitutional Law: How Early Post Office Policy Shaped Modern First Amendment Doctrine, 58 Hastings L.J. 671 (2007).

44. *See, e.g.,* Randall P. Bezanson, *The Developing Law of Editorial Judgment,* 78 Neb. L. Rev. 754 (1999).

45. Ansell, *supra* note 20, at 28.

4. Institutions and Institutionalism

1. 378 U.S. 184 (1964).

2. *See, e.g.,* Steven Alan Childress, *Constitutional Fact and Process: A First Amendment Model of Censorial Discretion,* 70 Tul. L. Rev. 1229, 1246–1247 (1996).

3. *See* Bob Woodward & Scott Armstrong, *The Brethren: Inside the Supreme Court* 198 (1976); Ronald K. L. Collins & David M. Skover, *The Pornographic State,* 107 Harv. L. Rev. 1374, 1390 (1994).

4. *Jacobellis,* 378 U.S. at 197 (Stewart, J., concurring). This is virtually the whole of Stewart's opinion. Perhaps not coincidentally, Stewart was one of the early advocates of an institutional approach to the freedom of the press; *see* Chapter 6.

5. Paul Gewirtz, *On "I Know It When I See It,"* 105 Yale L.J. 1023, 1024–1025 (1996).

6. *Cf.* Frederick Schauer, *A Critical Guide to Vehicles in the Park,* 83 N.Y.U. L. Rev. 1109, 1125–1126 (2008) (discussing Bertrand Russell's use of the example of a bald man to explore questions about boundaries, in which Russell "asked us to recognize that although there might be some cases in which we would be unsure about whether a man was bald or not, this does not mean that there are not men who are clearly bald and men who are clearly not"); *id.* at 1134 (drawing on the classic example of a rule prohibiting "vehicles in the park" and observing that although the difficulty in determining whether something is a "vehicle" within the terms of such a rule "tells us something important about modern common law legal systems, so too does the automobile that is plainly a vehicle"); Lawrence B. Solum, District of Columbia v. Heller *and Originalism,* 103 Nw. U. L. Rev. 923, 976 (2009) ("Vague words and phrases reveal borderline cases, but the very idea of a borderline entails that there are cases that are not in the vicinity of the border.").

7. *Branzburg v. Hayes,* 408 U.S. 665, 703 (1972).

8. Along similar lines, Andrew Koppelman has noted that "[r]eligion is a category that is hard to delimit," that "[t]here is no set of necessary and sufficient conditions that will make something a 'religion.'" And yet, he observes, "it is remarkable how few cases have arisen in which courts have had real difficulty in determining whether something is a religion." Andrew Koppelman, *Corruption of Religion and the Establishment Clause,* 50 Wm. & Mary L. Rev. 1831, 1906–1907 (2009).

9. Jack M. Balkin, *The Future of Free Expression in a Digital Age,* 36 Pepperdine L. Rev. 427, 432 (2009).

10. Richard W. Garnett, *The Story of Henry Adams's Soul: Education and the Expression of Associations,* 85 Minn. L. Rev. 1841, 1854 (2001).

11. Robert Post, *Participatory Democracy and Free Speech,* 97 Va. L. Rev. 477, 483 (2011). James Weinstein takes a similar approach: "Public discourse consists of speech on matters of public concern, or, largely without respect to its subject matter, of expression in settings dedicated or essential to democratic self-governance, such as books, magazines, films, the internet, or in public forums such as the speaker's corner of the park." James Weinstein, *Participatory Democracy as the Central Value of Free Speech Doctrine,* 97 Va. L. Rev. 491, 493 (2011). By singling out of particular "media of communication" and "essential settings," both definitions already take us some of the way toward the institutional turn.

12. Post, *supra* note 11, at 482–483.

13. *See* Symposium, 97 Va. L. Rev. 477 (2011). The symposium contains the articles by Post and Weinstein cited in note 11, a series of criticisms of those views by a variety of distinguished commentators, and useful replies by Post and Weinstein.

14. Post, *supra* note 11, at 484 (emphasis added).

15. *Cf.* Paul Q. Hirst, *Introduction,* in *The Pluralist Theory of the State: Selected Writings of G. D. H. Cole, J. N. Figgis, and H. J. Laski* 1, 30 (Paul Q. Hirst ed., 1989) (noting the British pluralist critique of political theories that "vest in a specific political body, the state, what could in fact only be contained in the whole of society itself"). I discuss the relevance of the British pluralists to First Amendment institutionalism in Chapter 7.

16. T. M. Scanlon, *Why Not Base Free Speech on Autonomy or Democracy?,* 97 Va. L. Rev. 541, 544 (2011) (quoting Post, *supra* note 11, at 483).

17. *Id.* (emphasis added).

18. Cynthia L. Estlund, *Working Together: The Workplace, Civil Society, and the Law,* 89 Geo. L.J. 1, 1–2 (2000).

19. The charge is captured by the title of a recent article by Eugene Volokh, *The Trouble with "Public Discourse" as a Limitation on Free Speech Rights,* 97 Va. L. Rev. 567 (2011). Volokh argues that under such an approach, public discourse will end up serving as "a *precondition* for extremely rigorous [constitutional] protection," while "other speech [will] lack[ ] full protection." *Id.* at 567, 570 (quotations and citation omitted).

20. *See, e.g.,* Post, *supra* note 11, at 485 (citing Robert Post, *The Constitutional Concept of Public Discourse: Outrageous Opinion, Democratic Deliberation, and* Hustler Magazine v. Falwell, 103 Harv. L. Rev. 601, 668–672 (1990)).

21. *Id. See also* C. Edwin Baker, *Is Democracy a Sound Basis for a Free Speech Principle?*, 97 Va. L. Rev. 515, 520 (2011) (describing Post as using the concept of public discourse to provide courts in First Amendment cases with a "guide" that is "theoretical and normative" in nature, "not sociological or empirical").

22. John R. Searle, *Making the Social World: The Structure of Human Civilization* xi (2010); *see also id.* at 16 ("Once you see the power of [language] to create an institutional reality, a reality of governments, universities, marriages, private property, and all the rest of it, you can see that social reality has a formal structure as simple and elegant as the structure of the language used to create it.").

23. Despite his initial focus on normative questions about public discourse, Post recognizes this point, I believe. Once he moves further away from his normative starting point, his argument is as much sociological and infrastructural as it is theoretical. *See* Post, *supra* note 11, at 486 ("Public discourse depends on the maintenance of the public sphere, which is a sociological structure that is a prerequisite to the formation of public opinion. Media like newspapers are major components of this structure and indeed are the historical grounds for its emergence.").

24. Frederick Schauer, *Towards an Institutional First Amendment*, 89 Minn. L. Rev. 1256, 1274 (2005).

25. *See, e.g., The Future of Academic Freedom* (Louis Menand ed., 1996); David Rabban, *Can Academic Freedom Survive Postmodernism?*, 86 Cal. L. Rev. 1377 (1998).

26. Emily M. Calhoun, *Academic Freedom: Disciplinary Lessons from Hogwarts*, 77 U. Colo. L. Rev. 843, 844 (2006).

27. *See, e.g.,* Paul Horwitz, *Grutter's First Amendment*, 46 B.C. L. Rev. 461, 472–481 (2005).

28. For exceptions, see, *e.g.,* Christina E. Wells, *Questioning Deference*, 69 Mo. L. Rev. 903 (2004); Daniel J. Solove, *The Darkest Domain: Deference, Judicial Review, and the Bill of Rights*, 84 Iowa L. Rev. 941 (1999); Note, *Deference to Legislative Fact Determinations in First Amendment Cases after Turner Broadcasting*, 111 Harv. L. Rev. 2312 (1998); Symposium, *One Hundred Years of Judicial Review: The Thayer Centennial Symposium*, 88 Nw. U. L. Rev. 1 (1993).

29. James B. Thayer, *The Origin and Scope of the American Doctrine of Constitutional Law*, 7 Harv. L. Rev. 129 (1893).

30. *See* Paul Horwitz, *Three Faces of Deference*, 83 Notre Dame L. Rev. 1061, 1078–1106 (2008).

31. 467 U.S. 837, 865 (1984).

32. Gary Lawson & Christopher D. Moore, *The Executive Power of Constitutional Interpretation*, 81 Iowa L. Rev. 1267, 1271 (1996).

33. U.S. Const., art. I, § 8, cl. 13.

34. *Rostker v. Goldberg*, 453 U.S. 57, 70 (1981).

35. *See generally* Alexander Bickel, *The Least Dangerous Branch: The Supreme Court at the Bar of Politics* (1962).

36. *Chevron*, 467 U.S. at 866.

37. *Rostker*, 453 U.S. at 112 (Marshall, J., dissenting).

38. Paul Horwitz, *Universities as First Amendment Institutions: Some Easy Answers and Hard Questions*, 54 UCLA L. Rev. 1497, 1504 (2007).

39. Horwitz, *supra* note 30, at 1066.

40. *Grutter v. Bollinger*, 539 U.S. 306, 327 (2003).

41. *United States v. American Library Association*, 539 U.S. 194 (2003); *Arkansas Educational Television Commission v. Forbes*, 523 U.S. 666 (1998); *National Endowment for the Arts v. Finley*, 524 U.S. 569 (1998).

42. *See, e.g., Univ. of Pa. v. EEOC*, 493 U.S. 182, 199 (1990); *Regents of Univ. of Mich. v. Ewing*, 474 U.S. 214, 225 (1985).

43. *See, e.g., Hazelwood Sch. Dist. v. Kuhlmeier*, 484 U.S. 260, 273 (1988); *Board of Education of Hendrick Hudson Central School Dist., Westchester Cty. v. Rowley*, 458 U.S. 176, 206 (1982); Bruce C. Hafen, *Hazelwood School District and the Role of First Amendment Institutions*, 1988 Duke L.J. 685.

44. *See* Randall P. Bezanson, *The Developing Law of Editorial Judgment*, 78 Neb. L. Rev. 754 (1999).

45. *Grutter*, 539 U.S. at 328. *Grutter* actually involved the Equal Protection Clause of the Fourteenth Amendment, but the Court's decision was heavily influenced by what it saw as the strong entitlement of universities to judicial deference under the First Amendment.

46. At least that is what the Court *said*. For an argument that its deference to the university in that case swept much more broadly than this, *see* Horwitz, *supra* note 27.

47. *See, e.g., Parker v. Levy*, 417 U.S. 733, 743 (1974).

48. *Goldman v. Weinberger*, 475 U.S. 503, 515 (1986) (Brennan, J., dissenting) (citations omitted).

49. Ernest A. Young, *The Rehnquist Court's Two Federalisms*, 83 Tex. L. Rev. 1, 14 (2004) (quoting 1 *Oxford English Dictionary* 575 (2d ed. 1989)).

50. Schauer, *supra* note 24, at 1274, 1275.

51. Horwitz, *supra* note 38, at 1511.

52. Young, *supra* note 49, at 14 (quoting Bernard Bailyn, *The Ideological Origins of the American Revolution* 198 (2d ed. 1992)).

53. *See, e.g.,* Paul Horwitz, *Churches as First Amendment Institutions: Of Sovereignty and Spheres*, 44 Harv. C.R.-C.L. L. Rev. 79 (2009); Franklin G. Snyder, *Sharing Sovereignty: Non-State Associations and the Limits of State Power*, 54 Am. U. L. Rev. 365 (2004); Franklin G. Snyder, *Nomos, Narrative, and Adjudication: Toward a Jurisgenetic Theory of Law*, 40 Wm. & Mary L. Rev. 1623 (1999).

54. *See* Robert M. Cover, *Foreword:* Nomos *and Narrative*, 97 Harv. L. Rev. 4 (1983).

55. Robert C. Post, *Foreword: Fashioning the Legal Constitution: Culture, Courts, and Law*, 117 Harv. L. Rev. 4, 8 (2003).

56. *See, e.g.*, Laurence R. Iannaccone, *Introduction to the Economics of Religion*, 36 J. Econ. Literature 1465 (1998); Laurence R. Iannaccone, *Sacrifice and Stigma: Reducing Free-Riding in Cults, Communes, and Other Collectives*, 100 J. Pol. Econ. 271 (1992); Laurence R. Iannaccone, *The Consequences of Religious Market Structure: Adam Smith and the Economics of Religion*, 3 Rationality & Soc'y 156 (1991). *See also* Paul Horwitz, *Act III of the Ministerial Exception*, 106 Nw. U. L. Rev. 973 (2012).

57. Snyder, *supra* note 53.

58. *See* Horwitz, *supra* note 53, at 96–98, 111–113.

59. *Cf.* Lee Anne Fennell, *Between Monster and Machine: Rethinking the Judicial Function*, 51 S.C. L. Rev. 183, 202 (1999).

60. David Aram Kaiser, *Entering onto the Path of Inference: Textualism and Contextualism in the Bruton Trilogy*, 44 U.S.F. L. Rev. 95, 99 (2009).

61. Michael C. Dorf, *Foreword: The Limits of Socratic Deliberation*, 112 Harv. L. Rev. 4, 82 (1998).

62. *See, e.g.*, Richard Warner, *Why Pragmatism?: The Puzzling Place of Pragmatism in Critical Theory*, 1993 U. Ill. L. Rev. 535, 536 n.6 (citing Ronald Dworkin, *Pragmatism, Right Answers, and True Banality*, in *Pragmatism in Law & Society* 359, 370 (Michael Brint & William Weaver eds., 1991)).

63. Recall from Chapter 3 that a major influence on First Amendment institutionalism is democratic experimentalism or New Governance theory, both of which draw on pragmatist theory to advocate more contextual, reflexive, and responsive approaches to the law. For a discussion of the relationship between these approaches and pragmatism, *see* Christopher K. Ansell, *Pragmatist Democracy: Evolutionary Learning as Public Philosophy* (2011).

64. *See, e.g.*, Richard A. Posner, *Law, Pragmatism, and Democracy* (2003); Michael C. Dorf, *Create Your Own Constitutional Theory*, 87 Cal. L. Rev. 593 (1999).

65. *See generally* Neil H. Komesar, *Imperfect Alternatives: Choosing Institutions in Law, Economics, and Public Policy* (1994).

66. The term "legal particularism" can also be found in a related context in debates within comparative constitutional law; *see, e.g.*, Sujit Choudhry, *The Lochner Era and Comparative Constitutionalism*, 2 Int'l J. Const. L. 1 (2004). I do not have that use of the term in mind here. There is also a considerable philosophical literature on "moral particularism," and it surely influences discussions of particularism in law; but again, that literature lies outside the scope of my discussion.

67. R. George Wright, *Dreams and Formulas: The Roles of Particularism and Principlism in the Law*, 37 Hofstra L. Rev. 195, 196 (2008).

68. I am grateful to an anonymous reviewer for the Harvard University Press for suggesting this formulation.

69. In this sense, it is closer to the insistence of some Legal Realists that certain legal categories, such as those governing tort and contract law, are often "applied quite differently," and that the differences in application "track distinctions in fact patterns . . . having to do with subject matter or parties—insurance, employment, or construction in contracts; shippers, passengers, or bystanders in railway torts." Robert W. Gordon, *American Law through English Eyes: A Century of Nightmares and Noble Dreams*, 84 Geo. L.J. 2215, 2224–2225 (1996). It also bears some relation to Max Weber's description of earlier legal regimes, prior to law becoming more bureaucratized and the state having become an "all-embracing coercive institution," as having recognized "[o]ther forms of law" and the important status of "particular constellations of individuals or objects." John P. McCormick, *Max Weber and the Legal-Historical Ramifications of Social Democracy*, 17 Can. J.L. & Juris. 143, 163–164 (2004) (quotations and citations omitted).

70. Or so it is commonly said. Of course, many have expressed their doubts that this is really so.

71. William N. Eskridge, Jr., *Relationships between Formalism and Functionalism in Separation of Powers Cases*, 22 Harv. J.L. & Pub. Pol'y 21, 21–22 (1998).

72. In particular, as I emphasize in Chapters 7 and 9, it shares with the British legal pluralists the view that First Amendment institutions, and the infrastructure of public discourse generally, should be understood according to the function performed by particular institutions within public discourse. *See, e.g.*, David Nicholls, *The Pluralist State: The Political Ideas of J. N. Figgis and His Contemporaries* 31, 46 (2d ed. 1994); Martin Loughlin, *The Functionalist Style in Public Law*, 55 U. Toronto L.J. 361, 391–397 (2005); David Schneiderman, *Harold Laski, Viscount Haldane, and the Law of the Canadian Constitution in the Early Twentieth Century*, 48 U. Toronto L.J. 521, 533–535 (1998). This approach is evident in my suggestion earlier in this chapter that the boundaries of First Amendment institutions' autonomy should be drawn in large measure by asking whether their conduct is consistent with these institutions' particular roles in public discourse.

73. *See, e.g.*, Frederick Schauer, *Formalism*, 97 Yale L.J. 509 (1988).

74. Frederick Schauer, *Institutions as Legal and Constitutional Categories*, 54 UCLA L. Rev. 1747, 1763, 1764 (2007).

75. *Id.* at 1764 (emphasis added).

76. *See, e.g.*, Post, *supra* note 55.

77. 334 U.S. 1 (1948).

78. *See, e.g.*, Louis Michael Seidman & Mark V. Tushnet, *Remnants of Belief: Contemporary Constitutional Issues* 61 (1996).

79. 376 U.S. 254 (1964).

80. *See, e.g., Curtis Publishing Co. v. Butts,* 388 U.S. 130 (1967).

81. J. Peter Byrne, *Academic Freedom: A "Special Concern of the First Amendment,"* 99 Yale L.J. 251, 300 (1989).

82. *See, e.g., Nadel v. Regents of the Univ. of Calif.,* 34 Cal. Rptr. 2d 188 (Cal. Ct. App. 1994); *County of Suffolk v. Long Island Lighting Co.,* 710 F. Supp. 1387, 1390 (E.D.N.Y. 1989).

83. *See, e.g.,* Mich. Const., art. VIII, § 5.

84. *See, e.g., State v. Schmid,* 423 A.2d 615 (N.J. 1980); *Commonwealth v. Tate,* 432 A.2d 1382 (Pa. 1981); Cal. Educ. Code § 94367.

85. *See, e.g.,* Gregory C. Sisk, *Returning to the* PruneYard: *The Unconstitutionality of State-Sanctioned Trespass in the Name of Speech,* 32 Harv. J.L. & Pub. Pol'y 389 (2009); Gregory C. Sisk, *Uprooting the* Pruneyard, 38 Rutgers L.J. 1145 (2007); J. Peter Byrne, *Constitutional Academic Freedom after* Grutter: *Getting Real about the 'Four Freedoms' of a University,* 77 U. Colo. L. Rev. 929, 946 (2006); Julian N. Eule & Jonathan D. Varat, *Transporting First Amendment Norms to the Private Sector: With Every Wish There Comes a Curse,* 45 UCLA L. Rev. 1537 (1998).

86. *See* Horwitz, *supra* note 27, at 587–588.

87. Frederick Schauer & Richard H. Pildes, *Electoral Exceptionalism and the First Amendment,* 77 Tex. L. Rev. 1803, 1803–1804 (1999).

5. Where Ideas Begin

1. George Washington, *Message to Congress,* Jan. 8, 1790, excerpted in Judith Areen, *Higher Education and the Law: Cases and Materials* 29 (2009).

2. 347 U.S. 483, 493 (1954).

3. *See, e.g.,* Harold T. Shapiro, *A Larger Sense of Purpose: Higher Education and Society* 1–6 (2005).

4. *See* Areen, *supra* note 1, at 29, 38–41, 62–64.

5. *See, e.g., id.* at 54–55.

6. *See, e.g.,* Walter P. Metzger, *Profession and Constitution: Two Definitions of Academic Freedom,* 66 Tex. L. Rev. 1265, 1269 (1988).

7. *See id.* at 1270; Richard Hofstadter & Walter P. Metzger, *The Development of Academic Freedom in the United States* 386–387 (1955); Matthew W. Finkin, *On "Institutional" Academic Freedom,* 61 Tex. L. Rev. 817, 822, 823 (1983).

8. Louis Menand, *The Marketplace of Ideas: Reform and Resistance in the American University* 131 (2010).

9. American Association of University Professors, *General Report of the Committee on Academic Freedom and Academic Tenure* (1915), reprinted in *Freedom and Tenure in the Academy* 398 (William W. Van Alstyne ed., 1993) [hereinafter *1915 Declaration*].

10. *See* Paul Horwitz, Grutter's *First Amendment*, 46 B.C. L. Rev. 461, 476, 477 (2005).

11. 1915 Declaration, *supra* note 9, at 401.

12. *See, e.g.,* Matthew W. Finkin & Robert C. Post, *For the Common Good: Principles of American Academic Freedom* 40–41 (2009).

13. *Gertz v. Robert Welch, Inc.,* 418 U.S. 323, 339 (1974).

14. *See, e.g.,* Finkin & Post, *supra* note 12, at 44; Menand, *supra* note 8, at 130.

15. *See, e.g.,* Metzger, *supra* note 6; J. Peter Byrne, *The Threat to Constitutional Academic Freedom*, 31 J.C. & U.L. 79 (2004).

16. 354 U.S. 234 (1957). The concept had been cited by Justice William Douglas in a dissent in an earlier case, *see Adler v. Bd. of Educ.,* 342 U.S. 485, 509 (1952) (Douglas, J., dissenting), but it did not appear in a majority opinion of the Court until *Sweezy.*

17. Byrne, *supra* note 15, at 86; *see also* Paul Horwitz, *Universities as First Amendment Institutions: Some Easy Answers and Hard Questions*, 54 UCLA L. Rev. 1497, 1500–1501 (2007).

18. *Sweezy,* 354 U.S. at 250.

19. *Sweezy,* 354 U.S. at 261–263 (Frankfurter, J., concurring in the result).

20. 385 U.S. 589, 603 (1967).

21. *See, e.g.,* Robert M. O'Neil, *Academic Freedom in the Wired World: Political Extremism, Corporate Power, and the University* 49 (2008).

22. *Keyishian,* 385 U.S. at 603 (quoting *United States v. Associated Press,* 52 F. Supp. 362, 372 (S.D.N.Y. 1943)).

23. *Regents of the University of Mich. v. Ewing,* 474 U.S. 214, 226 n.12 (1985); *see also Piarowski v. Illinois Community College Dist. 515, 759* F.2d 625, 629 (7th Cir. 1985).

24. *See generally* Robert C. Post, *Democracy, Expertise, and Academic Freedom: A First Amendment Jurisprudence for the Modern State* (2012); *see also* Stanley Fish, *Save the World on Your Own Time* 70, 110 (2008).

25. J. Peter Byrne has made this argument in a number of articles. *See also* Judith C. Areen, *Government as Educator: A New Understanding of First Amendment Protection of Academic Freedom and Governance*, 97 Geo. L.J. 945 (2009).

26. Emily M. Calhoun, *Academic Freedom: Disciplinary Lessons from Hogwarts*, 77 U. Colo. L. Rev. 843, 844 (2006).

27. *Ewing,* 474 U.S. at 225, 226 (quoting *Bd. of Curators, Univ. of Mo. v. Horowitz,* 435 U.S. 78, 89–90 (1978)).

28. *See, e.g.,* J. Peter Byrne, *Academic Freedom: A "Special Concern of the First Amendment,"* 99 Yale L.J. 251, 289–291 (1989). For contrasting views, *see, e.g.,* David M. Rabban, *A Functional Analysis of "Individual" and "Institutional" Academic Freedom under the First Amendment,* 53 L. & Contemp. Probs. 227 (1990); Richard H. Hiers, *Institutional Academic Freedom or Autonomy Grounded upon the First Amendment: A Jurisprudential Mirage,* 30 Hamline L. Rev. 1 (2007).

29. *Gertz*, 418 U.S. at 339.

30. *See Widmar v. Vincent*, 454 U.S. 263, 277–280 (1981) (Stevens, J., concurring).

31. Frederick Schauer, *Towards an Institutional First Amendment*, 89 Minn. L. Rev. 1256, 1274 (2005).

32. *See, e.g.*, Robert M. O'Neil, *Judicial Deference to Academic Decisions: An Outmoded Concept?*, 36 J.C. & U.L. 729, 737–741 (2010); Areen, *supra* note 25, at 995–996; Neil Kumar Katyal, *The Promise and Precondition of Educational Autonomy*, 31 Hastings Const. L.Q. 557 (2003).

33. *Ewing*, 474 U.S. at 225.

34. *See* Areen, *supra* note 25, at 995–996.

35. *See, e.g.*, Paul Horwitz, *Three Faces of Deference*, 83 Notre Dame L. Rev. 1061, 1104–1105 (2008); Horwitz, *supra* note 17, at 1541–1542.

36. 8 F. Supp. 2d 82, 85, 87, 90 (D. Mass. 1998) (quotation and citation omitted).

37. To take one example, a university might dismiss a faculty member on purely political grounds, but assert that its decision was wholly academic and followed normal academic processes. Whether that claim would succeed might depend on the evidence: lacking any evidence to support the university's claim that the decision was academic, even a deferential court could reasonably find that the decision did not merit deference, or that it so departed from the usual or best practices of the university as to deserve skepticism. But other cases might provide sufficient evidence that the university *did* observe academic criteria and processes in dismissing the individual, and in such cases the court might be obliged to defer even if the faculty member protested that the real reasons for his dismissal were political. Those decisions are not always unreasonable— Ward Churchill was arguably a politically controversial figure *and* someone whom a meaningful academic review process found to be unworthy of tenure—and when in doubt, the court should defer rather than intervene. Even in those cases, however, we must remember that the courts are not the only avenue for monitoring or redress; academics themselves, and the public, should closely scrutinize what their university does and take substantial responsibility for ensuring that it lives up to its principles and its function in public discourse.

38. *See* Areen, *supra* note 25.

39. Byrne, *supra* note 28, at 333, 338.

40. J. Peter Byrne, *Constitutional Academic Freedom after* Grutter: *Getting Real about the "Four Freedoms" of a University*, 77 U. Colo. L. Rev. 929, 939, 952 (2006).

41. *See, e.g.*, Joseph Blocher, *Institutions in the Marketplace of Ideas*, 57 Duke L.J. 812, 863 (2008).

42. *See, e.g.*, Horwitz, *supra* note 17, at 1542; Byrne, *supra* note 15, at 91 n.77.

43. Byrne, *supra* note 40, at 941.

44. *See* http://www.aboutmcdonalds.com/mcd/corporate_careers/training_and _development/hamburger_university.html.

45. For a measured account, *see* David L. Kirp, *Shakespeare, Einstein, and the Bottom Line: The Marketing of Higher Education* 240–254 (2003).

46. For a discussion of the similarities and differences between nonprofit and for-profit universities, pointing out a number of aspects of convergence between the two, *see* Brian Pusser & Sarah E. Turner, *Nonprofit and For-Profit Governance in Higher Education,* in *Governing Academia* 235 (Ronald G. Ehrenberg ed., 2004); *see also* Kirp, *supra* note 45.

47. *See, e.g.,* Robert J. Tepper & Craig G. White, *Speak No Evil: Academic Freedom and the Application of Garcetti v. Ceballos to Public University Faculty,* 59 Cath. U. L. Rev. 125, 134 n.58 (2009).

48. *See, e.g., Nieman v. Yale Univ.,* 851 A.2d 1165, 1172 (Conn. 2005); *Berkowitz v. President & Fellows of Harvard College,* 58 Mass. App. Ct. 262, 269 (2003).

49. *See, e.g.,* Scott A. Moss, *Against "Academic Deference": How Recent Developments in Employment Discrimination Law Undercut an Already Dubious Doctrine,* 27 Berkeley J. Emp. & Lab. L. 1 (2006).

50. *See, e.g., id.;* Mary Gray, *Academic Freedom and Nondiscrimination: Enemies or Allies?,* 66 Tex. L. Rev. 1591 (1988).

51. Amy Gajda, *The Trials of Academe: The New Era of Campus Litigation* 80 (2009).

52. 493 U.S. 182 (1990).

53. Byrne, *supra* note 28, at 319.

54. *See, e.g.,* James D. Gordon III, *Individual and Institutional Academic Freedom at Religious Colleges and Universities,* 30 J.C. & U.L. 1 (2003); Douglas Laycock, *Academic Freedom, Religious Commitment, and Religious Intensity,* 78 Marq. L. Rev. 297 (1995); Michael W. McConnell, *Academic Freedom in Religious Colleges and Universities,* 53 L. & Contemp. Probs. 303 (1990).

55. *See generally* William H. Buss, *Academic Freedom and Freedom of Speech: Communicating the Curriculum,* 2 J. Gender Race & Just. 213 (1999).

56. 1915 Declaration, *supra* note 9; *see also* Areen, *supra* note 25, at 956–958.

57. *See generally* Evelyn Sung, Note, *Mending the Federal Circuit Split on the First Amendment Right of Public University Professors to Assign Grades,* 78 N.Y.U. L. Rev. 1550 (2003).

58. *See Parate v. Isibor,* 868 F.2d 821, 828 (6th Cir. 1989).

59. *See, e.g., Garcetti v. Ceballos,* 547 U.S. 410, 425 (2006); *Adams v. Trustees of Univ. of N.C. Wilmington,* 2011 WL 1289054 (4th Cir. April 6, 2011).

60. *See, e.g.,* Areen, *supra* note 25, at 975, 999–1000.

61. *See, e.g.,* Jerome Karabel, *The Chosen: The Hidden History of Admission and Exclusion at Harvard, Yale, and Princeton* (2005).

62. *See, e.g.,* Norman Dorsen, *John T. Noonan, Jr.: Renaissance Man in the Catholic Tradition,* 76 Notre Dame L. Rev. 843, 846–847 (2001).

63. *Regents of the University of California v. Bakke,* 438 U.S. 265, 311, 312, 314 (1978) (opinion of Powell, J.).

64. *Gratz v. Bollinger,* 539 U.S. 244 (2003).

65. *Grutter v. Bollinger,* 539 U.S. 306, 328, 329 (2003).

66. *Id.*

67. *See, e.g.,* Byrne, *supra* note 40, at 935–936; Byrne, *supra* note 28, at 315; Mark G. Yudof, *The Three Faces of Academic Freedom,* 32 Loy. L. Rev. 831, 856–857 (1987).

68. *See, e.g., Adarand Constructors, Inc. v. Pena,* 515 U.S. 200 (1995); *Richmond v. J.A. Croson Co.,* 488 U.S. 469 (1989).

69. *See generally* Timothy C. Shiell, *Campus Hate Speech on Trial* (1998).

70. *See, e.g., Dambrot v. Cent. Mich. Univ.,* 55 F.3d 1177 (6th Cir. 1995); Robert M. O'Neil, *Free Speech in the College Community* 20–21 (1997).

71. *Doe v. Univ. of Mich.,* 721 F. Supp. 852, 863 (E.D. Mich. 1989).

72. Avern Cohn, *A Federal Trial Judge Looks at Academic Freedom,* in *Unfettered Expression: Freedom in American Intellectual Life* 117, 131 (Peggie J. Hollingsworth ed., 2000).

73. *See, e.g.,* Mari J. Matsuda, *Public Response to Racist Speech: Considering the Victim's Story,* in Mari J. Matsuda et al., *Words That Wound: Critical Race Theory, Assaultive Speech, and the First Amendment* 17, 44–45 (1993).

74. *See, e.g.,* Mary Becker, *The Legitimacy of Judicial Review in Speech Cases,* in *The Price We Pay: The Case against Racist Speech, Hate Propaganda, and Pornography* 208, 211 (Laura J. Lederer & Richard Delgado eds., 1995).

75. *See, e.g.,* J. Peter Byrne, *Racial Insults and Free Speech within the University,* 79 Geo. L.J. 399 (1991); W. Bradley Wendel, *A Moderate Defense of Hate Speech Regulations on University Campuses,* 41 Harv. L. on Legis. 407 (2004) (defending campus hate speech regulations insofar as they reflect considered judgments by a university about its mission).

76. One justice, at least, has acknowledged this point. In *Board of Regents of University of Wisconsin System v. Southworth,* 529 U.S. 217 (2000), Justice David Souter noted in a concurring opinion that a genuinely institutional approach to academic freedom, one modeled on the "four freedoms" of the university identified by Justice Frankfurter in *Sweezy,* "might even be thought to sanction student speech codes in public universities." *Id.* at 239 n.5 (Souter, J., concurring in the judgment).

77. Largely, but not entirely. In a valuable study, Jon B. Gould suggests that the data show that "hate speech policies not only persist, but they have actually increased in number," despite the decisions striking down those policies at public universities. Jon B. Gould, *The Precedent That Wasn't: College Hate Speech*

Codes and the Two Faces of Legal Compliance, 35 L. & Soc'y Rev. 345, 345 (2001). Gould's study is an important caution against overstatement, but it should not be accepted unreservedly without more careful examination. For one thing, many of the colleges studied were private universities, and thus not bound by those court decisions—although, as Gould points out, many private universities hold themselves out as trying to maintain policies that are consistent with First Amendment law. *See id.* at 352. For another, it is difficult to draw strong conclusions about a counterfactual. We do not know whether the rate of adoption of campus hate speech codes would have increased under different circumstances, and my view is that, despite outliers, the general popularity of campus hate speech codes has dwindled among academics, and certainly among leading academics, since its peak period. Finally, as the qualitative portion of Gould's study suggests, the reasons that universities either got rid of existing hate speech policies, or maintained existing policies or wrote new ones, appear to have had as much or more to do with academic policy, including considerations of public relations, than with a reaction to what the courts were doing. *See id.* at 365–384.

78. *See, e.g.,* Chi Steve Kwok, *A Study in Contradiction: A Look at the Conflicting Assumptions Underlying Standard Arguments for Speech Codes and the Diversity Rationale,* 4 U. Pa. J. Const. L. 493 (2002). *See also* Kelly Sarabyn, *Free Speech at Private Universities,* 39 J. Legal Educ. 145 (2010). Sarabyn notes the tensions between private universities that "promote themselves as institutions of free speech and thought" yet insist on "policies that explicitly restrict speech," and argues that in some cases contract law might be used to hold universities to their promises. Whether that approach would be successful or not, Sarabyn rightly takes the same general view I advance here: that universities promising one thing but doing another can and should be asked to explain the apparent contradiction.

79. *See, e.g.,* Byrne, *supra* note 75; Robert M. O'Neil, *Bias, 'Balance,' and Beyond: New Threats to Academic Freedom,* 77 U. Colo. L. Rev. 985 (2006); Cheryl A. Cameron, *Academic Bills of Rights: Conflict in the Classroom,* 31 J.C. & U.L. 243 (2005).

80. Fish, *supra* note 24, at 70, 118, 119 (emphasis added).

81. O'Neil, *supra* note 70, at 251 (quotations and citations omitted).

82. *See id.* at 256–257.

83. Fish, *supra* note 24, at 119.

84. Bylaws of the Ass'n of Am. Law Sch., Inc. § 6-3(b) (2005), available at http://www/aals.org/about_handbook_requirements.php. Separate requirements apply to religiously affiliated law schools.

85. *See* 10 U.S.C. § 654 (2000) (mandating the discharge of members of the armed forces who engage in "homosexual acts"). That policy is in the process of being eliminated at the time of this writing.

86. *See, e.g., Forum for Academic & Inst'l Rights, Inc. v. Rumsfeld,* 291 F. Supp. 2d 269, 281–288 (D.N.J. 2003).

87. *See National Defense Authorization Act for Fiscal Year 1996,* Pub. L. No. 104-106, 110 Stat. 186 (codified as amended at 10 U.S.C. § 983(b)).

88. *See* 10 U.S.C. § 983(b), (d).

89. *Rumsfeld v. Forum for Academic and Institutional Rights,* 547 U.S. 47, 62, 66, 70 (2006) [hereinafter *FAIR*].

90. *See, e.g.,* Richard A. Posner, *A Note on* Rumsfeld v. FAIR *and the Legal Academy,* 2006 Sup. Ct. Rev. 47, 47.

91. *See* Horwitz, *supra* note 35; Dale Carpenter, *Unanimously Wrong,* 2006 Cato Sup. Ct. Rev. 217.

92. *United States v. Am. Library Ass'n,* 539 U.S. 194, 213 (2003) (discussing *Legal Servs. Corp. v. Velazquez,* 531 U.S. 533 (2001)).

93. *Rust v. Sullivan,* 500 U.S. 173, 200 (1991).

94. Carpenter, *supra* note 91, at 228.

95. *See id.* at 254.

96. *See FAIR,* 547 U.S. at 58.

97. *See e.g.,* Diane H. Mazur, *A Blueprint for Law School Engagement with the Military,* 1 Nat'l Security L. & Pol'y 473 (2005); Posner, *supra* note 90, at 55, 57. The law schools might respond that students were not prevented from engaging with the military, even on campus; the military was only prevented from enjoying the same access rights as nondiscriminatory employers. But the knife cuts both ways: if military recruiters *were* allowed on campus, albeit under slightly less favorable conditions, then the law schools' recruitment restrictions are rendered vanishingly small, a matter of punctiliousness rather than proof of a genuine commitment to equality.

98. *See* Katyal, *supra* note 32, at 566.

99. *Cf.* Kathleen M. Sullivan, *First Amendment Intermediaries in the Age of Cyberspace,* 45 UCLA L. Rev. 1655, 1656 (1998) ("[S]ome private communities have expressive identities that themselves ought to be permitted to be diverse, including with respect to the diversity of speech they tolerate within themselves.").

100. *See, e.g.,* Byrne, *supra* note 28, at 941.

101. 530 U.S. 640 (2000).

102. *See, e.g.,* Brief for Respondents, *Rumsfeld v. Forum for Academic and Institutional Rights, Inc.,* at 33–35, available at 2005 WL 2347175 (Sept. 21, 2005).

103. 130 S. Ct. 2971, 2979, 2980 (2010) [hereinafter *CLS*].

104. *Id.* at 2986, 2990 (quotations and citations omitted), 2993–2994.

105. *Id.* at 2988 (quoting *Bd. of Educ. of Hendrick Hudson Central Sch. Dist., Westchester Cnty. v. Rowley,* 458 U.S. 176, 206 (1982)).

106. *Id.* at 2997–2998 (Stevens, J., concurring).

107 *Id.* at 2984 n.11 (quoting *Pleasant Grove City v. Summum,* 129 S. Ct. 1125, 1127 (2009)).

108. *Id.* at 2990–2991.

109. *Grutter,* 539 U.S. at 328.

110. *See Runyon v. McCrary,* 427 U.S. 160 (1976).

111. *See Bob Jones Univ. v. United States,* 461 U.S. 574 (1983).

112. *See, e.g.,* Horwitz, *supra* note 17, at 1532 n.205; Byrne, *supra* note 28, at 941.

113. *Id.* at 941.

114. One possibility that has been raised by readers is that a public university in the South, during the era in which those institutions practiced both *de jure* and *de facto* segregation, might have been allowed to maintain a policy of hiring only white faculty members or admitting only white students. The example is rightly troubling, but also somewhat counterfactual and limited in application. It is true that I consider the public status of these universities less determinative of the outcome than the fact that they were universities (although, as I note in the text above and in Chapter 9, if there were ever a time for a strict institutionalist reading of the First Amendment to bend, it would involve the American dilemma of race). But I can think of few universities that would have full-throatedly justified such decisions on *academic* grounds as opposed to nonacademic grounds, and to that extent such decisions would be less entitled to deference. Furthermore, this hypothetical ignores the role of academic culture itself in forcing change at such universities, including not only internal faculty resistance to such policies but, perhaps more important, the need to seek support, resources, and accreditation from broader educational organizations that oppose such policies. And it fails to recognize the degree to which the resistance to desegregation was led not by academics themselves, but by state legislatures and lay individuals such as the members of university governing boards—who, under First Amendment institutionalism, would have less power to enforce those policies against academic wishes. *See* John R. Thelin, *A History of Higher Education* 305–306 (1st ed. 2004).

In short, even if an institutionalist reading *might* support some judicial deference in *some* such cases, it would leave open the institutional and cultural pressures that might convince such a university to change its policies. *See, e.g.,* Melissa Kean, *Desegregating Private Higher Education in the South: Duke, Emory, Rice, Tulane, and Vanderbilt* (2008) (discussing the resistance of the gatekeepers at those universities to desegregation, but also noting the pressure on them to change if they wished to receive both private and public funding and to join the upper echelon of American universities).

115. 347 U.S. 483, 493 (1954).

116. *Tinker v. Des Moines Indep. Community Sch. Dist.,* 393 U.S. 503, 506, 511, 508 (1969).

117. *Bethel Sch. Dist. No. 403 v. Fraser,* 478 U.S. 675, 681 (1986) (quoting *Ambach v. Norwick,* 441 U.S. 68, 76–77 (1979)).

118. *Id.* at 683.

119. *Hazelwood Sch. Dist. v. Kuhlmeier,* 484 U.S. 260, 273 (1988).

120. Josie Foehrenbach Brown, *Representative Tension: Student Religious Speech and the Public School's Institutional Mission,* 38 J.L. & Educ. 1, 3 (2009).

121. *See, e.g., id.;* Richard W. Garnett, *Can There Really Be "Free Speech" in Public Schools?,* 12 Lewis & Clark L. Rev. 45 (2008); Martin H. Redish & Kevin Finnerty, *What Did You Learn in School Today?: Free Speech, Values Inculcation, and the Democratic-Educational Paradox,* 88 Cornell L. Rev. 62 (2002).

6. Where Information Is Gathered

1. Potter Stewart, *"Or of the Press,"* 26 Hastings L.J. 631, 631 (1975).

2. *Id.* at 632.

3. *Id.* at 633, 634.

4. *Id.* at 634, 636.

5. 435 U.S. 765, 796 (1978) (Burger, C.J., concurring).

6. *Id.* at 796.

7. *Id.* at 796, 797, 800.

8. *Id.* at 801, 802.

9. *Branzburg v. Hayes,* 408 U.S. 665, 683, 703–704 (1972) (quoting *Associated Press v. NLRB,* 301 U.S. 103, 132 (1937)).

10. In particular, that is truer of the lower federal courts, which have had to deal with a myriad of cases, and thus practical facts, involving the press, than of the Supreme Court, whose caseload involving the Press Clause is close to nonexistent.

11. *See, e.g.,* Alex S. Jones, *Losing the News: The Future of the News That Feeds Democracy* 128 (2009).

12. *See, e.g.,* Jason M. Shepard, *After the First Amendment Fails: The Newsmen's Privilege Hearings of the 1970s,* 14 Comm. L. & Pol'y 373, 398 (2009); Anthony L. Fargo, *The Year of Leaking Dangerously: Shadowy Sources, Jailed Journalists, and the Uncertain Future of the Federal Journalist's Privilege,* 14 Wm. & Mary Bill Rts. J. 1063, 1118–1119 (2006); David A. Anderson, *Freedom of the Press in Wartime,* 77 U. Colo. L. Rev. 49, 95–96 (2006).

13. *Bellotti,* 435 U.S. at 799–800.

14. Eugene Volokh, *Freedom of the Press as an Industry, or for the Press as a Technology?: From the Framing to Today,* 160 U. Pa. L. Rev. 459, 463 (2012). Coincidentally or not, Volokh is also an exemplar of a doctrinalist approach to First Amendment law, one that seeks to draw as much coherence as possible from the rules as presently constituted—with, to be sure, exceptions here and there as the

doctrine grows too complex to be governed completely by general rules. *See generally* Eugene Volokh, *The First Amendment and Related Statutes: Problems, Cases and Policy Arguments* (4th ed. 2011); Eugene Volokh, *The Trouble with "Public Discourse" as a Limitation on Free Speech Rights*, 97 Va. L. Rev. 567, 584 (2011) (defending a "presumptive all-inclusive approach" to free speech doctrine under which "all speech is presumptively protected against content-based restrictions imposed by the government, unless the speech falls within an exception to protection"); *id.* at 592 (acknowledging that "exceptions" to general rules "must be created under any theory" of First Amendment law).

15. *See generally* Randall P. Bezanson, *Whither Freedom of the Press?*, U. of Iowa Legal Studies Research Paper No. 12-01, Jan. 2012, at 2, available at http://papers .ssrn.com/sol3/papers.cfm?abstract_id=1982616 (acknowledging the value of Volokh's historical research but arguing that he is "wrong, historically and constitutionally").

16. Paul Starr, *The Creation of the Media: Political Origins of Modern Communications* 31–33 (2004). I draw heavily on Starr's account here.

17. *Id.* at 52.

18. *Id.* at 70.

19. *See id.* at 88–89, 86, 48 (quoting Tocqueville).

20. Merrill Jensen, *The New Nation: A History of the United States during the Confederation, 1781–1789* 430 (1958) (quoted in David A. Anderson, *The Origins of the Press Clause*, 30 UCLA L. Rev. 455, 466 (1983)).

21. Starr, *supra* note 16, at 84.

22. *See, e.g.*, Edward Lee, *Freedom of the Press 2.0*, 42 Ga. L. Rev. 309, 341 (2008); Mary-Rose Papandrea, *Citizen Journalism and the Reporter's Privilege*, 91 Minn. L. Rev. 515, 521 (2007); Eric Burns, *Infamous Scribblers: The Founding Fathers and the Rowdy Beginnings of American Journalism* (2006).

23. Starr, *supra* note 16, at 76.

24. Anderson, *supra* note 20, at 464–465, 478 (quoting Madison), 487.

25. *See generally* Robert W. T. Martin, *The Free and Open Press: The Founding of American Democratic Press Liberty 1640–1800* (2001).

26. Timothy E. Cook, *Freeing the Presses: An Introductory Essay*, in *Freeing the Press: The First Amendment in Action* 1, 8 (Timothy E. Cook ed., 2005).

27. Diana Owen, *"New Media" and Contemporary Interpretations of Freedom of the Press*, in *Freeing the Press, supra* note 26, at 139, 142.

28. David A. Anderson, *Freedom of the Press*, 80 Tex. L. Rev. 429, 466 (2002).

29. *See, e.g.*, David S. Allen, *The Institutional Press and Professionalization: Defining the Press Clause in Journalist's Privilege Cases*, 34 Free Speech Y.B. 49 (1996).

30. Stephen J. A. Ward, *The Invention of Journalism Ethics: The Path to Objectivity and Beyond* 188 (2004).

31. *See id.* at 195, 188–189.

32. *See* Maria Petrova, *Newspapers and Parties: How Advertising Revenues Created an Independent Press,* 105 Am. Pol. Sci. Rev. 790 (2011).

33. Ward, *supra* note 30, at 194.

34. *See, e.g., id.* at 214–215.

35. Blake D. Morant, *The Endemic Reality of Media Ethics and Self-Restraint,* 19 Notre Dame J.L. Ethics & Pub. Pol'y 595, 613 (2005).

36. Bill Kovach & Tom Rosenstiel, *The Elements of Journalism: What Newspeople Should Know and the Public Should Expect* 12, 17 (2001).

37. The longstanding analogy between journalism and physical infrastructure is discussed in Ward, *supra* note 30, at 176.

38. Frederick Schauer, *Institutions as Legal and Constitutional Categories,* 54 UCLA L. Rev. 1747, 1754 (2007).

39. *See, e.g.,* Joel D. Eaton, *The American Law of Defamation through* Gertz v. Robert Welch, Inc. *and Beyond,* 61 Va. L. Rev. 1349, 1406–1407 (1975); *Dun & Bradstreet v. Greenmoss Builders,* 472 U.S. 749, 771 (1984) (White, J., concurring).

40. *See* Randall P. Bezanson, *The Developing Law of Editorial Judgment,* 78 Neb. L. Rev. 754 (1998).

41. *New York Times v. Sullivan,* 376 U.S. 254, 280 (1964).

42. *Id.* at 272 (quotations and citations omitted).

43. Brian C. Murchison *et al., Sullivan's Paradox: The Emergence of Judicial Standards of Journalism,* 73 N.C. L. Rev. 7, 12 (1994).

44. Lyrissa Barnett Lidsky, *Prying, Lying, and Spying: Intrusive Newsgathering and What the Law Should Do About It,* 73 Tul. L. Rev. 173, 200 (1998).

45. Amy Gajda argues that the courts are now less likely to defer to the press in these sorts of cases. *See* Amy Gajda, *Judging the Press: The Turn toward Privacy and Judicial Regulation of the Press,* 97 Cal. L. Rev. 1039 (2009). Her argument does not disturb the general point that the standards for torts of these kinds have been far more sensitive to the institutional nature and functional role of the press than the institutionally agnostic model would predict.

46. *See, e.g., Cohen v. Cowles Media Co.,* 501 U.S. 663 (1991); *Branzburg,* 408 U.S. 665.

47. *Grosjean v. Am. Press Co.,* 297 U.S. 233, 249–250 (1936) (quotations and citations omitted).

48. Ernest A. Young, *The Constitution Outside the Constitution,* 117 Yale L.J. 408, 414 (2007). For a different form of this idea, *see, e.g.,* Henry P. Monaghan, *Foreword: Constitutional Common Law,* 89 Harv. L. Rev. 1 (1975).

49. Anderson, *supra* note 28, at 430.

50. *Id.* at 431, 431 n.8, 432; *see also Richmond Newspapers, Inc. v. Virginia,* 448 U.S. 555, 581 n.18 (1980).

51. Frederick Schauer, *Towards an Institutional First Amendment*, 89 Minn. L. Rev. 1256, 1275 (2005).

52. *See id.* at 1275 n.91.

53. *See* Sonja West, *Awakening the Press Clause*, 58 UCLA L. Rev. 1025, 1068–1070 (2011) (arguing that the boundary questions involved in defining the "press" for purposes of institutional constitutional protection should be resolved by focusing on "those [unique institutional] functions that a free press fulfills in our democracy" and suggesting that the press serves two such unique functions: it "gathers and conveys information to the public about newsworthy matters," and it "serves as a check on the government by conveying information to the voters").

54. Before becoming a lawyer and legal academic, I trained at Columbia University's Graduate School of Journalism and worked as a journalist. My view of journalism's status as a unique institution is surely colored by my own experience.

55. Erik Ugland, *The New Abridged Reporter's Privilege: Policies, Principles, and Pathological Perspectives*, 71 Ohio St. L.J. 1, 8 (2010).

56. *See also* West, *supra* note 53, at 1028–1031 (arguing that the primary value of an independent reading of the Press Clause would be its potential to offer the press greater protection for newsgathering).

57. 408 U.S. 665 (1972). For a narrow and skeptical reading of *Branzburg, see* Judge Richard Posner's opinion in *McKevitt v. Pallasch*, 339 F.3d 530 (7th Cir. 2003).

58. It is common enough, certainly, to hear arguments that the institutional press has failed utterly in its professional and ethical obligations, followed by a string of anecdotes. Again based on my own past and continuing experience in journalism, I think those claims are overstated and tend to understate the degree to which even the very public mistakes made by the press have met with *professional* criticisms and reforms.

59. *See* David Abramowicz, Note, *Calculating the Public Interest in Protecting Journalists' Confidential Sources*, 108 Colum. L. Rev. 1949, 1971–1974 (2008).

60. *See, e.g.,* Schauer, *supra* note 51, at 1270–1271.

61. Michael C. Dorf & Charles F. Sabel, *A Constitution of Democratic Experimentalism*, 98 Colum. L. Rev. 267, 351 (1998).

62. *In re Grand Jury Subpoena, Judith Miller*, 397 F.3d 964, 997 (D.C. Cir. 2005) (Tatel, J., concurring in the judgment).

63. *See, e.g.,* Daniel J. Solove & Neil M. Richards, *Rethinking Free Speech and Civil Liability*, 109 Colum. L. Rev. 1650 (2009); Randall P. Bezanson, *Means and Ends and Food Lion: The Tension between Exemption and Independence in Newsgathering by the Press*, 47 Emory L.J. 895 (1998).

64. *See New York Times v. United States*, 403 U.S. 713 (1971).

65. *See, e.g., Food Lion, Inc. v. Capital Cities/ABC, Inc.*, 194 F.3d 505 (4th Cir. 1999).

66. *See, e.g., Cohen v. Cowles Media Co.*, 501 U.S. 663 (1991).

67. *Id.* at 669.

68. *Id.* at 677 (Souter, J., dissenting) (quoting *Employment Division v. Smith*, 494 U.S. 872, 901 (1990) (O'Connor, J., concurring in the judgment)).

69. *Id.*

70. *Id.* at 666.

71. *Cohen v. Cowles Media Co.*, 457 N.W.2d 199, 204 (Minn. 1990), *rev'd*, 501 U.S. 663 (1991).

72. *Cohen*, 501 U.S. at 677–678 (Souter, J., dissenting).

73. *See, e.g.,* West, *supra* note 53, at 1031 (arguing that as long as the general protections of the Speech Clause exist as a "fallback," then those "fallback protections [will] lessen the impact of excluding some [from the Press Clause] but not others as well as the costs of any definitional mistakes"); *id.* at 1032 ("Even a wrongly excluded speaker [under the Press Clause] will be able to express himself and will be protected by the myriad speech safeguards [of current free speech doctrine] such as protections against prior restraints and content-based discrimination."). In sum, even if the institutional treatment of the press presents some boundary questions, those questions should not be fatal. Individuals and groups that do not qualify will still receive constitutional protection, and the public as a whole will still benefit from the enhanced newsgathering abilities of the institutional press.

74. *See, e.g.,* Gallup, *Confidence in Institutions,* July 8–11, 2010, available at http://www.gallup.com/poll/1597/Confidence-Institutions.aspx.

75. William P. Marshall & Susan Gilles, *The Supreme Court, the First Amendment, and Bad Journalism,* 1994 Sup. Ct. Rev. 169, 171.

76. *See, e.g.,* Leonard Downie, Jr. & Robert G. Kaiser, *The News About the News: American Journalism in Peril* 240–242, 245 (2002).

77. *See, e.g.,* Hugh Heclo, *On Thinking Institutionally* (2008).

78. Scott Gant, *We're All Journalists Now: The Transformation of the Press and Reshaping of the Law in the Internet Age* 204 (2007).

79. *See, e.g.,* Bill Mitchell, *Journalists Are More Likely to Be College Graduates,* April 10, 2003, at http://www.poynter.org/content/content_view.asp?id=28790.

80. *See, e.g.,* Richard A. Posner, *Past-Dependency, Pragmatism, and Critique of History in Adjudication and Legal Scholarship,* 67 U. Chi. L. Rev. 573, 590 (2000); Marc Galanter, *Lawyers in the Mist: The Golden Age of Legal Nostalgia,* 100 Dick. L. Rev. 549, 555–556 (1996).

81. *See, e.g.,* Dean Colby & Robert Trager, *Using Communication Theory to Understand Cyberlaw and Its Discontents,* 2005 U. Ill. J.L. Tech. & Pol'y 187, 240–243.

82. *See, e.g.,* Pew Research Center for the People and the Press, *Americans Spending More Time Watching the News,* Sept. 12, 2010, http://people-press.org/reports/pdf/652.pdf.

83. *See, e.g.,* Marvin Ammori, *Another Worthy Tradition: How the Free Speech Curriculum Ignores Electronic Media and Distorts Free Speech Doctrine,* 70 Mo. L. Rev. 59 (2005).

84. *See, e.g.,* Matthew L. Spitzer, *Controlling the Content of Print and Broadcast,* 58 S. Cal. L. Rev. 1349, 1352–1353 (1985).

85. Starr, *supra* note 16, at 384.

86. Lee C. Bollinger, *Images of a Free Press* 108–120, 117, 85 (1991).

87. 395 U.S. 367, 386, 390 (1969).

88. 418 U.S. 241, 258 (1974).

89. *See* Ronald H. Coase, *The Federal Communications Commission,* 2 J.L. & Econ. 1 (1959).

90. *See, e.g.,* Jim Chen, *Conduit-Based Regulation of Speech,* 54 Duke L.J. 1359 (2005); Christopher S. Yoo, *The Rise and Demise of the Technology-Specific Approach to the First Amendment,* 91 Geo. L.J. 245 (2003).

91. *FCC v. Pacifica Foundation,* 438 U.S. 726, 748–749 (1978).

92. *Id.* at 751. The words, taken from a George Carlin monologue and helpfully listed in an appendix to the Court's decision, were "shit, piss, fuck, cunt, cocksucker, motherfucker, and tits."

93. *See, e.g.,* Yoo, *supra* note 90, at 254.

94. *See, e.g.,* Cass R. Sunstein, *Television and the Public Interest,* 88 Cal. L. Rev. 499 (2000); Owen M. Fiss, *The Censorship of Television,* 93 Nw. U. L. Rev. 1215 (1999).

95. *See* Yoo, *supra* note 90.

96. Bollinger, *supra* note 86, at 109, 119, 118.

97. Geoffrey R. Stone, *Imagining a Free Press,* 90 Mich. L. Rev. 1246, 1257 (1992).

98. *See, e.g.,* Radio Television Digital News Association, *Code of Ethics and Professional Conduct,* available at http://www.rtnda.org/pages/media_items/code -of-ethics-and-professional-conduct48.php; *see also* Downie & Kaiser, *supra* note 76, at 132 (noting the establishment by a former CBS News executive of a set of news standards that "could easily be embraced in any good newsroom").

99. *See, e.g.,* Jonathan Weinberg, *Broadcasting and Speech,* 81 Cal. L. Rev. 1101 (1993); Timothy B. Dyk, *Full First Amendment Freedom for Broadcasters: The Industry as Eliza on the Ice and Congress as the Friendly Overseer,* 5 Yale J. Reg. 299 (1988); William W. Van Alstyne, *The Möbius Strip of the First Amendment,* 29 S.C. L. Rev. 539 (1978); Lucas A. Powe, Jr., *"Or of the [Broadcast] Press,"* 55 Tex. L. Rev. 39 (1976).

100. *See, e.g.,* Jonathan M. Phillips, Comment, *Freedom by Design: Objective Analysis and the Constitutional Status of Public Broadcasting,* 155 U. Pa. L. Rev. 991 (2007).

101. *Arkansas Television Commission v. Forbes,* 523 U.S. 666, 671 (1998).

102. *CBS, Inc. v. FCC,* 453 U.S. 367, 395 (1981) (quoting *Columbia Broadcasting System, Inc. v. Democratic National Committee,* 412 U.S. 94, 110 (1973)).

103. *See, e.g.,* Tim Greene, *Metaphor Mania: The Internet Is . . . ,* NetworkWorld, Jan. 7, 2008, http://www.networkworld.com/news/2008/010708-metaphors.html.

104. This is one traditional view of the Internet and its creation; *see, e.g.,* Katie Hafner & Matthew Lyon, *Where Wizards Stay Up Late: The Origins of the Internet* (1996). For important cautions about the accuracy of this view, however, *see, e.g.,* Christopher S. Yoo, *Free Speech and the Myth of the Internet as an Unintermediated Experience,* 78 Geo. Wash. L. Rev. 697 (2010); Moran Yemini, *Mandated Network Neutrality and the First Amendment: Lessons From* Turner *and a New Approach,* 13 Va. J.L. & Tech. 1, 16 (2008) (noting that the physical infrastructure of the Internet, and access to it, is essentially controlled by private companies); Jack Goldsmith & Timothy Wu, *Digital Borders,* Legal Affairs, Feb. 2006, at 40, 44 ("Underneath the mists and magic of the Internet lies an ugly physical transport infrastructure: copper wires, fiber-optic cables, and the specialized routers and switches that direct information from place to place. The physical structure is an asset owned by phone companies, cable companies, and other Internet Service Providers.").

105. *Cf.* Adam Gopnik, *The Information: How the Internet Gets Inside Us,* New Yorker, Feb. 14, 2011, at 124 (describing the holders of typical views on the Internet as the utopian "Never-Betters," the dystopian "Better-Nevers," and the "Ever-Wasers," who insist that there is nothing new to see here).

106. Yochai Benkler, *The Wealth of Networks: How Social Production Transforms Markets and Freedom* 29 (2006).

107. William E. Lee, *The Priestly Class: Reflections on a Journalist's Privilege,* 23 Cardozo Arts & Ent. L.J. 635 (2006).

108. Gant, *supra* note 78.

109. Benkler, *supra* note 106, at 2, 9, 10.

110. *Id.* at 12.

111. *See, e.g.,* Tung Yin, *Legal Blogs and the Supreme Court Confirmation Process,* 11 NEXUS 79, 80–81 (2006).

112. Benkler, *supra* note 106, at 77.

113. Although, as one anonymous reviewer of this manuscript pointed out, the broader set of networks that constitute the "Internet" is also "the product of an autonomous set of governance institutions," such as the Internet Corporation for Assigned Names and Numbers, or ICANN, and its Internet Engineering Task Force. In that sense, it is possible one could argue that the broader Internet *is* a First Amendment institution. That argument is intriguing, but beyond the scope of this chapter. I focus here only on one piece of the Internet that may be considered an emerging First Amendment institution.

114. Larry Ribstein, *Initial Reflections on the Law and Economics of Blogging,* 11 Ill. L. & Econ. Working Papers Ser., Working Paper No. Le05-008, Draft of Sept. 21, 2005, at 3, http://www.ssrn.com/abstract=700961.

115. *See, e.g.,* Beth S. Noveck & David R. Johnson, *Society's Software,* 74 Fordham L. Rev. 469 (2005); Larry E. Ribstein, *From Bricks to Pajamas: The Law and Economics of Amateur Journalism,* 48 Wm. & Mary L. Rev. 185 (2006).

116. *See* Bezanson, *supra* note 63.

117. *See, e.g.,* Richard A. Posner, *Bad News,* New York Times, July 31, 2005, Book Review, at 1.

118. There are exceptions, of course. I have been writing at the legal blog *Prawfs-blawg* since 2005, and my posts have been completely spot-on the entire time.

119. For detailed discussion, *see, e.g.,* Yochai Benkler & Aaron Shaw, *A Tale of Two Blogospheres: Discursive Practices on the Left and Right,* Berkman Center For Internet and Society, April 27, 2010, available at http://cyber.law.harvard.edu/publications/2010/Tale_Two_Blogospheres_Discursive_Practices_Left_Right (discussing variations in blog linking practices that appear to track ideological affiliation); *but see* Eszter Hargittai *et al., Cross-Ideological Discussions Among Conservative and Liberal Bloggers,* 134 Public Choice 67 (2008) (finding evidence of linking between ideologically divided bloggers).

120. *See, e.g.,* Ribstein, *supra* note 114, at 4–6.

121. Benkler, *supra* note 106, at 265.

122. *See, e.g.,* David S. Ardia, *Reputation in a Networked World: Revisiting the Social Foundations of Defamation Law,* 45 Harv. C.R.-C.L. L. Rev. 261 (2010); Glenn Harlan Reynolds, *Libel in the Blogosphere: Some Preliminary Thoughts,* 84 Wash. U. L. Rev. 1157 (2006).

123. *See, e.g.,* Linda L. Berger, *Shielding the Unmedia: Using the Process of Journalism to Protect the Journalist's Privilege in an Infinite Universe of Publications,* 39 Hous. L. Rev. 1371, 1373–1374 (2003); Laurence B. Alexander, *Looking Out for the Watchdogs: A Legislative Proposal Limiting the Newsgathering Privilege to Journalists in the Greatest Need of Protection for Sources and Information,* 20 Yale L. & Pol'y Rev. 97, 101 (2002); Anderson, *supra* note 28, at 529.

124. *See, e.g.,* Posner, *supra* note 117; Katherine Q. Seelye, *Study Finds More News Media Outlets, Covering Less News,* New York Times, March 13, 2006, at C3.

125. *See, e.g.,* Papandrea, *supra* note 22; Berger, *supra* note 123.

126. Yochai Benkler, *A Free Irresponsible Press: Wikileaks and the Battle Over the Soul of the Networked Fourth Estate,* 46 Harv. C.R.-C.L. L. Rev. 311 (2011). Benkler's article is not uncritical of the established press, which, he argues, sought to "denigrate the journalistic identity of the new kids on the block to preserve their own identity." *Id.* at 315. But his broader point is more measured and entirely relevant to this discussion: that new and traditional media may be converging around practices that "combine elements of both traditional and novel forms of news media" and that "'professionalism' and 'responsibility' can be found on both sides of the divide, as can unprofessionalism and irresponsibility." *Id.*

An institutionalist approach that views these emerging practices as vital to our infrastructure of public discourse but distinct in some ways from traditional practices, and whose contours of legal protection or autonomy are responsive to their emerging best practices, is consistent with an acknowledgment of both the virtues and the flaws of these emerging practices.

127. *See, e.g.,* C. Edwin Baker, *The Media That Citizens Need,* 147 U. Pa. L. Rev. 317 (1998).

128. *See* Benkler, *supra* note 126, at 315 (drawing on the Wikileaks episode and speculating that the emergence of new forms of "networked" journalism may result in "an improved watchdog function").

129. *See* Bollinger, *supra* note 86.

130. *See, e.g.,* Lawrence Lessig, *Code and Other Laws of Cyberspace* 4–14 (1999).

7. Where Souls Are Saved

1. Ira C. Lupu & Robert Tuttle, *The Distinctive Place of Religious Entities in Our Constitutional Order,* 47 Vill. L. Rev. 37 (2002).

2. *Kedroff v. St. Nicholas Cathedral of Russian Orthodox Church in North America,* 344 U.S. 94, 116 (1952).

3. *Corporation of Presiding Bishop of Church of Jesus Christ of Latter-Day Saints v. Amos,* 483 U.S. 327, 342 (1987) (Brennan, J., concurring in the judgment).

4. *Hosanna-Tabor Evangelical Lutheran Church & School v. EEOC,* 132 S. Ct. 694, 703-704 (2012) (quoting a veto statement by President James Madison, 22 Annals of Cong. 982–983 (1811)).

5. Michael W. McConnell, *The Problem of Singling Out Religion,* 50 DePaul L. Rev. 1, 3 (2000).

6. *See, e.g.,* Caroline Mala Corbin, *Above the Law? The Constitutionality of the Ministerial Exemption from Antidiscrimination Law,* 75 Fordham L. Rev. 1965 (2007); Marci A. Hamilton, *God vs. the Gavel: Religion and the Rule of Law* (2005); Marci A. Hamilton, *Religious Institutions, the No-Harm Doctrine, and the Public Good,* 2004 BYU L. Rev. 1099; Jane Rutherford, *Equality as the Primary Constitutional Value: The Case for Applying Employment Discrimination Laws to Religion,* 81 Cornell L. Rev. 1049 (1996).

7. *See, e.g.,* Christopher L. Eisgruber & Lawrence G. Sager, *Religious Freedom and the Constitution* 63 (2006).

8. Steven D. Smith, *Discourse in the Dusk: The Twilight of Religious Freedom?,* 122 Harv. L. Rev. 1869, 1873 (2009).

9. *See, e.g.,* Lupu & Tuttle, *supra* note 1, at 39; Thomas C. Berg, *Religious Structures under the Federal Constitution, in Religious Organizations in the United States: A Study of Identity, Liberty, and the Law* 129, 129 (James A. Serritella *et al.* eds., 2006).

10. *See, e.g.,* Steven D. Smith, *Freedom of Religion or Freedom of the Church?*, in *Matters of Faith: Religious Experience and Legal Response* (Austin Sarat ed., forthcoming), available at http://papers.ssrn.com/sol3/papers.cfm?abstract_id=1911412; Smith, *supra* note 8.

11. Robert Post, *Participatory Democracy and Free Speech*, 97 Va. L. Rev. 477, 482 (2011) (emphasis added).

12. David Nicholls, *The Pluralist State: The Political Ideas of J. N. Figgis and His Contemporaries* xx (2d ed. 1994). I explore these ideas further in Chapter 9.

13. Abraham Kuyper, *Lectures on Calvinism* 88 (reprint 2007) (1931).

14. Peter S. Heslam, *Creating a Christian Worldview: Abraham Kuyper's Lectures on Calvinism* 104 (1998).

15. Abraham Kuyper, *Sphere Sovereignty*, in *Abraham Kuyper: A Centennial Reader* 461, 467 (James D. Bratt ed., 1998).

16. Kuyper, *supra* note 13, at 96–97, 91.

17. Kuyper, *supra* note 15, at 472 (emphasis omitted).

18. Kuyper, *supra* note 13, at 94, 97.

19. Richard J. Mouw, *Some Reflections on Sphere Sovereignty*, in *Religion, Pluralism, and Public Life: Abraham Kuyper's Legacy for the Twenty-First Century* 87, 89–90 (Luis E. Lugo ed., 2000).

20. Kuyper, *supra* note 13, at 93, 94, 97–98.

21. *Id.* at 106.

22. *Id.* at 108.

23. Kent van Til, *Abraham Kuyper and Michael Walzer: The Justice of the Spheres*, 40 Calvin Theological J. 267, 276 (2005).

24. *See, e.g.,* John Witte, Jr., *The Reformation of Rights: Law, Religion, and Human Rights in Early Modern Calvinism* 143–207 (2007). Carl Esbeck traces the roots of religious autonomy further still, to the fourth century. *See* Carl H. Esbeck, *Dissent and Disestablishment: The Church-State Settlement in the Early American Republic*, 2004 BYU L. Rev. 1385, 1392.

25. Witte, *supra* note 24, at 196.

26. Henk E. S. Woldring, *Multiform Responsibility and the Revitalization of Civil Society*, in Lugo, ed., *supra* note 19, at 178, 179.

27. *Id.* at 179, 180.

28. *See, e.g.,* Witte, *supra* note 24, at 152, 205, 324; John Witte, Jr., *How to Govern a City on a Hill: The Early Puritan Contribution to American Constitutionalism*, 39 Emory L.J. 41, 50–51 (1990); John Witte, Jr., *Blest Be the Ties That Bind: Covenant and Community in Puritan Thought*, 36 Emory L.J. 579, 594 (1987).

29. Witte, *supra* note 24, at 287, 309 (quoting *Laws and Liberties of Massachusetts Bay* A2 (1648) (Max Farrand ed., 1929)), 310.

30. *Id.* at 310–311.

31. *Id.* at 277, 292–293.

32. Philip A. Hamburger, *A Constitutional Right of Religious Exemptions: An Historical Analysis,* 60 Geo. Wash. L. Rev. 915, 936 (1992).

33. Michael W. McConnell, *The Supreme Court's Earliest Church-State Cases: Windows on Religious-Cultural-Political Conflict in the Early Republic,* 37 Tulsa L. Rev. 7, 42 (2001).

34. Lupu & Tuttle, *supra* note 1, at 38.

35. Alexis de Tocqueville, 2 *Democracy in America* 106 (Alan Ryan ed., 1994).

36. *See* John O. McGinnis, *Reviving Tocqueville's America: The Rehnquist Court's Jurisprudence of Social Discovery,* 90 Cal. L. Rev. 485 (2002).

37. Paul Q. Hirst, *Introduction,* in *The Pluralist Theory of the State: Selected Writings of G. D. H. Cole, J. N. Figgis, and H. J. Laski* (Paul Q. Hirst ed., 1989), at 1–2, 17.

38. Carol Weisbrod, *Emblems of Pluralism: Cultural Differences and the State* 112 (2002); *see generally id.* at 111–115.

39. Nicholls, *supra* note 12, at 81.

40. *Id.* at 14; *see also* J. N. Figgis, *The Church and the Secular Theory of the State,* in Nicholls, *id.,* at 157 ("In a word, when the Church asks the State to acknowledge that it has real powers for developing itself, it is not asking for a privilege to be conceded, but for the facts to be realized.").

41. Robert M. Cover, *Foreword:* Nomos *and* Narrative, 97 Harv. L. Rev. 4 (1983); Mark DeWolfe Howe, *Foreword: Political Theory and the Nature of Liberty,* 67 Harv. L. Rev. 91 (1953).

42. *Id.* at 91.

43. Peter L. Berger, *Facing Up to Modernity: Excursions in Society, Politics and Religion* 134 (1977).

44. Peter L. Berger & Richard John Neuhaus, *To Empower People: The Role of Mediating Structures in Public Policy* 2, 138 (emphasis omitted) (1977).

45. Paolo G. Carozza, *Subsidiarity as a Structural Principle of International Human Rights Law,* 97 Am. J. Int'l L. 38, 43, 41 (2003).

46. Kyle Duncan, *Subsidiarity and Religious Establishments in the United States Constitution,* 52 Vill. L. Rev. 67, 72 (2007).

47. Figgis, *supra* note 40, at 159.

48. 2 Tocqueville, *supra* note 35, at 108–109.

49. Kuyper, *supra* note 13, at 107 (quotations and citations omitted), 108 (emphasis omitted), 97.

50. *See, e.g., Meyer v. Nebraska,* 262 U.S. 390 (1923); *Pierce v. Soc'y of Sisters,* 268 U.S. 510 (1925).

51. *See, e.g.,* Kwame Anthony Appiah, *Global Citizenship,* 75 Fordham L. Rev. 2375, 2388–2389 (2007).

52. *Cf.* Nicholls, *supra* note 12, at 110 ("[A] pluralist state can exist very well without an established church").

53. Kuyper, *supra* note 13, at 106.

54. 80 U.S. 679 (1871).

55. *Id.* at 728, 729, 725.

56. *See id.* at 727.

57. *Presbyterian Church in the United States v. Mary Elizabeth Blue Hull Mem'l Presbyterian Church*, 393 U.S. 440, 447, 449 (1969).

58. Kent Greenawalt, 1 *Religion and the Constitution: Free Exercise and Fairness* 267 (2006).

59. 443 U.S. 595 (1979).

60. *See Serbian E. Orthodox Diocese v. Milivojevich*, 429 U.S. 696 (1976).

61. *Employment Division v. Smith*, 494 U.S. 872, 881 (1990).

62. *Id.* at 888.

63. Corbin, *supra* note 6, at 1987.

64. Perry Dane, *"Omalous" Autonomy*, 2004 BYU L. Rev. 1715, 1740.

65. *Jones*, 443 U.S. at 603–604.

66. *See* Dane, *supra* note 64, at 1743–1744.

67. 42 U.S.C. § 2000e-1(a).

68. 483 U.S. 327, 341–342 (1987) (Brennan, J., concurring in the judgment).

69. *See, e.g., Rayburn v. Gen. Conference of Seventh Day Adventists*, 772 F.2d 1164, 1166 (4th Cir. 1985).

70. *Petruska v. Gannon Univ.*, 462 F.3d 294, 304 (3d Cir. 2006).

71. *Hosanna-Tabor*, 132 S. Ct. at 706.

72. Gregory A. Kalscheur, S.J., *Civil Procedure and the Establishment Clause: Exploring the Ministerial Exception, Subject-Matter Jurisdiction, and the Freedom of the Church*, 17 Wm. & Mary Bill Rts. J. 43, 101–102, 91 (2008) (quoting *Steel Co. v. Citizens for a Better Environment*, 523 U.S. 83, 102 n.4 (1998)).

73. Kuyper, *supra* note 13, at 108.

74. Where they *are* extrinsic. The Catholic Church's insistence that only men may serve as priests is well within its sovereign sphere.

75. *Hosanna-Tabor*, 132 S. Ct. at 715-716 (Alito, J., concurring). Alito's concurrence was joined by the Court's most recent appointee, Justice Elena Kagan.

76. A point emphasized by Justice Clarence Thomas in his concurring opinion in *Hosanna-Tabor* in terms that are consistent with the institutional turn's focus on judicial deference and institutional pluralism. *See id.* at 710 (Thomas, J., concurring) ("[I]n my view, the Religion Clauses require civil courts to apply the ministerial exception and to defer to a religious organization's good-faith understanding of who qualifies as its minister.").

77. I expand on this point in Paul Horwitz, *Act III of the Ministerial Exception,* 106 Nw. U. L. Rev. 973 (2012).

78. *See* Bob Jones University, *Statement About Race at BJU,* available at http://www .bju.edu/welcome/who-we-are/race-statement.php.

79. *See, e.g.,* Marci A. Hamilton, *Church Autonomy Is Not a Better Path to "Truth,"* 22 J.L. & Religion 215 (2006–2007).

80. *See, e.g.,* Ira C. Lupu & Robert W. Tuttle, *Sexual Misconduct and Ecclesiastical Immunity,* 2004 BYU L. Rev. 1789, 1792; Symposium, *The Impact of Clergy Sexual Misconduct Litigation on Religious Liberty,* 44 B.C. L. Rev. 947 (2003).

81. *See, e.g.,* Lupu & Tuttle, *supra* note 1; Kathleen A. Brady, *Religious Organizations and Free Exercise: The Surprising Lessons of* Smith, 2004 BYU L. Rev. 1633.

82. *See, e.g.,* Marci A. Hamilton, *The Catholic Church and the Clergy Abuse Scandal: Act Three,* Writ, Apr. 10, 2003, http://writ.news.findlaw.com/hamilton/20030410 .html.

83. The Court's decision in *Hosanna-Tabor* is consistent with this point, although it is decidedly unclear on the details. (Readers who remember the *FAIR* case from Chapter 5 will not be surprised to learn that both opinions were written by Chief Justice John Roberts, who is developing a skill for writing First Amendment opinions whose clarity is achieved by avoiding many of the most difficult issues.) While it upheld the ministerial exception, the Court cautioned that it took "no view on whether the exception bars other types of suits, including actions by employees alleging breach of contract or tortious conduct by their religious employers." And in the course of distinguishing its earlier decision in *Employment Division v. Smith,* it suggested that there was a distinction between "government interference with an internal church decision that affects the faith and mission of the church itself" and "government regulation of only outward physical acts." *Hosanna-Tabor,* 132 S.Ct. at 707, 710. The distinction between "internal church decisions" and "outward physical acts" is an imperfect one, to be sure; the ingestion of peyote, which was at issue in *Smith,* is both a physical act and a matter of internal church practice. But the general distinction is at least consistent with the idea that there is a difference between a church's decision that someone should or should not be a part of its community, and an action that causes concrete harms to another that would be considered harmful regardless of one's membership status.

84. Lupu & Tuttle, *supra* note 80, at 1816.

85. *Id.* at 1860–1861, 1862, 1860 (quotations and citations omitted).

86. *See, e.g.,* Brady, *supra* note 81; Dane, *supra* note 64.

87. Johan D. Van der Vyver, *Sphere Sovereignty of Religious Institutions: A Contemporary Calvinistic Theory of Church-State Relations,* in *Church Autonomy: A Comparative Survey* 645, 662 (Gerhard Robbers ed., 2001); Nicholas P. Wolterstorff,

Abraham Kuyper (1837–1920), in *The Teachings of Modern Protestantism on Law, Politics, & Human Nature* 29, 117 (John Witte, Jr. & Frank S. Alexander eds., 2007). As I observe below, this strand of doctrine is now much diminished.

88. *See* Paul Horwitz, *The Agnostic Age: Law, Religion, and the Constitution*, ch. 7 (2011).

89. *See* Wolterstorff, *supra* note 87, at 117.

90. Kuyper, *supra* note 13, at 106.

91. *See* Horwitz, *supra* note 88.

92. *See, e.g., Zelman v. Simmons-Harris*, 536 U.S. 639 (2002); *Mitchell v. Helms*, 530 U.S. 793 (2000).

93. *See, e.g., Good News Club v. Milford Cent. Sch. Dist.*, 533 U.S. 98 (2001); *Lamb's Chapel v. Ctr. Moriches Union Free Sch. Dist.*, 508 U.S. 384 (1993).

94. *See, e.g.*, Brady, *supra* note 81, at 1700–1704; Paul Horwitz, *The Sources and Limits of Freedom of Religion in a Liberal Democracy: Section 2(a) and Beyond*, 54 U. Toronto Fac. L. Rev. 1, 52–53 (1996).

95. *See, e.g.*, David Runciman, *Pluralism and the Personality of the State* 129 (1997) ("'[O]ut of conflicts and controversies, in essence religious, modern politics have developed themselves.'") (quoting J. N. Figgis) (citation omitted).

96. *See, e.g.*, Smith, *supra* note 8, at 1874–1875; Lupu & Tuttle, *supra* note 1, at 38.

97. *See, e.g.*, Horwitz, *supra* note 94, at 52–53; Stephen L. Carter, *God's Name in Vain: The Wrongs and Rights of Religion in Politics* (2000).

98. *See* Horwitz, *supra* note 77.

99. Esbeck, *supra* note 24, at 1390.

100. Cover, *supra* note 41, at 68.

8. Where Ideas Reside

1. Marc Jonathan Blitz, *Constitutional Safeguards for Silent Experiments in Living: Libraries, the Right to Read, and a First Amendment Theory for an Unaccompanied Right to Receive Information*, 74 UMKC L. Rev. 799, 800 (2006).

2. *Cf.* Rebecca Tushnet, *My Library: Copyright and the Role of Institutions in a Peer-to-Peer World*, 53 UCLA L. Rev. 977, 982 (2006) ("traditional libraries . . . are venerated in standard political and academic rhetoric").

3. *Brown v. Louisiana*, 383 U.S. 131, 142 (1966).

4. *U.S. v. American Library Ass'n*, 539 U.S. 194, 203 (2003) [hereinafter *ALA*].

5. *See, e.g.*, Mark C. Rahdert, *Preserving the Archives of Freedom: Justice Blackmun and First Amendment Protections for Libraries*, 97 Dickinson L. Rev. 437, 453 (1993) (observing that "the traditional first amendment proscription against content-based distinctions" does not fit well within the context of libraries); *id.* at 454 ("The nature of the library as an institution, and the interplay of competing

interests and concerns within it, necessitate a more delicate accommodation than is possible under the broad principles of access or content neutrality.") (quotations omitted).

6. *See, e.g., Neinast v. Bd. of Trustees of Columbus Metropolitan Library*, 346 F.2d 585 (6th Cir. 2003); *Kreimer v. Bureau of Police for Town of Morristown*, 958 F.2d 1242 (3d Cir. 1992); *Gay Guardian Newspaper v. Ohoopee Regional Library Sys.*, 235 F. Supp. 2d 1362 (S.D. Ga. 2002); *Sund v. City of Wichita Falls*, 121 F. Supp. 2d 530 (N.D. Tex. 2000); *American Council of the Blind v. Boorstin*, 644 F. Supp. 811 (D.D.C. 1986).

7. Culturally speaking, at least. The numbers are more complicated. Figures compiled by the American Library Association show a total of 122,101 libraries of all kinds in the United States. Of those, some 9,221 are public libraries, comprising about 16,671 central and branch buildings. There are about 8,476 "special libraries," including corporate, religious, law, and other libraries. The remainder of the number is made up of academic and school libraries, with public school libraries constituting the vast majority of that number. *See* American Library Association, *Number of Libraries in the United States*, ALA Library *Fact Sheet 1*, available at http://www.ala.org/ala/professionalresources/libfact-sheets/alalibraryfactsheet01.cfm (last updated August 2010).

8. *Reno v. ACLU*, 521 U.S. 844, 853 (1997).

9. *ALA*, 539 U.S. at 205, 203.

10. *See, e.g.*, Anne Klinefelter, *First Amendment Limits on Library Collection Management*, 102 Law Lib. J. 343, 344 (2010) ("[F]ew conflicts in law libraries lead to litigation."). A broader search for cases involving public libraries suggests the same conclusion.

11. *See id.* at 344 ("[P]ublicly funded law libraries rarely confront patron challenges or legislative restraints beyond requirements that collections be related to law."). As Klinefelter notes, First Amendment cases involving public school libraries are more common; I discuss one such case below. On the whole, though, there are relatively few straight First Amendment conflicts involving regular public libraries unaffiliated with schools.

12. Matthew Battles, *Library: An Unquiet History* 146 (2003).

13. Evelyn Geller, *Forbidden Books in Public Libraries 1876–1939: A Study in Cultural Change* 3–4 (1984).

14. *See* Susan Westberg Prager, *Law Libraries and the Scholarly Mission*, 96 Law Libr. J. 513, 532 n.34 (2004) (citation omitted).

15. Laura N. Gasaway, *Values Conflict in the Digital Environment: Libraries Versus Copyright Holders*, 24 Colum.-VLA J.L. & Arts 115, 128 (2000) (quoting Plummer Alston Jones, Jr., *American Public Library Service to the Immigrant Community, 1876–1948: A Biographical History of the Movement and its Leaders* 129 (1991)).

16. *Holmes and Frankfurter: Their Correspondence, 1912–1934* xii (Robert M. Mennel & Christine L. Compson eds., 1996).

17. *See* Anuj C. Desai, *The Transformation of Statutes into Constitutional Law: How Early Post Office Policy Shaped Modern First Amendment Doctrine,* 58 Hastings L.J. 671 (2007).

18. *Id.* at 727.

19. *See, e.g.,* Battles, *supra* note 12, at 9.

20. *See, e.g.,* Gregory K. Laughlin, *Sex, Lies, and Library Cards: The First Amendment Implications of the Use of Software Filters to Control Access to Internet Pornography in Public Libraries,* 51 Drake L. Rev. 213, 221–234 (2003).

21. Geller, *supra* note 13, at xv.

22. Blitz, *supra* note 1, at 836 (quoting J. P. Quincey, *Free Libraries,* in *Public Libraries in the United States of America: Part I, 1876 Report* 399 (Univ. of Ill., Graduate Sch. of Library Sci.)); *id.* at 839 (quoting Geller, *supra* note 13, at 46).

23. Battles, *supra* note 12, at 140.

24. Robert C. Berring, *Deconstructing the Law Library: The Wisdom of Meredith Willson,* 89 Minn. L. Rev. 1381, 1396 (2005).

25. Neil M. Richards, *Intellectual Privacy,* 87 Tex. L. Rev. 387, 420 (2008).

26. *See, e.g.,* Jennifer Rowley & Richard Hartley, *Organizing Knowledge: An Introduction to Managing Access to Information* (4th ed. 2008).

27. *See, e.g.,* Judith F. Krug, *ALA and Intellectual Freedom: A Historical Overview,* in American Library Association, Office for Intellectual Freedom, *Intellectual Freedom Manual* 14, 18–20 (7th ed. 2006).

28. *ALA,* 539 U.S. at 203, 204 (quoting Francis K. W. Drury, *Book Selection* xi (1930)).

29. *Pico,* 457 U.S. 853, 856, 857, 857–858 (1982). The books included several titles widely considered to be modern classics, such as *Slaughterhouse-Five* by Kurt Vonnegut, Jr., and *Black Boy* by Richard Wright. *See id.* at 857 n.3.

30. *Id.* at 862, 868 (quoting *Tinker v. Des Moines Sch. Dist.,* 393 U.S. 503, 506 (1969)).

31. *Id.* at 866, 867 (quoting *Stanley v. Georgia,* 394 U.S. 479, 482 (1969)), 869, 870, 872, 874.

32. *Id.* at 876, 879, 878, 880 (Blackmun, J., concurring in part and concurring in the judgment).

33. *Id.* at 894 (Powell, J., dissenting), 921 (O'Connor, J., dissenting).

34. A conclusion that may be compared to our discussion in Chapter 5 of *Keyishian v. Board of Regents,* 385 U.S. 589 (1967), one of the academic freedom cases. Recall that *Keyishian* used similar language, describing the classroom as "peculiarly the marketplace of ideas." *Id.* at 603 (quotations and citation omitted). Although *Pico* involved a school library and not a stand-alone library, and there is thus some justification for his language, Burger's description still exhibits some of the same problems that *Keyishian* does: it imports

a democratic model into what might have been treated as a professional or institutional context.

35. *Pico,* 457 U.S. at 888, 892, 891.

36. *Id.* at 907 (quotations and citations omitted), 909, 908–910, 920, 915 (Rehnquist, J., dissenting).

37. Mark G. Yudof, *Library Book Selection and the Public Schools: The Quest for the Archimedean Point,* 59 Ind. L.J. 527, 549 (1984). Even this point is dubious. Government can and does regularly declare orthodoxy. *See, e.g.,* Steven D. Smith, *Barnette's Big Blunder,* 78 Chi.-Kent L. Rev. 625 (2003). What it cannot do is *enforce* that orthodoxy against private citizens.

38. *See* Rahdert, *supra* note 5, at 453–454.

39. *Pico,* 457 U.S. at 868.

40. *ALA,* 539 U.S. at 198, 200, 201.

41. *Id.* at 203 (quotations and citations omitted), 204, 205.

42. *Id.* at 204, 210–211, 211.

43. *Id.* at 205, 206 (quotations and citations omitted), 214, 207–208.

44. *See id.* at 214–215 (Kennedy, J., concurring in the judgment).

45. *Id.* at 216, 217, 220 (Breyer, J., concurring).

46. *Id.* at 234, 235, 236 (Souter, J., dissenting).

47. *Id.* at 238, 241, 242.

48. *Id.* at 220 (emphasis added) (Stevens, J., dissenting).

49. *See id.* at 226.

50. *Id.* at 226–227, 228, 227, 229, 228.

51. Robert C. Post, *Foreword: Fashioning the Legal Constitution: Culture, Courts, and Law,* 117 Harv. L. Rev. 4, 80 (2003).

52. For these reasons, it should be clear that *ALA* is not only a decision about Internet speech. Libraries are certainly not the only public institution that might provide Internet access: publicly owned airports, for example, might provide free wireless access to people waiting within the terminal. But those sites do not serve the same specialized infrastructural role in public discourse that libraries do, and their function is generally unrelated to the provision of information. Libraries, on the other hand, function precisely toward that end. *ALA,* in short, deserves to be seen as a library case, at least in large measure, and not just as a garden-variety Internet law or public forum case. That is not to say no legal arguments would be available if, say, a public airport restricted access to the Internet on impermissible grounds. But that would be an area for general First Amendment doctrine, not for the deference and autonomy that form the central part of First Amendment institutionalism.

53. *See, e.g.,* Frederick Schauer, *Towards an Institutional First Amendment,* 89 Minn. L. Rev. 1256, 1262 (2005).

54. Robert M. O'Neil, *Libraries, Librarians and First Amendment Freedoms*, 4 Hum. Rts. 295, 309 (1975).

55. Rodney A. Smolla, *Freedom of Speech for Libraries and Librarians*, 85 Law Libr. J. 71, 73 (1993).

56. Jim Chen, *Mastering Eliot's Paradox: Fostering Cultural Memory in an Age of Illusion and Allusion*, 89 Minn. L. Rev. 1361, 1361–1362, 1379, 1376 (2005).

57. Blitz, *supra* note 1, at 807.

58. *Id.* at 842 (emphasis added), 843–864.

59. Schauer, *supra* note 53, at 1274.

60. Battles, *supra* note 12, at 211.

61. *See* Smolla, *supra* note 55, at 73.

62. *ALA*, 539 U.S. at 236 (Souter, J., dissenting).

63. *See, e.g.*, Frederick Schauer, *Is There a Right to Academic Freedom?*, 77 U. Colo. L. Rev. 907, 922–923 (2006).

64. *See, e.g.*, *Intellectual Freedom Manual*, *supra* note 27, at 111, 136–137, 357–359.

65. *ALA*, 539 U.S. at 241 (Souter, J., dissenting).

66. Bernard W. Bell, *Filth, Filtering, and the First Amendment: Ruminations on Public Libraries' Use of Internet Filtering Software*, 53 Fed. Comm. L.J. 191, 230 (2001).

67. *ALA*, 539 U.S. at 203, 204.

68. Frederick Schauer, *Principles, Institutions, and the First Amendment*, 112 Harv. L. Rev. 84, 115 (1998).

69. *See, e.g.*, *Kreimer v. Bureau of Police for the Town of Morristown*, 958 F. 2d 1255–1262 (3d Cir. 1992).

70. *See, e.g.*, *Intellectual Freedom Manual*, *supra* note 27, at 187 (noting that the ALA's Library Bill of Rights states that meeting rooms "should be made available to the public served by the given library 'on an equitable basis, regardless of the beliefs or affiliations of individuals or groups requesting their use.'").

71. *See* Smolla, *supra* note 55, at 73, 78.

72. *See, e.g.*, *ALA*, 539 U.S. at 211, 212.

73. In particular, it raises fewer procedural questions than one might imagine. Even if public libraries are not entitled to challenge restrictions imposed on them by the level of government that directly controls them, many restrictions are imposed by an entirely different level of government; *ALA*, which involved the imposition of *federal* spending conditions on *local* libraries, is one example. *See* Laura J. Hendrickson, *State Government Speech in a Federal System*, 6 Cardozo Pub. L. Pol'y & Ethics J. 691 (2008). Even regulations imposed directly on a library by an elected library board or a city government will generally provoke objections by library patrons, thus giving courts a viable plaintiff, with proper standing, to work with.

74. Blitz, *supra* note 1, at 882.

75. Lawrence Rosenthal, *The Emerging First Amendment Law of Managerial Prerogative,* 77 Fordham L. Rev. 33, 93 (2008).

76. *Grutter v. Bollinger,* 539 U.S. 306, 329 (2003).

9. Where People and Ideas Meet

1. *See* Jason Mazzone, *Freedom's Associations,* 77 Wash. L. Rev. 639, 691–693 (2002).

2. *See generally* Robert D. Putnam, *Bowling Alone: The Collapse and Revival of American Community* (2000).

3. *See, e.g.,* Amy Gutmann, *An Introductory Essay,* in *Freedom of Association* 3, 10 (Amy Gutmann ed., 1998); Mazzone, *supra* note 1, at 689–691.

4. John D. Inazu, *The Unsettling 'Well-Settled' Law of Freedom of Association,* 43 Conn. L. Rev. 149, 156 (2010).

5. *See Roberts v. United States Jaycees,* 468 U.S. 609, 634 (1984) (O'Connor, J., concurring). That distinction, too, raises difficult questions. *See, e.g.,* Larry Alexander, *What is Freedom of Association, and What Is Its Denial?,* 25 Soc. Phil. & Pol'y 1, 13–14 (2008).

6. 530 U.S. 640 (2000).

7. 130 S. Ct. 2971 (2010).

8. So did a third freedom of association case, *Rumsfeld v. Forum for Academic and Institutional Rights, Inc.,* 547 U.S. 47 (2006), which I discussed in Chapter 5.

9. *See, e.g.,* Akhil Reed Amar, *America's Constitution: A Biography,* ch. 12 (2005).

10. Taylor Branch, *Parting the Waters: America in the King Years 1954–63* 197 (1988).

11. *See, e.g.,* Pamela S. Karlan, *Introduction: Same-Sex Marriage as a Moving Story,* 16 Stan. L. & Pol'y Rev. 1, 9 (2005) (quoting King).

12. Aviam Soifer, *Law and the Company We Keep* 33 (1995).

13. *See, e.g.,* Mazzone, *supra* note 1, at 731–733; Theda Skocpol, *How Americans Became Civic,* in *Civic Engagement in American Democracy* 27 (Theda Skocpol & Morris P. Fiorina eds., 1999).

14. For Washington, *see* George Washington, *Farewell Address* (Sept. 17, 1796), in *George Washington: Writings* 968 (John Rhodehamel ed., 1997). For Madison, *see The Federalist No. 10* (James Madison) (Jacob E. Cooke ed., 1961).

15. Alexis de Tocqueville, 1 *Democracy in America* 191 (Alan Ryan ed., 1994) (1835); 2 *Democracy in America* 106 (Alan Ryan ed., 1994) (1835).

16. *See, e.g.,* William P. Marshall, *Discrimination and the Right of Association,* 81 Nw. U. L. Rev. 68, 69–70 (1986).

17. 1 Tocqueville, *supra* note 15, at 195; 2 Tocqueville, *supra* note 15, at 119.

18. Some especially helpful guides to this subject are David Runciman, *Pluralism and the Personality of the State* (1997); David Nicholls, *The Pluralist State: The*

Political Ideas of J. N. Figgis and His Contemporaries (2d ed. 1994); and *The Pluralist Theory of the State: Selected Writings of G. D. H. Cole, J. N. Figgis, and H. J. Laski* (Paul Q. Hirst ed., 1989). In my view, recent high-profile Supreme Court decisions like *Citizens United, Hosanna-Tabor,* and *Christian Legal Society,* each discussed in this book, suggest that the time is ripe for a scholarly reexamination of the British pluralists and their views.

19. Soifer, *supra* note 12, at 73, 75 (quoting *Maitland: Selected Essays* 233 (H. D. Hazeltine *et al.* eds., 1936)).

20. Carol Weisbrod, *Practical Polyphony: Theories of the State and Feminist Jurisprudence,* 24 Ga. L. Rev. 985, 1002, 1004 (1990) (quoting G. D. H. Cole & Margaret Cole, *A Guide to Modern Politics* 370 (1934)).

21. *See, e.g.,* J. N. Figgis, *The Church and the Secular Theory of the State,* which is included as an appendix to Nicholls, *supra* note 18, at 157, 159 ("The fact is, that to deny to smaller societies a real life and meaning, a personality, in fact, is not anti-clerical, or illiberal, or unwise, or oppressive—it is untrue.").

22. Nicholls, *id.* at 70.

23. *Id.* at 14.

24. Runciman, *supra* note 18, at 132 (quoting J. N. Figgis) (citation omitted). The whole quote is instructive: "What is needed nowadays is that as against an abstract and unreal theory of State omnipotence on the one hand and artificial view of individual independence on the other, the facts of the world with its innumerable bonds of association and the naturalness of social authority should be generally recognized, and become the basis of our laws, as it is of our life." *Id.* at 132–133.

25. *Id.* at 117.

26. 323 U.S. 530 (1945) (citing *De Jonge v. Oregon,* 299 U.S. 353, 364 (1937)).

27. Soifer, *supra* note 12, at 77–78.

28. 468 U.S. 609 (1984).

29. *Id.* at 617, 618.

30. *Id.* at 624, 627.

31. *Id.* at 632, 636, 631 (O'Connor, J., concurring in part and concurring in the judgment).

32. *Id.* at 618, 623.

33. *Id.* at 627.

34. Andrew Koppelman with Tobias Barrington Wolff, *A Right to Discriminate?: How the Case of* Boy Scouts of America v. James Dale *Warped the Law of Free Association* xi (2009) (emphasis added).

35. *Roberts,* 468 U.S. at 627.

36. Nancy L. Rosenblum, *Compelled Association: Public Standing, Self-Respect, and the Dynamic of Exclusion,* in Gutmann, ed., *supra* note 3, at 78.

37. *See Bd. of Directors of Rotary Int'l v. Rotary Club of Duarte,* 481 U.S. 537 (1987); *New York State Club Ass'n v. City of New York,* 487 U.S. 1 (1988).

38. *Hurley v. Irish-American Gay, Lesbian and Bisexual Group of Boston,* 515 U.S. 557, 569, 569–570, 573 (1995) (quoting *Pacific Gas & Elec. Co. v. Pub. Utilities Comm'n of Cal.,* 475 U.S. 1, 11 (1986)).

39. *Id.* at 574.

40. *Dale,* 530 U.S. 645.

41. *Id.* at 644, 648, 650.

42. *Id.* at 650.

43. *See id.* at 649 (majority opinion), 665–678 (Stevens, J., dissenting).

44. *Id.* at 653.

45. *Id.* at 655, 656, 659.

46. *See* Robert F. Nagel, *Six Opinions by Mr. Justice Stevens: A New Methodology for Constitutional Cases?,* 78 Chi.-Kent L. Rev. 509, 523–526 (2003).

47. *Dale,* 530 U.S. at 663, 664, 665 (quotations and citations omitted) (Stevens, J., dissenting).

48. *Id.* at 686, 687 (emphasis added).

49. *Id.* at 688, 694, 700 (quoting *New State Ice Co. v. Liebmann,* 285 U.S. 262, 311 (1932) (Brandeis, J., dissenting)). Readers of the British pluralists may see in Stevens's peroration an echo of the pluralist writer G. D. H. Cole's description of nineteenth-century political thought, which, he wrote, tended "to regard the association as, at the most, a necessary imperfection, to be tolerated rather than recognized, with no rights beyond those of expediency, and no powers beyond those conferred expressly by statute. From this point of view," Cole added, "we are now struggling slowly back to a saner doctrine." Nicholls, *supra* note 18, at 78 (quoting G. D. H. Cole) (citation omitted).

50. *See generally* Koppelman with Wolff, *supra* note 34.

51. Richard W. Garnett, *The Story of Henry Adams's Soul: Education and the Expression of Associations,* 85 Minn. L. Rev. 1841, 1850 (2001).

52. *See* George Kateb, *The Value of Association,* in Gutmann, ed., *supra* note 3, at 35, 45–50.

53. *See generally* Paul Horwitz, *Uncovering Identity,* 105 Mich. L. Rev. 1283 (2007).

54. *See* Richard A. Epstein, *The Constitutional Perils of Moderation: The Case of the Boy Scouts,* 74 S. Cal. L. Rev. 119, 127–130 (2000).

55. *See, e.g.,* Carl H. Esbeck, *The Establishment Clause as a Structural Restraint on Government Power,* 84 Iowa L. Rev. 1, 8 (1998).

56. Nicholls, *supra* note 18, at 29.

57. *See* Robert K. Vischer, *The Good, the Bad and the Ugly: Rethinking the Value of Associations,* 79 Notre Dame L. Rev. 949, 979–980 (2004); Meir Dan-Cohen, *Between*

Selves and Collectivities: Towards a Jurisprudence of Identity, 61 U. Chi. L. Rev. 1213, 1214 (1994).

58. *See, e.g.*, Heather K. Gerken, *Foreword: Federalism All the Way Down*, 124 Harv. L. Rev. 4, 30 (2010).

59. *See generally* Franklin G. Snyder, *Sharing Sovereignty: Non-State Associations and the Limits of State Power*, 54 Am. U. L. Rev. 365 (2004). *Cf.* Stephen L. Carter, *The Culture of Disbelief: How American Law and Politics Trivialize Religious Devotion* 35 (1993).

60. Robert M. Cover, *Foreword:* Nomos *and Narrative*, 97 Harv. L. Rev. 4, 32 (1983).

61. *See* Andrew Koppelman, *Should Noncommercial Associations Have an Absolute Right to Discriminate?*, 67 L. & Contemp. Probs. 27, 57 (2004). Even in the recent Court decision upholding the ministerial exception, *Hosanna-Tabor Evangelical Lutheran Church & School v. EEOC*, Justice Alito, in a concurring opinion that cited *Dale* and urged substantial judicial deference to churches in determining who constitutes a "minister," wrote that "[r]eligious groups are the archetype of associations formed *for expressive purposes*." 132 S. Ct. 694, 713 (2012) (Alito, J., concurring) (emphasis added). To reduce churches to "expressive" organs is to leave them considerably diminished.

62. *See, e.g.*, Madhavi Sunder, *Cultural Dissent*, 54 Stan. L. Rev. 495 (2001).

63. *See, e.g.*, Symposium, *Liberalism and Illiberalism*, 12 J. Contemp. Legal Issues 625 (2002); *see also* Nicholls, *supra* note 18, at 91 (arguing that the British pluralist writers did not give sufficient attention to the possibility that powerful groups might advance rather than resist state tyranny).

64. *See, e.g.*, Sunder, *supra* note 62; Nicholls, *supra* note 18, at 90–91.

65. Dale Carpenter, *Expressive Association and Anti-Discrimination Law after* Dale: *A Tripartite Approach*, 85 Minn. L. Rev. 1515, 1516 (2001).

66. Koppelman with Wolff, *supra* note 34, at 6.

67. Gerken, *supra* note 58, at 12.

68. A recent example is the Supreme Court's decision in *Citizens United v. Federal Election Commission*, 130 S. Ct. 876 (2010). That decision struck down campaign finance laws that distinguished between individual and corporate speakers. But its justification had nothing to do with the nature of the associations involved in the case; it was based instead on a general "mistrust of governmental power." *Id.* at 898.

69. Andrew Koppelman, *How "Decentralization" Rationalizes Oligarchy: John McGinnis and the Rehnquist Court*, 20 Const. Comment. 11, 18 (2003).

70. Abraham Kuyper, *Lectures on Calvinism* 96 (photo. reprint 2007) (1931).

71. *See generally* Larry Alexander, *Illiberalism All the Way Down: Illiberal Groups and Two Conceptions of Liberalism*, 12 J. Contemp. Legal Issues 625 (2002).

72. Cover, *supra* note 60, at 68.

73. Louis Michael Seidman, *The* Dale *Problem: Property and Speech Under the Regulatory State,* 75 U. Chi. L. Rev. 1541, 1599 (2008); *see also id.* at 1598 ("'the test of a sound legal rule is the extent to which it vindicates the practices and expectations embedded in, and generated by, dominant social institutions'") (quoting Bruce Ackerman, *Private Property and the Constitution* 12 (1977)).

74. *See, e.g.,* Frederick Schauer, *Towards an Institutional First Amendment,* 89 Minn. L. Rev. 1256, 1274 (2005).

75. *Dale,* 530 U.S. at 653.

76. *See* Ashutosh Bhagwat, *Associational Speech,* 120 Yale L.J. 978, 997 (2010).

77. Inazu, *supra* note 4, at 203.

78. *See, e.g.,* Philip Hamburger, *More Is Less,* 90 Va. L. Rev. 835 (2004).

79. *Cf.* Steffen N. Johnson, *Expressive Association and Organizational Autonomy,* 85 Minn. L. Rev. 1639, 1640–1641 (2001).

80. *See, e.g.,* Alexander, *supra* note 5, at 13–14.

81. *See, e.g.,* Epstein, *supra* note 54.

82. Seana Valentine Shiffrin, *What Is Really Wrong with Compelled Association?,* 99 Nw. U. L. Rev. 839, 879 (2005); *see also* Carpenter, *supra* note 65.

83. Peter de Marneffe, *Rights, Reasons, and Freedom of Association* at 154, in Gutmann, ed., *supra* note 3, at 145.

84. *Roberts,* 468 U.S. at 636 (O'Connor, J., concurring in part and concurring in the judgment).

85. Thus, an anonymous reviewer of this book, focusing on my discussion of the law firm, raises the concern that some firm might attempt to justify the refusal to hire or promote women, not by invoking sexism directly, but by arguing that it is animated by a concern with "family life" that requires women to take a less active role in the workplace. But the reviewer concedes that such an argument is much less likely to succeed in the modern marketplace. If, as the reviewer suggests, such an argument might have had greater traction several decades ago, I do not think the problem is the law; it is the salience, within and outside the marketplace, of background social views and conditions. The further back in time we go with such a hypothetical, the less likely it is that even a robustly acontextual approach to the freedom of association would have prevented such firms from operating as they chose.

86. *See* de Marneffe, *supra* note 83, at 155–156. In its recent ministerial exception decision, *Hosanna-Tabor,* the Supreme Court attempted to draw a similar distinction, albeit clumsily. *See Hosanna-Tabor,* 132 S. Ct. at 707 (distinguishing between "government interference with an internal church decision that affects the faith and mission of the church itself" and "government regulation of only outward physical acts"). Although the Court did a bad job of explaining

which "physical acts" should be treated as internal and which as "outward" acts, the distinction I draw in the text may do a better job of getting at what the Court ought to have said.

87. The classic text is Albert O. Hirschman, *Exit, Voice, and Loyalty: Responses to Decline in Firms, Organizations, and States* (1970).

88. Angela R. Riley, *Good (Native) Governance*, 107 Colum. L. Rev. 1049, 1066 (2007) (quoting Hanoch Dagan & Michael A. Heller, *The Liberal Commons*, 110 Yale L.J. 549, 568 (2001)).

89. Koppelman with Wolff, *supra* note 34, at 104; *see also* Sunder, *supra* note 62, at 557–558; Riley, supra note 88, at 1067–1068; Matt Zwolinksi, *Why Not Regulate Private Discrimination?*, 43 San Diego L. Rev. 1043 (2006).

90. *See, e.g.,* Vischer, *supra* note 57, at 1005.

91. *See also* Nicholls, *supra* note 18, at 84 ("'The hopeless confusion of thought between the right of the individual to choose for himself and his right to remain in [an association] pledged to one thing while he himself is pledged to its opposite would be incredible were it not so widespread, and would be the death-blow of all the political clubs that ever existed.'") (quoting J. N. Figgis) (citation omitted).

92. *See generally* Hirschman, *supra* note 87.

93. Nancy L. Rosenblum, *Membership and Morals: The Personal Uses of Pluralism in America* 36 (1998).

94. *U.S. Jaycees v. McClure*, 709 F.2d 1560, 1561 n.1 (8th Cir. 1983), *rev'd sub nom. Roberts v. United States Jaycees*, 468 U.S. 609 (1984). Similar internal dynamics occurred after the Boy Scouts' decision to emphasize the exclusion of gay scoutmasters. *See, e.g.,* Johnson, *supra* note 79, at 1654–1655.

95. *See, e.g.,* Jennifer Gerarda Brown, *Facilitating Boycotts of Discriminatory Organizations Through an Informed Association Statute*, 87 Minn. L. Rev. 481, 494 (2002).

96. *See also* Paul Horwitz, *Act III of the Ministerial Exception*, 106 Nw. U. L. Rev. 973 (2012) (discussing the role of internal reflection and public criticism in restraining groups such as churches in their exercise of legal autonomy).

97. Vischer, *supra* note 57, at 977–978.

98. *See id.* at 982 n.122.

99. *Grutter v. Bollinger*, 539 U.S. 306, 328 (2003).

100. *See, e.g.,* Carpenter, *supra* note 65, at 1516.

101. 427 U.S. 160 (1976).

102. *Id.* at 168, 167, 176 (quoting *McCrary v. Runyon*, 515 F.2d 1082, 1087 (4th Cir. 1975)).

103. Inazu, *supra* note 4, at 173.

104. *See* Richard A. Epstein, *Church and State at the Crossroads:* Christian Legal Society v. Martinez, 2010 Cato Sup. Ct. Rev. 105, 119.

105. *See* Inazu, *supra* note 4, at 184–186. For a recent article that offers a commendably thorough and candid effort to address these questions, although it does not mention *Runyon* itself, *see* Linda C. McClain, *Religious and Political Virtues and Values in Congruence or Conflict?: On Smith, Bob Jones University, and* Christian Legal Society, 32 Cardozo L. Rev. 1959 (2011).

106. *See* Paul Horwitz, *Universities as First Amendment Institutions: Some Easy Answers and Hard Questions,* 54 UCLA L. Rev. 1497, 1543–1544, 1532–1533 n.205 (2007); Koppelman with Wolff, *supra* note 34, at 43–59.

107. Evelyn Brody, *Entrance, Voice, and Exit: The Constitutional Bounds of the Right of Associations,* 35 U.C. Davis L. Rev. 821, 842 (2002); Maimon Schwarzchild, *Pluralism, Conversation, and Judicial Restraint,* 95 Nw. U. L. Rev. 961, 967 (2001).

108. *See* Inazu, *supra* note 4, at 172–173.

109. *See* John O. McGinnis, *Reviving Tocqueville's America: The Rehnquist Court's Jurisprudence of Social Discovery,* 90 Cal. L. Rev. 485, 536–537 (2002).

110. *See, e.g.,* Girardeau A. Spann, *Disintegration,* 46 U. Louisville L. Rev. 565, 600 n.187 (2008); Alex M. Johnson, Jr., *Bid Whist, Tonk, and* United States v. Fordice: *Why Integrationism Fails African-Americans Again,* 81 Cal. L. Rev. 1401 (1993).

111. *See* Horwitz, *supra* note 106, at 1544–1545.

112. 130 S. Ct. 2971 (2010).

113. *Id.* at 2979, 2980 (quotations and citations omitted), 2981.

114. *Id.* at 2984.

115. *See id.* at 2985.

116. *Id.* at 2989, 2990, 2993.

117. *Id.* at 2997, 2997–2998, 2998 (Stevens, J., concurring).

118. *See* B. Jessie Hill, *Property and the Public Forum: An Essay on* Christian Legal Society v. Martinez, 6 Duke J. Const. L. & Pub. Pol'y 49, 57 (2010).

119. *See* Toni M. Massaro, Christian Legal Society v. Martinez: *Six Frames,* 38 Hastings Const. L.Q. 569 (2011).

120. For similar criticisms, see John D. Inazu, *Justice Ginsberg and Religious Liberty,* Hastings L.J. (forthcoming).

121. *CLS,* 130 S. Ct. at 2997 (Stevens, J., concurring).

122. *Id.* at 3000 (Alito, J., dissenting).

10. The Borderlands of Institutionalism

1. Linda C. McClain, *Family Constitutions and the (New) Constitution of the Family,* 75 Fordham L. Rev. 833, 833 (2006).

2. *See* Robert A. Burt, *The Constitution of the Family,* 1979 Sup. Ct. Rev. 329; David D. Meyer, *The Constitutionalization of Family Law,* 42 Fam. L.Q. 529 (2008).

3. *Meyer v. Nebraska,* 262 U.S. 390 (1923); *Pierce v. Soc'y of Sisters,* 268 U.S. 510 (1925).

4. *Meyer*, 262 U.S. at 399.

5. Alice Ristroph & Melissa Murray, *Disestablishing the Family*, 119 Yale L.J. 1236, 1240 (2010).

6. Laurence H. Tribe, *Disentangling Symmetries: Speech, Association, Parenthood*, 28 Pepp. L. Rev. 641, 662 (2001).

7. *See, e.g.*, Ristroph & Murray, *supra* note 5.

8. *See, e.g.*, Stephen G. Gilles, *On Educating Children: A Parentalist Manifesto*, 63 U. Chi. L. Rev. 937, 1012–1019 (1996).

9. Michael Stokes Paulsen, *Scouts, Families, and Schools*, 85 Minn. L. Rev. 1917, 1943 (2001). For a novel effort to analogize family and parental rights to intellectual property law, see Merry Jean Chan, Note, *The Authorial Parent: An Intellectual Property Model of Parental Rights*, 78 N.Y.U. L. Rev. 1186 (2003).

10. *See, e.g.*, Stephen L. Carter, *Parents, Religion, and Schools: Reflections on Pierce, 70 Years Later*, 27 Seton Hall L. Rev. 1194 (1997).

11. *See generally Developments in the Law—The Law of Marriage and Family*, 116 Harv. L. Rev. 1996 (2003).

12. For discussions in the Supreme Court, see, *e.g.*, *Moore v. City of East Cleveland*, 431 U.S. 494 (1977); *Village of Belle Terre v. Boraas*, 416 U.S. 1 (1974).

13. *See, e.g.*, James G. Dwyer, *Religious Schools v. Children's Rights* (1998).

14. Kimberly A. Yuracko, *Education off the Grid: Constitutional Constraints on Homeschooling*, 96 Cal. L. Rev. 123, 133, 132 (2008).

15. *Prince v. Massachusetts*, 321 U.S. 158, 166 (1944).

16. *See, e.g.*, Martha Albertson Fineman, *The Autonomy Myth: A Theory of Dependency* 205 (2004).

17. Abraham Kuyper, *Lectures on Calvinism* 97 (photo. reprint 2007) (1931).

18. *See* Frederick Schauer, *Institutions as Legal and Constitutional Categories*, 54 UCLA L. Rev. 1747, 1758 (2007).

19. Michael R. Siebecker, *A New Discourse Theory of the Firm after* Citizens United, 79 Geo. Wash. L. Rev. 161, 169 (2010).

20. Cynthia L. Estlund, *Freedom of Expression in the Workplace and the Problem of Discriminatory Harassment*, 75 Tex. L. Rev. 687, 693–694 (1997).

21. *Zauderer v. Office of Disciplinary Counsel*, 471 U.S. 626, 637 (1985) (quotations and citations omitted).

22. *See, e.g.*, *Central Hudson Gas & Elec. Corp. v. Pub. Serv. Comm'n of New York*, 447 U.S. 557, 562–564, 566 (1980).

23. *Virginia State Bd. of Pharmacy v. Virginia Citizens Consumer Council, Inc.*, 425 U.S. 748, 764 (1976).

24. *See id.* at 769–770, 771 n.24.

25. *See Nike, Inc. v. Kasky*, 539 U.S. 654 (2003).

26. *Citizens United v. FEC*, 130 S. Ct. 876, 903 (2010).

27. *Id.* at 905.

28. *See, e.g.,* Seth Korman, *Citizens United and the Press: Two Implications,* 37 Rutgers L. Rec. 1, 6 (2010).

29. Robert C. Post, *Racist Speech, Democracy, and the First Amendment,* 32 Wm. & Mary L. Rev. 267, 289 (1991).

30. *See generally* Estlund, *supra* note 20; Cynthia L. Estlund, *Working Together: The Workplace, Civil Society, and the Law,* 89 Geo. L.J. 1 (2000).

31. *See, e.g.,* Cynthia L. Estlund, *Rebuilding the Law of the Workplace in an Era of Self-Regulation,* 105 Colum. L. Rev. 319 (2005).

32. *See, e.g.,* Robert C. Post, *Viewpoint Discrimination and Commercial Speech,* 41 Loy. L.A. L. Rev. 169 (2007).

33. James A. Brundage, *The Medieval Origins of the Legal Profession: Canonists, Civilians, and Courts* 2 (2008).

34. *See, e.g.,* Robert Post, *Informed Consent to Abortion: A First Amendment Analysis of Compelled Physician Speech,* 2007 U. Ill. L. Rev. 939, 944; Eugene Volokh, *Speech as Conduct: Generally Applicable Laws, Illegal Courses of Conduct, "Situation-Altering Utterances," and the Uncharted Zones,* 90 Cornell L. Rev. 1277, 1342–1343 (2005); David T. Moldenhauer, *Circular 230 Opinion Standards, Legal Ethics and First Amendment Limitations on the Regulation of Professional Speech by Lawyers,* 29 Seattle U. L. Rev. 843, 843 (2006); Robert Kry, *The "Watchman for Truth": Professional Licensing and the First Amendment,* 23 Seattle U. L. Rev. 885, 890 (2000).

35. *See, e.g.,* Frederick Schauer, *Facts and the First Amendment,* 57 UCLA L. Rev. 897, 915–916 (2010).

36. Daniel Halberstam, *Commercial Speech, Professional Speech, and the Constitutional Status of Social Institutions,* 147 U. Pa. L. Rev. 771, 772 (1999).

37. Michael Walzer, *Thinking Politically: Essays in Political Theory* 19 (2007).

38. It is no accident that academics are said to belong to the "learned professions" or that the rise of law and medicine has been intertwined with the university. Nor is it an accident that the modern profession of journalism has taken its place in the university as well. All of these activities combine knowledge and specialized skills with elite social status and a broad orientation toward public service.

39. *See, e.g.,* W. Bradley Wendel, *Free Speech for Lawyers,* 28 Hastings Const. L.Q. 305, 308 (2001).

40. Halberstam, *supra* note 36, at 773 (emphasis added).

41. *New York Times v. Sullivan,* 376 U.S. 254, 270 (1964).

42. American Medical Association, *Code of Medical Ethics: Principles of Medical Ethics,* Preamble.

43. *See, e.g.,* Paula Berg, *Towards a First Amendment Theory of Doctor-Patient Discourse and the Right to Receive Unbiased Medical Advice,* 74 B.U. L. Rev. 201, 231–240 (1994).

44. David Cole, *Beyond Unconstitutional Conditions: Charting Spheres of Neutrality in Government-Funded Speech*, 67 N.Y.U. L. Rev. 675, 711–712 (1992).

45. I draw here on Robert Post's discussion of this issue; *see* Post, *supra* note 34; Robert Post, *Democracy, Expertise, and Academic Freedom: A First Amendment Jurisprudence for the Modern State* (2012).

46. *See Bailey v. Huggins Diagnostic & Rehabilitation Center, Inc.*, 952 P.2d 768 (Colo. Ct. App. 1997).

47. *See* Halberstam, *supra* note 36, at 846. This is especially true where the ethical norms involved guard against self-interest on the professional's part: a dentist who persuades patients to undergo the possibly unnecessary removal of old fillings stands to turn a tidy profit.

48. *Lowe v. SEC*, 472 U.S. 181, 232 (1985).

49. S.D.C.L. § 34-23A-10.1.

50. *Planned Parenthood Minnesota, North Dakota, South Dakota v. Rounds*, 530 F.3d 724, 734–735 (8th Cir. 2008) (en banc); *id.* at 733 (quoting *Planned Parenthood of Southeastern Pennsylvania v. Casey*, 505 U.S. 833, 884 (1992)). On remand, the district court upheld the requirement on the physician to inform the patient that the abortion would terminate the life of a separate human being, but struck down provisions requiring additional statements that the "pregnant woman has an existing relationship with that unborn human being and that the relationship enjoys protection under the United States Constitution and under the laws of South Dakota," and that an increased risk of suicide was "associated" with abortion. *See Planned Parenthood of Minnesota, North Dakota, South Dakota v. Rounds*, 650 F. Supp. 2d 972 (D.S.D. 2009).

51. The situation would have been different, I think, if the same regulation had been passed by the medical regulatory authorities themselves after due deliberation about what their professional needs and norms demanded, provided at least that they did not act as a result of undue pressure from the state. Medical practitioners are, of course, already bounded in their professional speech by all kinds of regulatory requirements, as the dental filling case above demonstrates. A doctor who wanted to provide, or refrain from providing, certain kinds of information or advice about abortion (or any other medical procedure) in the face of direct opposition from the medical profession itself would, from an institutionalist perspective, stand on much weaker ground than the plaintiffs did in *Rounds*. But, of course, my point is that those decisions ought to be made by the responsible institutions themselves, in a way that reflects their own norms, practices, and expertise, and that those decisions will not be immune from either professional or public criticism even if the state itself cannot intervene. The likelihood that a professional medical association, exercising appropriate professional standards, would have required doctors to follow

the script set forth by the legislature in *Rounds* is vanishingly small. Even were it otherwise, the reason would have little to do with the law and a great deal to do with evolving norms and standards within the profession itself; an example is the American Psychological Association's declassification in 1973 of homosexuality as a mental disorder, which came not as a result of legal pressure but in response to changing professional views and broader social norms.

52. Cole, *supra* note 44, at 696.

53. Cass R. Sunstein, *Why the Unconstitutional Conditions Doctrine Is an Anachronism (with Particular Reference to Religion, Speech, and Abortion)*, 70 B.U. L. Rev. 593, 620 (1990).

54. *Rust v. Sullivan*, 500 U.S. 173, 178–181 (1991).

55. *Id.* at 199, 200.

56. Cole, *supra* note 44, at 681.

57. Halberstam, *supra* note 36, at 849.

58. *Legal Servs. Corp. v. Velazquez*, 531 U.S. 533, 537 (2001).

59. *Id.* at 543 (emphasis added), 544, 548.

60. I therefore disagree with Robert Post's argument that an institutional First Amendment approach to professional speech is "implausible" because if "[a]pplied literally, this approach suggests that . . . First Amendment coverage should be triggered by any political regulation of extant professional practices." Post, *supra* note 45, at 51. The point of the institutional approach is not to grant complete legal immunity to professional speech, but to align the First Amendment freedom with the functions and practices of professional speech, properly understood. In some cases that alignment may lead to greater immunity; in others it may lead to more regulation.

61. Samuel Issacharoff & Richard H. Pildes, *Politics as Markets: Partisan Lockups of the Democratic Process*, 50 Stan. L. Rev. 643, 644 (1998).

62. *See, e.g.,* Frederick Schauer & Richard H. Pildes, *Electoral Exceptionalism and the First Amendment*, 77 Tex. L. Rev. 1803 (1999).

63. Richard H. Pildes, *Formalism and Functionalism in the Constitutional Law of Politics*, 35 Conn. L. Rev. 1525, 1529 (2003); Heather K. Gerken, *Election Law Exceptionalism?: A Bird's Eye View of the Symposium*, 82 B.U. L. Rev. 737, 738 (2002).

64. *See generally* Richard H. Pildes, *Foreword: The Constitutionalization of Democratic Politics*, 118 Harv. L. Rev. 29 (2003). The seminal case was *Baker v. Carr*, 369 U.S. 186 (1962), in which the Court first entered what Justice Felix Frankfurter had earlier warned was a "political thicket." *Colegrove v. Green*, 328 U.S. 549, 556 (1946).

65. For examples see Gerken, *supra* note 63, at 739–741.

66. *See, e.g., Citizens United*, 130 S. Ct. 876.

67. *See, e.g.,* Schauer & Pildes, *supra* note 62, at 1806.

68. John Hart Ely, *Democracy and Distrust: A Theory of Judicial Review* 106 (1980). *See, e.g.*, Lillian R. BeVier, *The Issue of Issue Advocacy: An Economic, Political, and Constitutional Analysis*, 85 Va. L. Rev. 1761 (1999); Bradley A. Smith, *Faulty Assumptions and Undemocratic Consequences of Campaign Finance Reform*, 105 Yale L.J. 1049 (1996).

69. Although I cannot fully develop the point here, First Amendment institutionalism suggests one other point about corporate political speech and its regulation. At least in the popular discussion of the case, it is often assumed that if *Citizens United* was wrong, and if there are reasons to be concerned about the influence of unlimited corporate money in elections, the necessary remedy must be one of state regulation. From an institutionalist perspective, however, and from the perspective of the British pluralists we have examined elsewhere in this book, those who see the state as the first and best answer to this problem may be wrong. In "a unitary state with a centralized administration which can effectively claim unlimited sovereign power," there is a danger that a bare political majority, "dependent on the support of no more than a minority fraction of society," may use its laws corruptly or despotically. Paul Q. Hirst, *Introduction*, in *The Pluralist Theory of the State: Selected Writings of G. D. H. Cole, J. N. Figgis, and H. L. Laski* 4 (Paul Q. Hirst ed., 1989). We might find the disease worse than the cure. Consider that even as opponents of *Citizens United* have argued that a bare majority of Congress ought to be able to regulate the affairs of one form of institution—corporations and corporate political speech—we have seen, at the exact same time, a vigorous effort by bare majorities in state government to reduce the power and speech of a competing institution: unions. It may be that a better response to both problems is not to give government the ready authority to regulate corporate political speech, but to encourage the growth of a wider and more robust set of social institutions, "so that no mere mathematical majority could prevail over the complex web of interests in society." *Id.* at 6.

70. Robert C. Post, *Regulating Election Speech Under the First Amendment*, 77 Tex. L. Rev. 1837, 1839, 1838 (1999).

11. Critiques of First Amendment Institutionalism

1. *See, e.g.*, Owen M. Fiss, *Free Speech and Social Structure*, 71 Iowa L. Rev. 1405 (1986).
2. I emphasize the word "may." Although I do not aim here to eliminate the broad protections for non–First Amendment institutional speakers provided by current doctrine, in part because of the valuable backstop they offer for borderline or emerging First Amendment institutions and in part because of the continuing importance of individual speech, that does not mean the doctrine is not susceptible to criticism. In addition to Chapters 1 and 2 of this book, see, *e.g.*,

Robert Post, *Reconciling Theory and Doctrine in First Amendment Jurisprudence*, 88 Calif. L. Rev. 2353 (2000); Robert Post, *Recuperating First Amendment Doctrine*, 47 Stan. L. Rev. 1249 (1995).

3. *See, e.g.,* David McGowan, *Approximately Speech*, 89 Minn. L. Rev. 1416, 1432 (2005); Dale Carpenter, *The Value of Institutions and the Values of Free Speech*, 89 Minn. L. Rev. 1407 (2005).

4. *See, e.g.,* Gia B. Lee, *First Amendment Enforcement in Government Institutions and Programs*, 56 UCLA L. Rev. 1691 (2009).

5. Some versions of the argument from autonomy may believe that positive government action can be necessary to enhance individual autonomy; *see, e.g.,* Seana Valentine Shiffrin, *Reply to Critics*, 27 Const. Comment. 417, 418, 422 (2011). Other versions may simply see government-centered justifications for free speech as beside the point. *See* note 12, *infra*, and accompanying text. Nevertheless, many proponents of autonomy-based justifications for free speech base their arguments at least in part on distrust of government. *See, e.g.,* C. Edwin Baker, *Autonomy and Free Speech*, 27 Const. Comment. 251, 253 (2011) (arguing for a formal conception of autonomy under which "the constitution restrains the 'means' government uses to pursue even good ends as well as prohibits subordinating or enslaving people as permissible ends"), 257 ("As a bedrock libertarian principle, general opposition to paternalism (at least by government as applied to adults) connects closely to respect for autonomy—a person making choices about herself."). *See also* T. M. Scanlon, *Why Not Base Free Speech on Autonomy or Democracy?*, 97 Va. L. Rev. 541, 546–547 (2011) (argument by a former supporter of an autonomy-based conception of free speech that "Governments cannot justify restricting political speech on the grounds that it will lead citizens to form false beliefs about important political questions, because (a) we have an important interest in being able to make up our own minds about such matters and (b) giving goverments the power to regulate speech on these grounds is a clear threat to this interest.").

6. *See* Garry Wills, *Necessary Evil: A History of American Distrust of Government* (1999).

7. John Hart Ely, *Democracy and Distrust: A Theory of Judicial Review* 136 n.* (1980); Erwin Chemerinsky, *Amending the Constitution*, 96 Mich. L. Rev. 1561, 1567 (1998).

8. Frederick Schauer, *Free Speech: A Philosophical Enquiry* 86 (1982).

9. Dale Carpenter, *The Antipaternalism Principle in the First Amendment*, 37 Creighton L. Rev. 579, 586 (2004).

10. *See* Geoffrey R. Stone, *Autonomy and Distrust*, 64 U. Chi. L. Rev. 1171 (1993).

11. *See, e.g.,* Frederick Schauer & Richard H. Pildes, *Electoral Exceptionalism and the First Amendment*, 77 Tex. L. Rev. 1803, 1806–1807 (1999).

12. *See* Stone, *supra* note 10, at 1172.

13. Richard H. Fallon, Jr., *Ruminations on the Work of Frederick Schauer*, 72 Notre Dame L. Rev. 1391, 1392 (1997). *See, e.g.*, Frederick Schauer, *The Second-Best First Amendment*, 31 Wm. & Mary L. Rev. 1, 2 (1989); Frederick Schauer, *The Wily Agitator and the American Free Speech Tradition*, 57 Stan. L. Rev. 2157, 2168 (2005); Cass R. Sunstein, *Legal Interference with Private Preferences*, 53 U. Chi. L. Rev. 1129, 1140 (1986).

14. *See* Larry Alexander, *Banning Hate Speech and the Sticks and Stones Defense*, 13 Const. Comment. 71, 94–95 (1996).

15. Geoffrey R. Stone, *Content-Neutral Restrictions*, 54 U. Chi. L. Rev. 46, 56 (1987).

16. Carpenter, supra note 3, at 1411.

17. *See R.A.V. v. City of St. Paul*, 505 U.S. 377 (1992).

18. *See* Carpenter, *supra* note 9, at 582.

19. *See, e.g.*, Barry P. McDonald, *Speech and Distrust: Rethinking the Content Approach to Protecting the Freedom of Expression*, 81 Notre Dame L. Rev. 1347, 1352–1353 (2006); Martin H. Redish, *The Content Distinction in First Amendment Analysis*, 34 Stan. L. Rev. 113 (1981).

20. *See, e.g.*, Frederick Schauer, *Institutions as Legal and Constitutional Categories*, 54 UCLA L. Rev. 1747, 1763–1764 (2007).

21. *See* Frederick Schauer, *Principles, Institutions, and the First Amendment*, 112 Harv. L. Rev. 84, 119–120 (1998).

22. The classic example is *Branzburg v. Hayes*, 408 U.S. 665 (1972), which rejected a strong reporters' privilege under the Press Clause rather than force the courts to decide who qualifies for the privilege.

23. *See, e.g.*, Adam M. Samaha, *Litigant Sensitivity in First Amendment Law*, 98 Nw. U. L. Rev. 1291 (2004).

24. *Grutter v. Bollinger*, 539 U.S. 306, 329 (2003).

25. David Nicholls, *The Pluralist State: The Political Ideas of J. N. Figgis and His Contemporaries* xx (2nd ed. 1994).

26. *See, e.g.*, Joseph Blocher, *Institutions in the Marketplace of Ideas*, 57 Duke L.J. 821, 856 (2008); Christopher S. Yoo, *The Rise and Demise of the Technology-Specific Approach to the First Amendment*, 91 Geo. L.J. 245, 254 (2003).

27. *See* Glenn Reynolds, *An Army of Davids: How Markets and Technology Empower Ordinary People to Beat Big Media, Big Government and Other Goliaths* (2006).

28. *See, e.g.*, Larry Alexander, *Academic Freedom*, 77 U. Colo. L. Rev. 883 (2006).

29. *See, e.g.*, Marci A. Hamilton, *The Waterloo for the So-Called Church Autonomy Theory: Widespread Clergy Abuse and Institutional Cover-Up*, 29 Cardozo L. Rev. 225 (2007); Caroline Mala Corbin, *Above the Law?: The Constitutionality of the Ministerial Exemption from Antidiscrimination Law*, 75 Fordham L. Rev. 1965 (2007); Jane Rutherford, *Equality as the Primary Constitutional Value: The Case for Applying Employment Discrimination Laws to Religion*, 81 Cornell L. Rev. 1049 (1996).

30. *See, e.g.,* Andrew Koppelman, *Should Noncommercial Associations Have an Absolute Right to Discriminate?,* 67 L. & Contemp. Probs. 27, 47–50 (2004).

31. *See, e.g.,* Erwin Chemerinsky, *More Speech Is Better,* 45 UCLA L. Rev. 1635 (1998)

32. The closest we have come to such an argument is Scott A. Moss, *Students and Workers and Prisoners—Oh, My!: A Cautionary Note about Excessive Institutional Tailoring of First Amendment Doctrine,* 54 UCLA L. Rev. 1635 (2007). But Moss mostly steers clear of the kinds of institutions discussed in this book and concedes that arguments for greater judicial deference and awareness of institutional context may be stronger with respect to these institutions. *See id.* at 1671.

33. Steven H. Shiffrin, *The First Amendment, Democracy, and Romance* 5 (1990).

34. *See, e.g.,* Paul Horwitz, *Citizenship and Speech,* 43 McGill L.J. 445 (1998).

35. *See* Stone, *supra* note 15.

36. Roderick M. Hills, Jr., *The Constitutional Rights of Private Governments,* 78 N.Y.U. L. Rev. 144, 179 (2003).

37. *See, e.g.,* Stanley Ingber, *Rediscovering the Communal Worth of Individual Rights: The First Amendment in Institutional Contexts,* 69 Tex. L. Rev. 1, 22 (1990).

38. Alan Brownstein, *Protecting Religious Liberty: The False Messiahs of Free Speech Doctrine and Formal Neutrality,* 18 J. L. & Pol. 119, 181 (2002).

39. *See Univ. of Pa. v. EEOC,* 483 U.S. 182, 194 (1990).

40. *See, e.g.,* Eugene Volokh, *You Can Blog, But You Can't Hide,* New York Times, Dec. 2, 2004, at A39.

41. *See* Frederick Schauer, *Towards an Institutional First Amendment,* 89 Minn. L. Rev. 1256, 1266–1267 (2005).

42. Carpenter, *supra* note 3, at 1408.

43. *See, e.g.,* V. F. Nourse & Sarah A. Maguire, *The Lost History of Governance and Equal Protection,* 58 Duke L.J. 955, 1004 (2009).

44. Joseph Blocher, *Categoricalism in First and Second Amendment Analysis,* 84 N.Y.U. L. Rev. 375, 381 (2009).

45. *See, e.g.,* Schauer, *supra* note 41, at 1267–1268; Schauer, *supra* note 21, at 110–111.

46. *See, e.g.,* McGowan, *supra* note 3, at 1433.

47. *See generally* Frederick Schauer, *The Convergence of Rules and Standards,* 2003 N.Z. L. Rev. 303 (2003).

48. *See, e.g.,* Melville B. Nimmer, *The Right to Speak from* Times *to* Time: *First Amendment Theory Applied to Libel and Misapplied to Privacy,* 56 Cal. L. Rev. 935, 942 (1968).

49. *Branzburg,* 408 U.S. at 703.

50. *See, e.g.,* Carpenter, *supra* note 3, at 1410–1411; McGowan, *supra* note 3, at 1433–1435.

51. *See, e.g.,* Richard H. Pildes, *Why Rights Are Not Trumps: Social Meanings, Expressive Harms, and Constitutionalism,* 27 J. Legal Stud. 725 (1998).

52. Michael P. Van Alstine, *The Costs of Legal Change*, 49 UCLA L. Rev. 789, 793 (2002).

53. *See id.* at 793–794.

54. Carpenter, *supra* note 3, at 1411, 1411–1413.

55. *See* Oona A. Hathaway, *Path Dependence in the Law: The Course and Pattern of Legal Change in a Common Law System*, 86 Iowa L. Rev. 601, 614 (2001).

12. Institutionalism Beyond The First Amendment?

1. William H. Simon, *The Institutional Configuration of Deweyan Democracy*, Oct. 6, 2011, at 6 (describing Dewey's views), available at http://papers.ssrn.com/sol3/papers.cfm?abstract_id=1957332.

2. Frederick Schauer, *Principles, Institutions, and the First Amendment*, 112 Harv. L. Rev. 84, 84, 120 (1998).

3. Mitchell N. Berman, *Constitutional Decision Rules*, 90 Va. L. Rev. 1, 3 (2004) (emphasis added). This trend took wing with Richard H. Fallon, Jr., *Foreword: Implementing the Constitution*, 111 Harv. L. Rev. 54 (1997).

4. Richard H. Fallon, Jr., *Judicially Manageable Standards and Constitutional Meaning*, 119 Harv. L. Rev. 1274, 1276 (2006).

5. *See, e.g.*, Jennifer E. Laurin, *Rights Translation and Remedial Disequilibration in Constitutional Criminal Procedure*, 110 Colum. L. Rev. 1002, 1010 (2010).

6. Kermit Roosevelt III, *Constitutional Calcification: How the Law Becomes What the Court Does*, 91 Va. L. Rev. 1649 (2005).

7. *See* Daryl J. Levinson, *Rights Essentialism and Remedial Equilibration*, 99 Colum. L. Rev. 857 (1999); Roderick M. Hills, Jr., *The Pragmatist's View of Constitutional Implementation and Constitutional Meaning*, 119 Harv. L. Rev. F. 173, 175 (2006).

8. Fallon, *supra* note 4, at 1314.

9. Hills, *supra* note 7, at 181.

10. Roosevelt, *supra* note 6, at 1692.

11. *See id.* at 1689–1692.

12. Oliver Wendell Holmes, *Law in Science and Science in Law*, 12 Harv. L. Rev. 443, 460 (1899).

13. *See* Paul Horwitz, *Three Faces of Deference*, 83 Notre Dame L. Rev. 1061, 1144–1146 (2008).

14. Michael C. Dorf, *After Bureaucracy*, 71 U. Chi. L. Rev. 1245, 1266 (2004).

15. Mark Tushnet, *The New Constitutional Order* 171–172 (2003).

16. Michael C. Dorf & Charles F. Sabel, *A Constitution of Democratic Experimentalism*, 98 Colum. L. Rev. 267, 283 (1998).

17. Michael C. Dorf, *Legal Indeterminacy and Institutional Design*, 78 N.Y.U. L. Rev. 875, 961 (2003).

18. *See, e.g., id.*

19. Joanne Scott & Susan Sturm, *Courts as Catalysts: Re-Thinking the Judicial Role in New Governance,* 13 Colum. J. Eur. L. 565, 567, 571 (2007). *See also* Dorf, *supra* note 17, at 887–888 ("Experimentalist appellate courts self-consciously rely on the participation of affected actors to explore the implications of the framework rules that they create and use the record of such actors' efforts continually to refine such framework rules."); James S. Liebman & Charles F. Sabel, *A Public Laboratory Dewey Barely Imagined: The Emerging Model of School Governance and Legal Reform,* 28 N.Y.U. Rev. L. & Soc. Change 183, 278–283 (2003) (describing a model of "non-court-centric judicial review" that "allows the court to participate in a process of building a constitutional order, rather than imposing one or abandoning its obligation to do so").

20. *See, e.g.,* Douglas Nejaime, *When New Governance Fails,* 70 Ohio St. L.J. 323 (2009); David A. Super, *Laboratories of Destitution: Democratic Experimentalism and the Failure of Antipoverty Law,* 157 U. Pa. L. Rev. 541 (2008); William E. Scheuerman, *Democratic Experimentalism or Capitalist Synchronization?: Critical Reflections on Directly-Deliberative Polyarchy,* 17 Can. J.L. & Juris. 101 (2004).

21. William H. Simon, *New Governance Anxieties: A Deweyan Response,* 2010 Wis. L. Rev. 727, 727.

22. *See, e.g.,* Robert C. Post, *Foreword: Fashioning the Legal Constitution: Culture, Courts, and Law,* 117 Harv. L. Rev. 4, 8–9 (2003).

23. Heather K. Gerken, *Foreword: Federalism All the Way Down,* 124 Harv. L. Rev. 4, 8, 11 (2010).

24. *See id.* at 61.

25. *Id.* at 9.

26. *See* Symposium, *Non-State Governance,* 2010 Utah L. Rev. 1.

27. Michael W. McConnell, *Non-State Governance,* 2010 Utah L. Rev. 7, 7, 9.

28. Paul Schiff Berman, *Towards a Jurisprudence of Hybridity,* 2010 Utah L. Rev. 11, 12. *See generally* Patrick M. Garry, *Assessing the Constitutional Autonomy of Such Non-State Institutions as the Press and Academia,* 2010 Utah L. Rev. 141.

29. *Id.*

30. *See, e.g.,* Mark Tushnet, *Taking the Constitution Away From the Courts* 177–194 (1999).

31. *See* Larry D. Kramer, *The People Themselves: Popular Constitutionalism and Judicial Review* (2004).

32. Robert Post & Reva Siegel, *Roe Rage: Democratic Constitutionalism and Backlash,* 42 Harv. C.R.-C.L. L. Rev. 373, 379 (2007).

33. *Id.* at 374, 379.

34. Robert C. Post & Reva B. Siegel, *Democratic Constitutionalism,* in *The Constitution in 2020* 25, 27 (Jack M. Balkin & Reva B. Siegel eds., 2009).

35. *See, e.g.*, Daan Braveman, *On Law and Democratic Development: Popular Constitutionalism and Judicial Supremacy*, 33 Syracuse J. Int'l L. & Com. 41, 45 (2005); Erwin Chemerinsky, *In Defense of Judicial Review: A Reply to Professor Kramer*, 92 Cal. L. Rev. 1013 (2004); Barry Friedman, *The Cycles of Constitutional Theory*, 67 L. & Contemp. Probs. 149, 163 (2004); Erwin Chemerinsky, *In Defense of Judicial Review: The Perils of Popular Constitutionalism*, 2004 U. Ill. L. Rev. 673.

36. *See, e.g.*, Mark Tushnet, *Dialogic Judicial Review*, 61 Ark. L. Rev. 205, 211 (2008).

37. *See generally* Bradley C. Karkkainen, *"New Governance" in Legal Thought and in the World: Some Splitting as Antidote to Overzealous Lumping*, 89 Minn. L. Rev. 471 (2004).

38. Orly Lobel, *Setting the Agenda for New Governance Research*, 89 Minn. L. Rev. 498, 505 (2004).

39. Robert Post, *Recuperating First Amendment Doctrine*, 47 Stan. L. Rev. 1249, 1250 (1995).

40. J. N. Figgis, *The Church and the Secular Theory of the State*, in David Nicholls, *The Pluralist State: The Political Ideas of J. N. Figgis and His Contemporaries* 157, 158 (2nd ed. 1994).

41. Robert Cover, *Foreword: Nomos and Narrative*, 97 Harv. L. Rev. 4, 68 (1983).

42. Larry D. Kramer, *Popular Constitutionalism, Circa 2004*, 92 Calif. L. Rev. 959, 980 (2004).

Index